EPPP Fundamentals

Anne S. Klee, PhD, is a licensed psychologist in Connecticut. She works at VA Connecticut Healthcare System and is an assistant professor of psychology in the Department of Psychiatry, Yale School of Medicine. Dr. Klee contributes to psychology at the national level as the past president of the American Psychological Association's (APA) Division 18 (Psychologists in Public Service), and by serving on the APA Committee for Assessment and Training in Recovery. She is the 2002 recipient of the American Psychological Association Award for Distinguished Contributions by a Graduate Student, the 2007 APA Division of Psychologists in Public Service Early Career Achievement Award, and the 2012 APA Division of Psychologists in Public Service Michael S. Neale Award. She is also an Albert Schweitzer Fellow for Life and a Fellow of the Connecticut Health Foundation.

Bret A. Moore, PsyD, ABPP, is a licensed clinical psychologist in San Antonio, Texas. He is licensed as a prescribing psychologist by the New Mexico Board of Psychologist Examiners and is board certified in clinical psychology by the American Board of Professional Psychology. He is the 2007 recipient of the Arthur W. Melton Award from Division 19, which recognizes early-career achievements in military psychology, and the 2011 Early Career Achievement Award from Division 18, which recognizes achievements in public service psychology. He is the author and editor of 10 books, including *Pharmacotherapy for Psychologists: Prescribing and Collaborative Roles, Handbook of Clinical Psychopharmacology for Psychologists, The Veterans and Active Duty Military Psychotherapy Treatment Planner, Living and Surviving in Harm's Way, Wheels Down: Adjusting to Life After Deployment, Handbook of Counseling Military Couples,* and *The Veterans and Active Duty Military Homework Planner.* He also writes a biweekly newspaper column titled "Kevlar for the Mind," which is published by *Military Times.* His views and opinions on clinical and military psychology have been quoted in the *USA Today, New York Times, Boston Globe,* National Public Radio, the British Broadcasting Corporation, and the Canadian Broadcasting Corporation.

EPPP Fundamentals

Review for the Examination for Professional Practice in Psychology

Anne S. Klee, PhD
Bret A. Moore, PsyD, ABPP
Editors

SPRINGER PUBLISHING COMPANY
NEW YORK

Springer Publishing Company, LLC
11 West 42nd Street
New York, NY 10036
www.springerpub.com

Acquisitions Editor: Nancy S. Hale
Composition: Exeter Premedia Services Private Ltd.

ISBN: 978-0-8261-9973-7
e-book ISBN: 978-0-8261-9974-4

15 16 / 5 4 3 2

The author and the publisher of this Work have made every effort to use sources believed to be reliable to provide information that is accurate and compatible with the standards generally accepted at the time of publication. The author and publisher shall not be liable for any special, consequential, or exemplary damages resulting, in whole or in part, from the readers' use of, or reliance on, the information contained in this book. The publisher has no responsibility for the persistence or accuracy of URLs for external or third-party Internet websites referred to in this publication and does not guarantee that any content on such websites is, or will remain, accurate or appropriate.

Library of Congress Cataloging-in-Publication Data
Klee, Anne S.
    EPPP fundamentals : review for the examination for professional practice in psychology / Anne S. Klee & Bret A. Moore.
       p. ; cm
    ISBN 978-0-8261-9973-7
    1. Psychology–Practice–Examinations, questions, etc.   2. Psychologists–Certification.
    I. Moore, Bret A.   II. Title.
    BF75.K54 2014
    150.76–dc23

                                                                                                        2013033784

Special discounts on bulk quantities of our books are available to corporations, professional associations, pharmaceutical companies, health care organizations, and other qualifying groups. If you are interested in a custom book, including chapters from more than one of our titles, we can provide that service as well.

For details, please contact:
Special Sales Department, Springer Publishing Company, LLC
11 West 42nd Street, 15th Floor, New York, NY 10036-8002
Phone: 877-687-7476 or 212-431-4370; Fax: 212-941-7842
E-mail: sales@springerpub.com

Printed in the United States of America by Gasch Printing.

To Rob, Alex, and Jacob—for your unconditional love and support

—ASK

To my daughter, Kaitlyn, and wife, Lori; a perfect joy and loving partner

—BAM

Contents

Contributors

Rumeli Banik, MA   Graduate Student, Applied Developmental Psychology, Fordham University

John Beauvais, PhD   Associate Chief of Psychology, Director of Psychology Predoctoral Training, VA Connecticut Healthcare System; Assistant Professor, Department of Psychiatry, Yale University School of Medicine

Danette Beitra, MS   Doctoral Student, Clinical Psychology, Nova Southeastern University

Loretta E. Braxton, PhD   Chief Psychologist, Durham VA Medical Center; Assistant Professor, Psychiatry and Behavioral Sciences, Duke University Medical Center

Andrew J. Cavanagh, MA   Graduate Student in Applied Developmental Psychology, Fordham University

Daniel DaSilva, PhD   Clinical Neuropsychologist, Morris Psychological Group, Parsippany, New Jersey

Christian DeLucia, PhD   Associate Professor of Psychology, Nova Southeastern University

Amy E. Ellis, MA   Doctoral Student, Clinical Psychology, Nova Southeastern University

Miriam Frankel, MA   Graduate Student, Clinical Psychology PhD (Health Emphasis) Program, Ferkauf Graduate School of Psychology, Yeshiva University

David Gansler, PhD, ABPP/ABCN   Director of Clinical Training and Associate Professor of Psychology, Suffolk University

Ashley Gorman, PhD, ABPP   Clinical Neuropsychologist, Morris Psychological Group, Parsippany, New Jersey

Scott J. Hunter, PhD   Associate Professor, Departments of Psychiatry and Behavioral Neuroscience and Pediatrics, University of Chicago

Matthew Jerram, PhD   Assistant Professor, Psychology, Suffolk University

Cynthia Kane, PhD   Licensed Clinical Psychologist, University of Chicago

Samantha Kettle, PsyD   Staff Psychologist, Durham VA Medical Center

Dolores K. Little, PhD   Department of Veterans Affairs (retired)

Carlos Marquez, MA   Graduate Student, Clinical Psychology PhD (Health Emphasis) Program, Ferkauf Graduate School of Psychology, Yeshiva University

Walter Penk, PhD, ABPP   Professor, Psychiatry and Behavioral Sciences, Texas A&M College of Medicine

Christina J. Riccardi, PhD   Staff Psychologist, Operation Enduring Freedom/Iraqi Freedom/New Dawn Program, Durham VA Medical Center

Megan N. Scott, PhD   Assistant Professor, Department of Psychiatry and Behavioral Neuroscience, University of Chicago

Cheryl Seifert, PhD   Psychology Postdoctoral Resident, VA Connecticut Healthcare System

Wayne G. Siegel, PhD, ABPP   Director of Training and Psychology Supervisor, Minneapolis VA Medical Center Adjunct Professor of Psychology, University of Minnesota

Laura Stout Sosinsky, PhD   Assistant Professor of Psychology, Fordham University

Brenda Stepak, PhD   Psychologist, Atlantic Rehabilitation Institute, Morristown Medical Center

Sonia Suchday, PhD   Associate Professor and Program Director, Clinical Psychology PhD (Health Emphasis) Program, Ferkauf Graduate School of Psychology; Associate Clinical Professor and Associate Director, Center for Public Health, Albert Einstein College of Medicine, Yeshiva University

Jessica M. Valenzuela, PhD   Assistant Professor of Psychology, Nova Southeastern University

Robert Webb, PhD   Emeritus Professor of Psychology, Suffolk University

Preface

Most professions require some type of state or national examination before formal entrance into their respective fields can occur. For example, medicine requires completion of the U.S. Medical Licensing Exam. Prospective lawyers must pass the Bar. Accountants are required to take a test if they wish to become certified. And although it varies by state, to become a teacher, one must successfully navigate a certification exam. The profession of psychology is no different. Before one can practice psychology independently, the Examination for Professional Practice in Psychology (EPPP) must be passed.

The EPPP is a 225-question examination that focuses on eight content areas: biological bases of behavior; cognitive–affective bases of behavior; social and cultural bases of behavior; growth and life span development; assessment and diagnosis; treatment, intervention, prevention, and supervision; research methods and statistics; and ethical, legal, and professional issues. It is a broad-based test that assesses the individual's depth and breadth of knowledge of psychology. The underlying assumption behind inclusion of the exam content is that the questions assess the knowledge base required to successfully function as a psychologist in professional practice (ASPPB, 2012). It is not all encompassing of what an effective psychologist should know, only a mere sampling. (You can find detailed information about the EPPP and the examination process at www.asppb.net)

The EPPP is arguably one of the most anxiety-provoking milestones associated with becoming a psychologist. Without successful completion, it will delay one's entry into the profession leading to uncertainty, potential financial strain and, for some, thoughts of inadequacy and myriad negative emotions. Therefore, the anxiety is understandable. However, it is most often unwarranted and unnecessary. The truth is that the vast majority of individuals pass the test the first time they take it (Schaffer et al., 2012). And for those who don't, most all will pass it in a subsequent attempt. For the reasons mentioned above, passing the examination the first time is highly desirable. And the best way to maximize your chances of passing the examination right out of the chute is to adequately prepare.

EPPP Fundamentals: Review for the Examination for Professional Practice in Psychology provides a comprehensive review of core exam content and includes over 300 sample questions. *EPPP Fundamentals* goes beyond merely "teaching the test" through rote memorization. Instead, it covers the eight content domains of the EPPP and their representative knowledge areas in a stepwise, narrative, and review format. Another unique aspect of *EPPP Fundamentals* is that it is an edited volume. Consequently, it includes contributions from psychologists associated with some of the top psychology training and internship programs in the United States. The lead contributors are professors, training directors, and practitioners with expertise in the content areas of the chapters they authored. This combined approach helps users obtain the depth and breadth of knowledge required for passing the exam, and mirrors how doctoral level courses are commonly taught.

EPPP Fundamentals can be used in a variety of ways. We believe that the guide can serve as an instrumental text for supporting traditional systematic study methods or a stand-alone resource for those who are not able to invest in a formalized study program. Many students will find the textbook format of the guide useful as a primer at the beginning of the study process or as a review at the end. Questions found at the end of each chapter can serve as a gauge for successful review of the chapter material and the questions at the end of the text can serve as a review of the entire content of the book.

This book contains a considerable amount of information. If you have any questions or suggestions for updates or corrections, please email us at EPPPreview updates@yahoo.com.

Regardless of how you use *EPPP Fundamentals*, we wish you tremendous success with the exam and your future career as a psychologist. Passing the EPPP and becoming a professional psychologist will be one of the most memorable stages of your professional and personal life. We are honored to be a small part of that process.

References

Association of State and Provincial Psychology Boards. (2012). *ASPPB information for EPPP candidates: Examination for Professional Practice in Psychology*. Tyrone, GA: Author.

Schaffer, J. B., Rodolfa, E., Owen, J., Lipkins, R., Webb, C., & Horn, J. (2012). The Examination for Professional Practice in Psychology: New data-practical implications. *Training and Education in Professional Psychology*, 6(1), 1–7.

Acknowledgments

There are many people who make a book like this possible. We would like to thank Nancy S. Hale, Kathryn Corasaniti, and Shelby Peak from Springer Publishing Company and the production team at Exeter Premedia Services for all of their hard work and support during the publication process. We are grateful for the chapter authors who agreed to contribute to this volume. An edited book is only as good as those who write the chapters. We are grateful to Clare Gibson and Cheryl Seifert for providing suggestions and edits on earlier versions of the manuscript. There is no better perspective on a work of this nature than that of a student. Last, but certainly not least, we would like to thank our families for their patience and understanding while we spent late nights and early mornings in front of our computers. Editors are only as good as their loved ones.

Biological Bases of Behavior

Ashley Gorman, Daniel DaSilva, and Brenda Stepak

Broad Content Areas

- Biological and neural bases of behavior
- Psychopharmacology
- Methodologies supporting this body of knowledge

Biological processes are responsible, whether in isolation or concert with other processes, for all human and animal behavior. The biological system consists of highly complex, delicate, and integrated structures and mechanisms that are not fully understood by science. However, our knowledge in this area is growing at a rapid pace. Below we present the core components involved in the critical role biophysiological processes play in human and animal behavior with a focus on structures, functions, interventions, and methodologies.

Central Nervous System

It is important to understand that the brain forms only one part of what is also known as the central nervous system (CNS), which as a unit, comprises the brain and spinal cord. Elegant in design but complex in function, the brain and spinal cord make up the biological core of the human experience. To understand this system in terms of its functions and dysfunctions requires an understanding of the major structures and their role in the integration of our internal and external experiences.

Spinal Cord

The human spinal cord is a segmented cord linked with the organs and muscles of specific body regions. The spinal cord has four major divisions with 30 total segments, from the neck to the sacrum. The segments are identified according to their location in one of the three regions: cervical (C1–C8), thoracic (T1–T12), lumbar (L1–L5), and sacral (S1–S5). Fibers entering the dorsal portion of the spinal cord carry sensory information from the body to the brain. Descending fibers exiting the ventral portion of the spinal cord carry motor information to the muscles. When the spinal cord is damaged, a person loses the ability to feel and/or move the corresponding portion of his or her body at and below the site of the damage. For example, damage to the upper cervical regions of the spinal cord results in quadriplegia (inability to move the arms and legs), whereas damage to lower cervical regions results in paraplegia (inability to move the legs). Incomplete damage to the spinal cord may result in muscle weakness (paresis) as opposed to total immobility (paralysis). In addition to mediating voluntary movement, the spinal cord is also involved in involuntary movements such as reflexes (e.g., the withdrawal reflex from pain).

Brain

Skull and Cranial Meninges

The CNS, and the brain in particular, is guarded by several layers of protection. The most obvious is the skull, which is the bone structure forming the cranial vault. Just inside, and in various places, closely attached to the skull is the dura mater. This fibrous membrane also forms the falx cerebri, which extends down into the longitudinal fissure separating the two hemispheres of the brain. The arachnoid mater is a thinner and more delicate membrane separated from the dura by the subdural space through which passes a series of veins. Finally, the pia mater is the most delicate and highly vascular membrane, which closely follows the contours of the brain. The pia is separated from the dura by the subarachnoid space, which contains a network of arteries, veins, and connective tissue known as trabeculae.

Ventricles

Providing both protection and structural support, the internally located ventricular system comprises open chambers and channels filled with cerebral spinal fluid (CSF). This colorless fluid circulates through the two large lateral ventricles, located internally in each cerebral hemisphere, to the centrally located third ventricle, through the cerebral aqueduct and into the fourth ventricle in the dorsal brain stem. From there, the fluid flows in the subarachnoid space around the brain and spinal cord. The fluid is formed predominantly in the linings of the lateral ventricles known as the choroid plexus and then reabsorbed after its circulation. The CSF maintains the brain's neutral buoyancy in the cranial vault and plays an important role in protection from infection and regulation of cerebral blood flow.

Cerebrum

Gross examination of the human brain reveals that the surface comprises convolutions of fissures (the inward folds) and gyri (the smoothly curved hills), both serving to increase the surface area of the cortex. Comprising six layers of cell bodies and interconnections, the cortex forms the outer and most visible layer of the brain, also known as the cortex or gray matter. Although functionally significant, the fissures and gyri also form the definitions and boundaries of the major structures of the telencephalon, or cerebrum, which includes the four major lobes (frontal, temporal, parietal, and occipital). Each lobe is represented bilaterally in the right and left hemispheres.

Frontal Lobes

Located anterior of the central sulcus, the frontal lobe is the largest of the four lobes, governs output, and is considered the seat of higher cortical and cognitive functioning. Major anatomical subdivisions include the primary motor cortex, premotor cortex, orbitofrontal cortex, and prefrontal cortex. These regions are particularly devoted to attention, cognition, reasoning, problem solving, and voluntary movement.

Directly anterior to the central sulcus is the primary motor cortex. This gyrus, which runs laterally from superior to inferior, is crucial in the initiation of motor movements and isolated muscle groups are specifically represented along the surface of this gyrus. Moreover, the relative representation in this region corresponds directly to the requisite accuracy of motor control. For example, hands, fingers, lips, and tongue are heavily represented, whereas other regions such as the trunk and torso are not as heavily represented. Damage to this region will produce deficits in motor learning and more severe forms of lateralized damage will produce hemiparesis.

Directly anterior to the primary motor cortex is the premotor cortex, a region dedicated to the initiation and execution of limb movements in conjunction with input from other cortical regions. Mirror neurons located here have been associated with imitation and empathy and have been the focus of some autism studies (Schulte-Ruther, Markowitsch, Fink, & Piefke, 2007; Williams, Whiten, Suddendorf, & Perrett, 2001).

Prefrontal and orbitofrontal regions, located anterior to the primary motor cortex, are most often associated with higher-level cognitive functions also known as the executive functions, which includes reasoning, planning, and judgment. Dysfunction in this region has been associated with many disorders, including attention deficit hyperactivity disorder (ADHD) and schizophrenia. Inhibitory control is also most often associated with this region. The frontal lobe injury sustained by Phineas Gage in the mid-1800s, a railroad construction worker, is often considered an illustrative example of classic frontal lobe impairment.

For the majority of individuals, the inferior lateral region of the left frontal lobe is known as Broca's area. This area is particularly dedicated to the fluent production of oral and written speech, as well as grammar and comprehension of syntax. The dysfunction associated with a lesion here is most often recognized as Broca's (or expressive) aphasia (an acquired disorder of language).

Temporal Lobes

Located inferior to the lateral sulcus, the temporal lobes are divided into the superior, middle, and inferior temporal gyri. Located in the superior temporal gyrus is the site of primary auditory processing, where conscious perception of sound takes place. This region, typically found in the infolded region of superior temporal gyrus, is also known as Heschel's convolutions. Reception of stimuli in this region is considered "tonotopic," which corresponds to individual frequencies detected at the level of the cochlea located in the inner ear. Stimuli arrive here by way of the vestibulocochlear nerves and the medial geniculate nuclei of the thalamus and undergo only partial "decussation," the process by which incoming stimuli are transmitted to the contralateral hemisphere for processing. Because of partial decussation, or crossing of fibers, sound stimuli critical for auditory language comprehension will still arrive at the language-dominant hemisphere. Immediately adjacent and posterior to the primary auditory cortex is the auditory association cortex, where sound is further processed. In the language-dominant hemisphere, this region is known as Wernicke's area, which is dedicated to the comprehension of language. Lesions in this region will disrupt not only the ability to comprehend language but also the meaningful expression of language. This deficit is known as Wernicke's (or receptive) aphasia.

Parietal Lobes

The parietal lobes are located posterior to the central sulcus and include the site of primary somatosensory processing on the postcentral gyrus. Major neuroanatomical structures also include the inferior and superior parietal lobules. Within the parietal lobes are large regions of the heteromodal cortex, where different sensory modalities are integrated to construct a complete picture. The parietal lobes process visual information along dorsal and ventral pathways from the occipital lobes to help coordinate movements and behaviors with the environment. Damage to posterior regions of the parietal lobe can result in neglect syndromes such as hemispatial neglect, which is characterized by an inability to attend to features of the environment in the space contralateral to the lesion site.

As noted, primary somatosensory processing occurs on the postcentral gyrus where "somatotopic" detection of touch, pressure, pain, and temperature takes place. As on the primary motor cortex, regions of the sensory cortex proportionally represent body regions depending on their relative sensitivity, for example, there is heavy representation of the finger tips, face, and lips. Lateralized lesions here will result in hemisensory loss (loss of sensation on one side of the body).

Occipital Lobes

Located posterior to the temporal and parietal lobes, the occipital lobes are geographically defined by the parieto-occipital sulcus visible on the medial surface of the hemisphere. Primarily dedicated to visual processing, primary visual processing is located in the region of the occipital pole, posterior to the calcarine sulcus. Primary visual processing is phototopic in nature, receiving its stimuli from the retina and optic nerve by way of the lateral geniculate nucleus of the thalamus.

Properties such as color and movement are processed at the primary visual, or striate, cortex. They are then sent for further processing and integration along the dorsal stream to parietal regions for processing of object location and along the ventral stream to temporal regions for object identification. Areas adjacent to primary processing regions are considered visual associations areas, which further process and integrate visual stimuli. Lesions in primary visual processing regions result in cortical blindness. Other lesions can result in disturbances in color perception and inability to detect orientation or movement.

Subcortical Brain Regions

Hippocampus

The inferior temporal lobe curls in toward the midline and forms a region known as the hippocampus. As part of the limbic system, the hippocampus is critical for memory formation such as the transfer of memories to longer-term stores. The classic cases of a patient initially known as HM whose hippocampi were surgically removed to control seizures, and Clive Wearing, a British musician who contracted encephalitis, illustrate the debilitating memory impairments associated with bilateral hippocampal lesions.

Amygdala

Also part of the limbic system, the amygdala is located anterior of the hippocampus and is involved in processing olfactory stimuli. However, the amygdala is most often associated with processing emotions. Its connections to midbrain structures make the amygdala an essential component of the "fight-or-flight" response.

Thalamus

Located superior to and contiguous with the brain stem is the thalamus. This structure performs the critical relay functions between the cortex and the brain stem. Specific nuclei, or collections of nerve cells, form the specific transmission sites in the thalamus to and from specific cortical regions. Because of these very rich interconnections, the thalamus also performs important attention and perceptual functions.

Basal Ganglia

The basal ganglia is an important subcortical structure comprising a network of complex loops involved in motor output (i.e., descending motor pathways), emotions, cognition, and eye movements. The main components of the basal ganglia include the caudate nucleus, putamen, globus pallidus, subthalamic nucleus, and substantia nigra. The cerebral cortex provides most of the input to the basal ganglia, and the primary outputs of the basal ganglia are sent to the thalamus. Motor abnormalities due to basal ganglia do not involve paresis or paralysis, but rather the coordination and rhythm of movement. These syndromes are referred to as "extrapyramidal syndromes." For example, slow movements (i.e., bradykinesia) or excessive muscle rigidity result from basal ganglia dysfunction. Movement disorders such as Parkinson's disease (PD) and Huntington's disease result from abnormal activity in the basal ganglia.

Brain Stem

Comprising the medulla (also referred to as the medulla oblongata), pons, and midbrain, the brain stem forms the core of the brain. The midbrain and its component structures are surrounded by the cerebral hemispheres. Located caudally, or toward the tail, is the pons (or bridge), followed by the medulla, which is essentially contiguous with the spinal cord. Functionally, the brain stem, as a unit, is involved in the control and regulation of autonomic functions and maintaining the body's homeostasis, including breathing, heart rate, temperature regulation, and blood pressure. The reticular formation, including the reticular activating system, plays important roles in alertness, consciousness, and pain. It also plays important roles in regulating the respiratory and cardiovascular systems. Ascending sensory pathways from the spinal cord rise through dorsal regions, whereas descending, motor fibers pass through anterior regions of the brain stem.

Cerebellum

Attached to the posterior brain stem is the cerebellum. Rich in neurons, the cerebellum is structurally divided into the superior, middle, and inferior cerebellar peduncles. The middle cerebellar peduncle is the only structure visible on surface examination of the brain. The cerebellum comprises a gray matter cortex and subcortical white matter with rich interconnections to cortical regions of the other hemispheres of the brain. Functionally, the cerebellum is most often associated with the regulation of movement, including automatic and rhythmic movements, coordination of the limbs, and postural control. Studies have also associated the cerebellum with cognitive functions such as learning and attention (Helmuth, Ivry, & Shimizu, 1997).

The cerebellum is particularly vulnerable in multiple sclerosis, which can result in disruption of ocular movements such as nystagmus (a rapid rhythmic eye movement which is particularly enhanced when the gaze is in the same direction of the lesion site). Lesions of the cerebellum can also produce motor incoordination and a characteristic wide-based stance and gait.

Neurons

The neuron is the building block of the nervous system. Neurons vary in size and shape and are highly specialized to a specific function. A typical neuron consists of a cell body (containing the nucleus), dendrites (short processes emerging from the cell body which receive inputs from other neurons), and axons (long processes that carry output away from the cell body). Most neurons in the human brain are "multipolar," that is, they have multiple dendrites and axons. A myelin sheath, which is an insulating fatty layer, surrounds the axon and speeds up transmission. Axons can range in length from 1 mm to 1 m. The synapse is the space between two neurons in which chemical and/or electrical communication occurs. In most cases, the axon from one neuron communicates with the dendrites of another neuron.

Chemicals known as neurotransmitters are released "presynaptically" by the axon terminal of one neuron and bind to neurotransmitter receptors on the "postsynaptic" neuron, which may then cause postsynaptic excitation or inhibition. When postsynaptic excitation reaches a minimum threshold, that neuron then fires an action potential, causing that neuron to send the neural signal down its axon. The firing of a neuron is an "all-or-nothing" phenomenon, that is, the strength of neuronal firing does not vary in response to the strength of the input. In other words, a neuron either fires or it does not. After a neuron fires, there is a refractory period during which it is unable to fire again until it reestablishes an electrochemically based resting potential state. Different neurotransmitters have different effects on cells (excitatory or inhibitory), and the amount of a neurotransmitter that is available for binding to the postsynaptic neuron can be affected by various medications.

Neurotransmitters

Neurotransmitters are chemicals that transmit signals from one neuron to another and are classified according to their molecular size. Biogenic amines (e.g., acetylcholine [ACh] and serotonin), catecholamines (e.g., dopamine [DA], norepinephrine [NE], and epinephrine), and amino acids (e.g., gamma-aminobutyric acid [GABA] and glutamate) are smaller molecular messengers, whereas neuropeptides (e.g., vasopressin, oxytocin, and substance P) are larger molecules. Neurotransmitters fit into a receptor site like a lock and key, although a variety of neurotransmitters may fit into a single type of receptor (Zillmer & Spiers, 2001). The most significant neurotransmitters to psychopharmacology include NE, serotonin, DA, GABA, ACh, and glutamate (Wegman, 2012).

Norepinephrine or "noradrenalin" is a catecholamine and functions as a hormone and a neurotransmitter. It is formed in the brain stem at a site called the "locus coeruleus" and is found in the sympathetic nervous system and CNS. It regulates mood, memory, alertness, hormones, and the ability to feel pleasure. Elevated levels may lead to anxiety, whereas low levels may cause depression (Wegman, 2012). NE also underlies the "fight-or-flight" response and is released into the blood as a hormone by the adrenal gland in response to stress or arousal. It is primarily considered an excitatory neurotransmitter, but may result in inhibition in some areas.

Dopamine is also a catecholamine and can be both excitatory and inhibitory. The majority of DA neurons are in the substantia nigra. Dopamine pathways extend to the frontal lobes, basal ganglia, and hypothalamus. Overactivity of DA in the pathway to the frontal lobes has been implicated in schizophrenia, and the loss of DA-producing neurons in the basal ganglia pathway is the underlying cause of PD. Underactivity of DA has also been implicated in ADHD (Wegman, 2012). Dopamine plays a role in emotions, movement, endocrine functioning, as well as attention, sociability, motivation, desire, pleasure, and reward-driven learning.

Serotonin (5-HT) is a biogenic amine and is primarily inhibitory. It is widely distributed throughout the brain and originates in the raphe nuclei in the brain stem. Pathways extend to the limbic system, and serotonin levels are associated with the regulation of mood, anger, aggression, anxiety, appetite, learning, sleep, sexual functioning, level of consciousness, and pain. Low levels of serotonin are associated with depression, obsessive-compulsive disorder, and anxiety disorders (Wegman, 2012).

Acetylcholine is also a biogenic amine and plays a major role in the parasympathetic nervous system and autonomic nervous system (Zillmer & Spiers, 2001). It is the primary neurotransmitter at the neuromuscular junction (the synapse between neuron and muscle cells) and is involved in movement. Degeneration of ACh in the striatum of the brain is associated with a movement disorder called Huntington's disease. ACh also plays a major role in activating the brain through the reticular activating system and regulates alertness and attention. Another cholinergic system involving the hippocampus influences attention, learning, and memory (Zillmer & Spiers, 2003).

Gamma-aminobutyric acid is an amino acid and is the major inhibitory neurotransmitter of the CNS. It is widely distributed throughout the CNS but is most concentrated in the striatum, hypothalamus, spinal cord, and temporal lobes. GABA is associated with emotion, balance, and sleep patterns. Low levels of GABA are associated with high anxiety and agitation, and higher levels are associated with a reduction in anxiety (Wegman, 2012). GABA deficiencies are also implicated in epilepsy, and many antiepileptic drugs increase GABA activity.

Glutamate is also an amino acid and is the brain's primary excitatory neurotransmitter. It is widely distributed throughout the CNS. It is a basic building block of proteins and plays an important role in learning and memory (Wegman, 2012). Excessive glutamate causes excitotoxicity (cell death due to excessive stimulation and excitation), and is implicated in cell death following traumatic brain injury and stroke.

Psychopharmacology

Clinical psychologists may or may not have prescription privileges depending on whether they have specialized training and whether this training is recognized by the state in which they practice. It is imperative for even nonprescribing psychologists to possess a general understanding of psychotropic agents and whether they may be indicated. Often the psychologist will act as the intermediary between the patient and a prescribing clinician. It is necessary to be able to recognize when an evaluation for psychotropic medication (or for termination of medication) may be beneficial to the patient. Each patient is unique and will have different requirements based on age, sensitivities to medications, and other characteristics.

Pharmacokinetics and Pharmacodynamics

Psychotropic medications cross the blood–brain barrier and cause physiological and biochemical changes. The mechanism of action for these medications is complex. To put it simply, these medications alter the activity of neurotransmitter communication between neurons by doing one or more of the following: disrupting the action of the neurotransmitter at the synapse (thus blocking the action of the neurotransmitter), inhibiting the enzymes that break down neurotransmitters in the synaptic cleft (thus boosting the overall transmission of that neurotransmitter), changing the sensitivity of postsynaptic neurons to neurotransmitters, or increasing the amount of neurotransmitter produced and available at the synapse.

Psychoactive drugs are able to cause downstream biochemical and physiological changes by binding to receptor sites on neurons and either boosting the action of a particular neurotransmitter system or blocking the action of a neurotransmitter system. An agonist is a chemical that binds to a receptor site and mimics the activity of a neurotransmitter, thus causing the same downstream effects as that neurotransmitter and boosting the overall system. A partial agonist also binds to a receptor site and mimics the activity of a neurotransmitter, but cannot produce 100% of the effect of a full agonist, even at very high doses. An inverse agonist binds to the same receptor site as an agonist but has the opposite effect of full agonists by causing a reduction in the overall efficacy of a neurotransmitter system. An antagonist also blocks or reverses the effect of agonists or inverse agonists, but when an agonist is not present, they have no effect of their own (Stringer, 2011).

Pharmacodynamics describes the biochemical and physiological effects of drugs on the body. Pharmacokinetics describes how the body handles the drug through absorption, distribution, metabolism, and elimination. Absorption is the process through which drugs reach the bloodstream. This process occurs mainly in the small intestine and results in the drug's onset and degree of action. A poorly absorbed drug may not reach the minimal effective concentration required in the blood for clinical efficacy. The blood stream transporting a drug to its site of action serves as the distribution. The speed of distribution varies depending on how the drug is administered. For example, drugs taken orally must first travel through the digestive system, whereas drugs injected intramuscularly have a faster response. When a drug enters the bloodstream, metabolism begins. The body recognizes the drug as a foreign substance and attempts to eliminate it via chemical transformation. Metabolism occurs primarily in the liver. People metabolize psychotropic agents differently, and the sensitivities and preferences of each individual patient must be considered to get optimum risk–benefit ratios. For example, children and the elderly may metabolize drugs differently than young adults, and therefore dosage or scheduling adjustments may be required to achieve the best risk–benefit ratios. Once a drug is in circulation, elimination is a function of renal and hepatic processes. The elimination half-life of the drug is the time it takes for drug concentration to decrease by half due to excretion and metabolic change. In the steady state, the rate of elimination is equal to the rate of administration of the drug.

A therapeutic window is defined by the range of a drug dose that can result in desired clinical efficacy without resulting in unsafe side effects. For example, if a drug has a narrow therapeutic window, then there is only a small range of dosages that can result in the desired benefit before it becomes unsafe. A therapeutic index is the ratio of the amount of drug that causes the desired benefit to the amount of the drug that produces dangerous side effects. It is more desirable for a drug to have a high therapeutic index, as it is a measure of drug safety.

Psychoactive drugs can be classified according to the clinical disorders that they treat (e.g., anxiolytics, antidepressants, antipsychotics, stimulants, and pain medications). All psychoactive drugs have a unique mechanism of action, even those that treat similar clinical disorders, and all have notable side effects and possible drug interactions that must be considered. The following section summarizes the primary psychoactive drug classifications, their mechanism of action, side effects, and drug interactions.

Anxiolytics

Anxiolytics refer to the psychotropic medications that may be used to treat anxiety disorders and can be classified into benzodiazepines and nonbenzodiazepines. Examples of anxiolytics that are benzodiazepines are alprazolam (Xanax), clonazepam (Klonapin), diazepam, (Valium), and lorazepam (Ativan). Buspirone (Buspar) is an example of a nonbenzodiazepine anxiolytic. Some benzodiazepines are used as sleep agents and others may treat seizure disorders and alcohol withdrawal (Pies, 2005). Anxiety disorders that may be treated with benzodiazepines include generalized anxiety disorder, panic disorder, phobic disorders, adjustment disorder with anxiety, anxiety disorder due to a general medical condition, and substance-induced anxiety disorder (Pies, 2005; Wegman, 2012).

Benzodiazepines act through the CNS and cause muscle relaxation as well as sedative, anxiolytic, and anticonvulsant effects. They enhance the action of GABA (which is an inhibitory neurotransmitter) and block the rapid release of stress hormones associated with anxiety and panic. These medications are rapidly and completely absorbed after oral administration and distributed throughout the body. Some are short acting and some are long acting.

The most significant side effects of benzodiazepines include drowsiness, confusion or feelings of detachment, dizziness, imbalance, and high potential for dependence. When discontinued, they must be tapered slowly to prevent withdrawal symptoms. In regard to drug interactions, benzodiazepines increase the effects of alcohol and other CNS depressants. They should be used cautiously in patients with liver disease and avoided in patients with a history of substance abuse (Stahl, 2011).

Since the 1990s benzodiazepines have been increasingly replaced by selective serotonin reuptake inhibitors (SSRIs) and other antidepressants as clinicians' first choice for the treatment of anxiety disorders due to their increased safety, lower side effect profile, and decreased likelihood of dependence (Asho & Sheehan, 2004).

Barbiturates are medications that were formerly used for sedation and to induce sleep, but have now been essentially replaced by benzodiazepines. The side effects of barbiturates are extreme, including tolerance, physical dependency, and very severe withdrawal symptoms. They also enhance the function of GABA in the CNS (Stringer, 2011).

Antidepressants

Antidepressants are a diverse group of medications that have different mechanisms of action. The primary classifications of antidepressants include monoamine oxidase inhibitors (MAOIs), tricyclic antidepressants (TCAs), SSRIs, and newer agents such as norepinephrine–dopamine reuptake inhibitors (NDRIs) and serotonin–norepinephrine reuptake inhibitors (SNRIs). In general, antidepressants do not cause dependence, tolerance, or addiction. These medications are used to treat disorders such as unipolar major depression, dysthymic disorder, adjustment disorders, and mood disorder due to general medical condition. These medications are also used in the treatment of many anxiety disorders (Pies, 2005), ADHD, and eating disorders (Stein, Lerer, & Stahl, 2012). The use of antidepressants is contraindicated in patients with bipolar disorder, as they may induce mania.

The medications listed above target a class of neurotransmitters called the monoamines, which include NE, serotonin, and DA. The "monoamine hypothesis" of depression dates back to the 1960s and postulates that depression is caused by abnormal functioning of these neurotransmitters. Based on this hypothesis, antidepressant medications are thought to increase the availability of these neurotransmitters at the synaptic level. However, a simple deficiency of monoamines at the synaptic level is no longer thought to explain the mechanisms of action of these medications in full (Patterson, McCahill, & Edwards, 2010), and antidepressants likely affect many biological systems in addition to neurotransmitter uptake (Mycek, Harvey, & Champe, 1997).

Tricyclic antidepressants These drugs are categorized on the basis of their chemical three-ring structure (Pies, 2005). Examples of TCAs include amitriptyline (Elavil), nortriptyline (Pamelor and Aventyl), imipramine (Tofranil), and desipramine (Norpramin). Absorption of the tricyclic drugs occurs in the small intestine, and peak levels occur within 2 to 8 hours following ingestion (Golan, Tashjian, Armstrong, & Armstrong, 2008). Tricyclics block the reuptake of serotonin and NE (thus increasing the activity of these neurotransmitter systems by making them more available for binding to postsynaptic neurons); however, the precise mechanism of action of the TCAs is unknown (Stringer, 2011).

Unfortunately, this class of medications has side effects that make them unattractive. Side effects of TCAs fall into three categories: cardiac/autonomic, anticholinergic, and neurobehavioral. Orthostatic hypotension (a drop in standing blood pressure) is one of the most common reasons for discontinuation of this medication (Pies, 2005).

Monoamine oxidase inhibitors Monoamine oxidase inhibitors (MAOIs) are rarely used today because of serious drug–drug and drug–food interactions. They block the reuptake of monoamine neurotransmitters (serotonin, NE, and DA) by blocking their respective monoamine transporters, thus increasing the levels of these neurotransmitters in the synaptic cleft (Keltner & Folks, 2005). Examples of MAOIs include phenelzine (Nardil) and tranylcyromine (Parnate). The most dangerous side effect of MAOIs is hypertensive crisis, which can occur when an MAOI is taken with tyramine (Stahl, 2011).

Selective serotonin reuptake inhibitors These medications, which block the reuptake of serotonin by selective binding, are especially effective for the treatment of depression with agitation and/or comorbid anxiety. The term "selective" is used because they have weaker affinity for blocking the action of other monoamines. Examples of SSRIs include fluoxetine (Prozac), paroxetine (Paxil), fluvoxamine (Luvox), setraline (Zoloft), citalopram (Celexa), and escitalopram (Lexapro). SSRIs are less likely to cause anticholinergic and cardiac/autonomic side effects than the TCAs; however, side effects do include gastrointestinal side effects, headache, sexual dysfunction, insomnia, psychomotor agitation, and occasional extrapyramidal reactions.

Norepinephrine–dopamine reuptake inhibitors These antidepressants are relatively newer antidepressants, and they work by blocking the reuptake of NE and DA. An example of an NDRI is bupropion (Wellbutrin).

Serotonin–norepinephrine reuptake inhibitors These medications block the reuptake of serotonin and NE. An example of an SNRI is venlafaxine (Effexor).

Over-the-counter products St. John's wort, S-adenosyl methionine (SAMe), 5-HTP, Omega-3 fatty acids, and folic acid have all been shown to have some efficacy in treating depression. Omega-3 fatty acids and folic acid are typically used in conjunction with antidepressants (Preston & Johnson, 2012). However, it is important to note that these alternative remedies can also have negative side effects and adverse drug interactions. For example, St. John's wort can reduce the effectiveness of oral contraceptives and Omega-3 fatty acids can increase the risk of bruising and bleeding especially when combined with blood thinners (Wegman, 2012).

Antipsychotics

Antipsychotics are primarily used to treat schizophrenia, schizophreniform disorder, schizoaffective disorder, brief psychotic disorder, bipolar disorder, and agitation (Pies, 2005). Several neurochemical abnormalities are associated with schizophrenia but the DA system is the most studied (Patterson et al., 2010). All traditional (or first-generation) antipsychotic medications block DA receptors, whereas atypical (or second generation) also block serotonin receptors (Patterson et al., 2010).

Conventional antipsychotics ("typical" or "first generation") First developed in the 1950s, all of the drugs in this group seem to have equal efficacy but differ in potency and side effects. Examples of conventional antipsychotics include haloperidol (Haldol), thioridazine (Mellaril), molinidine (Moban), thiothixene (Navane), fluphenazine (Prolixin), trifluoperazine (Stelazine), and chlorpromazine (Thorazine).

Conventional antipsychotics may cause extrapyramidal symptoms (EPSs), including parkinsonism, acute dystonia, akathisia, and tardive dyskinesia. The first three EPSs are early drug reactions. The fourth, tardive dyskinesia, results from long-term use. Parkinsonism includes bradykinesia (slowed movements), tremor, and rigidity. Acute dystonia includes muscle spasms in the tongue, face, neck, and back. Akathisia is characterized by restless movements and symptoms of anxiety and agitation. Tardive dyskinesia is characterized by abnormal involuntary, stereotyped movements of the face, tongue, trunk, and extremities. Unfortunately, this syndrome may be irreversible, even when antipsychotic medications are discontinued (Lehne, 2013).

Another potential side effect is neuroleptic malignant syndrome (NMS), a rare but life-threatening reaction characterized by catatonia, stupor, fever, and autonomic instability. Additional side effects of the antipsychotics may include orthostatic hypotension, sexual dysfunction, and sedation, as well as anticholiner-gic effects such as dry mouth, constipation, and difficulty with urination (Lehne, 2013).

Atypical antipsychotics (second generation)   Atypical antipsychotics became available in the 1990s. In addition to blocking DA receptors in the CNS, the atypicals also block serotonin receptors (Patterson et al., 2010). Initially, the atypical anti-psychotic medications were thought to be more effective than the typical or first-generation antipsychotics; however the Clinical Antipsychotic Trials of Intervention Effectiveness (CATIE), a National Institutes of Health- (NIH) funded, nationwide clini-cal trial, revealed that the typical or first-generation antipsychotics may indeed be just as effective as some of the newer atypical antipsychotic medications (Lieberman et al., 2005). The newer atypical drugs may produce milder extrapyramidal symptoms than the typical antipsychotics; however, they may also cause dangerous metabolic effects such as weight gain, diabetes, and dislipidemia (Lehne, 2013).

Atypical antipsychotics include olanzapine (Zyprexa), quetiapine (Seroquel), ziprasidone (Geodon), aripiprazole (Abilify), paliperidone (Invega), iloperidone (Fanapt), asenapine (Saphris), clozapine (Clozaril), and risperidone (Risperdal). Clozapine is actually one of the more effective atypical antipsychotics although it is also the most dangerous. Fatal agranulocytosis (dangerously low white blood cell count causing decreased ability to fight infection) is a potential side effect. There-fore, testing of white blood counts is done on a regular basis, which improves out-come. Risperdal (risperidone) is a first-line medication for new onset schizophrenia and is also well accepted for treatment of agitation and aggression in dementia and in bipolar disorders. Risperdal is also Food and Drug Administration– (FDA) approved for minimizing self-harm in autism and disruptive behavior disorders in children and adolescents (Stringer, 2011).

Mood Stabilizers

Lithium was the first mood-stabilizing medication approved by the FDA for the treatment of acute mania and hypomania. It has well-documented efficacy in pre-venting relapse in bipolar disorder. Lithium's mechanism of action is complex and simply a theory. It is suspected to involve NE and serotonin (Wegman, 2012). Unfortunately, lithium has a slow onset of action and a narrow therapeutic index (i.e., the therapeutic dose is close to toxic).

Common side effects of lithium include nausea, diarrhea, vomiting, thirst, excessive urination, weight gain, and hand tremor. A reversible increase in white blood cell count frequently occurs with lithium use. Chronic use side effects include hypothyroidism, goiter, and rarely, kidney damage. Toxicity may result in lethargy, ataxia, slurred speech, shock, delirium, coma, or even death (Wegman, 2012). Drug interactions with diuretics can increase plasma lithium concentration, and those with nonsteroidal anti-inflammatory agents can increase serum lithium levels (Stahl, 2011).

Antipsychotics and anticonvulsant medications may also be used as mood stabilizers and are considered first-line treatments for bipolar disorder (Wegman, 2012). For example, the atypical antipsychotics Zyprexa and Abilify are both FDA approved for acute and maintenance treatment of bipolar mania. Symbyax is FDA approved for treatment of depression associated with bipolar disorder (Wegman, 2012). Examples of anticonvulsants used as mood stabilizers include divalproex (Depakote), lamitrogine (Lamictal), carbamezepine (Tegretol), and topiramate (Topamax). Anticonvulsants work by enhancing the actions of GABA, the brain's major inhibitory neurotransmitter (Wegman, 2012). One example of a serious side effect of an anticonvulsant medication (Lamictal) is Stevens–Johnson syndrome, a potentially fatal skin rash.

Opiates (Narcotic Analgesics)

Opiates refer to natural or synthetic compounds obtained from the juice of the opium poppy that are used as drugs. Natural opiates include opium, morphine, and codeine. Semisynthetic derivatives of opiates include morphine, heroin, Percodan (oxycodone hydrochloride and aspirin) and Dilaudid (hydromorphone hydrochloride). Drugs with opiumlike mechanism of action are called opioids. The brain produces its own version of opiates called endogenous opiates (Mycek et al., 1997), and there are naturally occurring binding sites in the brain called opiate receptors.

Opiates are used to relieve intense pain and the anxiety that goes along with it. They also induce sleep. Some opiates are prescribed for severe diarrhea or coughs (Stringer, 2011). Opiates are often manufactured in combination with nonopiate analgesics, such as aspirin and acetaminophen (e.g., Percodan or oxycodone hydrochloride and aspirin). The two work well in combination because these different classes of drugs affect pain pathways via different mechanisms of action (Stringer, 2011).

Long-term opiate use changes the way nerve cells work in the brain, which can lead to withdrawal symptoms when they are suddenly discontinued. These withdrawal symptoms may include diarrhea, vomiting, chills, fever, tearing and runny nose, tremor, abdominal cramps, and pain (Stringer, 2011). Opiates may be abused for their euphoric effects. Regarding drug interaction, the depressant actions of morphine are enhanced by MAOIs and TCAs (Mycek et al., 1997).

Psychostimulants

Psychostimulants increase prefrontal cortex levels of NE and DA (Pies, 2005) and are primarily used to treat ADHD. Some examples of psychostimulants include amphetamine (Adderall), methylphenidate (Concerta), and modafinil (Provigil), which is also used for sleep disorders such as narcolepsy. Some antidepressants can be used in treating ADHD because they also enhance the actions of NE and DA in the prefrontal cortex; however, SSRIs are considered a poor choice for treating ADHD due to their effects on serotonin (Wegman, 2012).

Side effects of the psychostimulants may include insomnia, headache, tics exacerbation, nervousness, irritability, overstimulation, tremor and dizziness, weight loss, abdominal pain or nausea, possibly slow normal growth in children, and blurred vision (Stahl, 2011). There are numerous potential drug interactions. For example, they should not be used with MAOIs as they may cause hypertensive crisis (Stahl, 2011).

Combined Treatments: Psychopharmacology and Beyond

It is important to note that the psychoactive medications described above often complement other nonmedication approaches to treatment for many psychiatric and neurological illnesses. For example, in the treatment of mild depression, cognitive behavioral therapy (CBT), antidepressants, and their combination have been shown to result in equal benefit (Otto, Smits, & Reese, 2005). For the treatment of severe depression, antidepressants used in combination with CBT have been shown to be better than either CBT or medication alone (Keller et al., 2000). Cognitive behavioral therapy for insomnia is shown to be equally effective and have longer lasting effects than psychotropic medication when active treatment is discontinued (Perlis, 2011)

Psychoactive medications are almost always used in the treatment of psychotic disorders. Unfortunately, schizophrenia and other forms of psychoses continue to be very difficult to treat. Psychotherapy, family therapy, skills training, psychoeducation, and vocational training often complement medication management (Patterson et al., 2010). Antipsychotics and anticonvulsant medications are also commonly used as first-line treatments for bipolar disorder, although they are commonly used in combination with psychotherapy (Wegman, 2012). Psychostimulants, which are primarily used to treat ADHD, are commonly used as part of a treatment plan involving multiple therapy modalities, including behavioral modification, parent and social skills training, and school-based interventions. Finally, environmental, social, and psychological interventions are crucial when managing patients with dementia.

Neuroimaging

The types of brain imaging techniques that can be used to visualize neuroanatomy and assess for neurological disorders are usually divided into "structural" and "functional" imaging techniques.

Structural Imaging

Computerized Tomography

Computerized tomography (CT) uses x-rays to look at slices of the brain, providing information on the density of brain tissue. There are two primary features that distinguish CT scans from traditional x-rays. First, rather than taking one view, the x-ray beam in CT is rotated around the patient to take many different views from different angles. Then, x-ray data are reconstructed by a computer to obtain detailed images of soft tissues, liquid, air, and bone.

The appearance of brain tissue on a CT scan depends on the tissue density. Very dense tissue, such as bone, appears white. Less dense tissue, such as air, appears black. The term *hyperdense* refers to brighter areas and *hypodense* refers to darker areas. Areas of intermediate density are referred to as *isodense*. Brain tissue that is rich in cells has a different density than areas rich in axons. White matter is slightly darker than gray matter due to its high myelin content. Cerebral spinal fluid is denser than air and is usually dark gray in color. In some instances, *intravenous contrast* material containing iodine is injected into the patient prior to obtaining the CT scan for better visualization of certain tissues. This contrast material is denser than brain tissue and will therefore appear hyperdense (white) in areas of increased vascularity or breakdown of the blood–brain barrier. CT images are often obtained with and without contrast for comparison. An *enhancing lesion* refers to areas that are absorbing this contrast material and may be indicative of brain neoplasms, abscess, infarct (area of dead tissue resulting from obstructed blood flow), demyelinating disease, resolving hematoma, or vascular malformation.

Clinically, CT is often used in the emergency room to detect acute hemorrhage or skull fracture following trauma. Fresh intracranial hemorrhage coagulates almost immediately and shows up as hyperdense (white) areas. Acute cerebral infarcts often cannot be seen with CT, although areas of abnormality resulting from cell death after a cerebral infarct are later visible. CT scans are also useful in the detection of neoplasms, (tumor), mass effect, or ventricular enlargement, for example, in the context of hydrocephalus.

Magnetic Resonance Imaging

Magnetic resonance imaging (MRI) was developed in the 1980s and uses powerful magnetic fields that cause protons to align themselves in response to the magnetic field's line of force. Unlike CT scans, MRI scans are not described in terms of density, rather they are described in terms of intensity, or brightness, of the signal. The term "hyperintense" refers to a brighter area, and the term "hypointense" refers to a darker area.

Clinically, MRI provides high-contrast, high-resolution imaging with good anatomical detail. MRI is the preferred method for detecting small lesions such as plaques found in patients with multiple sclerosis, subtle tumor, or chronic hemorrhage. CT is not as sensitive in detection of white matter or neurodegenerative disorders. However, MRI costs more and takes longer. CT is preferred in urgent assessment of head trauma with suspected intracranial hemorrhage, and it is better at visualizing bony structures (e.g., skull fracture). CT is also preferred for patients who have metallic implanted devices, such as a pacemaker. MRI is preferred in nonurgent situations in which a higher-resolution imaging method is required for better anatomical detail (Blumenfeld, 2010).

Neuroangiography

Neuroangiography is used to visualize lesions of blood vessels through the use of radiographs and injection of contrast material into the vasculature. It is the gold standard for evaluating vascular diseases in head, neck, and spine, such as atherosclerotic plaques and other vessel narrowings, aneurysms, and arteriovenous malformation (AVM). Angiography is often invasive and requires general anesthesia.

Wada Test

The Wada test is an example of neuroangiography that is helpful in localizing language function and aiding in presurgical planning, particularly in patients with epilepsy who are undergoing brain resection. For this procedure, amobarbital is selectively infused into each carotid artery while the patient is awake, essentially "putting to sleep" the contralateral hemisphere, so that various cognitive functions (e.g., memory and language) can be assessed in that hemisphere.

Functional Neuroimaging

Electroencephalography

Electroencephalography (EEG) is considered the original method for measuring brain activity. To measure brain activity using an EEG, a small metal disk that records the electrical activity of the neurons in the underlying brain area is attached to the scalp. These small electrical impulses are amplified and displayed on paper using a chart recorder called an electroencephalograph. EEG is useful in detecting widespread abnormality in brain function in a variety of contexts (e.g., sleep, anesthesia, coma, traumatic brain injury, and epilepsy), but its sensitivity and spatial resolution for detecting brain lesions are poor.

Positron Emission Tomography

Positron emission tomography (PET) uses small amounts of injected radioactive material to measure regional cerebral blood flow via glucose metabolism or oxygen consumption. The idea is that areas of the brain that are more active will use more glucose (and hence become radioactive) than less active areas. However, the brain is always active, so the brain's normal background activity is usually measured first to establish a baseline, which is then "subtracted" from the activity measured during the test. PET scans are useful for mapping the distribution of neurotransmitters and identifying brain dysfunction due to stroke, epilepsy, tumor, dementia, and other brain-impairing conditions.

Functional Magnetic Resonance Imaging

Functional magnetic resonance imaging (fMRI) was developed directly from MRI and can detect functionally induced changes from blood oxygenation. The basic idea is that oxygen distribution varies with brain activity and the amount of oxygen in the blood changes the magnetic properties of the blood without having to inject any radioactive materials, such as with PET or CT. Like MRI, fMRI has excellent resolution and provides a detailed structural map, while also providing functional information. fMRI can be used to measure the brain's real-time response to motor activities or neuropsychological tests.

Disorders

Aphasia

Aphasia refers to an acquired disorder of language (as opposed to a developmental language disorder) and can affect expressive speech, receptive speech, reading (alexia), and/or writing (agraphia). Aphasia syndromes can be subdivided into three major classifications: fluent aphasia (in which speech is fluent but there are difficulties with comprehension and/or repetition of words or phrases spoken by others), nonfluent aphasia (in which expressive speech is notable for poor articulation or poor grammar, but comprehension is relatively preserved), and pure aphasia, in which select aspects of language are affected, such as reading or writing.

Under the category of fluent aphasia is Wernicke's aphasia (aka sensory aphasia or receptive aphasia), in which the primary deficit is the inability to understand language. Speech is usually fluent (with normal rate and articulation) but the content of the speech is often nonsensical and meaningless, often containing neologisms (nonwords) or incorrect combinations of words ("word salad"). People with Wernicke's aphasia often have poor insight into their deficit and may expect others to understand what they are saying. The ability to repeat what others say is also impaired. The lesion typically associated with Wernicke's aphasia is in the left temporal lobe.

Transcortical sensory aphasia is similar to Wernicke's aphasia in that it is also a fluent aphasia in which comprehension is poor, but the individual can repeat what others say (unlike Wernicke's). The lesion is usually in the border zones between the parietal and temporal lobes.

Broca's aphasia (also known as motor or expressive aphasia) is a nonfluent aphasia in which the person speaks in a slow, halting manner, with poor grammar and limited prosody. Only keywords are used, and use of verbs or connecting words is limited. Damage is usually in the left frontal lobe around Brodmann areas 44 and 45, also known as "Broca's area." Writing is usually slow and effortful. Repetition is also impaired. Auditory comprehension and reading comprehension are relatively preserved.

Transcortical motor aphasia is similar to Broca's aphasia (and is sometimes referred to as "little Broca's") in that it is also a nonfluent aphasia, but the person is able to repeat what others say (unlike Broca's aphasia). Damage usually occurs in the left frontal areas surrounding Broca's area, leaving Broca's area and its connections to Wernicke's area intact.

Conduction aphasia is a specific disorder in which people can speak normally (therefore it is considered a fluent aphasia), name objects, and understand speech, but the sole deficit is in the repetition of what others say. Conduction is considered a "disconnection syndrome" in which the expressive speech center of the brain and the receptive speech center are disconnected. Damage is thought to affect the arcuate fasciculus, which is the large white matter tract connecting Broca's area and Wernicke's area.

Anomic aphasia consists of a focal deficit in naming objects, although the person can adequately produce meaningful speech, comprehend speech, and repeat speech. The angular gyrus is thought to be affected in this type of aphasia, although some degree of anomia, or problems with word finding, is present is most types of aphasias and is not consistently localized to a particular brain region.

In global aphasia, all aspects of language are impaired, including expressive speech, comprehension, repetition, reading, and writing.

Alexia

Alexia is the acquired inability to read (as opposed to dyslexia, which refers to a developmental disorder of reading starting in childhood). Pure alexia refers to impairments with reading, whereas the ability to write is relatively preserved. The pathology is usually a stroke in the posterior region of the left hemisphere, affecting the posterior region of the corpus callosum, disconnecting the visual centers of the brain from the language centers of the brain.

Agraphia

Agraphia refers to an acquired disorder of writing (as opposed to a developmentally based writing disorder beginning in childhood). Agraphia may affect a variety of components of writing, including spelling, grammar, letter formation, or visuospatial errors (e.g., poor spacing or orientation of letters). Different types of agraphia are usually classified based on accompanying symptoms such as alexia, apraxia, or visuospatial disorders. The site and extent of damage can range from parietal lobe, frontal lobe, corpus callosum, and subcortical structures.

Apraxia

Apraxia is an acquired disorder of skilled, purposeful movement that is not due to a primary motor or sensory impairment such as paresis or paralysis. For example, a person may not be able to demonstrate how to brush his or her hair or wave good-bye on command. There are many types of apraxia. In some cases, the action may be carried out accurately but in a clumsy manner, and in other forms of apraxia, the person may commit errors such as performing sequenced actions in the wrong order (such as sealing an envelope before placing the letter inside). The lesion site may vary depending on the type of apraxia but is usually in the left hemisphere.

Dementia

Dementia is an umbrella term that refers to a decline in two or more areas of cognitive functioning resulting in significant impairments in activities of daily living. The term *dementia* does not imply a specific cause and could be due to progressive, static, or reversible etiologies (National Institute of Neurological Disorders and Stroke (NINDS)—National Institutes of Health, n.d.). Although cognitive functions do decline with age, dementia is not a normal part of the aging process. Dementia is also distinct from delirium, which is an acute and potentially reversible form of cognitive decline. The term dementia has recently been replaced by the term "neurocognitive disorder" in the *DSM-5* (American Psychiatric Association, 2013).

Alzheimer's disease (AD) is the most common cause of dementia in those aged 65 and older. Approximately 10% of people over the age of 65 are living with AD in the United States, and nearly half of those older than 85 have the disease (www.ninds .nih.gov/disorders/dementias/dementia.htm). A neurocognitive disorder due to AD is defined by the *DSM-5* as a decline in memory and at least one other cognitive domain and a progressive, steady decline in cognition, and no evidence of mixed etiology. The onset must be insidious with gradual progression over time. These features should not be better accounted for by an Axis I disorder, medical disorder, or delirium.

AD is considered a "cortical dementia" because it primarily results in neuronal loss and atrophy of the cerebral cortex, namely, the medial temporal areas, including the amygdala, hippocampal formation, and entorhinal cortex. In later stages of the disease, the following brain areas may also be affected: basal temporal cortex, parietal–occipital cortex, posterior cingulate gyrus, and frontal lobes. The primary motor, somatosensory, visual, and auditory cortices are relatively spared. The primary pathological changes in AD are beta-amyloid plaques (insoluble protein cores) and neurofibrillary tangles (intracellular protein tangles) which can be found throughout the cortex, although primarily in the limbic cortex region (e.g., the hippocampus), which is involved in memory. Neurotransmitter changes are also present, with primary dysfunction in the cholinergic neurons, which are involved in learning and memory.

Current medications used to treat AD, such as cholinesterase inhibitors, prevent the breakdown of ACh. These medications include galantamine, rivastigmine (Exelon), and donepezil (Aricept). Weight gain, sedation, and rarely, seizures, are some of the side effects. These drugs should not be combined with other cholinesterase inhibitors (Stahl, 2011).

Another medication known as memantine (Namenda) works by regulating glutamate, which, in excess, can lead to cell death. These medications typically slow the progression of AD, rather than restore previously lost cognitive functions. Side effects include dizziness, headache, and constipation (Stahl, 2011).

The diagnosis of AD is based on clinical presentation, obtained through a detailed clinical history and evaluation of cognitive abilities (McKhann et al., 2011). Sophisticated imaging and biomarker techniques, such as PET and CSF assays, are also being developed to identify the pathological hallmarks of the disease, which develop years before the clinical signs of memory loss appear (Sperling et al., 2011). Not everyone who has these pathological changes in their brain will go on to develop AD.

In the early stage of the disease (1–3 years), mild impairments may be seen in memory, particularly new learning and retention of new memories over time, with remote memory being relatively spared. Other cognitive areas affected include visuospatial functioning (e.g., topographic disorientation and difficulty with construction) and language (e.g., word finding and naming). Increased frustration and irritability may also be present. In the intermediate stage (2–10 years), increased impairments in memory, visuospatial skills, and language are present, with the emergence of apraxia, acalculia, aphasia, or agnosia. In the later stages (8–12 years), intellectual functions may be severely impaired, verbal output may be minimal, and the patient may develop problems with his or her gait and motor control.

The greatest risk factor for developing AD is age. Most cases of AD are sporadic, although several risk genes have been implicated. The risk gene with the strongest influence is called apolipoprotein E-e4 (APOE-e4). Scientists estimate that APOE-e4 may be a factor in 20% to 25% of Alzheimer's cases. There is also a rare form of "familial" AD, which is caused by an autosomal dominant gene and often onsets before age 60.

Pick's disease is a rare form of cortical dementia that is caused by degeneration of the frontal and temporal lobes of the brain. Pick's disease is one specific cause of a heterogenous group of dementias referred to as frontotemporal dementia (FTD). Pathologically, Pick's disease is distinguishable on autopsy by characteristic Pick inclusion bodies usually found in cortical and hippocampal neurons in the frontal and anterior temporal lobes (as opposed to the amyloid plagues and neurofibrillary tangles, which are the hallmark of AD; Heilman & Valenstein, 2003). Dementia due to Pick's disease, as well as other types of FTDs, are characterized by personality changes such as behavioral disinhibition, which often occur early in the course of the disease, as well as executive dysfunction and language abnormalities. Memory problems are also present, but tend to become more obvious later in the disease (as opposed to AD where memory loss is typically the primary presenting problem). Onset is typically younger than that of AD, occurring between ages 50 and 60. There is no treatment for Pick's disease.

Cerebrovascular disease is the second leading cause of acquired dementia following AD and is caused by multiple infarcts, or strokes, in either large vessels or smaller vessels which penetrate deeper in the brain. Dementia due to cerebrovascular disease tends to begin earlier than AD and is more common in men than women. Alternative terminology includes "multi-infarct dementia," "vascular dementia," or "vascular cognitive impairment." The onset is typically abrupt with a "stepwise" or fluctuating course. Risk factors include hypertension, abnormal lipid levels, smoking, diabetes, obesity, cardiovascular disease, or previous stroke or transient ischemic attacks. Cerebrovascular disease may co-exist with other causes of dementia, including AD (O'Brien et al., 2003). The types of deficits present in vascular dementia are variable and depend on the nature, type, and extent of the cerebrovascular lesions. Focal deficits may be present, as well as gait disturbance or psychomotor retardation. Depression or mood changes are also common. Cognitive deficits common in vascular dementia include psychomotor processing speed, complex attention, and executive functioning. Diagnostic criteria are similar to that of AD but differ in the onset and course of the disease, and focal neurological signs (e.g., gait abnormalities or weakness of an extremity) or evidence of cerebrovascular disease on neuroimaging is required (American Psychiatric Association, 2013). Treatments are often preventive, focusing on the underlying risk factors (e.g., smoking cessation, exercise, and dietary modifications) as well as aspirin, anticoagulants, or antihypertensive medications.

Parkinson's disease (PD) is a progressive neurodegenerative condition that is characterized clinically by tremor, rigidity, bradykinesia (slowed movement), and postural instability. PD is considered a movement disorder and is caused by the degeneration of the substantia nigra, which is a nucleus in the basal ganglia, and the loss of DA, which is produced by this nucleus. The basal ganglia is a subcortical structure involved in regulating voluntary movement. Lewy bodies are often present in the substantia nigra on autopsy.

Dementia occurs in 20% to 60% of patients (American Psychiatric Association, 2013). Parkinson's dementia is considered a "subcortical" dementia and may be characterized by deficits in executive functioning, learning and recall aspects of memory, slowed psychomotor speed, and bradyphrenia (slowed thinking). There are typically no cortical disturbances such as aphasia or apraxia. Depression is relatively common and affects approximately 30% of patients with PD.

The major motoric symptoms of PD can be broken down into "positive" and "negative" symptoms. The positive symptoms (actions that are not seen in "normals") include a resting tremor that often has a "pill rolling" quality, muscular rigidity, or increased muscle tone, and involuntary movements, or akathisia. The negative symptoms (the inability to engage in behaviors that "normals" can do) include difficulty with positioning, difficulty standing from a sitting position, shuffling gait, bradykinesia or slowed movement, and blankness in facial expression (e.g., masked facies).

Treatment includes medications that boost the DA system in the brain, such as levodopa (L-DOPA), a precursor to DA. These medications may become less effective over time as the disease progresses, and there is less and less DA available. Dopamine agonists such as L-DOPA primarily help with the motor symptoms of the disease, but the cognitive symptoms are not improved. Neurosurgery such as deep brain stimulation (DBS) uses a surgically implanted device called a neurostimulator to deliver electrical stimulation to block the abnormal electrical signals within the basal ganglia. This type of treatment treats the motor symptoms of the disease and is used with patients whose symptoms are not adequately controlled with medication (NINDS, n.d.).

Huntington's disease or Huntington's chorea is also a movement disorder and is caused by a degenerative loss of neurons in the basal ganglia, particularly the caudate nucleus. Neurotransmitters such as GABA and NE, which normally inhibit the DA pathways, die during the course of the disease, thus creating a hyperactive DA system.

It is an autosomal dominant genetic disorder affecting approximately 5/100,000. The defect causes a part of DNA, called a cytosine, adenine, guanine repeat, to occur many more times than normal.

Offspring have a 50% chance of developing this disorder. The disorder typically appears in the third or fourth decade of life. Dementia almost always occurs and is characterized by a decline in memory retrieval and executive functioning, with more severe deficits in memory and global intellectual functioning later in the disease. Behavioral disturbances occur in up to 50% of cases and are often the initial feature of the disease. These behavioral changes may include depression, personality changes, anxiety, irritability, restlessness, or psychosis (NINDS, n.d.). The abnormal movements associated with this disease include "choreiform movements" (frequent, brisk jerks of the pelvis, trunk, and limbs), athetosis (slow uncontrolled movements), and unusual posturing. These motor symptoms often present months to a year after the disease onsets. Subtle changes in personality, memory, and coordination are often the first symptoms of the disease. There is no treatment for Huntington's disease. Genetic counseling plays an important role for those with a family history of Huntington's disease.

Dementia due to HIV disease is primarily a subcortical dementia caused by direct pathophysiological changes in the brain due to HIV. Alternative terminology includes AIDS dementia complex (ADC) or HIV/AIDS encephalopathy. Neuropathological findings include diffuse, multifocal destruction of white matter and subcortical structures, resulting in cognitive, behavioral, and motor symptoms. Cognitive symptoms include forgetfulness, slowness, concentration problems, and problem-solving difficulties. Behavioral manifestations include apathy and social withdrawal as the primary features, although some individuals may experience visual hallucinations, delusions, or delirium. Motor symptoms include tremors, balance problems, impaired repetitive movements, ataxia, and hypertonia.

CD4 counts are an important biomarker of HIV disease, and dementia due to HIV disease is more likely to occur as CD4+ count levels fall below 200 cells per microliter. With the advent of highly active antiretroviral therapy (HAART), the frequency of dementia due to HIV disease has declined from 30% to 60% of people infected with HIV to less than 20%.

Pseudodementia

The term "pseudodementia" has been used in the past to describe a dementia-type presentation in a variety of psychiatric illnesses, although depression tends to be the most common cause. This type of dementia may occur in a subset of patients with mood disorders and these features may resemble other neurological etiologies of dementia. Individuals with depression may report various cognitive problems in their daily lives, including slowed processing speed, memory problems, and attention problems. The onset of these cognitive symptoms can sometimes be linked to a precise date of onset (perhaps associated with onset of a life stressor or emotional upset), and the course tends to progress more rapidly than in dementia. Subjective cognitive complaints in depression are typically greater in severity than the actual impairment on testing. Conversely, patients with AD may underestimate their impairments due to the poor insight that is often a hallmark of the later stages of the disease.

Several presenting features can distinguish "organic" dementia from dementia due to depression. First, cortical signs such as aphasia, apraxia, and agnosia are typically absent in depression. Second, depressed patients may exhibit psychomotor slowing and inconsistent effort or attention during neuropsychological testing, rather than primary problems with retentive memory or visuospatial functioning. Cognitive impairments occurring during the acute stages of depression are typically reversible with treatment for the depressive symptoms. However, it is important to note that depression may also co-occur in the early stages of dementia, and cognitive symptoms in this context would be less likely to improve with antidepressant treatments.

Mild Cognitive Impairment

The term *mild cognitive impairment* (MCI) has been coined to capture the transitional time period between normal aging and dementia. MCI is defined as the state in which at least a single cognitive domain, usually memory, is impaired to a greater extent anticipated for someone's age, although the patient does not meet criteria for dementia and does not exhibit significant changes in their everyday, functional abilities (Peterson, 1995). These individuals are at an increased risk for developing dementia in subsequent years. Since the conception of MCI, four clinical subtypes of MCI have been defined: amnestic MCI-single domain, amnestic MCI-multiple domains, nonamnestic MCI-single domain, and nonamnestic MCI-multiple domain (Busse, Hensel, Gühne, Angermeyer, & Riedel-Heller, 2006).

The course of MCI can last for up to 5 years (Peterson, 1997). When followed longitudinally, individuals with MCI have a significantly increased rate of developing dementia, with conversion rates ranging from 8% to 15% per year, compared to a rate of 1% to 2% per year for the "normal" aging population (Devanand et al., 2008; Peterson et al., 1997). Individuals with amnestic MCI have the highest risk of progressing to AD (Busse et al., 2006).

Delirium

Delirium, or acute confusional state, is defined as a disturbance in consciousness accompanied by a change in cognition that cannot be better accounted for by a dementia process. Delirium differs from dementia in that its onset is typically abrupt (developing over the course of hours or days), the course is often fluctuating, and it is oftentimes reversible. A delirium state can be caused by a general medical condition (e.g., infection or metabolic disturbance), substance intoxication, or withdrawal, medication, toxin exposure, or a combination of factors. Delirium is common in inpatient hospital settings, affecting up to 30% of medically hospitalized patients. It is more common in the elderly.

The hallmark feature of delirium is impairment in the ability to focus or sustain attention. A patient with delirium may have difficulty focusing on a conversation or may be easily distracted. In addition to this attention disturbance, the patient may demonstrate a change in memory, orientation, language, or perception.

Concussion

Concussion, which is a form of mild traumatic brain injury, is the result of a direct or indirect trauma to the head. Although a loss of consciousness may occur, it is not necessary for diagnosis. Although many diagnostic frameworks have been developed, all require an identified trauma to the head, as well as at least some *alteration* of consciousness, posttraumatic amnesia (or amnesia for the event), or some focal neurological deficit.

Most of the literature suggests the presence of concussion-related symptoms for a few hours to several days after the injury. However, a more enduring syndrome of symptoms can occur and is known as postconcussion syndrome (PCS). For most, this syndrome will also resolve usually within the first 3 months. However, there is a smaller group of individuals who can remain symptomatic for over 3 months and, sometimes, up to several years following the injury. Post-concussion syndrome can be associated with a triad of somatic, cognitive, and behavioral symptoms. Somatic symptoms can include disordered sleep, fatigue, headaches, sensitivity to light and/or noise, vertigo or dizziness, and/or nausea. Personality/emotional changes can include anxiety, depressed affect, irritability, and/or apathy. Residual cognitive disturbances can include impaired attention and concentration, diminished short-term memory, slowed learning, decreased processing speed, lack of initiation, and poor planning, organization, and problem solving.

Seizure Disorders

A seizure is an episode of abnormal electrical firing of neurons resulting in abnormal behavior or experience of the individual (NINDS, 2004; Zillmer, Spiers, & Culbertson, 2008). The abnormal neuronal firing that occurs during a seizure may result in strange sensations, emotions, behavior, or sometimes convulsions or loss of consciousness. Epilepsy is a condition in which an individual experiences two or more unprovoked seizures. An unprovoked seizure means there is no identifiable cause or trigger. Having a seizure is not the same as being diagnosed with epilepsy. For example, someone may experience an isolated seizure without going on to develop epilepsy. Some children experience *febrile seizures,* in which a seizure occurs in the context of a high fever. However, most children with febrile seizures do not go on to develop epilepsy. Approximately 1% of the U.S. population has experienced an unprovoked seizure or has been diagnosed with epilepsy (NINDS, 2004). There are many causes of epilepsy. Anything that disrupts the normal pattern of neuronal activity may cause a seizure, for example, brain damage, abnormal development, illness, infection, toxins, drugs, or trauma. In about half of the cases of epilepsy, the exact cause is *idiopathic,* or unknown (NINDS, 2004).

There are several classifications of seizures. The first main classification is *generalized* versus *partial* or *focal.* In a generalized seizure, both sides of the brain are affected, resulting in loss of consciousness (or altered consciousness), falls, or muscle spasms. There are several types of generalized seizures. In a *tonic–clonic generalized seizure,* formally known as a *grand mal seizure,* the individual typically loses consciousness and exhibits stiffening of the body and repetitive jerking of the arms and/or legs. In an *absence seizure,* formally known as a *petit-mal seizure,* the person may appear to be staring into space.

Focal seizures, also called *partial seizures,* affect only one part of the brain. In a *simple partial* seizure, the individual does not lose consciousness. A person with a *simple partial* seizure may experience sudden and unexplained joy or anger or may hear, smell, or see things that are not real. In a *complex partial seizure,* the person experiences an alteration or loss of consciousness. A person having a complex partial seizure may display repetitive movements or behaviors, such as blinks, twitches, mouth movements, or more complicated actions. *Temporal lobe epilepsy* is the most common type of recurring focal seizures and may be associated with memory problems due to involvement of the hippocampus. Some people with partial or focal seizures experience an *aura*, or unusual sensation that warns a seizure is about to happen.

Not all seizures are distinctly partial or generalized. Some seizures may begin as a partial seizure and then spread to the entire brain. In addition, some people may appear to have a seizure, but there is no evidence of seizure activity in their brain. These events are referred to as *nonepileptic seizures*, formally referred to as *pseudoseizures*. The cause of these nonepileptic seizures may be psychogenic in origin, and sometimes people with epilepsy also have psychogenic seizures. It can be difficult to distinguish between epileptic and nonepileptic seizures, and careful evaluation and monitoring are required.

Epilepsy is usually diagnosed with EEG monitoring, brain scans, blood tests, neurological or behavioral tests, and a thorough check of medical history. Epilepsy is usually treated with antiseizure medication, although not all individuals with epilepsy respond well to these medications. When medications are not effective in controlling seizures, surgery to remove the affected brain tissue may be considered, depending on the nature and type of seizures.

References

American Psychiatric Association. (2013). *Diagnostic and statistical manual of mental disorders* (5th ed.). Arlington, VA: American Psychiatric Association.

Asho, K. R., & Sheehan, D. (2004). Benzodiazepines. In F. A. Schatzberg, & C. B. Nemeroff (Eds.), *The American psychiatric publishing: Textbook of psychopharmacology* (3rd ed., pp. 371–389). Washington, DC: American Psychiatric Press.

Blumenfeld, H. (2010). *Neuroanatomy through clinical cases* (2nd ed.). Sunderland, MA: Sinuaer Associates.

Busse, A., Hensel, A., Gühne, U., Angermeyer, M. C., & Riedel-Heller, S. G. (2006). Mild cognitive impairment: Long term course of four clinical subtypes. *Neurology, 67*, 2176–2185.

Devanand, D. P., Liu, X., Tabert, M. H., Pradhaban, G., Cuasay, K., Bell, K., ... Pelton, G. H. (2008). Combining early markers strongly predicts conversion from mild cognitive impairment to Alzheimer's disease. *Biological Psychiatry, 64*, 871–879.

Golan, D. E., Tashjian, A. H., Jr., Armstrong, E. J., & Armstrong, A. W. (2008). *Principles of psychopharmacology: The pathophysiologic basis of drug therapy* (2nd ed.). Baltimore, MD: Lippincott Williams and Wilkins.

Heilman, K. M., & Valenstein, E. (Eds.). (2003). *Clinical neuropsychology* (4th ed.). New York, NY: Oxford University Press.

Helmuth, L. L., Ivry, R. B., & Shimizu, N. (1997). Preserved performance by cerebellar patients on tests of word generation, discrimination learning, and attention. *Learning and Memory, 3*, 456–474.

Keller, M. B., McCullough, J. P., Klein, D. N., Arnow, B., Dunner, D. C., Gelenberg, A. J., ... Zajecka, J. (2000). A comparison of nefazodone, the cognitive behavioral-analysis system of psychotherapy, and their combination for the treatment of chronic depression. *New England Journal of Medicine, 342*(20), 1462–1470.

Keltner, N. L., & Folks, D. G. (2005). *Psychotropic drugs* (4th ed.). St. Louis, MO: Elsevier/Mosby.

Lehne, R. (2013). Antipsychotic agents and their use in schizophrenia. In *Pharmacology for nursing care* (8th ed.). St. Louis, MO: Elsevier/Saunders.

Lieberman, J. A., Stroup, T. S., McEvoy, J. P., Swartz, M. S., Rosenheck, R. A., Perkins, D. O. et al.; Clinical Antipsychotic Trials of Intervention Effectiveness (CATIE) Investigators. (2005). Effectiveness of antipsychotic drugs in patients with chronic schizophrenia. *New England Journal of Medicine, 353*(12), 1209–1223.

McKhann, G. M., Knopman, D. S., Chertkow, H., Hyman, B. T., Jack, C. R., Jr., Kawas, C. H., … Phelps, C. H. (2011). The diagnosis of dementia due to Alzheimer's disease: Recommendations from the National Institute on Aging-Alzheimer's Association workgroups on diagnostic guidelines for Alzheimer's disease. *Alzheimer's & Dementia: The Journal of the Alzheimer's Association, 7*(3), 263–269.

Mycek, M. J., Harvey, R. A., & Champe, P. C. (1997). *Lippincott's illustrated reviews: pharmacology* (2nd ed.). Philadelphia, PA: Lippincott Raven Publishers.

National Institute of Neurological Disorders and Stroke–National Institute of Health (NINDS). (2004). *Epilepsy: Hope through research*. In National Institute of Neurological Disorders and Stroke–National Institute of Health (Ed.). Retrieved December 28, 2012, from http://www.ninds.nih.gov/disorders /epilepsy/detail_epilepsy.htm

National Institute of Neurological Disorders and Stroke–National Institute of Health (NINDS). (2006). *Parkinson's disease: Hope through research*. In National Institute of Neurological Disorders and Stroke–National Institute of Health (Ed.). Retrieved December 16, 2012, from http://www.ninds.nih.gov /disorders/parkinsons_disease/detail_parkinsons_disease.htm#221523159

National Institute of Neurological Disorders and Stroke–National Institute of Health (NINDS). (n.d.). *Dementia: Hope through research*. In National Institute of Neurological Disorders and Stroke–National Institute of Health (Ed.). Retrieved December 16, 2012, from http://www.ninds.nih.gov/disorders /dementias/detail_dementia.htm

O'Brien, J. T., Erkinjuntti, T., Reisberg, B., Roman, G., Sawada, T., Pantoni, L., … DeKosky, S. T. (2003). Vascular cognitive impairment. *Lancet Neurology, 2*(2), 89–98.

Otto, M. W., Smits, J. A. J., & Reese, H. E. (2005). Combined psychotherapy and pharmacotherapy for mood and anxiety disorders in adults: Review and analysis. *Clinical Psychology: Science and Practice, 12*, 72–86.

Patterson, J. A. A., McCahill, M. E., & Edwards, T. M. (2010). *The therapist's guide to psychopharmacology: Working with patients, families, and physicians to optimize care*. London, UK: Guilford Press.

Perlis, M. L. (2011). BSM treatment protocols for insomnia. In M. L. Perlis, M. S. Aloia, & B. L. Kuhn (Eds.), *Behavioral treatments for sleep disorders: A comprehensive primer of behavioral sleep medicine interventions* (pp. 1–7). Oxford, UK: Elsevier.

Peterson, R. C. (1995). Normal aging, mild cognitive impairment, and early Alzheimer's disease. *The Neurologist, 1*, 326–344.

Peterson, R. C., Smith, G. E., Wering, S. C., Ivnik, R. J., Kokmen, E., & Tangelos, E. G. (1997). Aging memory, and mild cognitive impairment. *International Psychogeriatrics, 9*(S1), 65–69.

Pies, R. W. (2005). *Handbook of essential psychopharmacology* (2nd ed.). Washington, DC: American Psychiatric Press.

Preston, J., & Johnson, J. (2012). *Clinical psychopharmacology made ridiculously simple* (7th ed.). Miami, FL: Medmaster.

Schulte-Ruther, M., Markowitsch, H. J., Fink, G. R., & Piefke, M. (2007). Mirror neuron and theory of mind mechanisms involved in face-to-face interactions: A functional magnetic resonance imaging approach to empathy. *Journal of Cognitive Neuroscience, 19*(8), 1354–1372.

Sperling, R. A., Aisen, P. S., Beckett, L. A., Bennett, D. A., Craft, S., Fagan, A. M., ... Phelps C. H. (2011). Toward defining the preclinical stages of Alzheimer's disease: Recommendations from the National Institute on Aging-Alzheimer's Association workgroups on diagnostic guidelines for Alzheimer's disease. *Alzheimer's & Dementia: The Journal of the Alzheimer's Association, 7*(3), 280–292.

Stahl, S. (2011). *The prescriber's guide: Stahl's essential psychopharmacology* (4th ed.). New York, NY: Cambridge University Press.

Stein, D., Lerer, B., & Stahl, S. M. (Eds.). (2012). *Essential evidence based psychopharmacology* (2nd ed.). New York, NY: Cambridge University Press.

Stringer, J. L. (2011). *Basic concepts in pharmacology: What you need to know for each drug class* (4th ed.). New York, NY: McGraw Hill.

Wegman, J. (2012). *Psychopharmacology: Straight talk on mental health medications* (2nd ed.). Eau Claire, WI: Premier Publishing.

Williams, J. H., Whiten, A., Suddendorf, T., & Perrett, D. I. (2001). Imitation, mirror neurons and autism. *Neuroscience and Behavioral Reviews, 25*(4), 287–295.

Zillmer, E. A., & Spiers, M. V. (2001). *Principles of neuropsychology*. Belmont, CA: Wadsworth Thomas Learning.

Zillmer, E. A., Spiers, M. V., & Culbertson, W. C. (2008). *Principles of neuropsychology* (2nd ed.). Belmont, CA: Thomas Wadsworth.

Review Questions

1. All of the following may occur following damage to the basal ganglia, EXCEPT:
   A. Bradykinesia
   B. Rigidity
   C. Paralysis
   D. Tremor

2. The primary function of the myelin sheath is to:
   A. Increase the strength of the nerve impulse
   B. Determine whether the postsynaptic neuronal response is excitation or inhibition
   C. Determine whether the postsynaptic nerve will fire an action potential
   D. Increase the speed of neuronal firing

3. An acute intracranial hemorrhage will appear _____ on a CT scan, which is often referred to as a _____.
   A. White/hyperdensity
   B. White/hypodensity
   C. Black/hyperdensity
   D. Black/hypodensity

4. Your patient is a 7-year-old child. His mother reports that he frequently exhibits staring spells during which time he is unresponsive. These spells last several seconds, and he subsequently appears lethargic. The first diagnostic tool you should recommend is:
   A. A WADA test
   B. The Glasgow Coma Scale
   C. An EEG
   D. A neuroangiogram

5. The person who spontaneously utters the following phrase, "window... break...ball" but who cannot repeat the phrase, "The ball broke the glass window" most likely has which of the following disorders of speech:
   A. Wernicke's aphasia
   B. Conduction aphasia
   C. Transcortical motor aphasia
   D. Broca's aphasia

6. The primary site of brain deterioration in Alzheimer's dementia is usually the:
   A. Medial temporal lobe
   B. Medial parietal lobe
   C. Frontal–temporal lobes
   D. Temporal–parietal lobes

7. Which of the following answers correctly pairs the stage of Alzheimer's disease with the corresponding symptom presentation?

   A. Stage 1: Aphasia, apraxia, and/or acalculia
      Stage 2: Agnosia
      Stage 3: Declines in memory, visuospatial functioning, and language

   B. Stage 1: Declines in memory, visuospatial function, and language
      Stage 2: Apraxia, aphasia, and/or acalculia
      Stage 3: Impaired intellectual functioning and minimal verbal output

   C. Stage 1: Declines in memory and intellectual functioning
      Stage 2: Emergence of apraxia, aphasia, and/or acalculia
      Stage 3: Agnosia

   D. Stage 1: Impaired intellectual functioning, memory problems, and apraxia
      Stage 2: Minimal verbal output
      Stage 3: Declines in visuospatial functioning and language

8. Personality changes and executive dysfunction are primary features of which following disease?

   A. Parkinson's disease
   B. Alzheimer's disease
   C. Huntington's disease
   D. Pick's disease

9. The primary brain region affected in Huntington's disease is the:

   A. Caudate nucleus
   B. Putamen
   C. Substantia nigra
   D. Globus pallidus

10. Which of the following statements is NOT true?

    A. Delirium is marked by an abrupt onset and fluctuating course.
    B. The hallmark feature of a delirium state is impaired attention.
    C. Delirium is relatively uncommon among patients hospitalized for non-neurological conditions.
    D. Delirium can be caused by prescription medications, toxin exposure, or metabolic disturbance.

11. A seizure that is due to abnormal electrical activity in the left temporal lobe and is characterized by an alteration in consciousness and repetitive movements such as lip smacking or undoing a button would most likely be referred to as what type of seizure?

    A. Absence seizure
    B. Generalized tonic–clonic seizure
    C. Complex partial seizure
    D. Simple partial seizure

12. Which of the following is NOT a protective covering of the brain?

    A. Arachnoid
    B. Sphenoid
    C. Dura
    D. Pia
    E. C and B

13. Which of the following are regions of primary sensory processing?

    A. Occipital lobe

    B. Thalamus

    C. Temporal lobe

    D. A and B

    E. A and C

14. Which of the following structure is NOT considered part of the basal ganglia?

    A. Globus pallidus

    B. Pineal

    C. Subthalamic nucleus

    D. Putamen

15. An impulse traveling away from the cell body of the neuron travels along the
_____.

    A. Axon

    B. Dendrite

    C. Soma

    D. Terminal button

16. The process by which incoming stimuli cross over and are transmitted to the contralateral hemisphere is known as:

    A. Myelination

    B. Differentiation

    C. Propagation

    D. Decussation

17. The lateral geniculate nucleus of the thalamus _____.

    A. Maintains balance and coordination

    B. Relays visual information to the occipital lobe

    C. Processes auditory information

    D. Secretes cerebral spinal fluid

18. The telencephalon, or cerebrum, includes which of the following structures?

    A. Frontal Lobes

    B. Occipital lobes

    C. Pons

    D. A, B, and C

    E. A and B

19. The role of mirror neurons has been associated with _____.

    A. Empathy

    B. Primary visual processing

    C. Hand–eye coordination

    D. Imitation

    E. A and D

20. As part of the limbic system, the hippocampus is most often associated with
_____.

    A. Memory formation and transfer to longer-term storage
    B. The regulation of emotional responses to the environment
    C. Relaying of sensory information to primary processing regions
    D. Hunger

21. Multiple sensory modalities are integrated in cortical regions known as
_____.

    A. The parietal lobes
    B. The midbrain
    C. Heteromodal cortex
    D. The falx cerebri

22. Typically located in the language-dominant hemisphere, _____
is a secondary processing region dedicated to the comprehension of
language.

    A. The parastriate region
    B. Broca's area
    C. The orbitofrontal cortex
    D. Wernicke's area

23. _____ has/have increasingly replaced _____ for the first-line
treatment of chronic anxiety.

    A. Barbiturates, SSRIs
    B. Benzodiazepines, SSRIs
    C. SSRIs, benzodiazepines
    D. Alcohol, barbiturates

24. Cardiac/autonomic, severe anticholinergic, and neurobehavioral are types of
side effects of _____.

    A. TCAs
    B. Anticonvulsants
    C. SSRIs
    D. Anxiolytics

25. A drug known for having a narrow therapeutic index is_____.

    A. Lithium
    B. Ambien
    C. Cymbalta
    D. Concerta

26. Fatal agranulocytosis is a side effect of _____.

    A. Clozapine (Clozaril)
    B. Alprazolam (Xanax)
    C. Dextroamphetamine (Adderall)
    D. Buspirone (BuSpar)

27. SAMe is _____.

A. An alternative remedy for depression
B. An antipsychotic
C. A stimulant
D. A cognitive enhancing drug

28. SSRIs are used to treat _____.

A. Anxiety
B. Depression
C. Anxiety and depression
D. Psychosis

29. Barbiturates are _____.

A. Essentially replaced by other psychotropic medications, including benzodiazepines
B. Sleep medication
C. Antidepressants
D. Cognitive enhancing drugs

30. Pharmacokinetics refers to _____.

A. How the body handles a drug, including absorption, distribution, and elimination and metabolism
B. A drug's mechanism of action
C. Amino acids, biogenic amines, and peptides
D. How a drug brings about unwanted side effects

Answers to Review Questions

1. C. Paralysis

Motor abnormalities due to basal ganglia dysfunction do not involve paresis or paralysis, but rather refer to abnormal coordination and rhythm of movement. These syndromes are referred to as extrapyramidal syndromes.

2. D. Increase the speed of neuronal firing

The myelin sheath increases the speed of neuronal firing down the axon. Whether a postsynaptic nerve is excited or inhibited depends on the neurotransmitters binding to that neuron. The relative threshold of postsynaptic excitation determines whether an action potential will fire. The action potential is an all-or-nothing phenomenon, and the strength of neuronal firing does not vary in response to the strength of the input.

3. A. White/hyperdensity

*The appearance of brain tissue on a CT scan depends on the tissue density. Very dense tissue, such as bone, appears white. Less dense tissue, such as air, appears black. The term **hyperdense** refers to brighter areas and **hypodense** refers to darker areas. Fresh intracranial hemorrhage coagulates almost immediately and shows up as a hyperdense (white) area.*

4. C. An EEG

This child could be having seizures, and an EEG is the primary diagnostic tool used to diagnose epilepsy. The Glasgow Coma Scale is used to determine the severity of traumatic brain injury. The WADA test helps to determine relative hemispheric capabilities underlying language and memory and is often used in patients with epilepsy prior to undergoing brain resection. A neuroangiogram is used to detect lesions of blood vessels.

5. D. Broca's aphasia

Broca's aphasia is considered a nonfluent aphasia in which the person speaks in a slow, halting manner, with poor grammar and limited prosody. Only keywords are used, and use of verbs or connecting words is limited. Damage is usually in the left frontal lobe around Brodmann areas 44 and 45, also known as Broca's area. Writing is usually slow and effortful. Repetition is impaired. Auditory comprehension and reading comprehension are relatively preserved.

6. A. Medial temporal lobe

The primary site of brain involvement in AD is the medial temporal lobes, including the amygdala, hippocampal formation, and entorhinal cortex. In later stages of the disease, the basal temporal cortex, parietal–occipital cortex, posterior cingulate gyrus, and frontal lobes are also affected. The primary motor, somatosensory, visual, and auditory cortices are relatively spared.

7. B. Stage 1: Declines in memory, visuospatial function, and language

Stage 2: Apraxia, aphasia, and/or acalculia

Stage 3: Impaired intellectual functioning and minimal verbal output

In the early stage of the disease (1–3 years), mild impairments may be seen in memory, particularly new learning and retention of new memories over time, with remote memory being relatively spared. Other cognitive areas affected include visuospatial functioning (e.g., topographic disorientation and difficulty with construction) and language (e.g., word finding and naming). In the intermediate stage (2–10 years), increased impairments in memory, visuospatial skills, and language are present, with the emergence of apraxia, acalculia, aphasia, or agnosia. In the later stages (8–12 years), intellectual functions may be severely impaired and verbal output may be minimal.

8. D. Pick's disease

Pick's disease is one specific cause of a heterogenous group of dementias referred to as FTD. Dementia due to Pick's disease, is characterized by personality changes such as behavioral disinhibition, which often occur early in the course of the disease, as well as executive dysfunction and language abnormalities. Memory problems are also present, but tend to become more obvious later in the disease (as opposed to AD where memory loss is typically the primary presenting problem). Onset is typically earlier than that of AD, occurring between ages 50 and 60.

9. A. Caudate nucleus

Huntington's disease is an autosomal dominant genetic movement disorder that is caused by a degenerative loss of neurons in the basal ganglia, particularly the caudate nucleus. The abnormal movements associated with this disease include choreiform movements (frequent, brisk jerks of the pelvis, trunk, and limbs), athetosis (slow uncontrolled movements), and unusual posturing.

10. C. Delirium is relatively uncommon among patients hospitalized for non-neurological conditions.

Delirium can be caused by a variety of general medical conditions and occurs and affects up to 30% of medically hospitalized patients.

11. C. Complex partial seizure

Temporal lobe epilepsy is the most common type of complex partial seizure, in which the seizure activity is localized to the temporal lobe, and the person experiences an alteration of or loss of consciousness during the seizure.

12. B. Sphenoid

The sphenoid is a sinus. The dura, arachnoid, and pia are the three layers of the cranial meninges that form the cranial meninges and protective coverings of the brain.

13. **E. A and C**

   The thalamus is typically considered a relay for pathways between cortex and lower brain regions. On the other hand, the occipital lobe is the site of primary visual processing and the temporal lobe is the site of primary auditory processing.

14. **B. Pineal**

   The pineal is a small gland between the hemispheres. However, the globus pallidus, subthalamic nucleus, and putamen are all recognized as structures of the basal ganglia.

15. **A. Axon**

   Only the axon carries the nerve impulse away from the cell. The impulse ends at the terminal buttons, which are located at the ends of the axons. The soma is the cell body and the dendrite carries impulses toward the cell body.

16. **D. Decussation**

   Decussation refers to the structural crossing of fibers, which accounts for contralateral control and perception.

17. **B. Relays visual information to the occipital lobe**

   The sensory pathways travel through modality-specific nuclei located in the thalamus. The lateral geniculate nuclei are specific to vision.

18. **E. A and B**

   The pons is a midbrain structure. From these choices, only the frontal and occipital lobes are part of the telencephalon, which comprises the four lobes.

19. **E. A and D**

   Research has suggested that mirror neurons located in premotor cortex are associated with empathy and imitation.

20. **A. Memory formation and transfer to longer-term storage**

   Damage to the hippocampus, located in the inferior temporal lobe, is associated with severe impairments in memory because of its important role in the transfer of information to long-term storage.

21. **C. Heteromodal cortex**

   Only the heteromodal cortex processes and integrates multiple sensory stimuli.

22. **D. Wernicke's area**

   Wernicke's area represents a higher level of processing but is still modality specific. Therefore, it is considered a secondary processing region.

23. **C. SSRIs, benzodiazepines**

   Because benzodiazepines have the potential to be addictive, SSRIs are now the first-line treatment for chronic anxiety.

24. **A. TCAs**

These are the serious side effects of the TCAs.

25. **A. Lithium**

Lithium can be dangerous as the therapeutic dose is near fatal.

26. **A. Clozapine**

Fatal agranulocytosis is a risky side effect of clozapine (Clozaril).

27. **A. An alternative remedy for depression**

SAMe is an over-the-counter remedy for depression.

28. **C. Anxiety and depression**

SSRIs are used to treat anxiety and depression.

29. **A. Essentially replaced by other psychotropic medications, including benzodiazepines**

Barbiturates are now rarely used as psychotropic medication.

30. **A. How the body handles a drug, including absorption, distribution, and elimination and metabolism**

Pharmacokinetics is the study of the mechanisms of absorption, distribution, metabolism, and excretion of a drug in the body.

2

Cognitive–Affective Bases of Behavior

Matthew Jerram, David Gansler, and Robert Webb

Broad Content Areas

- Cognitive functions, including sensation, perception, attention, intelligence, and executive functions (EFs)
- Learning and memory
- Emotion and motivation
- Interaction of cognition, emotion, and motivation

The current chapter focuses of four broad content areas: (a) cognitive functions, including sensation, perception, attention, intelligence, and EFs; (b) learning and memory; (c) emotion and motivation; and (d) interaction of cognition, emotion, and motivation, including theories with clinical application. Several levels of headings are used to provide organization and guidance as you move through the chapter. To provide further explication, some concepts are represented graphically. Generally, within each broad content area, information is presented in increasing complexity. In the sections on emotion and motivation, and the interaction of cognition, emotion, and motivation, theories are generally presented chronologically in order of publication.

Many of the topics described in this chapter are covered in graduate courses in clinical psychology. We attempted to take this large content area and summarize it with a balance of depth and breadth. We also included recent and foundational research in the topic areas to provide a sense of the direction of the field.

Cognitive Functions

Sensation

Sensation is the detection of stimulation, the study of which commonly deals with the structure of sensory mechanisms (e.g., eye) and the stimuli (e.g., light) that affect those mechanisms. The study of both sensation and perception deals with the transduction of physical energy in one's environment into neural energy/ signals. How is meaningful information extracted from an environment that William James described as a booming buzzing confusion? Signal detection theory

(SDT; Green & Swets, 1966), part of the field of psychophysics, represents earlier efforts to explain how humans perform in sensory and perceptual tasks. More recently, optimal estimation theory or statistical decision theory, a Bayesian (probabilistic) approach (Simoncelli, 2009), has supplanted SDT, and will be described further in the next section on perception.

SDT deals with the observation that two individuals confronted with the same stimulus presentation may come to different conclusions, that is, they may not agree as to whether a simple stimulus was present. Disagreement may occur due to differences in discriminability or response bias (Robinson-Riegler & Robinson-Riegler, 2012). One observer could have greater *acuity* than the other, that is have more discriminatory capacity, or that observer could *be more willing* to report a stimulus observation (Robinson-Riegler & Robinson-Riegler, 2012). Discriminability (d') of the stimulus is described by the mathematical function of separation/spread, with separation representing signal strength and spread representing the background noise present during the stimulus presentation. Anyone traveling in a car listening to the radio has experienced the frustration of reduced signal strength and increased background noise as the vehicle gets farther from the broadcast tower. Response bias is a function of where the criterion for stimulus detection is set. The criterion can be set low to avoid false negatives at a more liberal threshold, or the criterion can be set high to avoid false positives at a more conservative threshold.

If we follow neural signals from the point of transduction in the retina, cochlea, skin, etc., through a series of synaptic connections to the primary sensory cortex, we can think of the information as represented first very briefly in short-term sensory stores whose capacity has been shown to exceed that of short-term memory (STM; Sperling, 1960). The large but transitory capacity of short-term sensory stores provides the time it takes to extract critical information features for further processing and action, the more elaborative process known as perception.

Perception

Perception is the branch of psychology that deals with the detection and interpretation of sensory stimuli. In order to understand how we make interpretations about external stimuli, say for a visual stimulus, we will return to the short-term sensory store of the previous example. It should be kept in mind, however, that the principles of perceptual processing presented here apply to other sensory modalities as well. Should our visual stimulus win the competition for attention, "grasp" attentional resources, and enter STM, it will be processed further at a conscious level for its location, shape, or object identity, and a number of other features such as color, luminance, and direction and speed of motion if relevant. The processing of these distinct visual features will be conducted in hierarchical, functionally segregated, and parallel units of the visual cortex (the occipital lobe and bordering parts of the temporal and parietal lobe as well), with these units having access to each other's contents as stimulus processing proceeds from coarser to finer grained analysis (bottom-up processing) and as they return to coarser levels (top-down processing) (Pinel, 2011). It is probably worth elaborating on what is meant by hierarchical, functionally segregated, and parallel perceptual processing. *Hierarchical processing* means that a perceived stimulus will undergo successive elaboration. For a visual stimulus this means edge and orientation processing at early stages, the detection of features such as corners or curves or shapes at middle stages, and the identification of an object from a memory store at a later stage. *Functional segregation* means that there is a separate central nervous system unit for processing each visual feature (i.e., shape, color, and motion). At one time it was thought there was an "integration" area at the top of a serial processing stream, but that does not seem to be the case, rather, integration occurs by the simultaneous activity of processing units gaining access to each other's contents (parallel and distributed processing). *Feature binding* (FB) is a newer term for sensory/perceptual integration, and is defined as the cognitive process by which a unified internal representation of a stimulus is formed from the activity of multiple mental modules (Botly & DeRosa, 2008). FB requires greater attentional resources than single feature processing, is more likely to rely on the activity of the frontal and parietal cortex, and is supported by cholinergic activity (Botly & DeRosa, 2008). Finally, according to Pinel, parallel processing means "the simultaneous analysis of a signal in different ways by the multiple parallel pathways of a neural network" (Pinel, 2011).

If we follow perceptual processing to the point of FB, the ultimate goal of the process is typically object recognition. As pointed out earlier, SDT was developed to understand the process of deciding whether external stimuli were present or what they represented, but more recently optimal estimation theory (Bayesian approaches) has been used to understand sensory/perceptual processes (Brainard, 2009; Simoncelli, 2009). By applying optimal estimation theory (also known as statistical decision theory) to a simple example, such as color recognition, we can outline its basic principles and extrapolate to a more complex process such as objection recognition.

Color constancy is the idea that our experience of a color can remain the same despite the fact that "colors of objects do not remain constant in different illuminants and when various conditions of viewing are changed" (Helson & Jeffers, 1940). How do our sensory/perceptual mechanisms help us resolve this type of ambiguity? Brainard and colleagues propose that our visual system resolves ambiguity by "taking advantage of the statistical structure of natural scenes" (Brainard et al., 2006). Given several possible interpretations of a visual scene, the visual system selects the most probable interpretation a priori (Brainard et al., 2006), or, put another way, the actual image data are combined with prior assumptions (Brainard, 2009).

Attention

The term *attention* has different meanings. Attention can refer to global states or selective processes (Gazzaniga, Ivry, & Mangun, 2009). Sleep and wakefulness are global states, and wakefulness itself can be divided into inattentive states such as drowsiness or relaxation versus an attentive/alert state. The term *attention* can also mean a process occurring during alert states by which a stimulus can either be attended to or ignored (i.e., the cocktail party phenomenon; Cherry, 1953). In this section, the word *attention* refers to its role as a selective mechanism (selective attention), and not as it would be applied to global states. Thus William James's (1890) definition of selective attention applies here: "Everyone knows what attention is. It is the taking possession by the mind, in clear and vivid form, of one out of what seem several simultaneously possible objects or trains of thought. Focalization, concentration of consciousness are of its essence."

Selective attention operates both by facilitation and inhibition of resources. The facilitating effects (i.e., valid cuing in the Posner paradigm) of selective attention have been demonstrated in increased accuracy and speed of target response, increased perceptual sensitivity for discrimination, and increased contrast sensitivity (Kastner, McMains, & Beck, 2009). The inhibitory effects of selective attention operating when a stimulus is ignored can be observed in reduction of distractor interference with increased attentional load (Kastner et al., 2009), by negative priming (i.e., invalid cuing in the Posner paradigm), and inhibition of return. The phenomenon of attentional blindness (Simons & Chabris, 1999) reveals the limits of selective attention. In the classic demonstration of attentional blindness, individuals who are actively tracking an aspect of a sports event fail to notice a person in a gorilla suit walking directly through the game—clearly, attention cannot be directed everywhere.

Attentional Resources

In keeping with the limits of attentional resources, when those are taxed through increased processing load, or by dividing them between two tasks, performance decrements are observed; however, those resources can be increased through practice (Treisman, 2009). Three reasons that limitations in attentional resources occur (Treisman, 2009) include:

- Structural interference—that is, the more similar tasks are, the more they compete for limited attentional resources. Similar tasks tend to share the same sensory/perceptual modality.

- General resource—there is a general limit to the extent of attentional resources. Evidence for this limit can be found even when attention is divided between two noninterfering (i.e., different modalities) tasks and performance decrements occur. These decrements are less than those occurring with high structural interference, but they are still meaningful enough to indicate a drain on a general attentional resource that is occurring.

- Behavioral coherence—the unity of our actions places limits on attentional resources in preparing responses.

Attentional Selection

Attention selects for objects (Duncan, 1984), location (Hoffman & Nelson, 1981), and attributes such as motion (Corbetta, Miezin, Dobmeyer, Shulman, & Petersen, 1991) within the visual field. The Stroop Effect (Stroop, 1935) is an example of attention to objects (i.e., word identity) taking precedence over attention to attributes (i.e., the color of ink the word is printed in). *Attentional load theory* (Lavie & Tsal, 1994) helps to explain the push–pull relationship of the facilitative and inhibitory mechanisms at work (Pinsk, Doninger, & Kastner, 2004). The theory posits the degree to which an ignored stimulus is processed depends on the extent of processing required by the attended stimulus. According to *attentional load theory,* reduction of interference caused by distractors is greatest when the processing demands to the attended stimulus are highest.

Attentional Control

Attention can be "captured" in a stimulus-driven fashion, referred to as bottom-up mechanisms or reflexive attention, or in a strategic fashion, referred to as top-down mechanisms (Treisman, 2009). Stimuli with high survival value, such as the odor of smoke indicating fire, and with high subjective value (Moray, 1959), such as one's name spoken from across a crowded room, are both quickly brought into the focus of attention, and exemplify the operation of bottom-up attention mechanisms. Anne Treisman's conjunction search paradigm (Treisman & Gelade, 1980) is an example of top-down mechanisms. In that paradigm, the participant is to search a broad stimulus array for the only stimulus that satisfies two conditions (i.e., find the letter *O* that is printed in red ink, in an array of *X*s printed in red or *O*s printed in green). Neuroscientists propose the existence of an attentional control system for top-down aspects of attention, communicating with, but distinct from sensory–motor systems, represented in the lateral parietal and frontal lobes. In contrast, stimulus-driven aspects of attentional control (bottom up) may be represented between the amygdala and ventral aspects of the frontal lobe. In day-to-day life, attentional selection is occurring among many stimuli, which automatically *compete* for attentional resources. Experimental evidence indicates that stimuli presented at the same time influence one another in a mutually suppressive manner. For example, a stimulus, which is presented on its own, is the subject of much greater brain activity than when it is presented simultaneously with three other stimuli (Beck & Kastner, 2005). Evidence is accumulating that *Gestalt* principles of perceptual organization (i.e., similarity, proximity, and common fate) are part of bottom-up attentional influences (Kastner et al., 2009). Top-down attentional control helps to resolve competition between stimuli by introducing *bias* toward one stimulus over another.

Executive Functioning

The EFs consist of those capacities that enable a person to engage successfully in independent, purposive, self-directed, and self-serving behavior (Lezak, Howieson, Bigler, & Tranel, 2012). EFs are often characterized as being activated in novel or unfamiliar circumstances, and are thus contrasted with routinized or more automatic behaviors (Shallice, 1990). EFs are increasingly important because they are the cognitive domains most strongly associated with emotional distress, and may reflect differing facets of underlying frontal lobe dysfunction common to cognitive and affective domains of disinhibitory psychopathology (Johnson-Greene, Adams, Gilman, & Junck, 2002). Specifically, EFs are important in diagnostic and treatment contexts, as an important functional domain in neuropsychological assessment (Lezak et al., 2012), as playing a specific role in geriatric depression and therefore in the use of problem-solving therapy as an appropriate modality in that context (Alexopoulos, 2003), in conceptualizing attention deficit hyperactivity disorder (ADHD) as a disorder of inhibitory control (Barkley, 1997), and as critical components of some intelligence tests such as the Cognitive Assessment System (CAS) based on the Planning, Attention, Simultaneous, and Successive (PASS) model from which interventions to boost planning skills in children have been developed (Naglieri & Das, 1988). Specific EFs may involve supervisory attention, working memory (WM), inhibitory control, or social problem solving. Latent variable analysis suggests that WM is a critical component of EFs, as there is a near perfect correlation of WM and non-WM executive functioning tasks, leading some experts to refer to a unitary underlying construct of executive attention (McCabe, Roediger, McDaniel, Balota, & Hambrick, 2010). "Cold" EFs are thought to involve cognitive functions, whereas "hot" EFs involve social and affective processing (Anderson, Jacobs, & Anderson, 2008). Of all the domains of the neuropsychological evaluation, only EFs have been shown to relate to measures of personality, a finding that lends credence to the notion of "hot" EFs (Johnson-Greene et al., 2002). Exemplars of EFs or their dysfunction have come from descriptions of psychiatric patients following frontal lobotomy, adult neurologic patients with lesions of the frontal lobe such as the prototypical case of Phineas Gage, and early childhood lesion of the frontal lobe resulting in primary social deficit. Frequently used clinical neuropsychological tests of EF include the Wisconsin Card Sort Test (set establishment and maintenance), the Stroop Color Word Test (attentional control), and the Controlled Oral Word Association Test (verbal fluency). The functional construct of EF is closely associated with the neuroanatomic construct of the prefrontal cortex, and a recent review indicates that clinical neuropsychological measures are sensitive, but not specific, to lesion of the frontal lobe (Alvarez & Emory, 2006).

Intelligence

It has been said that there are as many definitions of intelligence as there are intelligence theorists, and some of the variability stems from either the anthropologic or educational setting from which the definition arises. Anastasi (1986) emphasizes the individual operating in the environment—"intelligence is not an entity within the organism but a quality of behavior. Intelligent behavior is essentially adaptive, insofar as it represents effective ways of meeting the demands of a changing environment." In contrast, Carr (1910) provided a definition emphasizing intellectual processes—"intelligence is the power of using categories, it is knowledge of the relations of things." The differing traditions have had ramifications as the major models of intelligence, and the measures based on them (e.g., Stanford-Binet and Wechsler scales) have been criticized for focusing too much on the types of analytical and sequential thought processes required for academic success, while ignoring creative and practical abilities essential for broader life success (Sternberg, 1999). Gardner viewed intelligence tests as probing the limited range of linguistic, logical-mathematical, and spatial abilities, and so expanded to a theory of multiple intelligences to incorporate musical, bodily-kinesthetic, naturalistic, interpersonal and intrapersonal abilities (Gardner, 2011). Given the absence of an agreed upon definition, it is reasonable to note one of the better definitions as provided by the late Wechsler (1939), developer of the most widely used intelligence tests of the twentieth century, "Intelligence is the aggregate or global capacity of the individual to act purposefully, to think rationally and to deal effectively with his environment" (p. 3).

Research-Based Theories of Intelligence

Empirically based approaches to intelligence rely primarily on two kinds of evidence: (1) structural research relying on factor analysis and later hierarchical factor analysis that resolved some of the earlier controversies arising from differences in British and American factor analytic techniques; and (2) developmental research, dealing with the ways cognitive abilities develop with age (Horn and Blankson, 2012). One significant recent trend is the integration of the intellectual strains of cognitive neuroscience/neuropsychology with that of cognitive psychology models of intelligence. The PASS model (Naglieri & Das, 1988) is based on A. R. Luria's three-level theory of higher cortical functions in man (Luria, 1980), and represents an important alternative to the more purely cognitive British and

North American traditions stemming from the work of Charles Spearman and his student Raymond Cattell (see later descriptions of g and Gf–Gc theories). The three levels in Luria's (1980) theory, from the bottom up are: (1) regulation of cortical arousal and attention; (2) receiving, processing, and retention of information; and (3) programming, regulation, and verification of behavior.

Structural Research on Models of Intelligence

Within the first 30 years of research on tests of mental ability, it was discovered that all of the tests are positively correlated (Spearman, 1904), and this central tendency has come to be known as the positive manifold. Spearman, a student of Wilhelm Wundt, theorized that each mental ability represented by a mental test was influenced by a general factor and a specific factor, which he designated as lower case g and s (Spearman, 1927). Thurstone (1938), relying on North American traditions of conducting factor analysis, as opposed to Spearman's British statistical practices, came to a different conclusion when analyzing data on multiple tests of mental abilities. According to his theory of primary mental abilities (PMA), each of those belonged to between seven and nine ability categories that were independent of a higher-order g factor. The g theory versus PMA theory debate produced a great deal of scholarship. Cattell (1941) proposed that g was actually composed of general fluid (Gf) and general crystallized (Gc) ability. Gf was described as a facility for reasoning and adapting to new situations. Gc was described as accessible stores of knowledge. Vernon (1950) went on to define the relationship among the various factors that had been identified by proposing that g was a higher-order factor influencing lower-order factors (i.e., Gf and Gc). This thought process evolved further with the work of John L. Horn and then John Carroll's extensive work with hierarchical factor analytic models revealing that a three-stratum model best fit the 461 data sets he included (Carroll, 1993). The three-stratum model is often referred to as Cattell–Horn–Carroll (CHC) theory, and most, but not all, contemporary intelligence tests are based on it (Schneider & McGrew, 2012).

Developmental Research on Models of Intelligence

How does intelligence develop over time? Cattell (1987) proposed investment theory, in which a single relation perceiving faculty (Gf), is applied to the development of other abilities such as acquired knowledge (Gc), memory (Gsm), or sensory and or motor-related abilities (i.e., Ga). In addition to the structural evidence of a taxonomy of mental abilities, there is evidence of different developmental trajectories for these broad general abilities. There are abilities for which there is little or no aging decline (e.g., Gc), and abilities that decline with age (e.g., Gf) though physical exercise, social support and control beliefs can protect against this decline. In cognitive research, these abilities are sometimes referred to as maintained and vulnerable abilities, and in the neuropsychological literature as "hold" and "no-hold" functions. In addition to the effects of age, the vulnerable or no-hold functions, are, on average, more likely to be affected by neurologic insult. Studies indicate that Gc increases with age and is correlated with socioeconomic status and extent and quality of education. Abilities that decline with age include Gf (fluid reasoning), Gsm (short-term memory), and Gs (cognitive speed). Fluid reasoning tasks showing age-related decline include syllogisms, reasoning with analogies, concept formation, and series comprehension. Short-term memory (Gsm) is a label for a range of brief retention abilities of nonmeaningfully related information such as number or word series. Of those abilities, short-term WM, as epitomized by a backward digit span, declines significantly with age. Other types of STM, such as primacy and recency effects as obtained on list learning, or span of apprehension as epitomized by forward digit span, decline with age, but not as dramatically as WM. *Gs* (cognitive speed), like *Gf* and *Gsm*, declines with age.

Gender differences have also been observed in cognitive performance with women outperforming men on verbal abilities and men outperforming women on spatial cognition tasks. Women tend to perform better on vocabulary and arithmetic while men have an advantage on tasks of mental rotation and mathematical problem solving.

Applications of Research on Models of Intelligence Tests

The intelligence tests that follow from models of intelligence assess intellectual and cognitive functioning in children and adults. Intelligence testing has major educational, occupational, clinical, forensic, and treatment applications. Lubinski's (2004) review of criterion validity revealed g co-varied 0.70 to 0.80 with academic achievement measures, 0.70 with military training assignments, 0.20 to 0.60 with work performance with the higher correlations pertaining to the more complex jobs, 0.30 to 0.40 with income, 0.40 with socioeconomic status (SES) of origin, and 0.50 to 0.70 with achieved SES. Intelligence tests have applications in the identification of individuals with psychoeducational and/or developmental disorders (i.e., ADHD, learning disability [LD], autism, and intellectual disability [ID]), giftedness, neuropsychological or psychiatric disorders, the development of individualized instructional programming, and the identification of occupational performance and/or training potential (Wasserman, 2003). The major intelligence tests include the Wechsler Adult Intelligence Scale-IV often presented as combined with the Wechsler Memory Scale-IV, Wechsler Preschool and Primary Scale of Intelligence-3, Wechsler Intelligence Scale for Children-IV, Stanford-Binet Intelligence Scales-5, Kaufman Assessment Battery for Children-2, Woodcock Johnson-III, Differential Abilities Scales-2, Universal Nonverbal Intelligence Test, Cognitive Assessment System, and the Reynolds Intellectual Assessment Scales (Wasserman, 2003). As intelligence test administration takes between 1 to 2 hours before scoring and interpretation, depending on the test and the test taker, abbreviated versions of tests have been developed to provide reliable, valid estimates of intellectual ability (i.e., Wechsler Abbreviated Scale of Intelligence—WASI).

Psychometric Properties and Intelligence Tests

The current major intelligence tests produce composite and specific ability deviation scores, are generally based on standardization samples of 2,000 or more participants stratified by age, and are generally co-normed to an academic achievement battery, giving more coverage across the second level of CHC theory (broad general abilities). All report split-half and test–retest reliability, nearly all report convergent validity with at least one other intelligence test, and nearly all report the results of exploratory and confirmatory factor analysis to address construct validity of the more global and specific indices. Split-half reliability for composite scores tends to be above 0.9, with a range of 0.84 to 0.99, with lower reliabilities coming from the youngest samples. Test–retest reliabilities for composite scores range from 0.79 to 0.96. Test–retest reliabilities for subtests display a greater range from 0.38 to 0.9, with speeded tasks tending to produce lower reliabilities. Convergent validity, that is, correlations between the composite scores of major intelligence tests, tends to fall in the .70s, and range from 0.69 to 0.92.

Recent Trends in Intelligence Testing

A major concern in regard to intelligence testing involves intervention utility (Wasserman, 2003). *Treatment validity* refers to the value of an assessment in selecting and implementing interventions and treatments that will benefit the examinee. The CAS (Naglieri & Das, 1997), based on PASS theory, is unique among intelligence tests in fostering research on cognitive instruction. Planning facilitation is an empirically validated teacher-led classroom-based intervention to promote use of cognitive strategies that have been shown to lead to improved performance in mathematics, especially for children with low CAS planning standard scores (Naglieri & Das, 2000).

Bias in Intelligence Testing

On intelligence tests, African Americans differ from Caucasians by about 1.0 standard deviation, with Caucasians obtaining the higher scores, a finding that has been relatively consistent across time and assessment methods but is a difference that diminishes to a 0.5 standard deviation when socioeconomic status is accounted for (Reynolds & Ramsay, 2003). Research indicates that stigmatized groups' differences in cognitive abilities can also be understood as a function of factors such as stereotype threat (Stahl, Van Laar, & Ellemers, 2012), and quality and extent of education and acculturation (Manly, Byrd, Touradji, & Stern, 2004). Many cross-cultural clinical researchers recommend using the appropriate ethnic group measurement norm to improve diagnostic accuracy (e.g., Ardila, 1995). Some psychologists have raised concerns that the specific group norm approach fails to increase our understanding of underlying psychological processes, and could inadvertently encourage belief in a biological basis of ethnic differences in intellect, and so instead recommend adjusting cognitive test scores on the basis of degree of acculturation and quality of education (Manly et al., 2004). Sternberg (2003) has demonstrated in *Project Rainbow* that measures of practical and creative ability contribute significantly to predicting first-year undergraduate grade point average (GPA) above and beyond Scholastic Assessment Test (SAT) scores. Relative to ethnic differences in SAT and GPA, the Project Rainbow practical and creative ability measures reduced ethnic difference gaps, particularly for Hispanic Americans.

Learning

Learning is essentially the storage by the nervous system of information for its retrieval at a later time. There are two types of learning theory. One involves a focus on environmental events that influence behaviors, and the other focuses on changes that take place within the learner (Schwartz & Reisberg, 1991).

The dominant learning theory of the early 20th century was based on the work of Thorndike (1898), in the United States, and independently, Pavlov (1927), in Russia. Their findings were known as related forms of conditioning and became the cornerstone of behaviorism. Because behaviorism's conclusions were all based on observable qualities in either the environment or in behavior, it was well suited to studies of animals, particularly rats and pigeons. In fact, some strong behaviorists concluded that cognitive states were not only beyond the bounds of psychology, but also were essentially illusions. Notably such topics included thinking, feeling, and cognitive learning.

In the mid-20th century, as methods of working with human subjects developed, research in social and cognitive approaches began to be gradually more important and was aided by the introduction of the computer. The rise of cognitive psychology was a consequence, though it was a number of years before affect or feelings became acceptable as research topics.

Classical or Pavlovian Conditioning

Ivan Pavlov was a Russian physiologist working on the problem of what causes salivation. Food in the mouth of a hungry dog was readily seen to produce salivation (a saliva duct was brought outside to make it visible). But a new phenomenon presented itself when the dog salivated when the assistant getting the meat powder was merely walking down the hallway. Pavlov eventually worked out this necessary relationship and it became known as classical conditioning. Pavlov described the stimulus–response (S–R) paradigm in terms of an unconditioned stimulus (US; something to which an organism instinctively responds), an unconditioned response (UR; the instinctive response of the organism to the US), a conditioned stimulus (CS; a stimulus that is not responded to instinctively that is paired temporally with the US), and a conditioned response (CR; an organism's response to the CS that is similar to the UR). The basic paradigm is as follows.

CS/US > UR until conditioning has occurred, when the UR takes place as soon as the CS appears and the US is not needed any more, and the paradigm becomes simply CS > CR. Pavlov apparently tried to imitate the sound of the assistant in the hallway by using a metronome as his CS, though we all know him as having rung a bell. He would present the metronome (CS), and follow it with meat powder (US) in the dog's mouth. The dog would salivate (UR) in the course of eating the tiny amount of food. After a few trials, the dog salivated (CR) to the sound.

Watson, of course, is known for conditioning little Albert (Watson & Raynor, 1920, as cited by Hall, 1966) to fear white rats in very few trials. Moreover, the fear conditioning generalized to include white rabbits and other white furry objects. More everyday examples might show the acquisition of phobias, or anxiety in response to certain stimuli. Stimuli in these situations will probably not be as simple as Pavlov's, but rather complex elements of environmental context, such as standing before an audience, or driving across a high bridge, such that just talking about doing these things, or even thinking about having to be there, will produce responses of fear and anxiety. Many times adult reactions are due to childhood experiences that may have been forgotten. Fear of dogs, for example, may result from a child being threatened or even attacked by a dog. It seems that almost any emotion may become attached in this manner. The index in these cases is often some autonomic response such as increased blood pressure, heart rate, or GSR, the electrical measure of skin resistance.

In recent years, there has been an extension of classical conditioning as an important mechanism in drug and illness responses. For example, it was found that cues from the environment had a strong effect on response strength in the case of heroin. If a user administered his or her heroin shots in the same room every day, his or her body would begin an antagonistic response to it as soon as he or she entered that room. The drug's effect was lessened by this antagonistic reaction, becoming a factor in adaptation, so that higher doses gradually became necessary to achieve the high. However, if the shot was administered in a new room, the body would not begin reacting as soon, and an overdose would potentially ensue. (For more on this phenomenon, called conditioned place effects, see Tzschentke, 1998.)

Operant Conditioning

The basics of operant conditioning were discovered by Edward Thorndike (1898) and he called the relationship "the law of effect," because he found that random behaviors would be repeated only if they were followed by some sort of reward. The basic paradigm, which differs only slightly from the classical one, became as follows: CS > CR/US > UR. The paradigm is read as: a stimulus that precedes a behavior that leads to a "satisfying state of affairs" will tend to be repeated. The main difference from classical conditioning is that the CR moves ahead of the US, and indicates that the CR may or may not be made, depending on the nature of the consequence (the US). That is, CR still stands as in classical conditioning for CR, but now the response includes the element of choice, so that the response can be made if it leads to something desired, or one can refrain from making it if it does not, or if it leads to something aversive. Thus, pleasure and avoidance become crucial dimensions of the US, likely attributable to evolution in which animals were forced to approach food while avoiding predators. Negative outcomes of behavior in operant conditioning are called punishers, but, because they tend to make the CR *less* likely to happen, they *cannot* be called reinforcements. Note then that the term "negative reinforcement" has different meanings in the two forms of conditioning: in classical it increases the CR, whereas in operant it decreases its likelihood.

Much of the difference between classical and operant is caused by the addition to operant conditioning of some degree of choice for the person or animal involved. In classical conditioning, the animal cannot avoid the stimuli since they are under control of the experimenter. Because avoidance was not possible, the animals quickly learned whether the signal (CS) was leading to something good or bad, and CRs became faster than unconditioned ones. The index of response was the faster reaction time to the CS, or a secretion such as salivation that the animal could not willfully control. In operant conditioning, on the other hand, animals have a choice to respond or not, and the nature of the consequence influences their decision. They learn to respond when the consequence is desired and not to respond when it is aversive, and this is what makes operant conditioning probably as much about motivation as learning. It is an arguable question regarding how much choice different species, including our own, actually have, because behavior is nearly always in favor of the higher reward. For instance, B.F. Skinner (1971) maintained that none of us have free will.

Reinforcement Schedule

The learning situation in operant conditioning involves not only what the reinforcement will be but also how often it is likely to appear—this is the reinforcement schedule. If the reinforcer follows every instance of the CS, it is called continuous reinforcement, or CRF. CRF is the fastest way to learn, but, because it requires so many reinforcers, it is not efficient. But a rat pressing a lever, for example, does not need to be rewarded every time he presses, but only some proportion. If the schedule does not vary in proportion, say, consistently every fifth press is rewarded, it is called fixed ratio, or simply FR. It is found in human behavior control as piecework, or work on commission, where each piece produced earns a set amount of money. If the presses that are rewarded are randomly spaced, it is variable ratio (VR). Pop quizzes illustrate human use of this schedule. Both ratio schedules produce high rates of output. That is, they follow the rule that the more the work, the more the reward, or to maximize rewards, one maximizes output.

There are also two common schedules based on the passage of time, not on number of presses. They are known as interval schedules. Fixed interval (FI) means that the first press after a set interval is rewarded. Note that reinforcements are never given without some work, or work will simply stop. An FI schedule leads to intermittent behavior that, when graphed, looks scalloped because responses right after the reward are never rewarded, and as a result, responses stop for a time. After a while, the responses start again slowly, reaching a high rate just before the end of the interval. Responses are never rewarded at the beginning of an interval, but are always rewarded at the end, so responses stop at the beginning, and become rapid at the end. Responses stop again for a bit, and the cycle continues. Work on term papers nicely illustrates this schedule. Nothing relative to assigned papers happens at the beginning of a semester, but about mid-semester, topics are being chosen and a few books collected. The night before the paper is due, activity is high and may continue all night (we are obviously overgeneralizing!).

In the second interval schedule, intervals between reinforcements can be of unpredictable length. This is called variable ratio (VR), and a very steady response rate is produced, but of only medium speed. Again, this rate maximizes reinforcement, while minimizing work.

Verbal Learning

A line of research in learning predated Pavlov and Thorndike and involved experiments in verbal learning. Begun by Ebbinghaus (1885, as cited by Hall, 1966), the method with himself as subject involved memorizing nonsense syllables to see where the errors occurred. One approach presented a list in order over and over until there were no mistakes. It was called the anticipation method because after each syllable Ebbinghaus would try to anticipate the next syllable. He found lists in this manner to show both a primacy and recency effect. Primacy and recency effects referred to the first and last syllables being the easiest to remember, respectively. This finding proved to be similar to the distribution of errors in maze learning, likely due to the fact that a maze is a similar unchanging sequence. He concluded that items interfered with each other, and that there was less interference between items at the ends. Another Ebbinghaus method involved the presentation of pairs of syllables, with subjects attempting to report the second syllable of a pair when the first syllable was given. The order of the pairs was then shuffled among trials, but with the word pairing remaining constant. He called it the paired associate method, and it is still used today. The fewest errors were found when some sort of mental association between the syllables occurred.

Paired associate learning was later explained as an example of operant conditioning, but it seemed to be one of a number of behaviors involving learning without responding. That is, one might simply look at the pairs rather than orally responding. In such cases, the US–UR bond was missing and these were examples of learning without reinforcement. The problem was not only found in verbal learning, but also in operant behavior studies. In the early 1930s, E.C. Tolman extended Blogett's discovery of what he had called latent learning. In the simplest example, Tolman (1932) allowed animals to live in a maze in which no food was ever presented. When these animals were later rewarded for finding their way through the maze, they learned it in far fewer trials than naïve rats despite the absence of initial learning rewards. A number of other behaviors were later shown to be similarly learned without reward, such as Harlow's young monkeys that manipulated four types of puzzles, strings, and latches with no reinforcement. The time spent each day on this activity increased to an asymptote (Harlow, Blazer & McClearn, 1956). Butler (1954) showed that monkeys would press a lever for no other reinforcement than a chance to peek for 5 seconds into the adjoining room. He found they would work for a chance to see a still life of food, but would work harder for a moving electric train, and even harder to see another monkey. These and other studies showed that the concept of reinforcement had to be expanded to include cognitive and social reinforcements. Similarly, a number of human behaviors, such as solving puzzles; observing art; and expressing emotion in art, dance, or music, also call for expanded reinforcement concepts.

Studies showed that there were considerable individual differences in the value of reinforcements and in categories of reinforcements that could also be termed "needs." For example, Maslow (1970) developed his well-known pyramid of needs that reflected his findings that physiological needs were primary, with safety and social needs coming in the next two positions. Ego needs were next, with self-actualizing needs at the top. Prior to Maslow, Murray had developed a list of human motivations under the heading of needs (Murray, 1938). They can similarly be seen as a list of reinforcing activities, but here too there is huge variability in individual differences. Murray included "needs" such as aggression and other behaviors that are common among humans. The behaviorist position is that there must be something rewarding about it for the aggressors. Reinforcements can change with the time of day, with past experiences, with the presence of competing alternatives, with individual tastes, and with a host of other variables. Explaining human behavior, therefore, requires caution and cross-validation to guard against easy-but-wrong explanations based simply on reinforcement theory.

In the 1980s, the principle of Pavlovian conditioning was reinterpreted by Rescorla, who wrote, "Pavlovian conditioning is not the shifting of a response from one stimulus to another. Instead, conditioning involves the learning of relations among events that are complexly represented, a learning that can be exhibited in various ways" (Rescorla, 1988, p. 158). Rather than learning rote responses, human subjects may be learning the relationship between the two stimuli, resulting in wide flexibility rather than rigid reflexes. The stimulus-to-stimulus connection may be far more important than the CR. Rescorla focused on the content of learning instead of the learning environment (S–R). The same possibility applies to operant stimuli.

Pavlov discovered that stimuli associate even in the absence of any overt responses, and called this discovery sensory preconditioning, though it was overlooked and he is not often credited with its identification (Kimmel, 1977). A connection can be made between two stimuli (CS1 and CS2) by pairing them (step one) and no response is seen to occur. Now CS2, without the preceding CS1, is conditioned by adding a US in the standard way so that CS2 comes to produce a CR. The final step involves presenting the CS1 alone and observing that, without any discernible reinforcement (UR or CR), it too produces the CR. Note that step two does not have to be done to *produce* the connection between CS1 and CS2, it only has to be done to *demonstrate* the connection. Verbal learning, in that no responses are called for, shows some similarities.

However, in verbal learning, though no responses are called for, it might be argued that the responses were actually being made as verbalizations subvocally, and this would make the process standard S–R. However, it appears that this is only sometimes true. For example, consider the common pair, salt–pepper. When we were learning this combination we probably heard, "Please pass the salt and pepper" repeatedly, but we were not asked to say "pepper" in response to "salt." Nor when we hear the word "salt," do we immediately blurt out "pepper." We may if asked, but normally we do not verbalize at all. We learn the combination from simply hearing the words in conjunction repeatedly, just as happens with sensory preconditioning. Stimulus–stimulus (S–S) thus has also emerged as an important type of conditioning.

The difference between S–S and S–R is significant. A major distinction is evident in what is actually learned about the CS. In S–R, not only does the CR occur, but the CS tends to remain as simply a signal for the subsequent events. In S–S conditioning, on the other hand, the CS tends to take on the properties of the US. Here we see a real difference between the cognitive and the affective nature of the stimuli. Cognitive aspects are hard to condition unconsciously, but affective qualities do so readily. The affective qualities are the ones that particularly transfer back to the CS. This S–S characteristic means that if the US no longer appears, the learning about CS will generally begin to extinguish in S–R, but will show more resistance to extinction in S–S. Such a finding was recently documented by Walther, Weil, and Düsing (2011).

The complex nature of the CS was demonstrated by Janiszewski and Warlop (1993). Following the conditioning of a CS in what appears to be an S–S design, they reported finding subjects acting strangely toward the CS. They described the subject's behavior as "moving toward the CS" and "paying more attention to it." They noted that this was not the behavior that was conditioned and that it was very hard to explain using the old S–R model. However, this has come to be expected in the S–S model. Adult humans will be learning many things about their situation besides a restricted US–UR connection. The same should also be found in operant conditioning. It is now easier to understand Tolman's latent learning or learning without reinforcement as an operant instance of the S–S model. That is, while living in the mazes, the rats were engaged in S–S learning that was measured later when they were reinforced in a standard operant model. It suggests that some level of learning is going on much of the time, particularly when it relates to our personal environment.

The S–S model shows particular utility in cognitive learning situations. For instance, most advertising is classical conditioning (though often done incorrectly). That is, a new meaning is being attached to a brand (the CS), and some strong positively affective image might be the US (such as a beautiful person, a tropical beach, or a cute puppy), which produces a pleasant or positive feeling in the viewer. The US may not have anything to do with the brand; it just has to produce strong positive feelings, which are, of course, the UR. Measuring those feelings by means of a rating scale will confirm that the attitude toward the brand has indeed changed and the viewer has come to like the brand better. Note that this is not operant conditioning, because the viewer does not have to do anything to make the pairing happen (Olson & Fazio, 2001).

Just as vicarious reinforcement expanded the application of operant conditioning to cognitive reinforcement, the advent of S–S conditioning expanded the application of classical conditioning. Expectancy theory, for example, found a solid foundation in the S–S model in which the observation of behavior is sufficient to form the expectancy of reinforcement. Bandura and colleagues (1963), for instance, demonstrated that children will imitate adult behavior from simply observing it, and the phenomenon became known as observational learning. When animals were demonstrated watching other animals to find out how they were getting reinforcers, and then applying it themselves, it was called vicarious learning.

Memory

Although learning is considered the input to storage, memory is considered the output. However, the two topics are often blended or mixed up, because the measurement of learning is always through the mechanism of memory. Moreover, how something is learned has a strong influence on how it is remembered. This means that perception becomes important as well, for how it is perceived determines how it will be learned and, thus, remembered.

Past memory research reflected the influence of computer advances, as did learning research. The main force was epitomized as "information processing," which broke the neurological process into successive steps and sorted sensory inputs into categories represented by analogous cell groups. The "modal model" of information processing originated with Waugh and Norman (1965) and was expanded by Atkinson and Shiffrin (1968). It was composed of three levels: sensory memory, short-term memory, and long-term memory (LTM; Schwartz & Reisberg, 1991).

Sensory memory is probably too brief to be called memory (Schwartz & Reisberg, 1991). Experience involves a continuous flow of information (an analog), but the nervous system is built around discrete impulses (digital base) that is, a succession of separate packages of information and there is a need to transform the information from one form to the other. To our brains, experience flows without interruption, but memories are like still snapshots. Sensory memory involves chopping the flow into memories to compare to others in processing their meaning. Sensory memory is based on retaining visual images and auditory inputs for just milliseconds. In turn, these residual images can be used by the visual system. We notice this in the after-image of a flash when we see a spot everywhere we look. Sperling (1960) used this after-image by flashing a matrix of letters on a screen before subjects for about 50 milliseconds as they focused on a central letter. After the flash was gone, he asked what other letters in the matrix were seen. All the letters had been seen, but they faded away quickly, and the task was one of memory not perception. In short, it takes time to transfer information to memory.

Short-term memory (STM) represents storage of information that can be retained only for a brief time, and in limited amounts. "One is always very conscious of information in short-term memory" (Springer & Deutsch, 1998). In other words, in order to think about something, it has to have been brought into STM, which seems to be equivalent to consciousness. It will remain actively there only for a few minutes without being refreshed. It represents the material we are thinking about at a given moment, and has come to be called "working memory" (WM) today.

Long-term memory (LTM) refers to all the information that has been learned, but is not needed at the moment. It represents a relatively permanent memory bank. It is a vast library of information and comes in two main categories, declarative and nondeclarative. Declarative memory is composed of things one knows (explicit) and can access, and, according to the analysis of Squire (1992), it has two divisions. The first is semantic memory, which refers to knowledge of the world such as facts, meanings, concepts, and rules of culture. These are often learned in school, and as we all know, may require hard work to store. The second is called episodic memory. It was proposed by Tulving (1972) and is autobiographic memory. Everyday experiences are recorded here and are connected to other events of the day. These memories are essentially stored automatically, and this may be why hands-on learning is easier to retain than lecture. The more life is repetitious, the more these memories interfere with each other with some loss of sequence and specific times.

Nondeclarative memory consists of items the person is unaware of knowing (implicit), yet can still demonstrate knowledge of. For example, *priming* means presenting similar words or word parts previous to a test, which will reduce the time to identify a word fragment. It may be a form of cuing, in that both techniques involve activating associated brain areas, so that search there becomes faster and more efficient. It is an implicit characteristic when one is not aware of using the prime.

An interesting case illustrates the explicit–implicit difference. A man identified only as HM lost the use of his hippocampus and amygdala on both sides of his brain. The hippocampus is the main structure for consolidating LTM, and HM could, therefore, not store anything new in his explicit memory storage area, resulting in anterograde amnesia. His wife came to visit often, but each time she was out of the room for more than a few minutes, he greeted her return as though he had not seen her for weeks. In other words, his STM was working, as was his LTM from before his loss, but he had no memory after his loss. However, he was able to show improvement on learning lists and mazes in subsequent meetings, but each time he did not remember ever having seen them before.

Anderson proposed an ACT model of cognition (meaning Adaptive Control of Thought), in which procedural learning occurred through a series of If–Then connections (a concept perhaps borrowed from computer programming). Whenever the outcome was not as expected, additional If–Then clauses would be added to accommodate the new situation. Although the theory was quite powerful, with a number of applications, to some it was untestable (Leahey & Harris, 1993).

There is a possibility that affective memories will turn out to be stored in a different way from other memories. Greenwald and Leavitt (1984) worked out a theory of four levels of processing in perceiving stimuli, which they labeled as follows: Presensory (the catching-attention phase), Focal Attention (the paying-attention phase), Comprehension (the understanding phase), and Elaboration (making-connections and storing phase). Each level successively requires a bit more time than the previous. They supported the theory with evidence that showed the more the elaboration, the better the memory. In fact, it appeared that there was virtually no memory without some degree of elaboration. In this conclusion, Greenwald and Leavitt were following the path of Craik and Lockhart (1972), who had proposed that rather than discrete memory stores, memory was a function of cognitive level of processing. The deeper the level of processing, the better the recall would be. What drove the first stage of Greenwald and Leavitt's theory was not clear at the time, but now it appears that it is affect that directs attention. The affective system is faster than the cognitive system. Affect picks up the stimulus as a source of threat, and the cognitive system then analyzes it to find out why (Zajonc, 1980, 2000). Because affect is read so much faster than other memories, and because it has its own organization, it seems likely it has its own storage, but the necessary research has not yet been done.

Emotion and Motivation

Emotions are a central part of psychological experience and significantly contribute to the motivation of behavior. Generally speaking, psychologists understand emotions to contain the following components: physiological effects, including autonomic arousal, action urges, cognitive appraisals, facial expressions, and a subjective feeling of emotion. Motivation is often considered to be a component of emotion; however, it is also often considered a separate but related element of human experience.

Theories of Emotional Experience

The concept of emotion is one without a single overriding theory in psychology. Instead, there are several coexisting theories of emotion. To understand the prevailing theories, it is useful to approach them from an historical perspective.

William James was the first psychologist to propose a theory of emotional experience. His theory postulated that changes in physiological sensation are the primary elements of emotional experience (James, 1884). This theory is generally referred to as the James–Lange theory of emotion as the theory was independently proposed by Carl Lange, a Danish physician. In the simplest terms, the James–Lange theory models emotion as the psychological response to the changes in the physical systems of the body after the presentation of a stimulus. Fear is often used an example of this model:

1. The individual observes a threatening bear in the woods.
2. The individual runs away and has increased autonomic activity (increased heart rate, increased respiration, etc.).
3. The individual observes his increased autonomic activity and that he is running away from the bear.
4. The individual concludes that he is experiencing fear.

Several critiques of the James–Lange theory quickly emerged. Primarily, these critiques focused on the nature and response of the autonomic nervous system. Some of these critiques do not accurately reflect the James–Lange theory (i.e., the theory does not rely strictly on visceral responses to dictate emotion and the nature of the stimulus [a bear vs. an object of lust] is relevant to the reported emotion). However, they are sufficiently valid to indicate serious flaws in the theory as a comprehensive model of emotion. The first significant counterproposal to the James–Lange theory was presented by Walter Cannon and Philip Bard (Cannon, 1931).

The Cannon–Bard theory proposes that the physiological responses associated with emotion are a consequence of experiencing emotion, not a necessary precursor. As popularly understood, the Cannon–Bard theory states that one has the psychological experience of emotion and this experience generates a physiological change. To use the same example above, an emotional experience would take the following path:

1. The individual observes a threatening bear in the woods.
2. The individual processes the sensory information and recognizes a threatening situation.

3. The individual experiences fear.

4. The individual begins to experience physiological changes, such as autonomic arousal and an urge to flee.

However, this simplistic formulation of the Cannon–Bard theory neglects the important fact that perhaps the first theory of emotion not only centered the experience within the brain, but identified specific regions involved with the experience. In particular, the Cannon–Bard theory centers emotional experience on the thalamus, an area that we now think of as a sensory relay area, and one of many brain regions involved in emotional processing. The theory modeled the process of emotional experience in the following way:

Stimulus $\longrightarrow$ cortical processing $\longrightarrow$ thalamic processing $\longrightarrow$ behavior

Therefore, in contrast to the James–Lange theory, the Cannon–Bard theory requires processing within the brain prior to physiological changes. In terms of the perceived experience, the Cannon–Bard theory postulates that the conscious awareness of an emotional state and the physiological changes associated with that state occur simultaneously, such that the person would note the emotion and the physical changes as parallel, rather than sequential.

The James–Lange and Cannon–Bard theories remained the main models of emotional experience until the 1960s when Schachter and Singer published their seminal article, "Cognitive, Social and Physiological Determinants of Emotional State" (Schachter & Singer, 1962). In this study, Schachter and Singer demonstrated that similar physiological experiences would lead to different emotional experiences depending on the context. Through their research results, Schacter and Singer concluded that individuals must cognitively appraise a situation in order to determine their emotional states—they referred to this as the "two-factor" model of emotion:

Autonomic arousal $\longrightarrow$ Cognitive interpretation $\longrightarrow$ Emotion

Subsequently, this model of emotion has been subsumed in the broader term *cognitive appraisal*, which has been the dominant model of emotion since the 1960s.

Richard Lazarus developed a sophisticated appraisal model of emotion (1966, 1991) in which he theorized that each emotional experience arises from how an individual appraised ongoing interactions with the environment. His early work identified two stages of appraisal. In primary appraisal, the valence and threat of the stimulus are identified in a general sense (positive vs. negative; benign vs. stressful). During secondary appraisal, the individual identifies the resources and options that may be available to cope with the stimuli. Both processes combine into the experience of a particular emotion. The coping mechanisms of secondary appraisal may be identified as "emotion focused" (use of internal resources to cope with situation) or "problem focused" (intervene in the environment to solve a problem externally) (Folkman & Lazarus, 1980). This distinction has been found to be useful in the study of depression, for instance, in which individuals with depression are more likely to use emotion-focused coping (Folkman & Lazarus, 1985), as are those with executive functioning deficits (Krpan, Levine, Stuss, & Dawson, 2007).

Later adaptations of this theory by Lazarus (1991) have indicated that each emotion has a particular motivational function. In other words, the appraisal of the relationship between the individual and the stimuli is unique to each emotion experienced. This iteration of the model identifies multiple types of primary appraisal, including goal relevance, goal congruency, and ego involvement. There are also additions to the types of secondary appraisal, including identifying blame, coping resources, and expectations of the future. These adaptations were done to address criticisms of Lazarus's work, which suggested that his model was a theory of stress response more than a comprehensive theory of emotion.

In response to Lazarus's theory and the primacy of cognitive appraisal models, Zajonc (1980) described a model of emotion that allowed for the experience of affect without cognitive contribution. He challenged the idea that cognition is a necessary component of emotional experience, though he did not conclude that cognition never contributed to emotion.

Somatic Marker Hypothesis

A recent addition to theories of emotion is somatic marker hypothesis (SMH), which focuses on the emotion and its role in decision making (Damasio, Everitt & Bishop, 1996). Case reports of injury to the frontal lobe being associated with social conduct and decision-making deficits date back to the 19th century. More specifically, damage to the ventromedial prefrontal cortex (VMPFC) often results in significant changes in the ability to make opportune decisions in personal, social, and financial spheres. This led Antonio Damasio and colleagues (Damasio, Tranel, & Damasio, 1991) to propose that decision-making deficits following VMPFC damage result from the inability to draw on emotions to direct future behavior based on past experiences. The SMH proposes a mechanism by which emotional processes can influence behavior, predominantly decision making.

The central tenet behind the SMH is that decision making is influenced by marker signals that arise from multiple levels of operation, both consciously and unconsciously. Marker signals arise in bioregulatory processes (e.g., changes in heart rate, blood pressure, and glandular secretion) and in emotions and feeling. According to the SMH, the sensory mapping of visceral responses contributes not only to emotions, but is also vital for the implementation of goal-oriented behaviors. Subsequently, visceral responses operate by "marking" potential choices as beneficial or detrimental.

Emotional decision making can significantly affect individual's daily lives and, accordingly, the SMH has important clinical implications. In addiction, a deficit in the neural circuitry that subserves the action of somatic markers is implicated in dependent individuals' diminished ability to make favorable real-life decisions.

Dimensional/Basic Emotion Models

The determination of the appropriate model to classify and define emotions has focused on two competing theories. One side theorizes that all emotions can be described by a small group of specific emotions—usually referred to as the "basic emotion" model. The other side considers emotions to be a combination of several dimensions of physiological and psychological phenomena—usually referred to as the "dimensional" model. Each model has supporting research evidence and few efforts have been made to reconcile the opposing theories.

The main figure associated with the basic emotion model is Paul Ekman. In 1971, he and Wallace Friesen (Ekman & Friesen, 1971) published an article reporting the ubiquity of facial expressions related to emotion by studying facial expressions across several cultures. They identified six basic/primary emotions as defined by these facial expressions—happy, sad, surprised, disgusted, angry, and afraid. Basic emotion theory holds that these (usually) six emotions are the only emotions that humans experience. The basic emotions are "hardwired" into humans at birth. Therefore, "secondary" emotions that might be labeled other than happy, sad, surprised, disgusted, angry, or afraid are, in fact, combinations of some of the six basic emotions, and are influenced by cultural factors, among others. One of the main critiques of this theory is that, by setting a low limit on the number of "true" emotions, the theory is not sufficiently flexible to explain the complexity of human emotional experience.

Dimensional models of emotion attempt to incorporate flexibility into a simple model in an effort to provide a broader description of emotional experience. Dimensional models were described early in the development of psychology (Wundt, 1896), but did not begin to be well described and researched until Osgood, Suci, and Tannenbaum (1961) began work on the semantic differential. In this work, they had individuals rate their impression of stimuli on a Likert scale between two sematic opposites. Using factor analysis on these data, they identified three factors in the response patterns and they hypothesized that these factors represented the basic dimensions of emotional experience. Further research replicated this finding, though the first two factors were consistently much stronger than the third. Consequently, Russell (1977) and others have focused on two dimensions of emotion—usually identified as valence, the pleasantness of a stimulus, and arousal, the autonomic arousal in response to a stimulus. Russell and colleagues (1977) developed the circumplex model of emotion from these two dimensions, which is the dominant dimensional model currently. Much like the basic emotion model, the dimensional model has been criticized for not adequately describing the scope of human emotional experience. Dimensional models that are restricted to two axes, such as the circumplex model, have received similar criticism.

Brain Systems

The limbic system is a system of brain regions that is most commonly associated with emotion. This system is composed primarily of subcortical regions, including the following: amygdala, hippocampus, mammillary bodies, septal nuclei, parahippocampal gyrus, and cingulate gyrus. It is highly interconnected with the endocrine system and autonomic nervous system (Ulrich-Lai & Herman, 2009). Most of the regions of this system were first described by James Papez in 1937, and the term *limbic system* was coined by Paul MacLean in 1952 to describe the system. More recently, the concept of the limbic system has come under fire (LeDoux, 2003), but the regions included within the limbic system model have consistently been associated with emotional processing and experience.

Joseph LeDoux has focused much of the attention of emotion-related brain regions on the amygdala (LeDoux, 1996) through his research establishing the amygdala as the primary center of fear-related processing. The amygdala is reliably observed to activate in response to threatening or fearful stimuli but not for stimuli related to positive emotions (Feldman Barrett & Wager, 2006). As a result, the amygdala is often identified as the primary region involved in negative emotional experience, though research evidence does not always support this role (Phan, Wager, Taylor, & Liberzon, 2002).

More recently, other regions, including cortical regions, have been added to the more traditional network of the limbic system. Of particular importance are the orbitofrontal cortex and the nucleus accumbens. The orbitofrontal cortex has been implicated in the regulation of emotional behavior and is considered to provide an inhibitory influence on impulsive emotional responses (Bechara, Damasio, & Damasio, 2000). It has strong connections with the amygdala and the cingulate gyrus, providing evidence to support this role. Damage to the orbitofrontal cortex is associated with disinhibited behaviors, especially aggressive behaviors (Berlin, Rolls, & Kischka, 2004).

The nucleus accumbens, a small cluster of neurons within the basal ganglia, has been shown to be particularly important to the process of positive reinforcement and reward and is often identified as the brain's "pleasure center" (Breiter & Rosen, 1999). Research has demonstrated that it is active in response to rewarding stimuli, both physiological (i.e., drugs; Volkow, Fowler, Wang, & Swanson, 2004) and psychological (i.e., classical conditioning; Day & Carelli, 2007). Changes in activity in this region are associated with symptoms of depression (Nestler & Carlezon, 2006) and obsessive-compulsive disorder (Sturm et al., 2003).

Theories of Motivation

Motivation is the internal force that pushes the individual toward action and is generally considered to be composed of three components—arousal, direction, and intensity (Deckers, 2010). Motivation can either be directed toward internal rewards (intrinsic) or toward external rewards (extrinsic). The first theories of motivation focused on instinctual processes, such as Darwin's natural selection model and Freud's model, which postulates that motivation is a function of an organism's attempts to reduce the urge of a biological drive, such as hunger or sexual desire. In general, currently, instinctual models are not widely used as they have been found to be too simple to describe most human behavior. Other theories of motivation have focused on drives, needs, and cognitive processes.

Drive Theories

Drive theory revolves around the concept of homeostasis (Bouton, 2007), which is the idea that an organism works to keep a physiological equilibrium. When the equilibrium is upset, the organism has a need and is then motivated to engage in behavior that will reestablish equilibrium (drive reduction). For example, when the body is depleted of energy, this upsets the internal equilibrium and the organism will seek to find food.

A drive such as hunger is defined as a primary drive—these are drives that are biological and innate. Drives that are learned through experience, such as achieving wealth, are secondary drives, as they are not innate and do not directly support a biological need.

Clark Hull is among the most influential of motivational theorists who described a drive theory. Hull believed that there are internal drives that motivate behavior. The shape the behavior takes is, at first, random and is then honed by learning processes to a form that becomes habitual. He also stated that drive reduction through behavior is, in and of itself, reinforcing and successful reduction of a drive is sufficient to increase the probability of the behavior occurring in the future. He developed a formula to describe motivation using habit strength, drive strength, and excitatory potential (how likely is the individual to respond to the stimulus), though it has limited practical utility.

Drive theory has been extensively studied and has found a substantial amount of support. Attachment theorists have identified drive reduction as a mechanism behind attachment behavior in infants (Dollard & Miller, 1950). Zajonc (1965) used drive theory to develop an explanation of social facilitation. However, drive theory falls short when one considers the relationship between level of motivation and level of deprivation. Drive theory would suggest a linear relation between these variables—a very direct S–R interaction. Research has indicated that there is a cognitive component that intervenes in the S–R interaction in which the response becomes a habit only if it is reinforced and the organism will engage in that response only if it anticipates a positive outcome (Dickenson & Balleine, 1994). Thus, a pure drive theory is not sufficient to explain motivated behavior, but its focus on homeostasis is an important consideration.

Another consideration around drive theory is the concept of frustration and its impact on motivation. Work by Amsel and colleagues (Amsel & Roussel, 1952; Amsel & Ward, 1965) demonstrated that frustration can increase motivation more than reward. By frustration, they refer to thwarted anticipation of rewards and they showed that, in the context of the expectation of a large reward, no reward (or even a small reward) can lead to increased motivation to continue or complete a task. This research in frustration helps to explain paradoxical reward effects, which occur when a reward seems to weaken a response rather than strengthen it (Bouton, 2007).

Need-Based Theories

The most well known of the need-based theories is Maslow's hierarchy of needs. Maslow (1943) theorized that individuals are motivated to act based on certain needs and that these needs can be understood in hierarchical fashion, from the most basic physical needs, to more abstract intellectual and psychological needs. At its base are physiological needs such as food, water, and sleep. The individual will be motivated to engage in behavior to fulfill those needs and will not be motivated to engage in behavior that will fulfill a higher-level need, such as family or friends, until the lower-level needs are met. Maslow's hierarchy listed needs in the following order, from lowest to highest:

1. Physiological—food, water, sleep, and sex

2. Safety—shelter, employment, and health

3. Love/belonging—friendship and family

4. Esteem—self-esteem, achievement, and respect of others

5. Self-actualization—morality and creativity

Little research evidence supported Maslow's theory and it has generally fallen out of favor among motivation theorists (Jex & Britt, 2008). Need-based theories, however, have remained.

Herzberg, Mausner, and Snyderman (1959) developed a two-factor theory to explain workplace motivation—his two factors are intrinsic and extrinsic motivation. He also delineated motivators, which are elements, such as recognition and work challenges, that provide positive reward and satisfaction, and hygiene factors, such as security and status, which reduce motivation in their absence.

Atkinson and McClelland developed Need for Achievement theory, which postulates that motivation is governed by three considerations—achievement, authority, and affiliation (McClelland, 1965). Achievement is the need to find a sense of accomplishment through advancement and feedback. Authority is the need to lead and to make an impact. Affiliation is the need to be liked and to develop positive social interactions. According to the theory, people have varying degrees of each of the three motivational needs, and this theory is particularly relevant in industrial and organizational (I/O) psychology.

A more recent theory, self-determination theory (SDT), focuses on the idea that humans have "inherent growth tendencies" that lead to consistent effort (Deci & Vansteenkiste, 2004). This theory centers on intrinsic motivation and consists of three basic needs—competence, relatedness, and autonomy. *Competence* is the need to develop mastery. *Relatedness* is the need to develop relationships with others. *Autonomy* is the need to have control in one's own life while maintaining relationships with others.

Learning Theories

B.F. Skinner's description of operant conditioning (Skinner, 1938) can also be understood in the context of motivation. Skinner did not agree with Hull that a drive must be reduced in order for learning to occur. Skinner, instead, focused on the extrinsic reward as the motivation for behavior. Though he did not describe his thoughts as a theory, it is easy to understand why his model of behavioral modification informs the understanding of motivation as he took the focus of motivation from the internal forces that instinct and drive theories posit, and applied them to the external contingencies of behavior.

Cognitive Process Theories

The most well known of the cognitive process models is cognitive dissonance theory developed by Festinger (1957). In this theory, when individuals behave in a manner that is inconsistent with their values or beliefs, they will change their beliefs to manage the psychological tension created by the mismatch. This urge to cope with the dissonance generates motivation—either to change one's behavior or to change one's beliefs about the behavior. Most research indicates that people tend toward the latter solution.

Expectancy theory, developed by Victor Vroom in 1964, is another attempt to understand motivation, especially in decision making. Expectancy theory relies on three components—valence, expectancy, and instrumentality—to understand behavioral motivation. Valence refers to how much one values a particular consequence and will lead an individual to approach or avoid a behavior. Expectancy is the belief that one possesses the resources to achieve a certain goal, whereas instrumentality is the belief that completing a behavior will lead to a predictable outcome. Motivation is understood to be a combination of these three elements—individuals are motivated by a "motivational force" that is the product of the three elements.

Interrelationships Among Cognition, Affect, and Motivation

The interrelationships among cognition, emotion, and motivation are complex and cut across all areas of human functioning. Many of the observed interrelationships are based on the theories that have been outlined in the rest of this chapter. This section will describe some of the more important contributions to the understanding of these interrelationships.

Albert Ellis was the first psychologist to describe the importance of the interaction of cognition and emotion in normal and abnormal functioning, particularly in disorders like depression. In 1955, he established rational emotive behavior therapy (REBT), which focused on how thoughts determine emotion (Ellis, 1955). Ellis focused on "self-defeating" thoughts and postulated that these led to maladaptive behavior and pathological emotional states. He felt that helping an individual reduce these irrational thoughts would reestablish healthy emotions and behavior (Ellis, 1976).

Aaron Beck expanded on the influence of cognition on emotion when he developed cognitive therapy in 1967 with his seminal work, *Depression: Clinical, Experimental, and Theoretical Aspects*. In it, he introduced the concept of automatic thoughts and cognitive distortions and hypothesized that these concepts were primarily responsible for disruptions of normal emotional functioning. Automatic thoughts are thoughts that seem to occur spontaneously and are understood as accurate interpretations of reality by an individual. Automatic thoughts are not actually spontaneous but are well-learned interpretations. These automatic thoughts often interpret reality in ways that are biased and this bias is reflected in a cognitive distortion (Beck, Rush, Shaw, & Emery, 1979). Beck theorized that cognitive distortions lead to disrupted mood and disorders such as depression.

The theory of learned helplessness (Seligman & Maier, 1967) was developed to explain research that found that animals exposed to inescapable pain will eventually stop trying to avoid the pain, even when opportunities to escape were presented. This theory has been considered a possible explanation for depression, as individuals develop a sense that they are unable to escape pain and feel helpless, which eventually leads to depression (Seligman, 1975).

Attributional theory developed from Seligman's work based on research showing that learned helplessness was not a universal phenomenon (Cole & Coyne, 1977). Weiner developed the concept of attributional style and globality/specificity, stability/instability, and internality/externality (Weiner, 1986). Globality/specificity refers to whether an individual interprets events as a general response or a situation-specific response. Stability refers to the amount to which an individual expects a particular response to be consistent across time. Internality/externality refers to the extent to which an individual believes a result is caused by factors internal to the person or from the external environment.

Evaluative interactions between cognition and emotion have also been used to understand performance and job satisfaction. Equity theory (Adams, 1965) was among the first theories to apply cognitive/emotional interactions to these areas. This theory indicates that individuals assess the rewards from their work. If they feel under-rewarded or over-rewarded, they experience emotional distress and attempt to rectify these feelings through changing either their evaluations of or contributions to their work.

Goal-setting theory incorporated the fact that humans can plan for and form expectations about the future and that these expectations can assist individuals in reaching peak performance. Humans can set future goals that will then affect their behavior. According to Locke (1968), goals affect behavior in four ways:

1. by directing attention
2. by mobilizing efforts and resources for the task
3. by encouraging persistence
4. by facilitating the development of strategies to complete the goal

Goal-setting theory also holds that the individual must have a commitment to the goal in order to maintain motivation.

More recently, theories have been developed to understand the role of emotion and cognition in performance. Of particular interest is the role that anxiety (or autonomic arousal in general) plays in performance. The observable effects of anxiety on performance have been described with the Yerkes–Dodson law, which indicates that there is an optimal level of anxiety that will lead to peak performance (Yerkes & Dodson, 1908). If anxiety is too low or too high, performance will be negatively affected. Although the Yerkes–Dodson law describes the impact of anxiety on performance, it does not adequately explain the mechanisms at work.

Two competing theories proposed to understand the role of anxiety in performance are the Conscious Processing Hypothesis (CPH) and the Processing Efficiency Theory (PET). CPH postulates that increased anxiety associated with performance under pressure leads the individual to exert conscious control over a skill or activity that otherwise can be completed with automatic processing (Masters, 1992). This conscious focus on the skill disrupts the normally smooth automatic processing and leads to decrements in performance. Research has been equivocal for this theory (Mullen, Hardy, & Tattersall, 2005; Wilson, Smith, & Holmes, 2007). PET, on the other hand, focuses on the effect anxiety has on the cognitive resources available to the individual. PET predicts that increased stress will reduce the capacity of WM, thereby increasing the difficulty of completing the task for the individual (Eysenck & Calvo, 1992). PET also provides an explanation for maintained or improved performance under pressure by postulating that, concomitant with decreases in WM, there is an increase in the attention that is directed to the task. Research has generally been more supportive of PET over CPH (Hardy & Hutchinson, 2007; Wilson, Smith & Holmes, 2007).

Another resource-focused theory is Conservation of Resources (COR). COR postulates that the impact of stress and emotions on performance can be understood as a function of individual and group resources (Hobfoll, 1998). According to this theory, an individual is primarily motivated to build and maintain resources that will protect both the individual and the social system that supports the individual. Resources provide both the means to deal with stress and anxiety and the framework for an individual's appraisal of an event and ability to cope with the event (Buchwald, 2010). Individuals who already have reduced resources will be more vulnerable than those who have abundant resources; these vulnerable individuals will show reduced performance in the face of stress due to their depleted resources.

Recent research has also focused on the role of self-talk in performance. Self-talk is the verbalizations (internal or external) that an individual has toward him- or herself that allow that individual to regulate emotions, interpret perceptions, and provide instructions or feedback (reinforcement or punishment; Hackfort & Schwenkmezger, 1993). This phenomenon has been associated with Cognitive Interference Theory (Sarason, 1984), which postulates that negative self-talk unrelated to the task interferes with the individual's ability to perform adequately by drawing cognitive resources, such as attention, away from the task. This differs from the more contemporary understanding of self-talk in that current research tends to focus on self-talk related to the task. Self-talk has been a particular focus of research in sports psychology and has generally been found to be a significant predictor of performance, with negative self-talk leading to decrements in performance and positive self-talk improving performance (Van Raalte et al., 1994, 1995; Wrisberg & Anshel, 1997). Interventions to improve performance that incorporate training the individual in positive self-talk have been found to be more efficacious than interventions that do not (Hatzigeorgiadis et al., 2011).

References

Adams, J. (1965). Inequity in social exchange. *Advances in Experimental Social Psychology, 62,* 335–343.

Alexopoulos, G. S. (2003). Role of executive function in late life depression. *Journal of Clinical Psychiatry, 64,* 18–23.

Alvarez, J. A., & Emory, E. (2006). Executive function and the frontal lobes: A meta-analytic review. *Neuropsychology Review, 16*(1), 17–42.

Amsel, A., & Roussel, J. (1952). Motivational properties of frustration: I. Effect on a running response of the addition of frustration to the motivational complex. *Journal of Experimental Psychology, 43,* 363–368.

Amsel, A., & Ward, J. (1965). Frustration and persistence: Resistance to discrimination following prior experience with the discriminanda. *Psychological Monographs, 79,* 1–41.

Anastasi, A. (1986). Intelligence as a quality of behavior. In R. J. Sternberg, & D. K. Detterman (Eds.), *What is intelligence: Contemporary viewpoints on its nature and definition.* Norwood, NJ: Ablex.

Anderson, V., Jacobs, R., & Anderson, P. J. (2008). *Executive functions and the frontal lobes: A lifespan perspective.* New York, NY: Taylor & Francis.

Ardila, A. (1995). Directions of research in cross-cultural neuropsychology. *Journal of Clinical and Experimental Neuropsychology, 17,* 143–150.

Atkinson, R. C., & Shiffrin, R. M. (1968). Human memory: A proposed system and its control processes. In K. W. Spence, & J. T. Spence (Eds.), *The psychology of earning and motivation* (Vol. 2, pp. 89–105). New York, NY: Academic Press (as cited in Schwartz, & Reisberg, 1991).

Bandura, A., Ross, D., & Ross, S. A. (1963). Vicarious reinforcement and imitative learning. *Journal of Abnormal and Social Psychology, 67,* 601–607.

Barkley, R. A. (1997). *ADHD and the nature of self-control.* New York, NY: Guilford Press.

Bechara, A., Damasio, H., & Damasio, A. (2000). Emotion, decision making, and the orbitofrontal cortex. *Cerebral Cortex, 10,* 295–307.

Beck, A. T. (1967). *Depression: Clinical, experimental, and theoretical aspects.* New York, NY: Harper and Row.

Beck, A., Rush, A., Shaw, B., & Emery, G. (1979). *Cognitive therapy of depression.* New York, NY: Guilford Press.

Beck, D. M., & Kastner, S. (2005). Stimulus context modulates competition in human extrastriate cortex. *Nature: Neuroscience, 8,* 1110–1116.

Berlin, H., Rolls, E., & Kischka, U. (2004). Impulsivity, time perception, emotion and reinforcement sensitivity in patients with orbitofrontal cortex lesions. *Brain, 127,* 1108–1126.

Botly, L. C. P., & De Rosa, E. (2008). A cross-species investigation of acetylcholine, attention, and feature binding. *Psychological Science, 19*(11), 1185–1193.

Bouton, M. E. (2007), Learning and behavior: A contemporary synthesis, Sunderland, MA, Sinauer Associates.

Brainard, D. H. (2009). Bayesian approaches to color vision. In M. S. Gazzaniga (Ed.), *The cognitive neurosciences* (4th ed., pp. 395–408). MIT Press, Cambridge, MA.

Brainard, D. H., Longere, P., Delahunt, P. B., Freeman, W. T., Kraft, J. M., & Xiao, B. (2006). Bayesian model of human color constancy. *Journal of Vision, 6,* 1267–1281.

Breiter, H., & Rosen, B. (1999). Functional magnetic resonance imaging of brain reward circuitry in the human. *Annals of the New York Academy of Sciences, 877,* 523–547.

Buchwald, P. (2010). Test anxiety and performance in the framework of the conservation of resources theory. *Cognition, Brain and Behavior, 14,* 283–293.

Butler, R. A. (1954). Incentive conditions which influence visual exploration. *Journal of Experimental Psychology, 48*(1)19–23.

Cannon, W. B. (1931). Again the James-Lange and the thalamic theories of emotion. *Psychological Review* (38), 281–195.

Carr, H. W. (1910). Instinct and intelligence. *British Journal of Psychology, 3,* 230–236.

Carroll, J. B. (1993). *Human cognitive abilities: A survey of factor-analytic studies.* New York, NY: Cambridge University Press.

Cattell, R. B. (1941). Some theoretical issues in adult intelligence testing. *Psychological Bulletin, 38,* 592.

Cattell, R. B. (1987). *Intelligence: Its structure, growth and action.* New York, NY: Elsevier Science.

Cherry, E. C. (1953). Some experiments on the recognition of speech, with one and two ears. *Journal of the Acoustical Society of America, 25,* 975–979.

Cole, C., & Coyne, J. (1977). Situational specificity of laboratory-induced learned helplessness in humans. *Journal of Abnormal Psychology, 86*(6), 615–623.

Corbetta, M., Miezen, F. M., Dobmeyer, S., Shulman, G. L., & Petersen, S. E. (1991). Selective and divided attention during visual discrimination of shape, color, and speed—functional anatomy by positron emission tomography. *Journal of Neuroscience, 11*(8), 2383–2402.

Craik, F. I. M., & Lockhart, R. S. (1972). Levels of processing: A framework for memory research. *Journal of Verbal Learning & Verbal Behavior, 11,* 671–684.

Damasio, A., Everitt, B., & Bishop, D. (1996). The somatic marker hypothesis and the possible functions of the prefrontal cortex. *Philosophical Transactions: Biological Sciences, 351,* 1413–1420.

Damasio, A., Tranel, D., & Damasio, H. (1991). Somatic markers and the guidance of behaviour: Theory and preliminary testing. In H. S. Levin, H. M. Eisenberg, & A. L. Benton (Eds.), *Frontal lobe function and dysfunction.* New York, NY: Oxford University Press.

Day, J., & Carelli, R. (2007). The nucleus accumbens and Pavlovian reward learning. *Neuroscientist, 13,* 148–159.

Deci, E. L., & Vansteenkiste, M. (2004). Self-determination theory and basic need satisfaction: Understanding human development in positive psychology. *Ricerche di Psichologia, 27,* 17–34.

Deckers, L. (2010). *Motivation: Biological, psychological and environmental* (3rd ed.). Boston, MA: Pearson.

Dickinson, A., & Balleine, B. (1994). Motivational control of goal-directed action. *Animal Learning and Behavior, 22,* 1–18.

Dollard, J. & Miller, N. E. (1950). *Personality and psychotherapy.* New York, NY: McGraw-Hill.

Duncan, J. (1984). Selective attention and the organization of visual information. *Journal of Experimental Psychology: General, 113*(4), 501–517.

Ebbinghaus, H. (1885). *Memory: A contribution to experimental psychology* (H. A. Ruger, & C. E. Bussenius, 1913, trans.). New York, NY: Teachers College Columbia University. (As cited in Hall, 1966).

Ekman, P., & Friesen, W. (1971). Constants across cultures in the face and emotion. *Journal of Personality and Social Psychology, 17*(2), 124–129.

Ellis, A. (1955). New approaches to psychotherapy techniques. *Journal of Clinical Psychology: Monograph Supplement, 11,* 1–53.

Ellis, A. (1976). Basic clinical theory of rational-emotive therapy. In A. T. Beck (Ed.), *Cognitive therapy and emotional disorders.* New York, NY: International Universities Press.

Eysenck, M. W., & Calvo, M. G. (1992). Anxiety and performance: The processing efficiency theory. *Cognition and Emotion, 6,* 409–434.

Feldman Barrett, L., & Wager, T. (2006). The structure of emotion: Evidence from neuroimaging studies. *Current Directions in Psychological Science, 15*(2), 79–83.

Festinger, L. (1957). *A theory of cognitive dissonance.* Evanston, IL: Row, Peterson.

Folkman, S., & Lazarus, R. S. (1980). An analysis of coping in a middle-aged community sample. *Journal of Health and Social Behavior, 21,* 219–239.

Gardner, H. (2011). *Frames of mind: The theory of multiple intelligences* (30th year ed.). New York, NY: Basic Books.

Gazzaniga, M., Ivry, R. B., & Mangun, G. R. (2009). *Cognitive neuroscience: The biology of the mind.* New York, NY: Norton.

Green, D. M., & Swets, J. A. (1966). *Signal detection theory and psychophysics.* New York, NY: John Wiley.

Greenwald, A. G., & Leavitt, C. (1984). Audience involvement in advertising: Four levels. *Journal of Consumer Research, 11,* 581–592.

Hackfort, D., & Schwenkmezger, P. (1993). Anxiety. In R.N. Singer, M. Murphy, & L. K. Tennant (Eds.), *Handbook of research on sport psychology* (pp. 328–364). New York: Macmillan.

Hardy, L., & Hutchinson A. (2007). Effects of performance anxiety on effort and performance in rock climbing: A test of processing efficiency theory. *Anxiety Stress and Coping, 20,*147–61.

Harlow, H. F., Blazer, N. C., & McClearn, G. E. (1956). Manipulatory motivation in the infant rhesus monkey. *Journal of Comparative and Physiological Psychology, 49,* 444–448.

Hatzigeorgiadis, A., Zourbanos, N., Galanis, E., & Theodorakis, Y. (2011). Self-talk and sports performance: A meta-analysis. *Perspectives on Psychological Science, 6,* 348–356.

Helson, H., & Jeffers, V. B. (1940). Fundamental problems in color vision: II. Hue, lightness, and saturation of selective samples in chromatic illumination. *Journal of Experimental Psychology, 26,* 1–27.

Herzberg, F., Mausner, B., & Snyderman, B. B. (1959). *The motivation to work*. New York, NY: John Wiley.

Hobfoll, S. E. (1998). Stress, culture, and community: The psychology and philosophy of stress. New York, NY: Plenum.

Hoffman, J. E., & Nelson, B. (1981). Spatial selectivity in visual search. *Perception & Psychophysics, 30*(3), 283–290.

Horn, J. L., & Blankson, A. N. (2012). Foundations for better understanding of cognitive abilities. In D. P. Flanagan, & P. L. Harrison (Eds.), *Contemporary intellectual assessment: Theories, tests, and issues*. New York, NY: Guilford Press.

James, W. (1884). What is an emotion. *Mind, 9*, 188–205.

James, W. (1890). *Principles of psychology*. New York, NY: Holt.

Janiszewski, C., & Warlop, L. (1993). The influence of classical conditioning procedures on subsequent attention to the conditioned brand. *Journal of Consumer Research, 20*(2), 171–189.

Jex, S. M., & Britt, T. W. (2008). *Organizational psychology*. Hoboke, NJ: John Wiley.

Johnson-Greene, D., Adams, K. M., Gilman, S., & Junck, L. (2002). Relationship between neuropsychological and emotional functioning in severe chronic alcoholism. *Clinical Neuropsychologist, 16*(3), 300–309.

Kastner, S., McMains, S. A., & Beck, D. M. (2009). Mechanisms of selective attention in the human visual system: Evidence from neuroimaging. In M. S. Gazzaniga (Ed.), *The cognitive neurosciences* (4th ed.). Cambridge, MA: MIT Press.

Kimmel, H. D. (1977). Notes from "Pavlov's Wednesdays:" Sensory preconditioning. *American Journal of Psychology, 90*, 319–321.

Krpan, K. M., Levine, B., Stuss, D. T., & Dawson, D. R. (2007). Executive function and coping at one-year post traumatic brain injury. *Journal of Clinical and Experimental Neuropsychology, 29*(1), 36–46.

Lavie, N., & Tsal, Y. (1994). Perceptual load as a major determinant of the locus of selection in visual attention. *Perception & Psychophysics, 56*(2), 183–197.

Lazarus, R. (1966). *Psychological stress and the coping process*. New York, NY: McGraw-Hill.

Lazarus, R. (1991). Cognition and motivation in emotion. *American Psychologist, 46*(4), 352–367.

Leahey, T. H., & Harris, R. J. (1993). *Learning and cognition* (3rd ed.). Englewood Cliffs, NY: Prentice Hall.

LeDoux J. (1996). The Emotional Brain. New York: Simon & Schuster.

LeDoux J. (2003) The emotional brain, fear, and the amygdala. *Cell and Molecular Neurobiology, 23*, 727–38.

Lezak, M. D., Howieson, D. B., Bigler, E. D., & Tranel, D. (2012). *Neuropsychological assessment* (5th ed.). New York, NY: Oxford University Press.

Locke, E. A. (1968). Toward a theory of task motivation and incentives. *Organizational Behavior & Human Performance, 3*, 157–189.

Lubinski, D. (2004). Introduction to the special section on cognitive abilities: 100 years after Spearman's (1904) "General intelligence, objectively determined and measured." *Journal of Personality and Social Psychology, 86*(1), 96–199.

Luria, A. R. (1980). *Higher cortical functions in man* (2nd ed.). New York, NY: Basic Books.

Manly, J. J., Byrd, D. A., Touradji, P., & Stern, Y. (2004). Acculturation, reading level, and neuropsychological test performance among African American elders. *Applied Neuropsychology, 11*(1), 37–46.

Maslow, Abraham H. (1943). A theory of human motivation. *Psychological Review, 50*, 370–396.

Maslow, A. H. (1970). *Motivation and personality* (2nd ed.). New York, NY: Harper & Row.

Masters, R. S. W. (1992). Knowledge, knerves and know-how: The role of explicit versus implicit knowledge in the breakdown of a complex motor skill under pressure. *British Journal of Psychology, 83,* 343–358.

McCabe, D. P., Roediger, H. L., McDaniel, M. A., Balota, D. A., & Hambrick, D. Z. (2010). The relationship between working memory capacity and executive functioning: Evidence for a common executive attention construct. *Neuropsychology, 24*(2), 222–243.

McClelland, D. (1965). Toward a theory of motive acquisition. *American Psychologist, 20,* 321–333.

Moray, N. (1959). Attention in dichotic-listening—Affective cues and the influence of instructions. *Quarterly Journal of Experimental Psychology, 11*(1), 56–60.

Mullen, R., Hardy, L., & Tattersall, A. (2005). The effects of anxiety on motor performance: A test of the conscious processing hypothesis. *Journal of Sport and Exercise Psychology, 27,* 212–225.

Murray, H. A. (1938). *Explorations of personality.* New York, NY: Oxford.

Naglieri, J. A., & Das, J. P. (1988). Planning-arousal-simultaneous-successive (PASS): A model for assessment. *Journal of School Psychology, 26,* 35–48.

Naglieri, J. A., & Das, J. P. (1997). *Cognitive assessment system.* Itasca, IL: Riverside.

Naglieri, J. A., & Das, J. P. (2000). Effectiveness of a cognitive strategy intervention in improving arithmetic computation based on the PASS theory. *Journal of Learning Disabilities, 33,* 591–597.

Nestler, E., & Carlezon, W. (2006). The mesolimbic dopamine reward circuit in depression. *Biological Psychiatry, 59,* 1151–1159.

Olson, M. A., & Fazio, R. H. (2001). Implicit attitude formation through classical conditioning. *Psychological Science, 12*(5), 413–417.

Osgood, C. E., Suci, G. J., & Tannenbaum, P. H. (1961). *The measurement of meaning.* Champaign, IL: University of Illinois Press.

Pavlov, I. P. (1927). *Conditioned reflexes.* Oxford: Oxford University Press.

Phan, K. L., Wager, T. D., Taylor, S. F., & Liberzon, I. (2002). Functional neuroanatomy of emotion: A meta-analysis of emotion activation studies in PET and fMRI. *Neuroimage, 16,* 331–348.

Pinel, J. P. J. (2011). *Biopsychology* (8th ed.). Boston: Allyn & Bacon.

Pinsk, M. A., Doninger, G. M., & Kastner, S. (2004). Push-pull mechanism of selective attention in human extrastriate cortex. *Journal of Neurophysiology, 92*(1), 622–629.

Rescorla, R. A. (1988). Pavlovian conditioning: It's not what you think it is. *American Psychologist, 43*(3), 151–160.

Reynolds, C. R., & Ramsay, M. D. (2003). Bias in psychological assessment: An empirical review and recommendations. In J. R. Graham, & J. A. Naglieri (Eds.), *Handbook of psychology: Assessment psychology.* Hoboken, NJ: John Wiley.

Robinson-Riegler, B., & Robinson-Riegler, G. (2012). *Cognitive psychology: Applying the science of the mind* (3rd ed.). Boston, MA: Allyn & Bacon.

Russell, J. A. (1978). Evidence of convergent validity on the dimensions of affect. *Journal of Personality and Social Psychology, 36,* 1152–1168.

Sarason, Irwin G. (1984). Stress, anxiety, and cognitive interference: Reactions to tests. *Journal of Personality and Social Psychology, 46,* 929–938.

Schacter, S., & Singer, J. (1962). Cognitive, social and physiological determinants of emotional state. *Psychological Review, 69*(5), 379–399.

Schneider, W. J., & McGrew, K. (2012). The Cattell-Horn-Carroll model of intelligence. In D. Flanagan & P. Harrison (Eds.), *Contemporary intellectual assessment: Theories, tests, and issues* (3rd ed., p. 99–144). New York, NY: Guilford.

Schwartz, B., & Reisberg, D. (1991). *Learning and memory.* New York: W.W. Norton.

Seligman, M. (1975). *Helplessness: On depression, development, and death.* San Francisco, CA: W. H. Freeman.

Seligman, M., & Maier, S. (1967). Failure to escape traumatic shock. *Journal of Experimental Psychology, 74*, 1–9.

Shallice, T. (1990). *From neuropsychology to mental structure.* New York, NY: Oxford University Press.

Simoncelli, E. P. (2009). Optimal estimation in sensory systems. In M. S. Gazzaniga (Ed.), *The cognitive neurosciences* (4th ed.). Cambridge, MA: MIT Press.

Simons, D. J., & Chabris, C. F. (1999). Gorillas in our midst: Sustained inattentional blindness for dynamic events. *Perception, 28*(9), 1059–1074.

Skinner, B. F. (1938). *The behavior of organisms: An experimental analysis.* Cambridge, MA: B.F. Skinner Foundation.

Skinner, B. F. (1971). *Beyond freedom and dignity.* New York, NY: Alfred A. Knopf.

Spearman, C. (1904). "General Intelligence," objectively determined and measured. *American Journal of Psychology, 15*, 201–293.

Spearman, C. (1927). *The abilities of man: Their nature and measurement.* New York, NY: MacMillan.

Sperling, G. (1960). The information available in brief visual presentation. *Psychological Monographs, 74*.

Springer, S. P., & Deutsch, G. (Eds.). (1998). *Left brain, right brain: Perspectives from cognitive neuroscience* (5th ed.). New York, NY: W. H. Freeman.

Squire, L. (1987). *Memory and brain.* New York, NY: Oxford University Press.

Stahl, T., Van Laar, & Ellemers, N. (2012). The role of prevention focus under stereotype threat: Initial cognitive mobilization is followed by depletion. *Journal of Personality and Social Psychology, 102*(6), 1239–1251.

Sternberg, R. J. (1999). The theory of successful intelligence. *Review of General Psychology, 3*(4), 292–316.

Sternberg, R. J. (2003). *Wisdom, intelligence, and creativity, synthesized.* New York, NY: Cambridge University Press.

Stroop, J. R. (1935). Studies of interference in serial verbal reactions. *Journal of Experimental Psychology, 18*, 643–662.

Sturm, V., Lenartz, D., Koulousakis, A., Treuer, H., Herholz, K., Klein, J., & Klosterkötter, J. (2003). The nucleus accumbens: A target for deep brain stimulation in obsessive-compulsive- and anxiety-disorders. *Journal of Chemical Neuroanatomy, 26*, 293–299.

Thorndike, E. L. (1898). Animal intelligence: An experimental study of the associative process in animals. *Psychology Review Monographs, 2*(8).

Thurstone, L. L. (1938). *Primary mental abilities.* Chicago: University of Chicago Press.

Tolman, E. C. (1932). *Purposive behavior in animals and men.* New York, NY: Appleton-Century-Crofts.

Treisman, A. (2009). Attention: Theoretical and psychological perspectives. In M. S. Gazzaniga (Ed.), *The cognitive neurosciences* (4th ed.). Cambridge, MA: MIT Press.

Treisman, A., & Gelade, G. (1980). A feature-integration theory of attention. *Cognitive Psychology, 12*, 97–136.

Tulving, E. (1972). Episodic and semantic memory. In E. Tulving, & W. Donaldson (Eds.), *Organization of memory* (pp. 381–403). New York, NY: Academic Press.

Tzschentke, T. M. (1998). Measuring reward with the conditioned place preference paradigm: A comprehensive review of drug effects, recent progress, and new issues. *Progress in Neurobiology, 56*(6), 613–672.

Ulrich-Lai, Y., & Herman, J. (2009). Neural regulation of endocrine and autonomic stress responses. *Nature Reviews Neuroscience, 10*, 397–409.

Van Raalte, J. L., Brewer, B. W., Lewis, B. P., Linder, D. E., Wildman, G., & Kozimor, J. (1995). Cork! The effects of positive and negative self-talk on dart throwing performance. *Journal of Sport Behavior, 18*, 50–57.

Vernon, P. E. (1950). *The structure of human abilities*. London, UK: Methuen.

Volkow, N., Fowler, J., Wang, G., & Swanson, J. (2004). Dopamine in drug abuse and addiction: Results from imaging studies and treatment implications. *Molecular Psychiatry, 9*, 557–569.

Vroom, V. (1964). *Work and motivation*. New York, NY: John Wiley.

Walther, E., Weil, R., & Düsing, J. (2011). The role of evaluative conditioning in attitude formation. *Current Directions in Psychological Science, 20*(3), 192–196.

Wasserman, J. (2003). Assessment of intellectual functioning. In J. R. Graham, & J. A. Naglieri (Eds.), *Handbook of Psychology: Volume 10, Assessment Psychology*. Hoboken, NJ: John Wiley.

Watson, J. B., & Raynor, R. (1920). Conditioned emotional reactions. *Journal of Experimental Psychology, 3*, 1–4.

Waugh, N. C., & Norman, D. A. (1965). Primary memory. *Psychological Review, 72*, 89–104.

Wechsler, D. (1939). *The measurement of adult intelligence*. Baltimore, MD: Williams & Wilkins.

Weiner, B. (1986). *An attributional theory of motivation and emotion*. New York, NY: Springer-Verlag.

Wilson, M., Smith, N. C., & Holmes, P. S. (2007). The role of effort in influencing the effect of anxiety on performance: Testing the conflicting predictions of processing efficiency theory and the conscious processing hypothesis. *British Journal of Psychology, 98*, 411–428

Wrisberg, C. A., & Anshel, C. A. (1997). The use of positively-worded performance reminders to reduce warm-up decrement in the field hockey penalty shot. *Journal of Applied Sport Psychology, 9*, 229–240.

Wundt, W. (1896). *Grundriss der Psychologie*. Leipzig: Engelmann.

Yerkes, R. M., & Dodson, J. D. (1908). The relation of strength of stimulus to rapidity of habit-formation. *Journal of Comparative Neurology and Psychology, 18*, 459–482.

Zajonc, R. B. (1965). Social facilitation. *Science, 149*, 269–274.

Zajonc, R. B. (1980). Feeling and thinking: Preferences need no inferences. *American Psychologist, 35*(2), 151–175.

Zajonc, R. B. (2000). Feeling and thinking: Closing the debate over the independence of affect. In J. P. Forgas (Ed.), *Feeling and thinking: The role of affect in social cognition* (pp. 31–58). New York, NY: Cambridge University Press.

Review Questions

1. Which of the following statements regarding Signal Detection Theory (SDT) is true?
   A. SDT deals with the fact that when confronted with the same stimulus two people usually see the same thing.
   B. Discriminability (d′) is a mathematical function of signal strength and background noise.
   C. Response bias is a function of the diurnal variation phase of the respondent.
   D. Acuity is to response bias as willingness to report is to discriminability.

2. Which of the following statements regarding perceptual processes is false?
   A. Elaboration occurs in short-term sensory stores.
   B. Perceptual processing is conducted in hierarchical, functionally segregated, and parallel units.
   C. Feature binding occurs at later stages of perceptual processing.
   D. A functionally segregated unit has access to the contents of another unit.

3. All of the following terms are related to selective attention with the exception of:
   A. The cocktail party phenomenon
   B. Attentional blindness
   C. Wakefulness
   D. Reduction of distractor interference

4. Which of the following statements regarding executive functions (EFs) is false?
   A. EFs are measured in some intelligence tests
   B. The constructs of working memory and EF are closely related
   C. Hot and cold EFs have been described
   D. EF is not related to emotional distress

5. Which of the following is not part of David Wechsler's definition of intelligence?
   A. Capacity to act purposefully
   B. Capacity to think rationally
   C. Capacity to acquire information through acculturation
   D. Capacity to deal effectively with the environment

6. Which of the following is the only true statement applying to the field of intelligence?
   A. A.R. Luria's three-level theory of neuropsychological function is unrelated to intelligence test development.
   B. Spearman was a primary mental ability theorist.
   C. Cattell made a major contribution by identifying fluid and crystallized forms of intelligence.
   D. Structural research is to longitudinal studies as developmental research is to factor analysis.

7. Identify the one statement regarding intelligence tests that is not true:

   A. Composite intelligence scores correlate around 0.70 to 0.80 with academic achievement.
   B. Abbreviated tests of intelligence have not been developed due to validity concerns.
   C. Cattell–Horn–Carroll (CHC) theory is the theoretical basis for many intelligence tests.
   D. Split-half reliability for composite intelligence test scores tends to be above 0.90.

8. Which of the following statements regarding bias in intelligence testing is false?

   A. Cross-cultural psychologists discourage use of ethnic group measurement norms.
   B. Socioeconomic status accounts for some of the ethnic influences found on intelligence testing.
   C. Stereotype threat can influence test performance.
   D. Increasingly, cross-cultural psychologists view ethnic differences on intelligence tests as a proxy for the effects of quality of education and acculturation.

9. Of these the only one not identified as a protective factor against the deleterious effects of aging on cognition is:

   A. Physical exercise
   B. Control beliefs
   C. Social support
   D. Agreeableness

10. A negative reinforcer is found in _____ and causes response rates to _____.

    A. Operant conditioning; increase
    B. Classical conditioning; increase
    C. Operant conditioning; decrease
    D. Classical conditioning; decrease

11. To produce the fastest rates of response one would employ a/an _____ schedule of reinforcement.

    A. CRF
    B. VI
    C. Ratio
    D. Interval

12. For the fastest learning rates one would employ a/an _____ schedule of reinforcement.

    A. FR
    B. VI
    C. DRH
    D. CRF

13. The procedure using the anticipation method of Ebbinghaus showed that _____ trials were more efficient than _____ trials.

    A. Spaced; massed

    B. Recency; primacy

    C. Massed; spaced

    D. Operant; classical

14. Tolman had rats live in a maze where no food was ever introduced in order to demonstrate _____.

    A. The primacy effect

    B. Learning in spaced trials

    C. Latent motivation

    D. Learning without reward

15. B.F. Skinner argued that _____ free will.

    A. Contrary to belief, no one has

    B. Everyone starts out life with

    C. We will never know who has

    D. One has to attain a state of

16. "Working memory" is a newer term for _____.

    A. Sensory memory

    B. Short-term memory

    C. Long-term memory

    D. None of these

17. Which level of processing takes the longest to work?

    A. Comprehension

    B. Focal Attention

    C. Elaboration

    D. Presensory

18. Nondeclarative memory is characterized by being _____.

    A. Explicit in nature

    B. Memories we don't want to talk about

    C. Memories we don't know we have

    D. Memories too painful to recall

19. HM was a man who had lost his ability to form new memories. Damage to which structure in his brain was mainly responsible for this condition?

    A. Hippocampus

    B. Frontal cortex

    C. Hypothalamus

    D. Thalamus

20. This theory of emotion postulates that physiological sensations are the primary element of emotional experience:

A. Circumplex model
B. Cannon–Bard theory
C. James–Lange theory
D. Two-factor model

21. The interpretation of emotional experience through cognitive processes is known as:

A. Cognitive appraisal
B. Cognitive dissonance
C. Cognitive assessment
D. Emotional decision making

22. According to LeDoux, this brain region is the primary center of fear-related processing:

A. Hippocampus
B. VMPFC
C. Cingulate gyrus
D. Amygdala

23. Which of the following is NOT considered to be a component of motivation?

A. Arousal
B. Valence
C. Direction
D. Intensity

24. Clark Hull considered drive reduction to be _____.

A. Excitatory
B. Punishing
C. Reinforcing
D. Unnecessary

25. Which of the following is NOT part of cognitive therapy as described by Aaron Beck?

A. Cognitive distortion
B. Cognitive bias
C. Automatic thoughts
D. Self-defeating thoughts

26. Which theory has been postulated to explain depression as a function of inescapable pain?

A. Somatic marker hypothesis
B. Learned helplessness
C. Cognitive dissonance
D. Expectancy theory

27. Which of the following is NOT a component of Weiner's attributional style theory?
    A. Globality/specificity
    B. Internality/externality
    C. Equity/inequity
    D. Stability/instability

28. Somatic marker hypothesis postulates that this brain region is important to efficient emotional decision making:
    A. Hippocampus
    B. VMPFC
    C. Orbitofrontal cortex
    D. Amygdala

29. Paul Ekman is best known for the _____.
    A. Circumplex model of emotion
    B. Dimensional emotion model
    C. Basic emotion model
    D. Cognitive appraisal model

30. Achievement, affiliation, and authority are components of which theory of motivation?
    A. Self-determination theory
    B. Need for Achievement theory
    C. Expectancy theory
    D. Attributional theory

Answers to Review Questions

1. B. Discriminability (d') is a mathematical function of signal strength and background noise

SDT deals with the observation that two individuals confronted with the same stimulus presentation may come to different conclusions. Disagreement may occur due to differences in discriminability or response bias. Discriminability (d') of the stimulus is described by the mathematical function of signal strength to background noise.

2. A. Elaboration occurs in short-term sensory stores.

Short-term sensory stores are a concept associated with sensation, and not perception. Information is first represented there very briefly, and its capacity can exceed that of short-term memory.

3. C. Wakefulness

Attention can refer to global states or selective processes. Sleep and wakefulness are global states.

4. D. EF is not related to emotional distress.

EFs are increasingly important because they are the cognitive domain most strongly associated with emotional distress, and may reflect differing facets of underlying frontal lobe dysfunction.

5. C. Capacity to acquire information through acculturation

Given the absence of an agreed on definition, it is reasonable to note one of the better definitions as provided by the late David Wechsler (1939), developer of the most widely used intelligence test of the twentieth century—"intelligence is the aggregate or global capacity of the individual to act purposefully, to think rationally and to deal effectively with his environment."

6. C. Cattell made a major contribution by identifying fluid and crystallized forms of intelligence.

Cattell proposed that Spearman's g was actually composed of general fluid (Gf) and general crystallized (Gc) ability.

7. B. Abbreviated tests of intelligence have not been developed due to validity concerns.

As intelligence test administration takes between 1 to 2 hours before scoring and interpretation, depending on the test taker, abbreviated versions of tests have been developed to provide reliable, valid estimates of intellectual ability.

8. A. Cross-cultural psychologists discourage use of ethnic group measurement norms.

Many cross-cultural clinical researchers recommend using the appropriate ethnic group measurement norm to improve diagnostic accuracy.

9. D. Agreeableness

Protective factors against age-related decline in cognitive function include frequency of cognitive activity, control beliefs, social support, and physical exercise.

10. B. Classical conditioning; increase

In classical conditioning, negative reinforcement increases the CR.

11. C. Ratio

Ratio schedules produce high rates of output. That is, they follow the rule that the more the work, the more the reward, or to maximize rewards, one maximizes output.

12. D. CRF

If the reinforcer follows every instance of the CS, it is called continuous reinforcement or CRF, and it is the fastest way to learn.

13. A. Spaced; massed

Another Ebbinghaus method involved the presentation of pairs of syllables, with subjects attempting to report the second syllable of a pair when the first syllable was given. The order of the pairs was then shuffled among trials, but with the word pairing remaining constant. He called it the paired associate method, and it is still used today. He found fewest errors when he formed some sort of mental association between the syllables. Ebbinghaus also found that spaced trials were more efficient than massed.

14. D. Learning without reward

In the simplest example, Tolman (1932) allowed animals to live in a maze in which no food was ever presented. When these animals were later rewarded for finding their way through the maze, they learned it in far fewer trials than naïve rats, and it was clear that they had already learned much of it, although they had not been rewarded for doing so.

15. A. Contrary to belief, no one has

B.F. Skinner (1971) maintained that none of us has free will.

16. B. Short-term memory

Short-term memory represents the material we are thinking about at a given moment, and has come be called "working memory" (WM) today.

17. C. Elaboration

Perception goes through four stages, which were labeled as follows: Presensory (the catching-attention phase), Focal Attention (the paying-attention phase), Comprehension (the understanding phase), and Elaboration (making-connections and storing phase). Each successive level requires a bit more time than the previous.

18. C. Memories we don't know we have

Nondeclarative memory consists of items the knower is unaware of knowing (implicit), yet can still demonstrate knowledge of them.

19. A. Hippocampus

A man identified only as HM lost the use of his hippocampus and amygdala on both sides of his brain. The hippocampus is the main structure for consolidating long-term memories.

20. C. James–Lange theory

The theory that postulated that changes in physiological sensation are the primary element of emotional experience is generally referred to as the James–Lange theory of emotion, as the theory was independently proposed by William James and Carl Lange, a Danish physician.

21. A. Cognitive appraisal

Schacter and Singer concluded that an individual must cognitively appraise a situation in order to determine his or her emotional state. This model of emotion has been known by the term cognitive appraisal.

22. D. Amygdala

LeDoux established through his research that the amygdala is the primary center of fear-related processing. The amygdala is reliably observed to activate in response to threatening or fearful stimuli but not for stimuli related to positive emotions.

23. B. Valence

Motivation is the internal force that pushes the individual toward action and is generally considered to be composed of three components—arousal, direction, and intensity.

24. C. Reinforcing

Hull stated that drive reduction through behavior is, in and of itself, reinforcing and successful reduction of a drive is sufficient to increase the probability of the behavior occurring in the future.

25. D. Self-defeating thoughts

Self-defeating thoughts are part of rational emotive behavior therapy by Albert Ellis, not cognitive therapy.

26. B. Learned helplessness

The theory of learned helplessness was developed to explain research that found that animals exposed to inescapable pain will eventually stop trying to avoid the pain, even when opportunities to escape were presented. This theory has been considered a possible explanation for depression, as individuals develop a sense that they are unable to escape pain and feel helpless, which eventually leads to depression.

27. C. Equity/inequity

Weiner developed the concept of attributional style with the following components: globality/specificity, stability/instability, and internality/externality.

28. B. VMPFC

Damage to the ventromedial prefrontal cortex (VMPFC) often results in significant changes in the ability to make opportune decisions in personal, social, and financial spheres.

29. C. Basic emotion model

The main figure associated with the basic emotion model is Paul Ekman.

30. B. Need for Achievement theory

Atkinson and McClelland developed Need for Achievement theory, which postulates that motivation is governed by three considerations—achievement, authority, and affiliation.

3

Social and Cultural Bases of Behavior

Loretta E. Braxton, Christina J. Riccardi, and Samantha Kettle

Broad Content Areas

- Interpersonal, intrapersonal, intergroup, and intragroup processes and dynamics
- Theories of personality
- Diversity issues

Increasing our understanding of how people think, feel, and act is useful in interpreting cultural norms, group dynamics, and interpersonal relationships. Answering questions such as how people explain behavior and events, how people think about groups, what puts people in a more aggressive frame of mind, and what underlies prejudice and stereotypes provides a foundation for competent clinical practice and research. Examining theories focused on understanding how environmental forces impact our behavior, and studying the impact of evolution on our mating adaptations also add to our knowledge base of understanding human behavior. All of these topic areas are present as we negotiate our daily lives and raise interesting questions about our behavior and the behavior of those around us. As consumers of information, we benefit from learning about fundamentals such as error, bias, and reliability. The methods used to answer these questions are as rigorous and objective as in any scientific discipline. We learn from each other and our knowledge is transmitted within our current systems.

In this chapter, we review several broad areas, including group dynamics, theories of personality, environmental factors, and issues related to diversity. The chapter is divided with a number of heading levels to guide your understanding and exam preparation.

Social Cognition and Perception

Cognitive Structures and Processes

Sometimes called impression formation, social cognition is the study of how people make sense of their social world; that is, how we make sense of ourselves, others, and ourselves in relation to others. Social cognition research indicates that the ways we behave and interact in the social world are facilitated by cognitive representations called schemas (Fiske & Taylor, 1981). Schemas are organized patterns of thought and behavior that influence what we attend to and how we absorb new information. Schemas help us organize information in an efficient manner by providing tentative explanations about incoming stimuli and a sense of prediction and control of our social worlds. Schemas help us facilitate memory recall, are energy-saving devices, and are evaluative and affective. They are used for evaluation, role playing, identification, and prediction. For example, when we evaluate individuals who have a certain role, we compare their behavior to the identified schema for that role. Role playing is the script we use to help us decide how we will behave or how others should be behaving. Individuals are categorized and identified by the roles they have and role schemas help us place individuals into a certain category by matching their observed behavior with our role schema. We predict the future behavior of individuals once we place them in a specific category/role and we assume the individual will behave in accordance with our predictions of their behavior.

Types of Schema
Schema research has been applied to four main areas: person schema, event schema, role schema, and self-schema (Fiske & Taylor, 1991). Person schemas are attributes that we use to categorize people and make inferences about their behavior. We assess their skills, competencies, and values to make determinations about their personality traits. Event schemas, often referred to as cognitive scripts, provide the basis for anticipating the future, setting goals, and making plans. The cognitive scripts are the processes or practices we use to approach tasks or problems. Role schemas, often associated with stereotypes, include behavior sets and role expectations. These schemas tell us how we expect individuals in certain roles to behave. Self-schemas are cognitive representations about our self-concept, that is, perceptions of our traits, competencies, and values.

Models for Social Categorization
People rely on models of social categorization to facilitate their information processing—prototypical and exemplar models. Social objects, people, and events have typical or prototypical variables that represent the category. The more the features that are shared in a category, the more the efficiency and confidence that are associated with placing the social objects in the category. In contrast, exemplar models represent specific and concrete information about a category. Exemplar models represent the extreme instances within an overall general category. We tend to rely on both models—prototypical and exemplar—based on the conditions of information processing.

Attribution of Cause
Attributions provide explanations for behaviors and events. Heider theorized that people observe, analyze, and explain behaviors with explanations though people attribute different kinds of explanations to behaviors. He differentiated between two types of causal attribution—dispositional and situational. Dispositional attribution refers to characteristics such as personality traits, motives, and attitudes. Situational attribution refers to social norms, external pressures, random chance, acts of God, etc. Heider explained that we tend to overestimate dispositional factors and underestimate situational factors, which is known as the fundamental attribution error.

Attribution Theories

Correspondent Inference Theory

Jones and Davis introduced correspondent inference theory, which posits that people make inferences about others' behavior when they are looking for a cause of their behavior. People make correspondent inferences by reviewing the context of the behavior. Correspondent inference theory describes how people identify explanations of people's personal characteristics from behavioral evidence. For example, a correspondent inference would be to attribute an individual's frequent anger outburst to an underlying stable trait within the person.

Covariation Model of Attribution

Kelly introduced the theory of covariation model of attribution, which contends that we assess similarities (covariation) across situations to help us make causal attributions in a rational and logical fashion. Covariation of behavior is assessed using three types of information: consensus information—how other people act in the same situation and with the same stimulus; distinctiveness information—how similarly people act in different situations toward different stimuli; and consistency information—how frequently people perceive the same stimuli and respond the same.

Achievement attribution (motivation and emotion) was proposed by Weiner. He posits that attributions people make for success and failure elicit different emotional consequences that are characterized by three underlying dimensions: stable theory (stable vs. unstable)—the cause of the behavior is perceived as fixed (i.e., personality) or changeable (motivation or effort); internal and external (locus of control)—whether success or failure is attributed internally or externally; and controllable and uncontrollable (control)—whether we feel we have any control over the cause.

Bias and Errors in Attributions

While trying to find rational and logical explanations for people's behavior, there is a tendency to fall into biases and errors. Bias occurs when the perceiver systematically distorts what are thought to be correct and logical procedures. Recent research has found evidence of persistent biases in attribution processes (Fiske & Taylor, 1991). There are four pervasive forms of attribution biases: fundamental attribution error, actor–observer difference, the self-serving bias, and culture bias.

The fundamental attribution error is the tendency to overvalue personal/dispositional explanations for behavior while undervaluing situational explanations. Fundamental attribution error is most noticeable when we are trying to explain the behavior of others. For example, if a friend is late to a lunch meeting with you, you are more likely to assume that your friend does not value your time rather than taking into account other explanations of why your friend may be late.

The actor–observer effect occurs when we attribute dispositional factors to other people's behavior while attributing situational factors to our behavior. For example, when an individual gets a poor grade on a test, we tend to attribute internal factors such as laziness or failure to study. Alternatively, if we get a poor grade we tend to attribute it to situational factors that justify the outcome. For example, the test covered materials that were not addressed in the study guides.

The self-serving bias is the tendency to attribute dispositional factors for success and external, uncontrollable factors for failure. Sometimes called the self-enhancing bias, it refers to motivational factors that drive us to enhance our self-esteem when we succeed and protect it when we fail.

The self-serving bias also operates at the group level. There is a tendency to protect the groups(s) to which we belong, and research shows that we make attributions based on our group membership. For example, there are individualist and collectivist cultures; members of individualist cultures tend to engage in more self-serving bias than collectivist cultures.

Social Interaction

Affiliation and Attraction

Affiliation is the desire to be with others and form social relationships. There are a number of factors that affect how and when people affiliate with one another. Women tend to spend more time engaged in conversation, especially with individuals of the same sex, and tend to affiliate more in public places than men (Deaux, 1978; Latane & Bidwell, 1977). Relationships among women are more likely to rely on verbal communication and self-disclosure. In contrast, relationships among men tend to center around shared activities (Hays, 1985). Anxiety also increases the tendency to affiliate. In anxiety-provoking situations, social comparison often leads to affiliation more so than relief from discomfort.

Attraction is a type of affiliation based on "liking." Attraction is affected by a number of factors, including physical attractiveness, proximity and exposure, similarity, reciprocity, self-disclosure, and reinforcement. Gain–loss theory posits that attraction is maximized when an individual's evaluation of a person is at first negative and then changes to positive. Social exchange theory suggests that attraction occurs when the relationship's rewards exceed its costs and when the rewards and costs are reciprocal. People are likely to remain in a relationship when the rewards outweigh the costs and leave a relationship when the costs exceed the rewards. Equity theory also focuses on relationship rewards and costs but suggests that perceptions of equity in a relationship are more important than the magnitude of costs and rewards.

Aggression

Aggression is any form of behavior directed toward the goal of harming or injuring another who is motivated to avoid such treatment (Baron & Richardson, 1994). The frustration–aggression hypothesis proposes that aggression is the result of frustration, which is produced whenever the ability to achieve a desired goal is blocked (Dollard et al., 1939). The objective of aggression is to move the block, but if the block cannot be removed, then aggression may be directed on another object. This theory was modified due to the lack of evidence of a causal relationship between frustration and aggression. Berkowitz (1971) suggested that frustration creates a readiness for aggression; however, expression of aggression requires both anger arousal and the presence of external aggressive cues. In contrast, social learning theory states that aggressive behaviors arise through the observation of others. Research has supported social learning of aggression (e.g., Bobo doll studies; Bandura, 1983). Recent research on the effects of viewing violence in the media has produced inconsistent results; however, the majority of studies conclude that viewing violence increases aggression.

Expression of aggression is affected by a number of factors. Deindividuation refers to the tendency of people to act aggressively when they believe their actions are anonymous. Social roles and expectations are influential in determining aggressive and antisocial behavior. For example, in Zimbardo's prison study (1972) student participants were assigned to roles as either prisoner or guard. Participants strongly adapted to their roles, some of those in the guard condition went as far as to torture those in the prisoner role, many of whom passively accepted the torture. The threat of retaliation often decreases aggressiveness; however, when provocation is coupled with threat of retaliation people are more likely to act aggressively, but aggression may be displaced to someone other than the provocateur.

Altruism

Altruism is the motivation to increase another's welfare. There is debate over the capability of humans to be truly altruistic and place the welfare of others in front of their own. The social exchange theory suggests that altruism exists when benefits outweigh cost. However, others suggest four categories that motivate altruism: altruism to benefit the self (egoism), to benefit the other person (altruism), to benefit a group (collectivism), or to uphold a moral principal (principlism). The empathy–altruism hypothesis suggests that altruism is evoked by the desire to help someone who is suffering. Feelings of concern for the other person are contrasted with personal distress, which leads people to act to reduce the negative emotions, which are experienced when suffering is witnessed.

Social Influences on Individual Functioning

Social influence occurs when an individual's attitude, thoughts, feelings, or behaviors are affected by the persuasive effect of others. There are many responses to social influence. For example, people adjust their beliefs, attitudes, and behaviors based on their respect for others who have similar feelings. They also tend to adopt the attitudes of their social group if the majority of members hold particular beliefs. Kelman (1958) identified three effects: compliance, identification, and internalization. Compliance occurs when people change their behavior to obtain a reward or to avoid punishment. They appear to agree with others but actually keep their opposing thoughts and opinions private. Identification occurs when there is a behavioral change because of desired acceptance or to identify with another person. An example is when someone is influenced by an individual who is well regarded and respected, like a celebrity. Internalization is acceptance of a belief, attitude, or behavior that is expressed publicly and privately. People make changes based on the acceptance of others' beliefs and attitudes or behaviors. The most common form of social influence is conformity. Conformity occurs when an individual changes a belief or behavior to fit in with a particular group or to meet the expectations of others. Examples of conformity are informational conformity (accepting information from others as evidence), normative conformity (pressure to conform to the positive expectations of others), and peer pressure. People's willingness to conform is affected by group unanimity, group size, group cohesiveness, and ability to express opinion anonymously. Obedience occurs when a person submits to a request of authority. The Milgram shock experiments and Zimbardo's prison experiments are examples of study participants' willingness to obey authority figures even in the face of conflicted personal conscience. Reactance occurs when a person feels his or her choices or alternatives are being taken away or limited and the reaction is the opposite of what is desired (Brehm, 1972).

Social power is the exertion of influence over another person. French and Raven (1959) provided an early formulation of the bases of social power. They viewed social influence as the outcome of the exertion of social power from one of the five distinct bases: coercive, reward, expert, referent, and legitimate. An opinion or attitude change, usually conformity, was considered an instance of social influence whether it represented a true private change or not. A person's ability to influence someone is the result of two or more bases of power. The more varied the individual sources of power, the greater the ability to influence others.

Minority influence (Moscovici, 1985) occurs when the minority changes the opinion of the majority. Minority influence usually involves a shift in personal opinion. People often comply with the majority for normative reasons (to be liked or avoid punishment) and comply with the minority for informational reasons (e.g., minority has caused them to reevaluate their beliefs). Minority influence more likely occurs when the point of view is consistent, flexible, clear, and aligned with current social trends. Maass and Clark (1988) found that influence is more likely to occur when the majority or minority are a part of the "in-group" as influence is more likely among those who are similar.

Social impact theory provides a framework for understanding outcomes in social situations. This theory posits that the effect of any information source on an individual will increase with three factors: strength of the source of the impact, immediacy of the event, and the number of sources imposing the impact. Any impediment to any of these factors will attenuate the impact. A noted weakness of social impact theory is that it depicts people as passive recipients who accept social impact rather than as active pursuers. To expand on social impact theory, Latané and L' Herrou (1996) included group interactions to describe and predict the diffusion of beliefs through social systems. The new focus was called dynamic social impact theory, and it includes four components that influence how group dynamics operate and how ideas are diffused throughout the groups. The four components are consolidation—diversity reduced by minority opinion accepting the majority opinion; clustering—subgroups that emerge and hold differing opinions than the overarching population; correlation—previously disconnected ideas become connected in some way; and principle of continuing diversity—because there is clustering that causes subgroups to emerge, consolidation will not be able to wipe out minority opinion. This view explains that people influence each other in a dynamic and iterative way.

Persuasion is the process of guiding oneself or another toward the adoption of some attitude by some rational or symbolic means. Cialdini (2001) defines six principles of persuasion that can contribute to an individual's propensity to be influenced by a persuader: reciprocity—return favors and pay back; commitment and consistency; social proof—people do things when they see others doing them; authority—people obey authority figures; liking—people are persuaded by people they like; and scarcity—sense of scarcity generates demand.

Environmental/Ecological Psychology

The Social Environment

Environment can have a significant impact on individual behavior. The first social psychologist to recognize the importance of environment was Lewin, who proposed field theory. Field theory (Lewin, 1936) states that behavior is affected by both the person and concurrently the environment he or she is in, although their relative importance is different in different cases. Field theory was applied to a number of inter- and intrapersonal behaviors, including conflict, group dynamics, and leadership. Lewin (1931) identified three categories of intraindividual conflict, and later, a fourth category was added (Miller, 1944):

> *Approach–approach conflict* occurs when an individual must choose between two equally attractive or positive goals. This type of conflict tends to be the easiest to resolve because both outcomes are appealing.

> *Avoidance–avoidance conflict* occurs when an individual must choose between two equally unattractive or negative goals. This type of conflict is generally difficult to resolve and often leads to inaction, indecision, and withdrawal from the situation.

> *Approach–avoidance conflict* occurs when a single goal has both attractive and unattractive qualities. Individuals experiencing this conflict often feel increased avoidance as they move toward a goal and conversely experience increased desire toward the goal as they decide to move away from it.

> *Double approach–avoidance conflict* occurs when choosing between two goals that both have attractive and unattractive qualities. This tends to be the most difficult conflict to resolve and often results in moving between two alternatives.

Research on the impact of environment on behavior has also focused on the effects of crowding. *Crowding* refers to the state of mind that occurs when people are in high-population-density situations. The effects of crowding depend on the specific circumstances. Crowding can have positive effects in some situations and people tend to prefer it at sporting events (e.g., football games), rock concerts, and attention-grabbing movies (e.g., violent or humorous movies). Crowding has been linked with negative performance on complex tasks but has little or no impact on simple tasks. Densely populated residential areas have been linked with increased physical and mental health problems, poor academic performance, juvenile delinquency, and higher mortality rates.

A number of factors that contribute to the effects of crowding have been identified. When people perceive a sense of control they are better able to handle the stress of crowded situations. Additionally, when people anticipate that an environment will be crowded or when distracted by an event (e.g., games and movies) they experience less stress. The density intensity hypothesis suggests that differential effects of crowding occur because crowds increase positive experiences and situations and also make unpleasant experiences more negative (Deaux & Wrightsman, 1988). An individual's need for personal space also influences the effects of crowding. Intrusions of personal space commonly lead to anxiety, irritability, and increased aggression. The need for personal space varies with culture and Americans generally need more personal space than Latin Americans, Arabs, Greeks, and the French. Men and individuals with high authoritarianism or low self-esteem also report a greater need for personal space.

Organizational Culture

Organizational culture is the shared values, beliefs, and perceptions held by employees within an organization. It has been linked to high levels of job performance, satisfaction, and organizational commitment. Schein (1992) outlined three levels of organizational culture. The first level is observable artifacts and includes dress code, stories and rituals, and annual reports. The second level comprises espoused values and beliefs. These are the norms, goals, and ideologies held by the organization. The final level is the basic assumptions of the organization, which include the unconscious, beliefs, thoughts, and perceptions that are often considered the "unspoken rules" of the organization.

Person–organization fit is the extent to which an individual's values match those held by the organization's culture (Greenberg & Barron, 1993). Good fit is achieved through the selection and socialization process of the organization and is associated with greater job satisfaction, motivation, organization commitment, and lower levels of turnover.

National Culture

Organizational culture is embedded within the culture of nations and influenced by it. Hofetede's model of national culture (1993) identified five dimensions:

Power-distance: The extent to which people accept an unequal distribution of power.

Uncertainty avoidance: The ability or willingness of people to tolerate uncertainty.

Individualism: The extent to which individuals and social structures are the foundation of the social system.

Masculinity: The value placed on competitiveness, assertiveness, and independence.

Long-term orientation: The extent to which people focus on the past or present versus the future.

Evolutionary Perspectives on Social Behavior

Mate Selection

Buss (2007) refers to mating as "differential reproductive success" because of the natural selection that allowed modern humans to inherit the mating strategies of their ancestors. Darwin's sexual selection theory and Trivers's parental investment theory (Trivers, 1972) provide the conceptual framework for the evolution of mating adaptations. Darwin's sexual selection identifies same-sex competition and preferential mate choices as the driving force for mating adaptations. Years later, Trivers added parental investment theory that posits that animals are most selective of mates when the investment in offspring is the greatest. Females were identified as having the greatest investment.

Current evolutionary psychologists disagree about the fundamental mating strategies of humans. Having tackled different challenges in the mating domain, the sexes have emerged with different psychological mating solutions. Buss describes these psychological differences as "possessing distinct mate preferences, dissimilar desires for short-term mating, and distinct triggers that evoke sexual jealousy" (p. 502). Similarly, Schmitt (2005) outlines human mating strategies that are sex differentiated and sensitive to context. Schmitt explored the temporal context of short-term mating and long-term mating. Schmitt describes four mating strategies: monogamous, polygynous, polyandrous, and short term. Monogamous mating occurs when two people choose each other exclusively for reproductive efforts, and can be perennial or serial. Members of the opposite sex may choose one partner for life or serially choose different partners, but only one at a time. Polygynous mating occurs when one male mates with numerous females, but the females only mate with one male. Polygynous is the most preferred mating strategy. Polyandrous mating occurs when females compete for access to numerous males, and after mating with an individual male, abandon the male and offspring entirely. Polyandry is not a preferred mating arrangement as it is found in less than 1% of preindustrial cultures. It is found among humans in the Himalayas where the living conditions are harsh and do not support families. Evidence indicates that polyandry is not an evolved mating strategy in humans. Short-term mating strategies occur when females mate with multiple males and males mate with multiple females. These mating pairs tend to be brief and lack exclusivity though mate preferences for dominance, status, and health remain.

Empathy

Prosocial behavior occurs when one acts to help another when there is no goal other than to help a fellow person. Empathy is a prosocial emotion that has been researched by Batson (1991) who formulated the empathy–altruism hypothesis. The empathy–altruism hypothesis states: "If we feel empathy towards a person, we are likely to help them (in proportion to the empathy felt) without any selfish thoughts. Otherwise, we will help them only if the rewards of helping them outweigh the costs." In summarizing how empathy is enhanced, Baumeister and Finkel (2010) report that empathy for another person can be evoked by focusing on another's feelings; by sharing emotions, feeling, and sensations; by valuing another's welfare; and by recognition of kinship, similarity, or closeness. Batson, his colleagues, and detractors conducted numerous investigations to evaluate the motivations underlying empathy-induced behavior. They asserted that the motivation could be altruistic, egoist, or both. They found that participants in the low-empathy group opted out of helping a confederate when doing so was easy, but helped out half the time when opting out of the situation was difficult. Conversely, the high-empathy group opted to help the confederate whether the opting out was easy or difficult. In another series of experiments, Batson, Ahmad, and Lishner (2009) concluded that empathy-induced behavior motivated by the goal of avoiding social or self-punishments for failing to help has consistently supported the empathy–altruism hypothesis.

Major Research-Based Theories of Personality

Psychoanalytic/Psychodynamic Theories

Within psychology, there are a number of research-based theories of personality. One of the earliest conceptualizations was Freud's psychoanalytic theory. This structural theory comprises three distinct aspects of personality: the id, ego, and super ego. The id is present at birth and operates on the pleasure principle. It consists of both life (e.g., self-preservation and sexual gratification/libido) and death (e.g., destruction, anger, and aggression/thanatos) instincts. The id is also thought to be responsible for the primary process of thinking and basic instincts. At 6 months, the ego begins to develop in response to the id's inability to gratify all of its needs. The ego strives to mediate the conflicting demands of the id and reality and defer gratification until appropriate. The id is responsible for secondary process thinking, which is realistic and rational. Between the ages of 4 and 5, the super ego emerges and is an internalization of society's values and standards conveyed to a child through reward and punishment. The super ego attempts to permanently block the id's socially unacceptable drives and is driven by concepts of right and wrong. An overdeveloped ego occurs when the drive for pleasure is overindulged (overactive id) and can lead to addiction, anger, and other self-harming behaviors. Conversely, an overdeveloped superego (i.e., exaggerated sense of right and wrong) can lead to increased feelings of guilt, anxiety, and eating disorders.

Object relations theory is another psychodynamic theory that grew largely from the work of Klein. This theory emphasizes the process by which an infant assumes his or her own physical and psychological identity. Objects are conceptualized as internalized images, which assist the unconscious in making sense of people and the environment, most often based on the infant's mother or father. From birth to 1 month, a child is oblivious to the external world, which can be described as normal autism. At 2 to 3 months, an infant is fused with his or her mother and does not differentiate between "I" and "not-I," which is termed normal symbiosis. At this stage, infants mainly view the world as part objects, that is, viewing objects as good and bad and as separate rather than part of the same whole object. When a child reaches 4 months, the separation–individuation phase begins. During this phase, a child takes steps toward separation and sensory exploration. By 3 years, a child develops a permanent sense of self and object, also known as object constancy, and is able to perceive others as both separate and related. Disruption of this process is thought to cause an individual to carry that object in his or her unconscious during adulthood and expect similar interactions with others. For example, if a child is neglected or abused as an infant, he or she will expect similar outcomes from others and use that experience to understand his or her adult relationships.

Jungian theories are based on the work of Jung and conceptualize personality as a consequence of both the conscious and the unconscious mind. The conscious mind is orientated toward the external world. It is governed by the ego and is representative of individual thoughts, feelings, ideas, perceptions, and memories. The unconscious mind contains both the personal and collective unconscious. The personal unconscious comprises experiences that were once recalled, but are now repressed and forgotten. The collective unconscious consists of hidden memories that are passed down from one generation to the next.

A persona is a public mask that overemphasizes individuality, minimizes the collective psyche, and hides the true nature of the individual. Jung also introduced the notion of archetypes or "primordial images," which cause people to experience and understand certain phenomena in a universal way. The "self" strives for unity among different, and sometimes conflicting parts of personality, including feminine (anima) and masculine (animus) aspects of personality. Jung proposed that each individual has a personality type based on how he or she perceives things and how he or she makes decisions. There are four basic psychological functions that contribute to these processes: thinking, feeling, sensing, and intuiting. The function a person uses most frequently is referred to as dominant and may either be extroverted or introverted. The Myers–Briggs Type Indicator grew out of Jung's personality theory (Myers & Myers, 1980, 1995).

Adlerian theory (originally called Individual Psychology) postulates that basic mistakes originating from faulty perceptions, attitudes, and beliefs lead to myths, which strongly influence personality. Self-defeating perceptions and feelings of inferiority develop during childhood as the result of real or perceived biological, psychological, or social weakness. These beliefs may have been appropriate during childhood, but are no longer useful as the person ages. Adler suggested that people strive for superiority due to an inherent tendency toward becoming competent and achieving "perfect completion." Individuals follow a "style of life," which unifies various aspects of the personality. This style is affected by experiences in the family atmosphere during childhood. Thus, birth order is an important component of Adler's theory and he identified five psychological positions from which children view life: oldest, second of only two, middle, youngest, and only. A healthy style of life includes goals that reflect optimism, confidence, entail contributions to the welfare of others, and community feeling (i.e., social interest and a sense of being connected to humanity). An unhealthy (mistaken) style of life includes goals reflecting self-centeredness, competition, and striving for personal power.

Self psychology theory hypothesizes that an illness or personality disruption is the result of unmet developmental needs. This theory emphasizes the parent's ability to provide a child with factors that lead to a cohesive sense of self or "healthy narcissism." Key factors in healthy personality development include empathy and optimal frustration.

Humanistic/Existential Theories

Although there are a broad range of theories under the umbrella of humanistic and existential approaches, most emphasize subjectivity and self-reflection, particularly the importance of choice and self-determination. The existential view of the mind is based on the principle that humans are alone in the world yet long to be connected with others. Yalom identified anxiety arising when individuals are confronted with normal life experiences, including death, isolation, meaninglessness, and freedom. An individual's response to these four concerns may be functional or dysfunctional, as existentialists believe that every individual has a capacity of choice and direction in his or her life. A healthy personality is able to integrate these components, whereas an unhealthy personality becomes overwhelmed by either freedom or limitations and is unable to balance the realities of living.

Person-centered theories are often associated with the work of Rogers. The central concept of these theories is the notion of "self." The whole persona is composed of perceptions of the "I" or "me" and perceptions of the relationship of the "I"/"me" to others, as well as the values attached to these perceptions. Rogers believed that individuals have an inherent need for positive regard from others they depend on. In order to grow, self must remain unified and respond to environmental demands as a whole. Rogers identified two parts of the self that develop over time: the ideal self and the self-concept. The ideal self is how the person would like to be and the self-concept is how the person views him- or herself. Disruptions and conflicts between these parts can be minimized by openness to experience, which leads to a state of congruence and wholeness. If the individual is rigid and unwilling to be flexible in his or her perceptions, then he or she will often overgeneralize experience and have poor reality testing, sometimes leading to various personality disorders.

Gestalt theories postulate that personality consists of self and self-image. The self is the creative aspect of personality that promotes individuals' inherent tendency for self-actualization (ability to live a fully integrated life). On the other hand, the self-image is the "darker side" of personality. Personality depends on the person's early interactions with the environment. Perls emphasized choice and personal responsibility, although also including the social circumstance as important. There is often a balance that needs to be created between personal needs and values that are taken due to environmental demands. An introject is a value that is not assimilated into the self and creates conflict within the personality.

Cognitive and Behavioral Theories

Behavioral approaches generally conceptualize personality as a result of mutual interaction of the person or "the organism" with its environment. Skinner developed operant theory known as radical behaviorism. He believed children do bad things because the behavior obtains attention that serves as a reinforcer. The three-term contingency model or "Stimulus–Response–Consequence Model" was created as a method for analyzing behavior. This model suggests that we do the things because of learned consequences, sometimes called contingencies of reinforcement. These contingencies may be positive or negative, and may occur whether the behavior does or does not occur.

Social cognitive approaches grew out of behaviorism and social learning theory. Bandura focused on the reciprocal determinism between the interaction of personal factors, behavior, and the environment (Bandura, 1978). In social cognitive approaches, behavior is explained as being guided by cognitions (e.g., expectations) about the world, especially those about other people. Similar to other theories, the person and environment influence each other, yet heavy emphasis is placed on cognitive capabilities. Social cognitive theory emphasizes cognitive processes such as thinking and judgment.

Reality therapy was developed by Glasser and is often categorized as a form of cognitive behavioral therapy. This theory proposes that human behavior is purposeful and originates from within the individual rather than external forces. There are several basic innate needs: four psychological (belonging, power, freedom, and fun) and one physical (survival) needs. A success identity fulfills needs in a responsible manner, whereas a failure identity gratifies a need to be irresponsible.

Trait Theory

Trait theory focuses on the role of specific personality traits. Traits are thought to be relatively stable over time and are defined as patterns of behavior, thought, and emotion. Allport defined central traits as basic aspects of someone's personality, whereas secondary traits are less important. Cardinal traits are the characteristics by which an individual may be recognized. In recent years, there has been a shift to studying group statistics (nomothetic) rather than individual (idiographic) traits.

Interpersonal and Systematic Theory

Interpersonal and systematic theories of personality combine elements of both psychodynamic and cognitive behavioral theories. The common theme in these approaches is the focus on elements external to the individual (e.g., environment and other people) as largely contributing to behavior rather than aspects of personality. Therefore the social environment, both personal relationships and larger social systems, is of tantamount importance. Often the person's self is defined by various interactions, as noted in the work of Sullivan.

Social-Contextual Issues

Privilege is defined as a right or benefit that only belongs to one group and has a number of implications for psychotherapy and assessment. Hays (2001) provides the ADDRESSING acronym (see Table 3.1) to guide understanding of potential areas of holding or not holding privilege within the American power system.

Having self-awareness of personal privilege, as well as an understanding of the oppression that exists, are important aspects of being a competent provider of psychological services. Experiences of prejudice and discrimination are a daily reality for individuals who do not hold privilege in these domains. Oppression has often taught people in nondominant groups that it is not safe to self-disclose, and they develop an adaptive level of paranoia.

Holding privilege (regardless of being aware or unaware) may lead to "ethnocentric monoculturalism." Sue et al. (1998) identified five components of

TABLE 3.1 The ADDRESSING Acronym

CULTURAL INFLUENCES	DOMINANT GROUPS/HOLD PRIVILEGE
Age and generational influences	30–60 years old
Developmental or acquired **D**isabilities	Do not have disability
Religion and spiritual orientation	Secular or Christian home
Ethnicity	Euro-American heritage
Socioeconomic status	Middle or upper class
Sexual orientation	Heterosexual
Indigenous heritage	Not of indigenous heritage
National origin	Live in country where born/grew up
Gender	Male

ethnocentric monoculturalism: belief in superiority, belief in the inferiority of others, power to impose standards, manifestation in institutions, and the invisible veil (i.e., assumption that everyone experiences reality and truth). These components reinforce prejudice and discrimination and lead to labeling individuals in nondominant groups as being the ones with problems. This approach is problematic for a number of reasons and is starting to be challenged by various movements within psychology. One such movement is international or global psychology.

Global psychology is used to imply a worldwide scope, *international psychology* is used when discussing differences among nations, and *cross-cultural psychology* is used to refer to differences among cultures (regardless of within or outside nations). These branches of the field explore cross-cultural comparisons, including power structures, communication, and practice. Exploration may focus on a global issue (such as subjective well-being or gender roles), or compare how different approaches lead to different outcomes.

Another growing area of psychology focuses on religion and spirituality. The American Psychological Association (APA) identified religion as a type of diversity that should be ethically addressed (1992) and established Division 36, Psychology of Religion, in response to this need. This is not surprising as research suggests that "about 97% of U.S. residents believe in God, and about 90% pray" (Spilka, Hood, Hunsberger, & Gorsuch, 2003, p. 1). North America is home to countless religions and spiritual practices, the most common being Christian denominations. However, there is great variety in these religious practices. Richards and Bergin (2000) note that many religious and spiritual people have distrust about psychotherapy and often seek help within their faith rather than contacting a therapist. One way to increase psychotherapy engagement may be to increase training among psychologists about religion and spirituality.

Impact of Race/Ethnicity on Psychosocial, Political, and Economic Development of Individual, Families, Groups, Organizations, and Communities

Theories of Racial/Ethnic Identity

Over the past three decades, various theories on racial and ethnic identity development have emerged. Cross (1971, 1991, 2001) developed the Black Racial (Nigrescence) Identity Development Model. The first version of the model describes a shift from Black self-hatred to Black self-acceptance, which occurs through five stages of identity development: pre-encounter, encounter, immersion–emersion, internalization, and internalization–commitment. In 1991, a revision reduced the number of stages to four and introduced the ideal of "race salience." Racial identity salience is the extent to which an individual's race is currently a relevant part of his or her self-concept. The model was expanded in 2001 by Cross and Vandiver (see Table 3.2); four stages remained, but it expanded the pre-encounter stage to include assimilation, miseducation, and self-hatred identities and the internalization stage to include two multiculturalist orientations (racial and inclusive).

TABLE 3.2 Stages of the Black Racial Identity Development Model

Pre-encounter stage	Race and identity have low salience. In assimilation substage adopt mainstream identity, in the anti-Black substage accept negative beliefs about Black people and as a result are likely to have low self-esteem.
Encounter stage	Exposure to single significant race-related event or series of events leads to racial/cultural awareness and interest in developing a Black identity.
Immersion–emersion stage	Race and racial identity have high salience during this stage. Individuals in this immersion substage idealize Blacks and Black culture and feel a great deal of rage toward Whites as well as guilt and anxiety about his or her own previous lack of awareness of race. During the emersion substage intense emotions subside but individuals reject all aspects of White culture and begin to internalize a Black identity.
Internalization stage	Race continues to have high salience. Individuals in this stage have adopted one of three identities: pro-Black, nonracist (Afrocentric); biculturist orientation that integrates Black identity with White or another salient cultural identity; or multiculturalist orientation that integrates Black identity with two or more other salient cultural identities.

The White Racial Identity Development Model was created by Helms (1990, 1995) and comprises six distinct phases. Racism is a central part of being White in America and that identity development involves two phases: abandoning racism (statuses 1–3) and developing a nonracist White identity (statuses 4–6). Each phase or status (see Table 3.3) is characterized by a different information-processing strategy (IPS), which refers to the methods the individual uses to reduce discomfort related to racial issues.

Atkinson, Morten, and Sue (1993) proposed the Racial/Cultural Identity Development Model (see Table 3.4). This model distinguished among five stages that

TABLE 3.3 Stages of the White Racial Identity Development Model

STAGE	DESCRIPTION	IPS
Contact status	Little awareness of racism and racial identity and may exhibit unsophisticated behaviors that reflect racist attitudes and beliefs	Obliviousness and denial
Disintegration status	Increasing awareness of race and racism leads to confusion and emotional conflict. To reduce dissonance, person may overidentify with members of minority groups, act in paternalist ways toward them, or retreat into White society	Suppression of information and ambivalence
Reintegration status	Attempts to resolve moral dilemmas associated with the disintegration status by idealizing White society and denigrating members of minority groups	Selective perception and negative out-group distortion
Pseudoindependence Status	Personally jarring event or series of events causes person to question racist views and acknowledge role that Whites have in perpetrating racism; interested in understanding racial/cultural differences but only on an intellectual level	Selective perception and reshaping reality
Immersion–emersion status	Explores what it means to be White, confronts own biases, and begins to understand ways he or she can benefit from White privilege	Hypervigilence and reshaping
Autonomy status	Internalizes nonracist White identity that includes appreciation of and respect for racial/cultural differences and similarities	Flexibility and complexity

TABLE 3.4   Stages of the Racial/Cultural Identity Development Model

Stage 1	Conformity	Positive attitudes toward a preference for dominant cultural values and depreciating attitudes toward one's own culture
Stage 2	Dissonance	Confusion and conflict over the contradictory appreciating and depreciating attitudes that one has toward self and others of the same and different groups
Stage 3	Resistance and immersion	Active rejection of the dominant society; exhibits appreciating attitudes toward self and members of one's own group
Stage 4	Introspection	Uncertainty about the rigidity of beliefs held in stage 3 and conflicts between loyalty and responsibility toward one's own group and feelings of personal autonomy
Stage 5	Integrative awareness	Experience a sense of fulfillment with regard to cultural identity and has a strong desire to eliminate all forms of oppression; adopts a multicultural perspective and objectively examines the values, beliefs, etc. of one's own and other groups before accepting or rejecting them

people experience as they attempt to understand themselves in terms of their culture, the dominant culture, and the oppressive relationship among cultures.

Causes, Manifestations, and Effects of Oppression

Prejudice and Discrimination

The field of psychology has long focused on causes, manifestations, and effects of oppression. *Prejudice* can be defined as intolerant, unfair, or negative attitude toward an individual simply because of his or her group membership. Discrimination includes negative, unfair and often aggressive acts toward members of a particular group. In other words, prejudice includes more of an affective component, whereas discrimination focuses chiefly on the behavioral component.

There are many causes of prejudice and discrimination, including stereotyping and perceived threat. Stereotyping occurs when an individual holds schemas about entire groups that contain oversimplified, rigid, and generalized impressions of members. This is the cognitive component of prejudice. It is important to note that the individual may not be aware of these beliefs, leading to more complex and ambivalent racial expressions sometimes referred to as "aversive racism" (Gaertner & Dovidio, 1986). Another cause may be perceived threat, or when an individual believes that a particular group represents a direct threat to one's well-being.

Although overt racism persists, symbolic (modern) racism is more prevalent. These types of prejudice and discrimination are less blatant and may include rejections of obvious forms of prejudice and discrimination. For example, someone may say "I'm not a racist" but oppose busing, welfare, affirmative action, etc., which would counter White privilege. Sue et al. (1997) highlighted the use of racial microaggressions or "brief and commonplace daily verbal, behavioral, or environmental indignities, whether intentional or unintentional, that communicate hostile, derogatory, or negative racial slights and insults toward people of color."

Research on prejudice has traditionally focused on race and ethnicity; however, recent studies have also focused on sexism and heterosexism. The term *homophobia* was coined by Weinberg (1972) to refer to antigay attitudes and behaviors. It may also be used to imply an irrational fear of homosexuality or psychopathology. Heterosexism is an ideological system that denies, denigrates, and stigmatizes among nonheterosexual forms of behavior, identity, relationships, or community (Herek, 1991). Heterosexism contains both individual and cultural components (Herek & Berrill, 1992).

Sexual prejudice refers to negative attitudes based on sexual orientation, whether the target is homosexual, bisexual, or heterosexual. Research focused on correlates of sexual prejudice have generally found higher levels of sexual prejudice among heterosexual men, among individuals who are older, have lower levels of education, live in Southern or Midwestern states or in rural areas, or have limited personal contact with homosexuals (Herek, 2000).

Sexism was coined to label discrimination against men or women because of their identified sex. Studies indicate that "81% of 8th through 11th graders, 30% of undergraduates, and 40% of graduate students have been sexually harassed" (Sue & Sue, 2003, p. 407). Furthermore, several research studies have demonstrated that teachers may unwittingly promote sexism by responding differently to female and male students. For example, many studies show that math is considered to be a "male" domain, as well as communication being labeled differently (i.e., okay for boys to interrupt but girls should raise their hands).

Classism, or being discriminated against because of class or socioeconomic status, can also deeply affect individuals. Sue and Sue (2003) explored the role of class-bound values within the therapy room and clinicians' potential difficulty understanding a life "characterized by low wages, unemployment, underemployment, little property ownership, no savings and lack of food reserves" (p. 115). Without understanding this lifestyle, clinicians may overpathologize behavior. This is consistent with research that has shown a mental illness diagnosis is more likely to occur and a more negative prognosis is assumed when an individual comes from a lower rather than higher socioeconomic background.

Methods for Reducing Prejudice and Discrimination

Allport (1954) argues that intergroup prejudice arises from a combination of historical, cultural, economic, cognitive, and personality factors and proposes that because prejudice has multiple determinants, focusing on one will not lead to understanding and resolution of the problem. It is important to note that laws prohibiting discrimination can be effective even when they do not reflect public consensus.

Similar to the belief that aversive racism increases by staying in-group, contact hypothesis states that stereotypes will decrease when contact among members of different groups increases. However, this is not to say that contact alone is enough. People from both groups must have equal status and power and must have opportunities to disconfirm negative stereotypes about members of other groups. Additionally, contact should require intergroup cooperation to achieve mutual goals. This can be particularly challenging due to systematic and cultural components that perpetuate White privilege, heterosexism, and other dominant groups to stay in power.

Sexual Orientation and Identity

Sexual Identity Development

Along with models of racial identity development, the past few decades have produced standard models of sexual identity development. One of the most frequently cited is the Cass Identity Model (1979). This model was the first to normalize the process, rather than pathologize being gay and consists of six stages of identity development (see Table 3.5). Kaufman and Johnson (2004) criticized this model because of societal changes over the past 20 years, as well as lack of integration of other sociocultural factors, which may impact identity development.

Troiden (1979, 1988) proposed another model of homosexual identity development. This model of Gay Identity Acquisition (see Table 3.6) identified four stages.

Other models of gay identity development have been proposed and many of these models have a number of common elements. Generally the first stage of gay identity development models involves an initial awareness of being different than same-gender peers, and depending on the individual's age may include questioning one's sexual orientation. One example is Coleman's (1982) Developmental Stages of Coming Out, which has five stages: pre–coming out, coming out, exploration, first relationships, and integration. There is criticism of these models, including that most of the research was done on gay men (rather than lesbian women) and focused on White individuals rather than people of color. In addition, more categories than gay and lesbian have emerged, including bisexuality, pansexuality, and transgendered issues. Therefore, D'Augelli (1994) proposed a life span model (rather than linear) that includes other aspects of self, including

TABLE 3.5   The Cass Identity Model: Six Stages of Identity Development

Identity confusion	First awareness of gay or lesbian thoughts, feelings, and attractions; individuals often feel confused and disoriented
Identity comparison	Individual accepts possibility of being gay or lesbian and thinks of implications; may include grief, isolation, and self-alienation while trying to compartmentalize sexuality
Identity tolerance	Individual understands he or she is not alone; beginning to accept self and commit to being lesbian or gay; seeks out others and addresses own heterosexism and internalized homophobia
Identity acceptance	Individual accepts him- or herself and is hopeful—positive meaning; attempts to have congruent personal and public self—deciding how/if/when to disclose
Identity pride	World may be seen as divided between heterosexual and homosexual (us vs. them)
Identity synthesis	Individual integrates his or her sexual identity with other aspects of self

TABLE 3.6   Stages of the Gay Identity Acquisition Model

Stage 1	Sensitization; feeling different	During this stage (usually middle childhood) individual feels different from his or her peers
Stage 2	Self-recognition; identity confusion	Usually onset of puberty, individual realizes he or she is attracted to people of the same sex and attributes those feelings to homosexuality, which leads to confusion and turmoil
Stage 3	Identity assumption	Individual becomes more certain of his or her homosexuality and may deal with this realization in a variety of ways (e.g., try to "pass" as heterosexual, align with homosexual community, or act in ways consistent with stereotypes about homosexuality)
Stage 4	Commitment; identity integration	Adopt a homosexual way of life and publicly disclose as homosexual

family, peers, self-concept, and community. His six "identity processes" are not stages but interact independently. The six stages include exiting heterosexuality, developing a personal lesbian, gay, or bisexual (LGB) identity, developing an LGB social identity, becoming an LGB offspring ("come out" to family), developing an LGB intimacy status, and entering an LGB community. These processes may change over time, as well as retreat (such as during times of transition). For example, disclosure and management in the workplace can be tricky and partners may choose to stay "in the closet" while at a new job. In addition, an individual may have developed a large LGB community but then moved to a new town and may need to rebuild over time.

In 1973, the American Psychiatric Association removed "homosexuality" from its list of mental disorders (American Psychiatric Association, 1974). Of note, although families with lesbian and gay parents often experience prejudice, research does not indicate any impairment for lesbian or gay adults with regard to being parents (American Psychological Association [APA], 2005). In addition, some research indicates that lesbian mothers and gay fathers are likely to divide child care work evenly and report satisfaction in their partnership. Furthermore, some research indicates that lesbian mothers' and gay fathers' parenting skills may be even better than those of heterosexual parents (APA, 2005).

Psychology and Gender

Gender Identity

Gender identity refers to a person's sense of being male or female. Gender identity develops early. By age 3 most children label themselves as either "boy" or "girl" and are able to identify others as either the same or opposite gender. At this age children also have an understanding of what behaviors are considered appropriate for a boy or girl and show a preference for behaviors and activities consistent with their gender. These beliefs about behavior often reflect gender-role stereotypes, which are overgeneralized beliefs about what males and females are supposed to be like. Gender-role stereotypes affect children's play, memory, and attributions.

There are a number of theories that explain gender-role identity development, including the following.

Psychodynamic Theory
Freud's psychodynamic theory suggests that the development of gender identity relies on the successful resolution of psychosexual crisis that occurs in the phallic stage of development. Crisis resolution results in identification with the same-sex parent and gender identity.

Social Learning Theory
Social learning theory (Mischel, 1966) proposes that gender-role development is the result of observational learning and differential reinforcement. This theory is supported by research which demonstrates that parents play more roughly with male children and are more protective of female children (Santrock, 2006).

Cognitive Developmental Theory

Kohlberg's cognitive developmental theory (1966) suggests that gender-role development occurs in a series of stages that parallel cognitive development. First, children recognize they are either male or female (age 2 to 3), next they realize gender is stable over time (i.e., boys become men and girls become women), and then children understand gender is constant across situations and people cannot change gender by altering appearance or behavior (age 6 to 7).

Gender Schema Theory

Gender schema theory (Bem, 1981) suggests that the development of gender-role identity is the result of a combination of social learning and cognitive development. Children create schemas of masculinity and femininity based on their sociocultural experiences. These schemas organize how a person perceives the world.

Differences in gender roles appear to decrease in late adolescence and early adulthood. However, gender roles appear to increase when couples have children and the woman assumes primary child-rearing responsibilities (Gager, 1998). In middle age, gender roles may reverse such that males become more passive, expressive, sensitive, and dependent and women become more active, outgoing, competitive, and independent (Huyck, 1990).

Disability and Rehabilitation Issues

Models of Disability

A number of conceptual models have been proposed to understand and explain disability, including the medical and social models. The medical model suggests that disability is a problem directly caused by disease, trauma, or other health conditions that require sustained medical treatment provided by professionals. Treatment is focused on adjustment and behavior change that would "cure" the disability. In contrast, the social model views disability as a socially created problem that is the result of loss or limitation of opportunities to take part in the normal life of the community on an equal level because of physical and social barriers (Oliver, 1996). Management of the problem requires social and political solutions that would allow people with disabilities to fully participate in all areas of social life.

Inclusion of Persons With Disabilities in the Workplace

The Americans with Disabilities Act (ADA, 1991) prohibits employers from discriminating against qualified individuals with mental or physical disabilities. This legislation states that if a disabled person is able to perform the essential functions of a job, he or she is considered qualified and the employer must make "reasonable accommodations" as long as those accommodations do not place undue hardship on the employer. The ADA also requires that pre-employment measures be directly related to job requirements and prohibits a medical exam prior to an employment offer. If medical exams are administered they must be given to all applicants, not just those with disabilities. Drug tests are an exception and not considered a medical exam according to the ADA.

Acculturation of Immigrant, Refugee, and Political-Asylum-Seeking Populations

Acculturation

Acculturation refers to the extent to which a culturally diverse group accepts and adheres to the values, attitudes, and behaviors of their own group and the dominant or majority group. Berry et al. (1987) proposed four categories of acculturation status:

> *Integration*: A person maintains his or her own (minority) culture and also incorporates many aspects of the dominant culture.

> *Assimilation*: A person relinquishes his or her culture and accepts majority culture.

> *Separation*: A person withdraws from the dominant culture and accepts his or her own culture.

> *Marginalization*: A person does not identify with either his or her own culture or the majority culture.

Phinney and Devich-Navarro (1997) also proposed a model of acculturation that distinguishes among six categories: assimilated, fused, blended bicultural, alternating bicultural, separated, and marginal. Using these categories, they found that the majority of African American and Mexican American adolescents described themselves as either blended bicultural (strong integrated ethnic and American identities) or separated (only an ethnic identity).

Culturally Mediated Communication Patterns

High-Context and Low-Context Communication

Hall (1969) defined two styles of communication: high and low context. High-context communication is grounded in the situation, depends on group understanding, and relies heavily on nonverbal cues. This type of communication helps to unify cultures and changes slowly. Conversely, low-context communication depends on the explicit, verbal part of a message. It can change quickly and easily and is a less unifying form of communication. Low-context communication is characteristic of Euro-American cultures and high-context communication is typical of culturally diverse groups in the United States.

References

Allport, G. W. (1954). *The nature of prejudice*. Reading, MA: Addison-Wesley.

American Psychiatric Association. (1974). *The diagnostic and statistical manual of mental disorders* (2nd ed.). Washington, DC: American Psychiatric Press.

American Psychological Association (APA). (1992). Ethical principles of psychologists and code of conduct. *American Psychologist, 47*, 1597–1611.

American Psychological Association (APA). (2005). *Lesbian & gay parenting*. Washington, DC: American Psychological Association.

Americans With Disabilities Act of 1990, Pub. L. No. 101-336, §2, 104 Stat. 328 (1991).

Atkinson, D., Morten, G., & Sue, D. (1993). *Counseling American minorities: A cross-cultural perspective*. Madison, WI: Brown & Benchmark.

Bandura, A. (1978). The self system in reciprocal determinism. *American Psychologist, 33,* 344–358.

Bandura, A. (1983). Psychological mechanisms of aggression. In R. G. Green & E. I. Donnerstein (Eds.), *Aggression: Theoretical and Empirical Reviews*. New York, NY: Academic Press.

Baron, R. A., & Richardson, D. (1994). *Human aggression*. New York, NY: Plenum.

Batson, C. D. (1991). *The altruism question: Toward a social-psychological answer*. Hillsdale, NJ: Erlbaum.

Batson, C. D., Ahmad, N., & Lishner, D. A. (2009). Empathy and altruism. In C. R. Synder, & J. Lopez (Eds.), *Oxford handbook of positive psychology* (2nd ed., pp. 417–426). New York, NY: Oxford University Press.

Baumeister, R. F., & Finkel, E. J. (2010). *Advanced social psychology: The state of the science*. New York, NY: Oxford University Press.

Bem, S. L. (1981). Gender schema theory: A cognitive account of sex typing. *Psychological Review, 88,* 354–364.

Berkowitz, L. (1971). The contagion of violence: An S-R meditational analysis of some effects of observed aggression. In W. Arnold & M. Page (Eds.), *Nebraska Symposium on Motivation*, Vol. 18. Lincoln: University of Nebraska Press.

Berry, J. W., Kim, U., Minde, T., & Mok, D. (1987). Comparative studies of acculturative stress. *International Migration Review, 21,* 491–511.

Brehm, J. W. (1972). *Responses to loss of freedom: A theory of psychological reactance*. Morristown, NJ: General Learning Press.

Buss, D. M. (2007). The evolution of human mating. *Acta Psychologica, 37,* 502–512.

Cass, V. C. (1979). Homosexual identity formation: A theoretical model. *Journal of Homosexuality, 4,* 219–235.

Cialdini, R. B. (2001). *Influence: Science and practice* (4th ed.). Boston, MA: Allyn & Bacon.

Coleman, E. (1982). Developmental stages of the coming-out process. In W. Paul, J. D. Weinrich, J. C. Gonsiorek, & M. E. Hotvedt (Eds.), *Homosexuality: Social, psychological, and biological issues* (pp. 149–158). Beverly Hills, CA: Sage.

Cross, W. E., Jr. (1971). *Shades of black: Diversity in African-American identity*. Philadelphia, PA: Temple University Press.

Cross, W. (1991). *Shades of black*. Philadelphia: Temple University Press.

Cross, W. E., Jr., & Vandiver, B. J. (2001). Nigrescence theory and measurement: Introducing the Cross Racial Identity Scale (CRIS). In J. G. Ponerotto, J. M. Casas, L. M. Suzuki, & C. M. Alexander (Eds.), *Handbook of multicultural counseling* (2nd ed., pp. 371–393). Thousand Oaks, CA: Sage.

D'Augelli, A. R. (1994). Identity development and sexual orientation: Toward a model of lesbian, gay, and bisexual development. In E. J. Tricket, R. J. Watts, & D. Birman (Eds.), *Human diversity: Perspectives on people in context* (pp. 312–333). San Francisco, CA: Jossey-Bass.

Deaux, K. (1978). Sex differences. In T. Blass (Ed.), *Personality variables in social behavior*. Hilsdale, NJ: Erlbaum.

Deaux, K., & Wrightsman, L. S. (1988). *Social psychology*. Pacific Grove, CA: Brooks/Cole.

Dollard, J., Miller, N. E., Doob, L. W., Mowrer, O.H., & Sears, R. R. (1939). *Frustration and aggression*. New Haven, CT: Yale University Press.

Fiske, S. T., & Taylor, S. E. (1991). *Social cognition* (2nd ed.). New York, NY: McGraw-Hill.

French, J., & Raven, E. (1959). The bases of social power. In D. D. Cartwright (Ed.), *Studies on social power*. Ann Arbor: University of Michigan, Institute for Social Research.

Gaertner, S. L., & Dovidio, J. F. (1986). The aversive form of racism. In J. F. Dovidio, & S. L. Gaertner (Eds.), *Prejudice, discrimination, and racism* (pp. 61–89). Orlando, FL: Academic Press.

Gager, C. T. (1998). The role of valued outcomes, justifications, and comparison referents in perceptions of fairness among dual-earner couples. *Journal of Family Issues, 19*, 622–648.

Greenberg, J., & Baron, R. A. (1993). *Behavior in organizations*. Boston, MA: Allyn and Bacon.

Hall, E. T. (1969). *The hidden dimension*. Garden City, NY: Doubleday.

Hays, R. B. (1985). A longitudinal study of friendship development. *Journal of Personality and Social Psychology, 48*, 909–924.

Hays, P. A. (2001). *Addressing cultural complexities in practice: A framework for clinicians and counselors*. Washington, DC: American Psychological Association.

Helms, J. E. (1990). *Black and White racial identity: Theory, research, and practice*. New York, NY: Greenwood Press.

Helms, J. E. (1995). An update of Helms' White and People of Color racial identity models. In J. G. Ponterotto, J. M. Casas, L. A. Suzuki, & C. M. Alexander (Eds.), *Handbook of multicultural counseling* (pp. 181–191). Thousand Oaks, CA: Sage.

Herek, G. M. (1991). Stigma, prejudice, and violence against lesbians and gay men. In J. Gonsiorek, & J. Weinrich (Eds.), *Homosexuality: Research implications for public policy* (pp. 60–80). Newbury Park, CA: Sage.

Herek, G. M. (2000). The psychology of sexual prejudice. *Current Directions in Psychological Science, 9*, 19–22.

Herek, G. M., & Berrill, K. T. (1992). *Hate Crimes: Confronting violence against lesbians and gay men* (pp. 149–169). Newbury Park, CA: Sage.

Hofetede, G. (1993). Cultural constraints in management theories. *Academy of Management Executives, 7*, 81–94.

Huyck, M. H. (1990). Gender differences in aging. In J. E. Birren, & K. W. Schaie (Eds.), *Handbook of the psychology of aging*. San Diego, CA: Academic Press.

Kaufman, J., & Johnson, C. (2004). Stigmatized individuals and the process of identity. *Sociological Quarterly, 45*, 807–833.

Kelman, H. (1958). Compliance, identification, and internalization: Three processes of attitude change. *Journal of Conflict Resolution, 1*, 51–60.

Kohlberg, L. (1966). A cognitive-developmental analysis of children's sex-role concepts and attitudes. In E. E. Maccoby (Ed.), *The development of differences*. Stanford, CA: Stanford University Press.

Latané, B. (1981). The psychology of social impact. *American Psychologist, 36*, 343–356.

Latané, B. & Bidwell, L. D. (1977). Sex and affiliation in college cafeterias. *Personality and Social Psychology, Bulletin, 3*, 571–574.

Latané, B., & L' Herrou, T. (1996). Spatial clustering in the conformity game: Dynamic social impact in electronic games. *Journal of Personality and Social Psychology, 70*, 1218–1230.

Lewin, K. (1931). Environmental forces in child behavior and development. In C. Murchison (Ed.), *A handbook of child psychology* (pp. 590–625). Worcester, MA: Clark University Press.

Lewin, K. (1936). *A dynamic theory of personality.* New York, NY: McGraw-Hill.

Maass, A., & Clark, R. D. (1988). Social categorization in minority influence: The case of homosexuality. *European Journal of Social Psychology, 18,* 347–367.

Miller, N. E. (1944). Experimental studies of conflict. In J. M. Hunt (Ed.), *Personality and the behavior disorders* (pp. 431–465). New York, NY: Ronald Press.

Mischel, W. (1966). A social learning view of sex differences in behaving. In E. E. Maccoby (Ed.), *The development of sex differences.* Stanford, CA: Stanford University Press.

Moscovici, S. (1985). Social influence and conformity. In G. Lindzey & E. Aronson (Eds.), *The handbook of social psychology.* New York, NY: Random House.

Myers, I. B., & Myers P. B. (1980, 1995). *Gifts differing: Understanding personality type.*

Oliver, M. (1996). The social model in context. *Understanding disability: From theory to practice* (pp. 30–42). Basingstoke, UK: Macmillan.

Phinney, J. S., & Devich-Navarro, M. (1997). Variations in bicultural identification among African American and Mexican American adolescents. *Journal of Research in Adolescence, 7,* 3–32.

Richards, P. S., & Bergin, A. E. (2000). *Handbook of psychotherapy and religious diversity.* Washington, DC: American Psychological Association.

Santrock, J. W. (2006). *Lifespan development.* Boston, MA: McGraw-Hill.

Schein, E. (1992). *Organizational culture and leadership.* San Francisco, CA: Jossey-Bass.

Schmitt, D. (2005). Fundamentals of human mating strategies. In D. M. Buss (Ed.), *Handbook of evolutionary psychology* (pp. 258–291). Hoboken, NJ: John Wiley.

Spilka, B., Hood, R. W., Jr., Hunsberger, B., & Gorsuch, R. (2003). *The psychology of religion: An empirical approach.* New York, NY: Guilford Press.

Sue, D. E., & Sue, D. (2003). *Counseling the culturally diverse: Theory and practice* (4th ed.). New York, NY: John Wiley.

Sue, D. W., Capodilupo, C. M., Torina, G. C., Bucceri, J. M., Holder, A. M. B., Nadal, K. L., Torino, G. C. (1997). Racial microaggressions in everyday life: Implications for clinical practice. *American Psychologist, 62*(4), 271–286.

Sue, D. W., Carter, R. T., Casas, J. M., Fouad, N. A., Ivey, A. E., Jensen, M., ... Vazquez-Nutall, E. (1998). *Multicultural counseling competencies: Individual and organizational development.* Thousand Oaks, CA: Sage Publications.

Trivers, R. L. (1972). Parental investment and sexual selection. In B. Campbell (Ed.), *Sexual selection and the descent of man, 1871–1971* (pp. 136–179). Chicago, IL: Aldine.

Troiden, R. R. (1979). Becoming homosexual: A model of gay identity acquisition. *Psychiatry, 42,* 362–373.

Troiden, R. R. (1988). *Gay and lesbian identity: A sociological analysis.* Dix Hills, NY: General Hall.

Weinberg, G. (1972). *Society and the healthy homosexual.* New York, NY: St. Martin's Press.

Review Questions

1. Schemas are organized patterns of thought and behavior that help us derive hypotheses about incoming stimuli and provide a sense of prediction and control. Schemas function as ALL of the following except:
   A. Evaluation—uses information to compare to others
   B. Role playing—defines the scripts for how we should behave
   C. Identification—helps to categorize information about others
   D. Acculturation—defines how others are like you

2. Schemas are self-sustaining and exist in the face of contradictory evidence. Research has focused on four types of schemas though there are many types. Which below is not identified as a schema?
   A. Person
   B. Event
   C. Self
   D. Mental

3. In making attributions about behavior, we tend to commit biases and errors. Fundamental attribution error is a common bias that states:
   A. The tendency to overvalue personal factors and undervalue situational factors when explaining the behavior of others
   B. The tendency to attribute personal factors for success and external factors for failure
   C. The tendency to attribute personal factors to others' failure and situational factors to personal failure
   D. The tendency to undervalue personal factors and overvalue situational factors when explaining others behavior

4. There are several types of social influence. All except which of the following is not a type of social influence.
   A. Minority influence
   B. Dynamic social impact
   C. Persuasion
   D. Social power

5. The Zimbardo prison experiments represent which type of social influence:
   A. Informational conformity
   B. Internalization
   C. Obedience
   D. Peer pressure

6. Which of the following human mating strategies occurs when females compete for access to numerous males, and after mating with one male, leave him and the offspring?
   A. Monogamy
   B. Polygyny
   C. Polyandry
   D. Short term

7. Research on motivations underlying empathy-induced behavior includes:

   A. Altruistic
   B. Egoist
   C. Antisocial
   D. Both A and B

8. Empathy is evoked under the following situations except:

   A. Sharing emotions and feelings
   B. Valuing another's welfare
   C. Recognizing kinship
   D. Seeking others who are dissimilar

9. Freud's psychodynamic theory of personality posits that the _____ develops at 4 or 5 years of age to block the _____ socially unacceptable drives.

   A. Ego; id's
   B. Ego; super ego's
   C. Super ego; ego's
   D. Super ego; id's

10. A therapist who conceptualizes a client's behavior as the result of learned consequences likely ascribes to which theory of personality?

    A. Behavioral
    B. Social cognitive
    C. Humanistic
    D. Existential

11. Someone who views disability as the result of a loss of opportunities to take part in the normal life of the community likely ascribes to what model of disability?

    A. Medical model
    B. Market model
    C. Social model
    D. Economic model

12. Which of the following is not consistent with the requirements established by the Americans with Disabilities Act?

    A. Employers must make reasonable accommodations for disabled employees
    B. Drug tests must be given to all applicants, not just those with disabilities
    C. Pre-employment measures must be related to job requirements
    D. Disabled persons are considered qualified for a position if they are able to perform the essential functions of the job

13. According to Berry's (1987) model of acculturation, a woman who withdraws from the dominant culture and accepts her own culture is in what category of acculturation status?

    A. Marginalization
    B. Assimilation
    C. Integration
    D. Separation

14. The tendency of a patient to attribute his past job success to his intelligence, skill, and hard work, and attribute recent failures to situational factors can be described using the:

   A. Actor–observer bias
   B. Learned helplessness model
   C. Self-attribution effect
   D. Self-serving bias

15. Crowding has been linked with a number of negative outcomes, including all of the following except:

   A. Poor performance on simple tasks
   B. Juvenile delinquency
   C. Mental health problems
   D. Poor academic performance

16. A conflict that arises when a person must choose between two jobs that both have positive and negative aspects is what type of conflict?

   A. Double approach–approach
   B. Approach–approach
   C. Double approach–avoidance
   D. Approach–avoidance

17. A company that was striving to increase person–organization fit would have the most success by using which of the following strategies?

   A. Revising selection process of new employees
   B. Increasing financial compensation
   C. Increasing medical benefits
   D. Adapting a more relaxed work environment

18. According to Cross and Vandiver (2001), which stage of identity development is associated with an awareness and interest in developing a Black identity?

   A. Pre-encounter
   B. Immersion–emersion
   C. Internalization
   D. Encounter

19. Sexual prejudice is correlated with all of the following except:

   A. Older age
   B. Heterosexual women
   C. Lower levels of education
   D. Living in a rural area

20. The idea that the acquisition of a gender-role identity results from the combination of social learning and cognitive development is most consistent with which theory of gender identity development?

   A. Psychodynamic theory
   B. Social learning theory
   C. Cognitive behavioral theory
   D. Gender schema theory

21. According to Berry's model of acculturation, a person who does not identify with his or her own culture or the majority culture is in what status?

    A. Assimilation
    B. Integration
    C. Marginalization
    D. Separation

22. The gain–loss theory of attraction posits that attraction is maximized when the individual's evaluation of a person is at first _____ and then changes to _____.

    A. Neutral; positive
    B. Negative; positive
    C. Negative; neutral
    D. Positive; neutral

23. The Bobo doll studies demonstrated that aggressive behaviors arise through the observation of others. This research supports which theory of aggression?

    A. Social learning
    B. Deindividuation
    C. Frustration–aggression
    D. Role adaptation

24. _____ is defined as intolerant, unfair, or negative attitudes toward an individual because of his or her group membership.

    A. Discrimination
    B. Stereotyping
    C. Oppression
    D. Prejudice

25. Allport (1954) argued that intergroup prejudice arises from a combination of all the following factors except:

    A. Cultural
    B. Economic
    C. Historical
    D. Geographic

26. Myers–Briggs type indicators grew out of whose work on personality theory?

    A. Alder
    B. Jung
    C. Rogers
    D. Kelin

27. Anxiety _____ desire to affiliate and in anxiety-provoking situations social comparison is a _____ potent cause of affiliation than relief from discomfort.

    A. Increases; more
    B. Increases; less
    C. Decreases; more
    D. Decreases; less

28. A therapist who focuses on a patient's judgments and beliefs in treatment likely ascribes to which model of personality?

A. Behavioral
B. Psychodynamic
C. Structural
D. Cognitive

29. According to Troiden's model of homosexual identity development, during which stage do individuals begin to align with the homosexual community?

A. Stage 2
B. Stage 3
C. Stage 4
D. Stage 5

30. According to Cialdini, the propensity to be influenced by another person is increased due to all of the following factors except:

A. Authority
B. Abundance
C. Reciprocity
D. Liking

Answers to Review Questions

1. **D. Acculturation—defines how others are like you**

   Schemas help us organize information through the functions of evaluation, prediction, role playing, and identification.

2. **D. Mental**

   The most frequently identified types of schemas are person, event, self, and role.

3. **A. The tendency to overvalue personal factors and undervalue situational factors when explaining the behavior of others**

   When explaining the behavior of others, we tend to attribute their behavior to internal personality characteristics rather than situational factors.

4. **D. Social Power**

   Social power involves coercion, whereas social influence involves the process of change in someone's thoughts, attitudes, or behaviors.

5. **C. Obedience**

   Research shows that people tend to be obedient when there is a perceived legitimate authority figure regardless of the task they are being asked to perform.

6. **C. Polyandry**

   Polyandry occurs when a female mates with multiple males within or without marriage. It is different from group marriage where there are multiple partners of both sexes.

7. **D. Both A and B**

   Batson posits that both altruistic (other focused) and egoist (self-focused) motivation can result in empathy.

8. **D. Seeking others who are dissimilar**

   Empathy is evoked when we recognize others who are similar to us.

9. **D. Super ego; id's**

   Freud's personality theory identified three aspects of personality. The id is present at birth; the ego develops at 6 months to defer gratitude until appropriate; and the super ego is an internalization of society's values and standards.

10. **A. Behavioral**

    Behavioral theories are based on the idea that patterns of behavior are the result of learned behaviors and consequences.

11. C. Social model

The social model views disability as a socially created problem that is the result of loss or limitation of opportunities to take part in the normal life of the community on an equal level because of physical and social barriers.

12. B. Drug tests must be given to all applicants, not just those with disabilities

If medical exams are administered by employers they must be given to all applicants, not just those with disabilities. Drug tests are an exception and not considered a medical exam according to the ADA.

13. D. Separation

In the assimilation status, a person relinquishes his or her own culture and accepts the majority culture. In contrast, separation status is defined as withdrawing from the dominant culture and accepting one's own culture.

14. D. Self-serving bias

The self-serving bias is the tendency of a person to attribute his or her behavior to dispositional factors when the consequences are positive and to situational factors when the consequences are negative.

15. A. Poor performance on simple tasks

Crowding is associated with poor performance on complex rather than simple tasks.

16. C. Double approach–avoidance

An approach–avoidance conflict arises when a single goal has positive and negative consequences. Choosing between two goals, both of which have positive and negative consequences, is called a double approach–avoidance.

17. A. Revising selection process of new employees

Person–organization fit refers to the extent which values held by specific individuals match those of the organization's culture. Good fit is achieved through the selection and socialization process.

18. D. Encounter

Cross and Vandiver identified four stages of Black racial identity development. The second stage in the encounter is characterized by exposure to a single significant race-related event or a series of events leads to racial/cultural awareness and interest in developing a Black identity.

19. B. Heterosexual women

Sexual prejudice is correlated with heterosexual men rather than heterosexual women.

20. D. Gender schema theory

Bem's gender schema theory suggests that gender-role identity arises from the combination of social learning and cognitive development.

21. C. Marginalization

Berry identified four categories of acculturation status. A person in the marginalization status does not identify with either his or her own culture or the majority culture.

22. B. Negative; positive

Gain–loss theory states that attraction is maximized when a person initially views someone as negative and then changes the perception to positive.

23. A. Social learning

According to social learning theory, aggressive behavior is the result of observational learning. In the Bobo doll studies, children's behavior was affected by watching another child interact with the doll and receive a reward or punishment for their behavior.

24. D. Prejudice

Prejudice is intolerant, unfair, or negative attitudes toward an individual because of his or her group membership. Discrimination is negative and unfair acts toward members of a particular group. Stereotypes are schemas about entire groups that contain oversimplified, rigid, and generalized impressions of group members.

25. D. Geographic

Allport proposed that intergroup prejudice was the result of a combination of cultural, economic, cognitive, historical, and personality factors.

26. B. Jung

Jung's theory of personality included two attitudes (introversion and extroversion) and four basic psychological functions (thinking, feeling, sensing, and intuiting), which is an early foundation of Myers–Briggs type assessments.

27. A. Increases; more

Anxiety increases the desire to affiliate in anxiety-provoking situations. In such situations, comparison is a more likely motivator for affiliation than the reduction of anxiety or discomfort.

28. D. Cognitive

Cognitive models of personality focus on the way a person thinks about him- or herself and the world.

29. B. Stage 3

Troiden identified four stages of homosexual identity development. Stage 3 is characterized by developing certainty of sexuality and the assumption of a homosexual identity.

30. B. Abundance

Cialdini suggested that an individual's propensity to be influenced by a persuader is affected by six factors: reciprocity, commitment and consistency, social proof, authority, liking, and scarcity.

4

Growth and Life Span Development

Laura Stout Sosinsky, Rumeli Banik,
and Andrew J. Cavanagh

Broad Content Areas

- Development across the full life span
- Atypical patterns of development
- The protective and risk factors that influence developmental trajectories of individuals

Development is relatively enduring growth and change that makes an individual better adapted to the environment by enhancing the individual's ability to engage in, understand, and experience more complex behavior, thinking, and emotions. Simple growth and change are part of development, but development is more than growth and change. Development is "best described and studied as a variable process in which individual differences in cognitive, social, affective, language, neurobiological maturation, environment and life experiences, and genetics interact in complex ways" (National Institute of Child Health and Human Development, 2013). Virtually all developmentalists agree that development involves constant interplay between biology and the environment, occurs in a multi-layered context, is cumulative, and continues throughout life (Sameroff, 2010). The pathway that connects a person's past to his or her future is known as the developmental trajectory.

Organizing Concepts, Theories, and Models

Developmental science is organized around major concepts. For one, current science recognizes that development occurs as a function of "nature with nurture" (Steinberg, Vandell, & Bornstein, 2011). In the past, the concept was often put in terms of a debate about nature versus nurture. The current consensus among developmentalists is that the biological forces that govern development ("nature") interact with the environmental conditions and with the supports that influence development ("nurture"). Development will not occur without both, and they "interpenetrate" each other in that "one's nature changes one's nurture" and vice versa (Sameroff, 2010, p. 9).

Theories and models of development are often guided by additional major organizing concepts. All of these are complementary with the "nature with nurture" or interactive approach, but focus on more specific issues of timing of receptivity and the impact of events on the developmental trajectory, and on the relative contributions of the individual and environment within and between domains of development. These concepts include (1) sensitive or critical periods, (2) continuity and discontinuity, (3) risk and resilience, and (4) the active or passive role of the individual and environment.

Six age periods characterize major transitions in human development: the prenatal period (conception to birth), infancy (birth to 2 years), early childhood (ages 2–6), middle childhood (ages 6–11), adolescence (ages 11–20), and adulthood (above age 20). Recently, the age periods of emerging adulthood (ages 18–25), as well as old and very old (ages above 80) periods have begun to receive attention as individually significant periods of transition. These periods mark major developments, and the age markers are only approximate.

In this chapter, first, we expand on the major organizing concepts of developmental science. Second, we describe major theories, organized by historical and contemporary frameworks. Then, we expand on specific topics and provide definitions, terms, descriptions, and current evidence. This chapter takes a life span perspective, beginning prenatally and continuing through adulthood. Topic sections are organized by developmental domain and, within topic, by developmental chronology. Within domain, subtopics will be addressed. Within topic, we employ the following organization: (a) introduction to the topic (i.e., definition/explanation), (b) typical developmental course and/or implications of the topic for typical development, and (c) interactions with environment. Embedded within each section, relevant overall concepts and theoretical perspectives that pertain primarily only to that topic are included. Woven throughout, where relevant, we include key risk and protective factors with a major focus on poverty and, within the issue of poverty, related issues of access to services and supports for basic needs, exposure to violence and toxins, chronic issues of social support, depression, discrete positive or negative life events, and so forth.

Major Organizing Concepts

The interactive approach to development means that development results from the constant interplay of biology and the environment. Characteristics of both the child and the environment must be measured and taken into account to explain current and future behavior and adaptation. All children come into the world with the set of genes they inherit from their parents (genotype, or the 23 pairs of chromosomes one inherits from one's parents), but only a few traits are genetically "determined." The characteristics a child develops (phenotype, or one's observable appearance and characteristics) are the result of interaction between genetic and environmental influences over time (Gottlieb, Wahlstein, & Lickliter, 2006). The individual is characterized by physical attributes such as genetic, biological, hormonal, and anatomical make-up, descriptive characteristics such as age, sex, gender, or health status, cognitive and social–emotional features such as reactivity, cognitive capacities, motivation, and knowledge accrued over time through experience and learning.

The environment is characterized by the range of characteristics of the physical and social/relational contexts in which they are situated. These typically include home environments and primary and secondary caregivers such as parents, extended family members, including siblings, other children, including peers and friends, school and educational settings and associated nonparental caregivers, teachers and other adults, romantic partners, friends, and coworkers, plus the broader environment, including their caregivers' environments and supports, and the culture, laws, and norms of the whole.

The role of the environment diverges in models that are primarily focused on traits, on the environment, or on the interaction of the two (Lewis & Mayes, 2012). Trait models, also often called medical models, look to predict a later outcome based on earlier status features. Traits can be "innate" features such as genetic features or temperamental tendencies, or can be processes, coping skills, attributes, or other features not seen as readily malleable. Personality theory and research fit with trait models as well. Attachment, once established as part of an interactive process, is often treated as more of a status variable (Lewis & Mayes, 2012). However, evidence reveals some problems with trait models. For one, trait models are not often predictive of later behaviors, characteristics, or psychopathology. For example, early abuse and later depression (Cicchetti, Rogosch, Gunnar, & Toth, 2010), the APOE gene and later Alzheimer's disease (Borroni, Costanzi, & Padovani, 2010), and other pairings of early risk factors and later problems, are found to be correlated but not predictive of later psychopathology. In addition, individual traits tend to be situation specific, and trait models do not consider this impact of the situation (Lewis & Mayes, 2012).

Environmental models, at their simplest level, view development as occurring as a function of environmental forces acting continuously on the individual, with rewards and punishments from the environment directly predicting the individual's behavior. Consistent environments are seen as influencing consistent child behavior, and if a child's environment changes, so will the child's status and behavior. Modeling and observational learning fit within environmental models. The indirect effects of memories of earlier environmental forces on concurrent and later behavior also fit within this framework.

Interactional models have in common the active role of both the child and the environment in development over time. Characteristics of both the child and the environment must be measured and taken into account to explain current and future behavior and adaptation. The interactional approach is dominant in the field based on research evidence across the discipline of developmental science (Sameroff, 2010).

Five principles can be drawn from the accumulated research evidence (Steinberg et al., 2011, pp. 8–9):

1. *Development results from the constant interplay of biology and the environment.* All children come into the world with the set of genes they inherit from their parents, but only a few traits (such as eye color and blood type) are genetically "determined." The characteristics a child develops are the result of interaction between genetic and environmental influences over time (Gottlieb et al., 2006). A child may inherit a genetic tendency to be inhibited, for instance, but whether this leads to painful shyness or quiet confidence depends on the child's experiences.

2. *Development occurs in a multi-layered context.* Children are profoundly affected by their *interpersonal* relationships, the *social* institutions that touch their lives, their *culture,* and the *historical* period in which they are developing (Bronfenbrenner & Morris, 2006).

3. *Development is a dynamic, reciprocal process.* Children are not passive recipients of environmental influence. They actively shape their own development: by selecting the contexts in which they participate...; by imposing their subjective appraisal on the context...; and most of all by affecting what takes place in the context....

4. *Development is cumulative.* Development builds on itself. To understand an individual at one point in the life span, we need to look at earlier periods (Baltes, Lindenberger, & Staudinger, 2006). The quality of the infant's relationships at home lays the groundwork for the relationships she forms with school friends, which in turn shapes relationships she develops with intimate friends and lovers, and so on. Psychologists call the pathway that connects the past with the present and the future a developmental trajectory (Nagin & Tremblay, 2005). A child who has poor early relationships is not destined to have bad relationships throughout life, but one who is launched on a healthy trajectory clearly has an advantage.

5. *Development occurs throughout the life span.* The belief that the first years of life are a critical period in development has become part of our popular culture ... [however] development continues from birth to death, and change is almost always possible....

Several subconcepts further organize the understanding of human development. The first concepts described below, namely, sensitive or critical periods, plasticity, and continuity, are more concerned with time, chronology, and developmental trajectories, whereas the latter two, namely, risk/resilience and active/passive roles, are more concerned with the relative characteristics and roles of the individual and environment. However, these may all be at work in any given developmental process and across developmental processes over time.

Sensitive or Critical Periods

The concept of sensitive or critical periods encompasses the idea that individuals may have different possible developmental trajectories given the timing of an environmental experience or lack thereof (Bornstein, 1989). If a process, structure, or function is undeveloped at the time of the onset of an environmental experience, the experience may induce or prevent emergence of that process, structure, or function. Without any experience, the process, structure, or function will not develop. If a process, structure, or function is partially developed, experience may maintain, attune, facilitate or suppress further development. If a process, structure, or function is more fully developed, experience could maintain it, or lack of effective experience could eventuate in loss.

If an aspect of development is subject to a critical period, which could be also called an "all-or-nothing" period, this means that there is a period of growth when something specific must occur (or not occur) if development is to proceed normally. Research findings indicate that there are few truly critical periods in human development in which experience or lack thereof will eventuate in a permanent alteration of a typical developmental trajectory. Most of these appear to be in prenatal development and will be described in relevant sections below.

If an aspect of development is subject to a sensitive period, this means that there are times in an individual's development of heightened sensitivity to certain environmental stimuli when a particular experience (or lack of it) has a more pronounced effect on the organism than does the experience at another time. Research supports sensitive periods in several aspects of human development in which experiences can influence developmental trajectories, with the possibility that future experience can further influence that trajectory becoming smaller or requiring more profound experiences. Evidence of such sensitive periods will be described and presented in relevant sections throughout this chapter.

Plasticity

Related to the concept of critical or sensitive periods is the concept of malleability or plasticity. *Plasticity* can be defined as sensitivity to the environment engendered by experience, including the capacity of immature systems to take on different functions as a result of experience and the degree to which a developing structure or behavior is modifiable due to experience (Lewis & Mayes, 2012). This addresses the extent and under what conditions it is possible for the course of development to change as the result of intervention or accident. Certain aspects of development are more or less fixed and difficult to change, whereas other aspects of development are relatively malleable and easy to change. In the former, the environment may have less influence, or less influence over time, whereas in the latter, the environment can have great influence. However, the notion of sensitive periods also implies that the malleability or plasticity of some aspects of development changes. In other words, it becomes harder to change some aspects over time.

Continuity and Discontinuity

The concept of continuity involves the notion that development is a gradual, continuous process of change, whereas the concept of discontinuity involves the notion that development is punctuated by periods of rapid change and sudden emergence of new forms of thought and behavior. Formal developmental theories that take a discontinuous approach are also called stage theories (Lerner, 1997).

Risk and Resilience

In human development, a risk is any characteristic that is associated with an elevated probability of an undesirable outcome. A risk factor is a predictor of an undesirable outcome in a population. The probabilities of such undesirable outcomes are established by studying groups of people. An individual described as at risk is a member of a group in which research has shown an elevated probability of the negative outcome under consideration. Resilience can be defined most broadly as "the capacity of a dynamic system to withstand or recover from significant challenges that threaten its stability, viability, or development" (Masten, 2011, p. 494). "In research on psychology or human development, resilience in individual people is usually the focus of concern, with an emphasis on the processes that may account for individual differences in patterns of adaptation, function, or development that occur during or following experiences that pose significant threats to the individual. As a domain of inquiry, resilience science in human development refers to the study of the processes of, capacity for, or pathways and patterns of positive adaptation during or following significant threats or disturbances" (Masten, 2011, p. 494).

Active and Passive Roles of Individual and Environment

Some developmental models are classified by whether they consider individual children or persons and the environment as passive or active agents in development. They can also be classified by the way in which they consider traits, the environment, and the interaction between the individual and the environment (Lewis & Mayes, 2012). In a model with a passive child and an active environment, the environment is viewed as controlling the child's behavior and development. Operant conditioning processes fall into this view. This may include behavior modification treatment or parent education or parent guidance programs that aim to alter maladaptive behavior and/or guide parent behavior to shape child behavior. In a model with an active child and a passive environment, the child is viewed as extracting and constructing his or her knowledge and world. Piaget's cognitive development theory fits within this framework, as the child needs the environment to provide input and construct knowledge, but the environment itself does not play a major role. Most dominant in current developmental science and practice is the model with an active child and an active environment. Many approaches fit this model, including transactional, epigenetic, bioecological, and more.

Major Developmental Theories

A developmental theory is a broad framework or set of principles and ideas that can be used to guide the collection and interpretation of a set of facts. A theory describes, explains, predicts behavior, and provides testable hypotheses.

Historical Theories

The major theories with elements addressing human development that dominated aspects of developmental science and practice in the earlier phases of the discipline include psychoanalytic and personality theories, learning theories, and cognitive-developmental theories.

Psychodynamic theories, including Freud's theory of psychosexual development and Erikson's theory of psychosocial development, are historically important but no longer serve as the underpinnings of current developmental science and practice. Learning theories, including behaviorism, classical and operant conditioning, and social learning theory continue to play a role in some aspects of developmental science and practice (e.g., Kazdin, 2001), but a more limited role pertaining to comprehensive developmental processes. The cognitive-developmental theory of Piaget (1954) continues to influence some aspects of current research and practice, though many of the specific propositions have been revised in the face of later research evidence and other propositions have been critiqued as insufficient to describe observed child development.

Piaget's Cognitive-Developmental Theory   Through detailed observations of his own three children and subsequent observations and interviews with other children, Piaget developed his stage theory and changed people's perceptions about the way in which children think about the world. Children's thinking is not less intelligent than adults', just different. According to Piaget, cognitive development is not governed by internal maturation or external teachings alone; instead, children are "little scientists" who actively construct their cognitive worlds through exploration, manipulation, and trying to make sense of their environment. As children develop from birth through adolescence, they undergo a process of decentralization from an undifferentiated, concrete, perceptual world to one that is increasingly conceptual and is able to be symbolically represented. Through adaptation, children build mental structures, called schemas (singular form—schema), to organize knowledge, adapt to the world, and adjust to new environmental demands. In the process of assimilation, individuals incorporate new information or experiences into an existing schema. For example, a child who has learned the word "dog" for a four-legged animal may refer to other animals such as cats, zebras, and elephants as "dogs." In the process of accommodation, individuals adjust their schema to take into account new information or experiences. Thus, a child learns to fine-tune his "dog" schema to only include animals that are four-legged, furry, and bark. By a mechanism called equilibration, children attempt to create a balance between assimilation and accommodation. The internal search for equilibrium is the motivation for change and helps to explain children's shift from one stage of thought to the next. As a result of these processes, children undergo cognitive change.

Piaget proposed four stages of cognitive development (sensorimotor, preoperational, concrete operational, and formal operational), with each stage built on the preceding one and representing a qualitative difference in understanding. An individual undergoes the stages in a fixed order, and change does not result from more knowledge or experience but rather due to the pursuit of equilibrium. During the sensorimotor stage (birth to 2 years), infants learn about themselves and the environment by coordinating their sensory experiences with physical actions. Initially, the child uses primarily reflexive behaviors and by the end of the stage is able to employ complex sensorimotor patterns and simple symbols. The sensorimotor stage is further divided into six substages. During the simple reflexes substage (birth to 1 month), a newborn uses reflexes such as rooting and sucking to coordinate sensation and action. At first, the newborn will only suck if there is a nipple placed in his mouth. Within a month, he may start to suck when a bottle or nipple is near his mouth, initiating an action that resembles a reflex, and actively organizing his experience. In the second substage, first habits and primary circular reactions (1–4 months), the infant coordinates sensation with two types of schema: habits (reflexes that are separated from the eliciting stimulus) and primary circular reactions (creation of an event that initially occurred by chance). Thus, an infant may suck even when a bottle is not present or try to suck on his fingers again after accidentally sucking them when they were placed near his mouth (his fingers may not cooperate because he does not have the coordination yet). The primary focus remains on the infant's body and he does not look to the environment. During the third substage, secondary circular reactions (4–8 months), an infant moves beyond self-preoccupation and becomes more object oriented. An infant may accidentally shake a rattle and then repeat the action because he is interested in and satisfied with the sound it makes. In the fourth substage, coordination of secondary circular reactions (8–12 months), an infant's actions become outwardly directed and intentional. He is able to coordinate touch and vision to make hand–eye movements. Thus, he may simultaneously visually examine a rattle while exploring it tactilely. He may intentionally use a stick to bring an attractive toy within reach. During this substage, an infant becomes more capable of recognizing object permanence, the understanding that objects continue to exist even if they cannot be seen, heard, or touched. In tertiary circular reactions, novelty, and curiosity (12–18 months), the fifth substage, infants become interested in the various properties of objects and the things that can happen to them. They continually experiment to explore the results. For example, an infant may choose a block to throw, spin, slide across the ground, or hit another object to observe the consequences of these actions. During the sixth substage of the sensorimotor period, internalization of schemata (18–24 months), an infant develops the ability to use simple symbols and form lasting mental representations. This allows an infant to think about concrete events and represent them by using internalized sensory images or words. For example, a child who has never thrown a temper tantrum before sees another child throw a tantrum. He retains a memory of this event and throws a tantrum himself the next day. In short, the key cognitive-developmental achievement of the sensorimotor period is the ability to create symbolic representations of experiences and the environment.

The second stage of cognitive development in Piaget's theory is the preoperational stage (2–7 years). At this stage, children use mental representations, such as words, images, and drawings, to understand the world and begin to reason. A child is not yet able to complete operations, or reversible mental actions that are not preformed physically, such as mentally adding or subtracting numbers. This stage is dominated by egocentric thinking and magical beliefs. The preoperational stage is divided further into two substages, symbolic function and intuitive thought. During the symbolic function substage (2–4 years), a young child is able to mentally represent an object that is not present as evidenced by scribbling, language use, and pretend play. The three mountains task is used to demonstrate egocentrism, or the inability to differentiate one's own perspective from someone else's. A child and a doll sit on opposite sides of a model displaying three mountains of different sizes. When asked to point to the picture of the way the doll sees the three mountains, the child in the preoperational stage points to the picture showing his own perspective, demonstrating that he cannot take the doll's point of view. During this stage, a young child believes in animism, that inanimate objects have lifelike characteristics and are able to perform actions. Therefore, according to a child with preoperational thought, a car is not starting because it is sick or tired, and a piece of furniture must be punished because it is naughty since it hurt the child when he ran into it. A child in the second substage, intuitive thought (4–7 years), begins to use simple reasoning and asks "why" questions to figure out how the world works.

In the concrete operational stage (7–11 years), the third stage in Piaget's cognitive-developmental theory, children are able to reason logically in specific or concrete examples. Due to their ability to mentally reverse actions, they understand conservation and their thinking is no longer controlled by centration, focusing on one aspect to the exclusion of all others. Conservation is the understanding that changing the appearance of an object or substance does not change its basic properties. The beaker test is a task that demonstrates conservation. A child is shown two identical beakers with the same amount of liquid in each. As the child watches, an experimenter pours the liquid from one beaker into another beaker that is taller and thinner than the two identical beakers. When asked which beaker has more liquid, a child in the preoperational stage will point to the taller and thinner beaker, whereas a child in the concrete operational stage will understand that the amount of liquid has not changed in the transfer.

The fourth and final stage of Piaget's theory is the formal operational stage (appears between 11 and 15 years of age and continues through adulthood). This stage is characterized by abstract, idealistic, and logical thinking. Instead of relying on trial and error, individuals are capable of hypothetical-deductive reasoning, the ability to develop hypotheses and determine systematically the best way to solve a problem and arrive at a conclusion.

Although Piaget's theory has greatly influenced the current field of children's cognitive development, several points of criticism have been presented as a result of findings from subsequent research. Cognitive development is less abrupt and stagelike and more gradual and continuous than Piaget thought. Cognitive development is not necessarily a general process and new skills in one area may not translate to new skills in another area. Moreover, Piaget may have underestimated children's competence and overestimated adolescents' cognitive abilities. In particular, Piaget placed an over-reliance on the physical and motor skills of infants, and ignored learning through sensation, perception, and environmental input. Methodologically, Piaget required children to perform complex tasks and answer complex questions. When children are given real-world, less abstract tasks to complete, they are generally more successful at an earlier age than Piaget predicted. Finally, Piaget did not consider the influence of the environment, individual differences, cultural variations, and social trends on children's cognitive development. Neo-Piagetians (e.g., Case, 1987, 1999) believe that Piaget's theory needs considerable revision and place a greater emphasis on children's use of attention, memory, speed, and strategy to process information.

Vygotsky's Sociocultural Cognitive Theory   Like Piaget, Vygotsky believed children actively construct their knowledge and understanding of the world (Vygotsky, 1978). However, Vygotsky's theory emphasizes the importance of social interaction and cultural context in shaping children's thinking. Instruction plays a major role in cognitive development, as reflected in the concept of the zone of proximal development (ZPD). The ZPD encompasses the tasks that are too difficult for a child to complete on his own but can be learned and accomplished with the guidance of an adult or a more skilled child. The lower limit of the ZPD is the level of skill a child has while working independently and the upper limit is the level of additional capability with the assistance of an instructor. Scaffolding refers to the changing level of support an instructor provides as she adjusts to a child's current performance level based on his increasing skill level. Thus, in the beginning of a lesson, a teacher may use a great amount of direct instruction and offer less guidance as the student's competence increases. Some criticisms of Vygotsky's theory include not enough specifics about age-related changes, an inadequate explanation of how changes in socioemotional abilities translate to cognitive development, and an overemphasis on the role of language in thinking. However, some aspects of Vygotsky's ideas continue to be influential and shaped later thinking and research. For example, Rogoff (1990) drew on and expanded Vygotsky's ideas in developing her concept of guided participation in sociocultural activity as contributing to cognitive development.

Contemporary Theories

More recent approaches to development are described below. These approaches continue to shape current research and practice.

Bioecological Systems Theory   The bioecological systems theory (or ecological systems) proposed by Bronfenbrenner (Bronfenbrenner, 1979, 1986; Bronfenbrenner & Morris, 2006) emphasizes the influence of environmental factors and systems on individual development. Bronfenbrenner described four types of

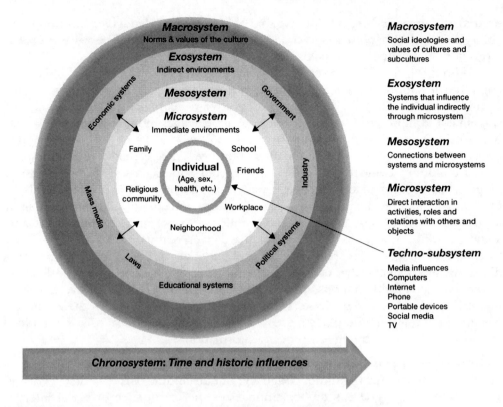

FIGURE 4.1   Bronfenbrenner's bioecological model of human development.

ecological systems nested within each other: the microsystem, mesosystem, exosystem, and macrosystem (see Figure 4.1). The individual is in the center, and the
biological influences of factors such as sex, age, and health that affect development
are considered. The microsystem includes all the settings with which the individual
directly interacts as well as the contexts that directly influence development, including family, peers, the school, and neighborhood. The individual actively constructs
his experiences in these settings and is not a passive participant. The mesosystem
consists of the connections among microsystems, such as the relationship between
the family and school or the family and peers. For example, a child's education and
experiences in school may be influenced by his parents' interactions with teachers
and the extent of their involvement with the school. The exosystem includes contexts within which the individual does not directly interact but has indirect influences on development. Thus, there may be increased parental conflict and changes
in interaction patterns with a child when a working mother receives a promotion
that necessitates more travel. The macrosystem describes the impact of the broader
social context in which an individual lives, including the laws, policies, and ideologies of that culture on development. For example, changes to welfare in 1996
resulted in more mothers returning to work and spending less time with their children as well as influenced child care policies and the quality of child care received
by welfare recipients. The chronosystem represents the developmental patterns
and transitions of the individual across time as well as the sociohistorical conditions of that time. Thus, parental divorce is a major transition that affects the child

in both negative and positive ways because the family initially experiences instability but tends to become more stable after about 2 years. These systems continue to function, albeit within different contexts, throughout adulthood. Here, microsystem settings in which individuals are proximally involved typically include their place of work, worship, and adult peer-group interactions. Though the specific nature of changes within the exo- and macrosystems may evolve over time from childhood to adulthood within the chronosystem, the theoretical structure of these influences remains stable over time.

Bronfenbrenner's bioecological systems theory is prevalent because it considers both the micro and macro influences on individual development and gives attention to the interactions among environmental systems. Two major criticisms of the theory include insufficient focus on both biological and cognitive factors, though later formulations presented theoretical innovations in form and content (Bronfenbrenner & Morris, 2006).

Dynamic Systems Theory   The dynamic systems theory of Esther Thelen (Thelen & Smith, 2006) posits that the child's mind, body, and physical and social worlds form an integrated system that guides mastery of new skills. Any change in one context or domain of development can disrupt the entire system, prompting a reorganization that leads to more adaptive functioning. In this model, *dynamic* refers to the concept that a change in any part disrupts the current organism–environment relationship, which leads to active reorganization so that the system's components work together again, but this time in a more complex, effective way. Development is viewed as nonlinear; rather, an image often used to visualize this perspective is one of development as a web, with processes and skills branching out. Dynamic processes are central during transitions.

For example, a child's first steps are highly influenced by physical maturation, as the child's muscles strengthen and balance improves. The change from nonwalker to walker is more than a physical change, however, in that it can disrupt the entire system within the child and in her broader environment. This prompts a reorganization that leads to more adaptive functioning. A newly walking child receives new perceptual and cognitive input, as she now has an upright perspective, can touch, see, and hear more, and this new input will then allow her to adjust her understanding of the world. Moreover, a new walker can reach something of interest on her own power, rather than having to passively wait or signal to others where she desires to go. This ability can reinforce her active interest in the world, her motivation to explore, and increase excitement and a sense of achievement. In the environment, a newly walking child prompts both praise and excitement and nervousness and anxiety in the child's parents or caregivers. Parents love to see their child's first steps, but then also worry about injury, reorganize the home with stair gates and dangerous items placed out of reach, and so forth. Parents may also become more restrictive of their child out of concern; thus the parent–child interactive system is also disrupted. Over time, as the transition to walking settles down, the child's system and her environment will adapt and reach a new, different normalcy, one that now supports the child's next developmental processes.

A number of developmentally salient transitions also emerge in adolescence and adulthood, including the transition from high school to a college or work setting, the transition from employment to retirement, and the transition from home to assisted living or nursing home care. Each of these transitions represents a significant strain on the motivational and adaptational resources of the individual. At each of these transitional phases, individuals are challenged by changes in the environment to call on personal and social resources (i.e., coping skills, and emotional and instrumental support from others) in order to adjust to their new contexts. Failure to successfully adapt to change has been associated with a number of poor developmental outcomes in adolescence and adulthood, including behavior problems, school dropout, anxiety, and depression.

Life Span Theory   In an effort to explain the positive behavioral adaptations that individuals evince in response to age-related losses, Paul Baltes and colleagues introduced the Selective Optimization with Compensation (SOC) model, which describes three factors critical to successful aging across the life span (Baltes, Reese, & Lipsitt, 1980; Freund & Baltes, 1998). These action-based processes include the selection of desired goals or strategies that one chooses to pursue, optimization of actions and abilities that can be used to achieve such goals, and compensation, or adjustment of goals and strategies in response to losses in capacity (Baltes & Baltes, 1990). The main premise of this theory is that while there is marked variability in both intra- and interindividual developmental trajectories, the utilization of SOC helps to mitigate the effects of losses in functioning, while providing the basis for adaptive functioning and positive adjustment. Baltes's SOC model is a life span developmental theory that describes the structure and direction of individual development over time, as well as a framework for understanding variations in the process of successful aging. Rather than viewing successful development as having a single path with a lone outcome for "normal" development (as in Freud's psychoanalytic theory), life span developmental psychology posits that a wide range of developmental pathways can lead to numerous positive developmental outcomes (Baltes, 1987). The changes that occur over time as we age involve a wide range of domains (i.e., are multidimensional), including social, emotional, and physical growth, that change over time to varying degrees (and are thus multi-directional; Baltes, 1987). SOC theory accounts for both age-graded (i.e., physical and cognitive transformations that occur in nearly all humans as they age) and non-normative changes (i.e., happen to select individuals, such as disease or mental disorder) that characterize growth and decline over time. Although individuals are likely to experience age-related declines in motor and cognitive abilities over time, including difficulty walking and decrements in processing speed and working memory, there are nonetheless opportunities to compensate for these losses at each stage in life. In adulthood, individuals show a propensity to increasingly rely on external aids such as reading glasses, note-taking, and mobility devices in order to maintain a stable level of everyday functioning.

Domains of Development

In this section, we review the major domains of development: physical development, cognitive development, and socioemotional development. The borders between these developmental domains are fuzzy rather than firm. Physical development includes genetic, neurocognitive, hormonal, motor, sensory and perceptual, and health and nutrition. Cognitive development includes sensation, perception, attention, and memory; milestones of skills, knowledge, and achievements; language development; theory of mind (ToM); and more. Social–emotional development includes self-concept; emotions; regulation; temperament; stress; attachment; moral development; prosocial behavior and aggression; social skills and relationships with siblings, friends, and peers; and identity.

We begin first with a section on prenatal development for which domains of development are highly intertwined. We then present sections on physical, cognitive, and social–emotional development.

Prenatal Development, Birth, and the Neonatal Period

Meiosis and Mitosis   Reproductive cells, or gametes, reproduce by meiosis. Meiosis produces cells with only half of a set of chromosomes, or half of the genetic material of the parent cell, producing sperm or ova. "Crossing over" is the first phase of meiosis, in which each of the 23 pairs of chromosomes line up, wrap around each other, and exchange genetic material. Reshuffling takes place in the second phase of meiosis, in which some of the mother's chromosomes align with the father's chromosomes and vice versa. The cell then divides into two, and the chromosomes with new, unique combinations of genetic material produce duplicates of themselves. Finally, these cells divide, producing four cells with 23 chromosomes each. Chromosomal abnormalities are often caused by mutations during meiosis. Down syndrome is the most common example.

At conception, the ovum and sperm unite to form a new cell called a zygote. During ordinary cell reproduction, or mitosis, a cell divides into a copy of itself. Each resulting cell receives a full copy of all 46 chromosomes. As the zygote travels toward the uterus, it begins to differentiate into cells with specialized roles, with the outer cells to become the placenta and the inner cells the embryo. Once the zygote reaches the uterus, implantation may occur. Sex differentiation begins at conception, with girls having two X chromosomes and boys an X and a Y chromosome.

Periods of Prenatal Development   After implantation, the embryo's cells form specialized layers in the embryonic period. The ectoderm will become the skin, nerves, and sense organs. The mesoderm will become the muscle, bones, circulatory system, and some organs. The endoderm will become the digestive system, lungs, urinary tract, and glands. During the embryonic period, the basic structure of a human being appears and organs begin to function. Neurogenesis begins; neurons are produced in the embryo's primitive neural tube, migrate to form the major parts of the brain, and then, once in place, they differentiate, establishing their unique functions by extending fibers and forming synaptic connections (see paragraph on brain development). By the end of the embryonic period, all the major organ and body parts have formed.

During the fetal period, the primitive organ and body parts develop and grow. Neurogenesis is typically complete by the end of the sixth month, and the brain begins to organize itself, allowing some neurons to die off while others make new connections.

Environmental Impact During Prenatal Development   The impact of the environment on prenatal development can be significant. The quality of maternal nutrition impacts the health of the embryo and fetus. Malnutrition in early pregnancy, particularly lack of folic acid, increases risk for birth defects such as spina bifida or anencelapathy. New evidence also suggests that prenatal folic acid deficiency is associated with increased risk for autism spectrum disorders (Surén et al., 2013). Malnutrition later in pregnancy is associated with lower birth weight, although the effects can be overcome by quality nutrition after birth in a stable, supportive environment. High stress in pregnancy increases the risk for premature birth.

A teratogen is any substance that can have a negative impact on fetal development. An agent is teratogenic if it has the potential for producing congenital malformations or problems depending on the dosage and timing of exposure during pregnancy (Brent, 2004). Exposure during a sensitive period may alter anatomy or function irreversibly. Although some environmental factors have immediate effects, others have sleeper effects that do not emerge until later in development.

The placenta protects the fetus from many bacteria but not viruses. Rubella contracted during the first 3 months of pregnancy can be devastating for the fetus. About one in four infants affected with HIV develops AIDS symptoms shortly after birth. An HIV-positive mother can protect her fetus by taking AZT and other drugs that slow the HIV duplication. Drugs with known teratogenic effects include corticosteroids, lithium therapy, retinoids, thalidomide, some anticonvulsants, and some hormone therapies, as well as nicotine/smoking. Chemicals with known teratogenic effects include carbon monoxide, lead, mercury, polychlorinated biphenyls (PCBs), and the insecticide DDT (dichlorodiphenyltrichloroethane). Controlled substances with teratogenic potential include alcohol, cocaine, and heroine (Brent, 2004). Fetal alcohol syndrome (FAS) is a pattern of mental disabilities and facial abnormalities found in infants with alcoholic mothers. FAS babies typically have some degree of impaired general intelligence, short attention span, worse language-based memory and poor functional communication skills, and emotional/behavioral disorders (Chasnoff, Wells, Telford, Schmidt, & Messer, 2010). Centers for Disease Control (CDC) studies have shown that 0.2 to 1.5 cases of FAS occur for every 1,000 live births in certain areas of the United States. Other studies using different methods have estimated the rate of FAS to be higher, at 0.5 to 2.0 cases per 1,000 live births. Rates of fetal alcohol spectrum disorders (FASDs), which are a group of conditions that can occur in a person whose mother drank alcohol during pregnancy, are less well known, but scientists believe that there are at least three times as many cases of FASDs as FAS (Centers for Disease Control and Prevention, 2012).

Birth Complications Complications during labor and delivery can occur even in healthy pregnancies. There are several risks to the neonate, or newborn, which can have lasting effects, some of which can be ameliorated or prevented with assessment and treatment.

Some birth complications are positional. The vertex, head-down, back-facing position is ideal for childbirth; other positions such as a breech or hammock position may be problematic and warrant a cesarean section. Anoxia is one of the most significant birth complications. It can be caused by the umbilical cord being pinched, or because of a placental abruption or placenta previa. Short-term anoxia is usually not a problem, but long-term oxygen loss can cause brain damage.

Preterm birth is one of the highest risk factors for child development. Full-term pregnancies are normally between 38 and 40 weeks; newborns born before 37 weeks are considered premature and are at risk of complications, including immature lungs, respiratory distress, and digestive problems.

Low-birth-weight babies weigh less than 5.5 pounds, and very-low-birth-weight is below 2.5 pounds. The reasons for preterm birth are numerous, including structural abnormalities to the uterus, maternal age, lack of spacing between a previous pregnancy, and maternal or fetal distress. Preterm babies often suffer from respiratory distress syndrome (RDS) and are vulnerable to infection. If preterm newborns are in a medical facility, they usually are fed intravenously or by feeding tube, and are at risk for brain hemorrhaging.

The Apgar assessment is given to newborns at 1 minute after birth and 5 minutes after birth if delivered in the care of a trained health professional. The test scores the infant on appearance, pulse, grimace, activity, and respiration, with a score of 0 to 2 for each that is then summed. Scores above 7 indicate a healthy baby, and below 4 indicate a baby in critical condition. The Neonatal Behavioral Assessment Scale uses reflexes and social interaction to assess the newborn's overall well-being, including motor capabilities, state changes, and central nervous system (CNS) stability (Brazelton & Nugent, 1995).

Failure to thrive (FTT) is a disorder of impaired growth (lack of weight gain). It can happen in older children who are seriously ill or undernourished, but it is most common and most dangerous during the earliest months and over the first 3 years. FTT can be caused by an organic underlying health problem that means the baby cannot obtain or make use of adequate nutrition, such as anemia or thyroid problems. Nonorganic FTT may be psychological or social, associated with the child or caregiver or the dyad.

Physical and Motor Development
This section on physical and motor development includes the genetic, neurocognitive, hormonal, motor, sensory and perceptual, and health and nutrition aspects of development.

Genetics   Detailed explanation of genetics is beyond the scope of this chapter. However, a key concept of genetics in developmental science is epigenesis, or the gradual process of increasing differentiation and complexity in an individual due to an interaction between his or her heredity and the environment. Genes affect development through gene expression, or through the proteins they "instruct" the body to produce. Gene expression depends on both the genetic instruction code and on the context in which the genetic instructions occur. Probabilistic epigenesis is the probability that a trait, characteristic, or behavior will develop depending on certain conditions in the environment in a reciprocal process (Gottlieb, 2007).

Brain Development   Similar to details of genetics, the details of neurological and neurocognitive functions are beyond the scope of this chapter. However, the development of the brain and CNS includes important processes of synaptogenesis, or the development of connections (synapses) between neurons through the growth of axons and dendrites, and synaptic pruning, or the process of elimination of unused and unnecessary synapses. Both of these processes, which begin prenatally and flourish throughout the early months and even years, are fundamental to plasticity and the degree to which the developing brain and CNS are modifiable due to experience. Experience plays a central role in the selection, maintenance, and strengthening of connections among many neurons. If a neuron is used, it forms more synapses or connections with other cells and becomes functional. Without stimulation and the opportunity to function, neurons are unlikely to establish or maintain many connections with other neurons. Thus, brain development is experience based. Two types of brain plasticity are experience-expectant processes, whereby some neurons grow and differentiate rapidly at about the time they can be expected to receive relevant stimulation with overproduction of synapses in expectation that a particular sensory stimulus will occur (for example, parts of the visual cortex involved in depth or pattern perception develop quite rapidly shortly before and after birth); and experience-dependent processes, which involve the active formation of new synapses based on individual experience, thus allowing for unpredictable opportunities for learning (Greenough, Black, & Wallace, 1987).

Hypothalamic–Pituitary–Adrenal Axis   The hypothalamic–pituitary–adrenal (HPA) axis is an important regulatory system that controls the levels of the stress hormone cortisol that are released in the body. The body's release of cortisol as a direct response to acute stress is an adaptive response that typically elevates the individual's ability to respond. However, sustained levels of cortisol are typically harmful, as the HPA axis may become dysregulated and lead to heightened stress and anxiety, as well as impaired cognitive, behavioral, and social functioning, particularly in the brain systems responsible for memory and emotion regulation. This system is of particular importance in early childhood development, when individuals develop expectations of the levels of stress that they will encounter in their daily lives. The consistent presence of environmentally induced stressors during childhood, including neglectful and abusive parenting, can also lead to greater susceptibility to genetic predispositions to a range of developmental disorders. Evidence in animal and human studies has revealed that sustained separation or abuse from one's primary caregiver can lead to hyperactivity in the HPA axis, resulting in elevated cortisol levels. Consistent, emotionally available parenting, on the other hand, can promote healthy HPA functioning and provide the individual with the ability to properly regulate his or her stress response systems.

Malnutrition   Malnutrition is the underlying contributing factor in over one third of all child deaths, making children more vulnerable to severe diseases, according to the World Health Organization (WHO, 2012). Malnourished children are more likely to contract a disease, and more likely to experience severe effects of disease. Children suffering from disease have reduced appetites and absorb less nutrition, in a vicious cycle of illness and delayed growth. Malnourishment and child mortality are linked to poverty, again in a vicious cycle. Poverty obviously contributes to malnourishment, but malnutrition and illness contribute to poverty by contributing to lower cognitive development, lower school achievement, reduced wages, and loss of income due to illness.

Motor Development   Motor development involves the development of the capacity for movement, action, and coordination of one's limbs, as well as the development of strength, posture control, balance, and perceptual skills, particularly that made possible by changes in the nervous system and muscles. Fine motor development includes the development of skills involving the smaller muscle groups, including the ability to manipulate small objects, transfer objects from hand to hand, and various hand–eye coordination tasks. Gross motor development includes the development of skills related to simple, large muscle group actions, including lifting one's head, rolling over, sitting up, balancing, crawling, and walking.

Motor development is an important part of developmental science and understanding. First, behavior *is* movement, including visual exploration, manipulation of objects, and navigation of the environment, and movements are a medium for making inferences about thoughts, perceptions, and intentions that are not directly observable, especially in infants and nonverbal individuals. Second, adaptive control of movement is coupled with perception, and provides new opportunities for learning (Adolph & Berger, 2005).

Motor skill development changes throughout the life span, but the period of the most rapid change is in the earliest months and years. Observations of infants and children show that motor development follows a fairly predictable pattern, with these patterns denoted by parents and practitioners in charts of norms of motor milestones including sitting, standing, and walking (see Table 4.1). Norms are average outcomes, not actual or ideal ones. Individual differences refer to variation among persons on a given characteristic. There is a wide range of timing in achieving these milestones, which is considered "normal," and cultural and familial expectations and practices can influence these averages. However, for many years, it was assumed that these milestones unfolded universally along predictable timetables because of maturation, but the traditional maturational account could not explain how children move from one skill level to another. More recent research from a dynamic approach investigates the changes that generate the shift into new skills, often by employing novel experimental tasks to explore how new skills, and thus also "universal" milestones, are learned through a child's process of exploring and selecting a wider range of possible behaviors and configurations to meet a goal. Motivation to accomplish a task is thus assumed to be the driving force for change in this domain, rather than genetic instructions and biological maturation. Thus, motor development studies demonstrate that each component in the developing system is both cause and product in a dynamic process, even if on different levels and time scales, where task motivates behavior, behavior enables new tasks, and biomechanical factors and changes both limit and facilitate movement (Thelen & Smith, 2006).

Directionality refers to how body proportions change, and somewhat to improvements in control and motor development. Change is generally *cephalocaudal* (from head to tail) and *proximodistal* (moves from the center of the body outward). The brain develops more rapidly, which regulates growth and development and influences basic drives (i.e., hunger and thirst). Gross motor development usually follows a pattern. Children gain control over the head, hands, and upper body before the lower body, and generally large muscles develop before smaller ones. Similarly, regions nearer the trunk tend to grow and become more differentiated earlier than those more peripheral. For example, children typically gain control of their arms and legs much earlier than their fingers and toes. Gross motor development is the foundation for developing skills in other areas (such as fine motor skills).

Early motor behaviors are marked by "rhythmical stereotypies," or repeated sequences of motions performed with no apparent goal. As infants make gains in movement, they show progress in coordinating postural control (the ability to maintain an upright orientation to the environment), locomotion (the ability to maneuver through space), and manual control (the ability to manipulate objects).

Milestones in postural control and locomotion are noted in Table 4.1. Notably, crawling is no longer considered a true "milestone" in the sense that there are many recognized crawling postures other than the traditional hands-and-knees position, and that a child can skip crawling with no consequences for motor development. In fact, rates of hands-and-knees crawling are dropping, which may be associated with the "Back-to-Sleep" public health campaign, which began in 1994 and recommends that infants be put on their back to sleep to reduce the occurrence of sudden infant death syndrome (SIDS). As more parents and caregivers follow this advice (and overall SIDS rates have declined by more than 50%), infants do not spend as much time on their fronts and do not develop as much arm strength and practice in that position.

Progression in manual control includes reaching, grasping, and writing. Reaching progresses from "prereaching" with no real intent or coordination between reaching and grasping to ballistic reaching in which the trajectory is not modified once reaching has begun until the hand contacts an object through guided reaching with more coordination between visual cues and motor movements. Grasping

TABLE 4.1   Percentiles and Mean in Months for Six Gross Motor Milestones

MOTOR MILESTONE	MEAN (SD)	AGE IN MONTHS		
		5TH PERCENTILE	50TH PERCENTILE	95TH PERCENTILE
Sitting without support	6.0 (1.1)	4.3	5.9	8.0
Standing with assistance	7.6 (1.4)	5.5	7.4	10.1
Hands-and-knees crawling	8.5 (1.7)	6.1	8.3	11.3
Walking with assistance	9.2 (1.5)	6.9	9.0	11.8
Standing alone	11.0 (1.9)	8.1	10.8	14.4
Walking alone	12.1 (1.8)	9.4	12.0	15.3

Source: WHO Multicentre Growth Reference Study Group (2006).

progresses from an ulnar–palmar grasp technique, pressing objects against the palm, around 5 or 6 months, to the pincer grasp, where the thumb and index finger can work independently of the other fingers, giving infants the fine dexterity useful for eating, manipulating objects, and, eventually, writing.

Sensory and Perceptual Development   Preferential looking or sucking and habituation paradigms are used to study newborn and infant sensory and perceptual skills and development. In a preference paradigm, two stimuli are presented side by side or alternating, and infant behavior is measured to determine preference. For example, a neonate's sucking amplitude, measured with a pacifier wired to a computer, changes when presented with the scent of her own mother's breast milk compared to that of another mother. Similarly, newborns look longer at high-contrast patterns than at indistinct patterns. In the case of two stimuli that may evoke no particular preference in an infant, in which looking time or other behaviors may be equal across two different stimuli, the habituation paradigm can be used. Habituation has occurred when the response to a stimulus decreases when the stimulus is repeatedly presented (i.e., the assumption is that habituation is similar to boredom). Dishabituation occurs when the response to a stimulus increases with presentation of a novel change in the stimulus. The most frequently employed response is infant looking time, though sucking and other behaviors have been used as well. If an infant dishabituates to presentation of a new stimulus, such as a different face or a new color, it can be concluded that he perceives the difference.

From such studies, there is evidence that the five senses develop at different rates. Hearing, touch, taste, and smell are well developed at birth. Sight is least well developed, with different aspects of vision developing over the first few months. There is some evidence of limited color vision by about 2 months and depth perception by 4 months beginning with sensitivity to kinetic cues, then binocular cues, and then pictorial cues. Visual acuity reaches near-adult levels by about 6 months of age.

Sensation and perception are tied to learning. Perception of objects and events that stimulate many senses at once is multimodal perception. Learning is enhanced by multimodal perception. Cross-modal perception is shown when infants demonstrate recognition of an object with one sense when only previously encountered with another, such as recognizing by sight a pacifier only previously experienced by touch through sucking, or recognizing when a sight and sound do not match, such as asynchronous sound and sight of a bouncing object. Early perception can aid with the beginnings of self-knowledge. For example, newborns may not show the rooting reflex if the stroke to their cheek comes from their own hand rather than another person or a pacifier. Although well organized at birth, additional improvements in perceptional abilities are associated with environmental input. For example, infants show a preference for looking at faces, but moreover, infants whose mothers smiled a lot showed more sensitivity to smiling faces in a laboratory setting.

Cognitive Development

Cognitive development includes attention and memory, milestones of skills, knowledge and achievements, language development, ToM, and more. In addition to the overall theoretical approaches to development described above, additional approaches to cognitive development are described in this section as well, where relevant.

The information-processing approach likens the brain to a computer, with cognitive development involving increasing capacity and efficiency of the brain's ability to process information in a continuous manner. Information is acquired (sensation and perception), selected (attention), stored (memory), and used to plan or solve problems.

Attention consists of focusing on some information and ignoring other information, avoiding distraction to achieve a goal.

Memory includes many elements and types. Working memory pertains to conscious, short-term representations of what a person is actually thinking about at a given time and may be brief, whereas long-term memory is potentially unlimited in capacity and duration. Long-term memory involves both recognition memory (association of an event or object with one previously experienced, generating a sense of familiarity) and recall memory (remembering a fact, event, or object not currently present, requiring retrieval of information from memory). Generic memory involves the development of scripts for familiar action sequences, episodic memory involves recall for events at a specific time and place, and autobiographical memory involves recall for events or episodes with personal meaning in one's life.

Children's early memories are more likely to last if they are of unique events, if the child was actively participating in the episode, and if the child talked about the episode with parents or others. Indeed, interaction with parents partially guides the development of memory. Over the course of the life span, semantic memory, or recall of general facts and knowledge, as well as procedural memory, or knowledge of how to perform routines and other organized actions, remains relatively stable. Although there are typically substantial variations in the rate and progression of memory decline with age, episodic memory tends to show the greatest age-related decreases in performance. Stress, anxiety, depression, and substance abuse are all associated with declines in memory performance in adulthood (Austin, Mitchell, & Goodwin, 2001; Davidson, Dixon, & Hultsch, 1991).

Language and Communication   Language development begins with the development of communication skills in infancy. The most intensive period for the development of speech and language skills is the first 3 years of life when the brain is developing most rapidly and with the greatest plasticity. The production and perception of sound (phonology) and learning of the meanings of words (semantics) and the grammatical set of shared rules (syntax) that allow people to communicate in a meaningful way must be mastered in infancy. There appears to be a sensitive period for speech and language development. If infants and young children are not exposed to language and the opportunity for communicative interaction during the earliest months and years, it will be more difficult to learn language later in childhood.

Receptive communication and language, or comprehension, nearly always precedes expressive language, or production. Early on, most infants produce prelinguistic vocalizations of cooing and babbling; even deaf babies babble, suggesting that auditory input is not necessary for babbling. However, communication skills develop best in a world rich with environmental input, the most important of which is the speech and language of others in regular communicative interaction. Prelinguistic vocalizations begin to differentiate with others' speech and feedback. All newborns universally babble all consonants, but by about 6 months of age, infants begin to sort out the speech sounds of the native language of the speakers in their environment, and infant babbles begin to favor the consonants found in that language and drop those not found in that language.

Children follow a natural progression for mastering the skills of language, but there is wide variation in the rate of language development. Individual differences are associated with many factors. Hearing loss may cause delay. Speech disorders such as apraxia may make it difficult to put sounds and syllables together in the correct order to form words. Children with specific language impairment (SLI) may not begin to talk until their third or fourth year.

Individual differences in language development are also highly associated with the child's environment. The fact that all normal children in normal environments learn to talk almost certainly reflects two critical ideas: humans have biological capacities for language acquisition and human social environments support language acquisition (Hoff, 2006). Variation in the support for language acquisition in the social environment is one of the key contributors to individual differences in language development. The socioeconomic status (SES) of a child's family is highly correlated with the quantity, variety, and quality of words children hear, as well as the amount of child-directed language. Children from high-SES families may hear three to four times as many words over the course of a week compared with children from families on public assistance (Hart & Risley, 1995), and the vocabulary of college-educated mothers is richer, the frequency of contingent replies is greater, and conversations are marked by fewer directives and more questions compared with high-school-educated mothers (Hoff, 2006). High-quality nonparental early care and education experiences are also associated with better child language outcomes (NICHD Early Child Care Research Network, 2002), yet again, children from low-SES families are less likely to have such high-quality child care experiences (Torquati, Raikes, Huddleston-Casas, Bovaird, & Harris, 2011). Early gaps in language proficiency can contribute to gaps in literacy and school readiness that may persist into and throughout the school years and beyond (Duncan et al., 2007).

Theory of Mind   Theory of Mind is an integrated, coherent understanding of what the mind is, how it works, and why it works that way. A child's awareness of her own and other people's thought processes and mental states must begin first with an understanding that others' thoughts are different from her own, and then can include an understanding that all people differ from one another in their thoughts, beliefs, desires, knowledge, and perspectives. A related concept is metacognition, or "thinking about thinking"; this is an understanding or knowledge that people have about their own thought processes. ToM develops rapidly in early childhood, and is correlated with cognitive and language abilities, as well as social interaction with adults and older children, including make-believe play.

Social–Emotional Development

Social–emotional development includes self-concept; emotions; regulation; temperament; stress; attachment; moral development; prosocial behavior and aggression; social skills; relationships with siblings, friends, and peers; identity; and more. As in the section on cognitive development, additional theoretical approaches to social–emotional development are described in this section as well where relevant, in addition to the overall theoretical approaches to development described at the beginning of this chapter.

Emerging Self-Concept   A major developmental task of childhood is for the individual to establish an understanding of who he or she is, or a unified conception of the self. Throughout childhood, physical, cognitive, and social demands place increasing importance on the role of self in relation to others. Allport (1955) conceived of this process of self-realization as a crucial component of development in infancy, in which the child establishes a sense of his or her own body, a nascent self-identity, and self-esteem. Recent research on the self-concept has divided this construct into two parts: knowledge components and evaluative components. Knowledge components describe aspects of the self that can be used to answer the question "Who am I?" and include understanding of one's physical and cognitive abilities, the roles that one plays in various social settings, and the goals that one wishes to pursue (Campbell et al., 1996). In contrast, evaluative components involve the self-assessment of the individual, and reflect one's self-esteem. As the individual develops from infancy through childhood and adolescence, he or she must continue to negotiate both individual and social demands on the self, and develop a self-concept across contexts (e.g., home, school, and peer settings). Once established, self-concept is a relatively stable characteristic in adolescence and adulthood. Discrepancies or conflicts in the conceptualization of self have been associated with poor outcomes, including depression, anxiety, and low self-esteem.

Gender Awareness, Identity, and Constancy   A person's sense of self as male or female, or gender identity, begins to develop very early with the ability in toddlerhood to discriminate between males and females and then label themselves and others by gender. However, gender identity is only a label at this age. It is not until age 6 or 7 that children show evidence of a sense of gender constancy, or the concept that gender is permanent and immutable (Ruble, Martin, & Berenbaum, 2006). In middle childhood, gender consciousness solidifies, functioning as an organizing framework for children's thoughts about themselves in relation to others, choices of friends and activities, and a guide for behavior. Gender plays a role in children's behavior and social interactions with adults and peers; similarities and differences in behaviors and interactions are discussed in the relevant topical sections below.

Emotional Development   Emotion can be defined as a complex, spontaneous process produced in response to some external or internal event involving physiological, expressive, and experiential components. Emotions function to organize and regulate behavior, influence cognitive processes, and initiate, maintain, or terminate interactions with others. Emotional development encompasses emotional expression, understanding, and regulation. Some emotional expressions, like an infant crying, are adaptive as they encourage others to respond. Emotions are a regulator of social interactions. Interactions that are characterized by synchrony— that are well timed, rhythmic, and appropriate—are positive, but only make up about 30% of infant–caregiver face-to-face interactions. The remainder of interactions, which are asynchronous, provide the infant the opportunity to adjust, learn rules, and repair interactions, which may give the infant a sense of mastery and agency (Tronick & Cohn, 1989).

Primary emotions are the first emotions that infants express, and appear to be universal and rooted in human biology. The six primary emotions are joy, surprise, sadness, anger, fear, and disgust; sometimes shyness and distress are included as primary emotions as well. Secondary emotions, sometimes called self-conscious or other-conscious emotions, involve evaluation of oneself and increase as the infant becomes self-aware. They do not emerge until the second or third year of life and depend on higher mental capacities, including an objective sense of the self as distinct from others, awareness of standards for behavior, and a sense of responsibility for one's actions. Secondary emotions include emotions like embarrassment, envy, guilt, or shame, but also positive emotions such as pride. Between 18 and 36 months of age, children begin to use language to describe feeling states and to label their own and others' emotions, which is associated with better social behaviors and more appropriate responses to emotions of friends.

Emotional understanding or comprehension begins with reading and recognizing emotional signals. Infants may imitate surprised, happy, and sad facial expressions as young as 3 days old, though there is some controversy about how to interpret such findings. Infants show preferences for facial expressions, preferring to look less at sad faces and more at angry faces compared to happy faces. Infants show resonating or matching of adult expressions, which may be related to mirror neurons, which are cells in the brain that are activated when we do something and when we see someone else do the same thing, like smile. Mirror neurons may play a role in empathy. Social referencing, or the use of others' emotional expressions to interpret ambiguous events, is another important part of social and emotional development.

There is evidence of cultural variation in the specifics of secondary emotions. There is also a role for adult instruction and family conversations about when to feel and how to express secondary emotions, expectations, and understanding of emotional experiences. When family relations are less positive, lacking warmth, supportiveness, or negotiation and reasoning, children's emotional understanding may be impaired. Children who have been abused or neglected may have difficulty discriminating among different emotions (Pollak, Klorman, Brumaghim, & Cicchetti, 2001). Children of mothers with chronic depression also have problems with emotional understanding and expression, but instead may experience more shame and guilt than other children (Zahn-Waxler & Radke-Yarrow, 1990).

Emotional regulation refers to the ability to adjust one's emotional state to a comfortable level of intensity in order to accomplish one's goals, and includes strategies and abilities to inhibit, enhance, maintain, and modulate emotional arousal (Eisenberg, Fabes, & Spinrad, 2006). Emotion regulation improves over early childhood, with associations with other benefits for interactions with other individuals and situations. Effortful control, a particular aspect of emotion regulation and of temperament, is the ability to withhold a dominant, reactive response in order to execute a more adaptive response and continue a social interaction and engage in planning (Rothbart & Bates, 2006). Effortful control is negatively associated with externalizing problems such as impulsive aggressive actions in response to frustration.

Temperament is an individual's behavioral style and characteristic way of responding, particularly to new or unfamiliar environments and situations. Research has demonstrated that infants are born with a temperament that remains moderately stable across the childhood years. There are both biological and environmental influences on temperament. Children may inherit physiological characteristics such as heart rate, cortisol level, and right frontal lobe activity that may bias them to a particular temperament. Twin and adoption studies suggest heredity has a moderate influence on temperament. Experience as well as developmental contexts such as gender and culture may also play a role in modifying temperament. It is important to focus on the goodness of fit, the match between a child's temperament and environmental demands, rather than emphasize the temperament classification itself. An awareness of goodness of fit has implications for parenting, including ensuring parents are sensitive and flexible to an infant's signals and needs, and structuring a child's environment so that children who are classified as difficult or slow to warm up have additional time to adjust to a crowded or noisy environment.

Through their research with the New York Longitudinal study, Thomas and Chess (1977, 1991) defined nine temperament traits in young children: activity, regularity, initial reaction, adaptability, intensity, mood, distractibility, persistence and attention span, and sensitivity. Based on their findings, 65% of infants could be classified into three temperament categories and 35% were unclassifiable. Easy children (40%) are generally in a positive mood, establish regular routines quickly, and adapt easily to new experiences. Difficult children (10%) often react negatively and cry frequently, have irregular routines, and are slow to accept change. Slow-to-warm-up children (15%) have low activity levels, are somewhat negative, and exhibit low mood intensity.

Other researchers have developed various temperament categories. Kagan (2002, 2008a, 2008b, 2010) classified temperament into two categories: uninhibited and inhibited. Uninhibited children are outgoing, extraverted, sociable, and bold. Inhibited children are timid, subdued, fearful, and shy around unfamiliar people (both adults and peers). Around 7 to 9 months of age, inhibited children begin to approach new and unfamiliar situations with avoidance, distress, apprehension, and passive affect. An inhibited temperament has been found to be relatively stable from infancy through about age 7 (Pfeifer, Goldsmith, Davidson, & Rickman, 2002).

Rothbart and Bates (2006) proposed that the structure of temperament can be characterized into three broad dimensions: extraversion/surgency, negative affectivity, and effortful control (self-regulation). Extraversion/surgency includes "positive anticipation, impulsivity, activity level, and sensation seeking" (Rothbart, 2004, p. 495). This temperament type parallels Kagan's uninhibited category. Negative affectivity includes "fear, frustration, sadness, and discomfort" (Rothbart, 2004, p. 495). Similar to Kagan's inhibited category, children who fit this temperament become easily distressed and often fuss and cry. Effortful control (self-regulation) includes "attentional focusing and shifting, inhibitory control, perceptual sensitivity, and low-intensity pleasure" (Rothbart, 2004, p. 495). Children with high effortful control do not allow their arousal level to become too high and have developed self-soothing strategies. Children with low effortful control have difficultly regulating their arousal and quickly become agitated and intensely emotional. Low effortful control in school-aged children has been correlated with externalizing problems, such as cheating, lying, being disobedient, and aggressiveness (Zhou, Lengua, & Wang, 2009).

In adulthood, lack of self-regulation is associated with overall difficulties in adaptation in various contexts, including interpersonal relationships and family and occupational settings. Poor self-regulatory skills are a hallmark of antisocial behavior and other psychiatric disorders, which typically emerge in adolescence, when a lack of self-control can lead to the violation of social norms and the personal liberties of others. The dual-processing theory describes the pathways by which adolescents tend to engage in higher frequency of risk behaviors compared to children and adults (Steinberg, 2008). According to this theory, risk behaviors can be explained, at least in part, to the rapid development of reward-seeking areas of the brain (located in the amygdala and orbitofrontal cortex), which mature prior to cognitive control mechanisms that promote effortful control and self-regulation. In adulthood, these cognitive control mechanisms (located in the lateral prefrontal cortex), broadly defined as executive functioning, include deliberate thinking, impulse control, and the strategic evaluation of risks and rewards, and provide the basis for individuals to make rational decisions to control their behavior (Steinberg, 2008).

Self-Regulation, Stress, and the Environment   Early environments can have a substantial impact on the developing child's ability to regulate his or her stress response system. Over time, dysregulation of the HPA axis can result in difficulties responding to stressful situations in adolescence and adulthood, as a consequence of either heightened or stunted HPA secretion of cortisol. Two settings that have consistently been found to influence children's stress response systems are the home rearing and out-of-home child care environments. In the home environment, abuse, maltreatment, and neglect from caregivers have all been shown to substantially impact children's cortisol levels. Chronic overactivation of the stress response system, such as that often experienced by children with inconsistent, abusive, or negligent caregivers can significantly impact child functioning, and has been linked to both major depression and recovery from disease in adults (Kudielka & Kirschbaum, 2005). Researchers have also shown that infants and toddlers placed in poor-quality childcare settings (i.e., unsafe environment, negative caregiving practices, and high child–staff ratios) display heightened levels of cortisol throughout the day (Vermeer & van IJzendoorn, 2006).

In adulthood, inability to regulate one's stress response is typically associated with two types of reactions. In the first, in which the stress response system is hyperactivated, individuals display more externalizing disorders, as well as antisocial behavior, in which individuals show a propensity to "act out" aggressively in response to heightened emotions. The second involves stress responses that are hypoactivated or "stunted," is associated with underdeveloped and passive responses to stress, as well as social withdrawal.

Attachment   Attachment is an emotional bond between a child and his primary caregivers that endures over the lifetime (Bowlby, 1969). Normal social and emotional development depends on the creation of a relationship with at least one primary caregiver (often the mother); multiple attachments may occur but one is always primary. Attachment occurs when adults are sensitive and responsive to a child's needs over a lasting period of time from 6 months to 2 years. Attachment behaviors include crying, smiling, babbling, sucking, grasping, and following, which help the infant remain in close proximity to the caregiver. Early attachment relationships become an internal working model for children, such that it affects their future relationships over the course of the life span via perceptions, emotions, and expectations about relationships. Attachment is one of the most significant developmental tasks and serves as a protective factor for growth and development under adverse circumstances.

Ainsworth (1979) operationalized Bowlby's attachment construct by developing the Strange Situation Procedure, a series of eight separations and reunions between a 12- to 18-month-old child and his caregiver, during which the child's amount of exploration, behaviors, and reactions are observed. Ainsworth used the Strange Situation to explore individual differences in patterns of attachment behavior and identified three major attachment types (see Table 4.2): secure, avoidant, and ambivalent/resistant. A fourth attachment type, disorganized/disoriented, was added by Main in 1996. About 65% of children in the general population are securely attached and the remaining 35% are divided among the insecure attachment categories. Table 4.2 provides typical child and caregiver behaviors displayed during the separations and reunions during the Strange Situation for each attachment classification (Bornstein & Lamb, 2002).

There are several points of criticism for attachment research: the way it was conducted for many years, the Strange Situation Procedure, and the associated attachment classifications. The characteristics of a healthy attachment are not universal and cultural variations have been observed. The most frequent classification of infants in the United States is a secure attachment; however, among insecurely attached children, German infants are more likely and Japanese infants are less likely to display avoidant attachment than U.S. infants. German children's attachment behaviors may be categorized as avoidant because German caregivers encourage independence. Moreover, Japanese infants may demonstrate a resistant attachment because these children are rarely cared for by anyone but their mothers and may become more stressed by a stranger than U.S. children. Furthermore, the Strange Situation has been criticized because children's attachment behaviors are observed in an unfamiliar, laboratory setting instead of in a natural environment such as the home. The Strange Situation also places too great an emphasis on attachment with the mother, and does not observe children's interactions with other caregivers (Lamb, 2005). Finally, by only coding the mother's behavior toward the child and not considering how the child's behavior may affect the mother, the Strange Situation approaches attachment from a unidirectional and not a bidirectional perspective.

Moral Development   A dominant paradigm in moral development is the stage theory presented by Lawrence Kohlberg (1976). Using the Moral Judgment Interview, Kohlberg was able to distinguish six stages of moral development, by identifying qualitatively different forms of moral thinking by individuals in response to moral dilemma vignettes. The first two stages, termed "preconventional" thinking, involve the individual progressing from a focus on obedience to authority and avoidance of punishment to a self-interest orientation, in which moral behaviors are viewed as those that represent the individual's best interest. In stage 3, the first stage of "conventional" thinking, individuals are concerned with interpersonal accord and conforming to social norms, and judge morality of actions and their consequences by the extent to which they promote or detract from social approval. Stage 4 thinking is characterized by a desire to adhere to laws in order to maintain stability and harmony in society. Stage 5 represents "postconventional" thinking, which emphasizes moral principles and values that should guide society through promoting democratic values. Stage 6 involves moral reasoning based on abstract, universal ethical principles that guide perceptions of actions as "right" or "wrong."

TABLE 4.2 Attachment Classifications and Associated Child and Caregiver Behaviors

ATTACHMENT TYPE	CHILD BEHAVIOR	CAREGIVER BEHAVIOR
Secure	Uses caregiver as a secure base from which to explore. Protests caregiver's departure and seeks closeness and is comforted on return, resuming exploration. May be comforted by a stranger but shows clear preference for caregiver.	Responds appropriately, promptly, and consistently to child's needs
Avoidant	Little affective sharing in play. Shows little or no distress after caregiver departure, and little or no visible response on return, turning away or ignoring with no effort to maintain contact if picked up. Interacts with stranger similarly to caregiver. Child feels there is no attachment and as a result is rebellious and develops a lower self-image and self-esteem.	Little or no response to distressed child; discourages crying and encourages independence
Ambivalent/Resistant	Unable to use caregiver as secure base, wanting closeness before separation occurs. Distressed on separation with ambivalence, anger, reluctance to be comforted by caregiver and resume play on return. Preoccupied with caregiver's availability, seeking contact but resisting angrily when it is offered. Not easily soothed by stranger. Child always feels anxious because caregiver's availability is inconsistent.	Inconsistent between appropriate and neglectful responses; in general, will only respond after child displays increased attachment behavior
Disorganized	Exhibits atypical behavior on return such as rocking or freezing. Lack of a coherent attachment strategy demonstrated by contradictory, disoriented behaviors such as approaching but with back turned.	Frightened or frightening behavior, intrusiveness, withdrawal, negativity, role confusion, affective communication errors, and maltreatment; often associated with several forms of abuse toward the child

Aggression and Prosocial Behavior   Research on aggression in youth has traditionally distinguished between two forms of aggression: overt and relational. Overt aggression describes behavior targeted toward inflicting physical harm on others, through striking, pushing, or using hostile and threatening language. Overt aggression is much more common in boys than girls, and children engaging in overt aggression tend to use these behaviors to establish dominance over others or to "get one's way."

Relational aggression is typically more likely to emerge in girls, and tends to include behaviors focused on manipulating others or damaging their social relationships. Research indicates that relational aggression is perceived as more likely to be successful in female peer-to-peer interactions, and can include gossip and spreading rumors, encouraging social exclusion of a peer, or making threats toward others. Both overt and relational aggression are strong predictors of future social and behavioral outcomes. Children who engage in high levels of aggression toward others are more likely to experience difficulties in adjustment, including poor psychosocial outcomes such as peer rejection, depression, anxiety, as well as school dropout (Crick, 1996; Samson, Ojanen, & Hollo, 2012).

In contrast to aggression, prosocial behavior in childhood describes behaviors that promote positive interactions with others (e.g., peers, siblings, and adults). Advances in social- and cognitive-developmental areas such as sympathy, empathy, and moral reasoning throughout childhood have been shown to predict increases in prosocial behavior such as caring for and helping others, sharing, and perspective taking. Prosocial behaviors have been associated with a wide range of positive developmental outcomes, including self-regulation, coping, positive emotionality, and positive social adjustment (Eisenberg et al., 1996). In addition, prosocial behavior has been linked with less aggressive behavior in youth, whereas antisocial behavior is associated with high levels of aggression.

Social Competence and Social Skills   An important theme of developmental theory in social development of children is the role of an individual's social network in contributing to ontogenic growth. Social competence is a critical area of early development that is representative of social influences on individual development. The two contexts that are specifically tasked with socializing children include the home and early childcare or school settings. At home, children's interactions with their caregivers serve as the basis for the formation of internal working models, or expectations about others and social relationships. Attachment theorists view the child's formation of a strong, positive relationship with his or her primary caregiver as necessary for normal social and emotional development. In the school setting, youth have the opportunity to interact with peers and adults, and are exposed to interactions that shape both their self-conception and their view of others. In the microsystem of the home, children interact with parents and siblings on a daily basis, in order to form cognitive schema about interpersonal relationships as well as social convention. Importantly, individuals are not viewed as passive receptors of environmental input. Sameroff's (Sameroff & Chandler, 1975; Sameroff & Fiese, 2003) Transactional Model understands development as a series of continuous reciprocal interactions between the individual and his or her context. Placing equal emphasis on individual and environmental influences in contributing to developmental outcomes, the Transactional Model accounts for the myriad social influences that help to shape changes in the individual over time. The development of social competence is affected in children with developmental delays such as mental retardation and autism, which inhibit individuals' ability to initiate and respond to social cues.

Identity   Scientific understanding of individual identity development has ben-efitted in large part from Erik Erikson's (1968) stage theory, which described the process of identity as unfolding across the life span in a series of eight stages (see Table 4.3). Each of these stages is characterized by a conflict, which must be resolved in order to promote positive development in future stages. In the early stages, individuals must establish trust in their caregivers in order to develop a sense of the world as a safe place. A sense of trust is likely to form if the home rearing environment is safe, and parents are responsive to the child's basic needs for food and comfort. In early childhood, individuals begin to establish a sense of individualism and autonomy stemming from the ability to walk and explore the world on their own. Here, the individual comes to see him- or herself as an individ-ual entity, separate from a mother or father. As childhood progresses, individuals gain increasing ability to act on the world in more sophisticated ways, eventu-ally mastering basic skills and integrating concepts. With adolescence comes an increased demand on the individual to establish a sense of self in relation to oth-ers. Failure to do so in multiple contexts (e.g., school, home, and work) can result in role confusion and a lack of a coherent self-concept. In adolescence, individu-als are typically subject to increasing amounts of peer influence, particularly with respect to identity development. In early adulthood, there is a growing emphasis for individuals in establishing an intimate bond with a significant other, or risk experiencing feelings of loneliness and isolation. As adulthood progresses, identity development is more intrinsically linked to a sense of contributing to others and retrospective rumination on having accomplished one's life goals.

Contexts of Development

Family

The family is a social system that consists of several subsystems that are defined in terms of generation, gender, and role as well as division of labor and attach-ments. Each member of the family is a participant in several subsystems that can be dyadic (involving two people) or polyadic (involving more than two people). For example, the mother and child make up one dyadic subsystem, the mother and father another, and mother–father–child and mother and two siblings create poly-adic subsystems. The family subsystems directly and indirectly influence each other through interactions within the marital relationship, parenting, and child behaviors. Family members are involved in reciprocal socialization, in which socialization is bidirectional and parents and children socialize each other. Parents who report they are happily married demonstrate more sensitivity, warmth, responsiveness, and affection toward their children than unhappily married parents (Grych, 2002). Support of the marital relationship and promotion of marital satisfaction through marriage-enhancement programs and interventions that enhance parenting skills increase intimacy, communication, and affection toward children. Family processes are impacted by various sociocultural and historical influences, such as increases in divorce, working mothers, stepparent families, gay and lesbian parents, multiethnic families as well as war, famine, and mass immigration, reflecting Bronfenbrenner's concepts of the exosystem, macrosystem, and chronosystem.

TABLE 4.3 Erikson's Psychosocial Stages

STAGE	BASIC CONFLICT	IMPORTANT EVENTS	OUTCOME
Infancy (birth to 18 months)	Trust vs. Mistrust	Feeding	Children develop a sense of trust when caregivers provide reliability, care, and affection. A lack of this will lead to mistrust.
Early Childhood (2 to 3 years)	Autonomy vs. Shame and Doubt	Toilet training	Children need to develop a sense of personal control over physical skills and a sense of independence. Success leads to feelings of autonomy and failure results in feelings of shame and doubt.
Preschool (3 to 5 years)	Initiative vs. Guilt	Exploration	Children need to begin asserting control and power over the environment. Success in this stage leads to a sense of purpose. Children who try to exert too much power experience disapproval, resulting in a sense of guilt.
School Age (6 to 11 years)	Industry vs. Inferiority	School	Children need to cope with new social and academic demands. Success leads to a sense of competence, whereas failure results in feelings of inferiority.
Adolescence (12 to 18 years)	Identity vs. Role Confusion	Social relationships	Teens need to develop a sense of self and personal identity. Success leads to an ability to stay true to oneself, whereas failure leads to role confusion and a weak sense of self.
Young Adulthood (19 to 40 years)	Intimacy vs. Isolation	Relationships	Young adults need to form intimate, loving relationships with other people. Success leads to strong relationships, whereas failure results in loneliness and isolation.
Middle Adulthood (40 to 65 years)	Generativity vs. Stagnation	Work and parenthood	Adults need to create or nurture things that will outlast them, often by having children or creating a positive change that benefits other people. Success leads to feelings of usefulness and accomplishment, whereas failure results in shallow involvement in the world.
Maturity (65 to death)	Ego Integrity vs. Despair	Reflection on life	Older adults need to look back on life and feel a sense of fulfillment. Success at this stage leads to feelings of wisdom, whereas failure results in regret, bitterness, and despair.

Gender, Family, and Peers

Children begin to self-segregate in their choice of playmates in early childhood. Gender or sex segregation, or the tendency of children to associate with others of the same sex, appears to be fairly universal, beginning at about age 2 to 3 years and becoming prominent after age 3. Furthermore, once children are in gender-segregated peer groups, they tend to show some differences in play styles and activities, number of playmates, and levels of physical aggression. For example, girls tend to play in smaller groups, in closer proximity to adults, and with more cooperative group dynamics. Boys tend to play in larger groups, farther away from adults, and with more rough-and-tumble play and with more competition (Ruble et al., 2006). By adolescence, children move away from peer groups that are highly sex segregated to adolescents with increasingly more contact with opposite-sex friends, including an increase in nonromantic friendships with other-sex peers. For most adolescents, friendships become more intimate. However, compared to adolescent boys, adolescent girls list more friends, are more likely to include intimacy as a defining aspect of close friendship, and show more complexity in their thinking about friendships.

Gender socialization or social norms conveyed to children concerning characteristics associated with being male or female, may contribute to observed gender differences in children's emotional and interactive styles. Adults may convey different messages to girls and boys about appropriate activities, interests, and friends, and may provide different messages about skills and achievements that are expected and valued. Children may form gender schemas about being male or female, and about perceived strengths of the differences between girls and boys. Meta-analyses of research on sex differences do find some support for some differences in areas such as physical aggression, which is found to be higher in boys than in girls, and some aspects of cognitive abilities, with boys found to be stronger in special abilities and girls found to be stronger in verbal skills (Ruble et al., 2006). However, these differences may be exaggerated in common understanding. Although adults' socialization practices and children's own gender schema may accentuate perceived gender differences, there is much more overlap between boys and girls in all areas than there are differences (Hyde, 2005).

Divorce and Stepfamilies

The rates of divorce have been increasing across all socioeconomic groups; however, factors such as low educational attainment, low income levels, no religious affiliation, a child before marriage, divorced parents, and marriage at a young age are associated with higher rates of divorce (Hoelter, 2009). Both divorced men and women experience loneliness, lower self-esteem, anxiety, stress, and difficulty in forming satisfying new intimate relationships (Eldar-Avidan, Haj-Yahia, & Greenbaum, 2009). Divorcees are at a higher risk for psychological disorders such as clinical depression, alcoholism, and sleep disorders (Rotterman, 2007) as well as chronic health problems (Waite, 2009). Due to a decrease from their predivorce income, divorced mothers experience increased workloads and rates of job instability, and residential moves to less desirable neighborhoods with lower quality schools (Sayer, 2006). Children of divorce are more likely to have academic difficulties, demonstrate both externalized (acting out and delinquency) and internalized (anxiety and depression) problems, be less socially adjusted, initiate sexual activity at an early age, drop out of school, take drugs, have antisocial peers, have low self-esteem, and have trouble in intimate relationships (Lansford, 2009). Adolescent girls with divorced parents are particularly vulnerable to depression (Oldehinkel, Ormel, Veenstra, De Winter, & Verhulst, 2008). Children who have experienced multiple divorces are at a greater risk for these issues. Children in stepfamilies show similar adjustment problems to those in divorced families (Hetherington & Kelly, 2002). Nevertheless, the majority of children in divorced and stepparent families do not have significant adjustment problems (Ahrons, 2007; Hetherington & Kelly, 2002).

Gay and Lesbian Parents

Due to donor insemination, surrogates, and adoption, the number of families of gay or lesbian couples with children has increased in the last few decades. Little differences have been found in adjustment in children of homosexual and heterosexual couples (Patterson, 2009). Children raised in gay or lesbian families are just as popular with peers, and have no differences in mental health or cognitive and social–emotional development than children growing up with heterosexual parents (Hyde & DeLamater, 2008). Organizations such as the American Academy of Pediatrics (AAP) have expressed their support for same-sex unions and civil marriage and cited evidence for the lack of differences in children's development in same- or different-gender parents (AAP, 2013).

Extended Families

Grandparents play an important role in many families, including providing advice, support, and child care, and the extent of their role and function in the family are influenced by ethnic, cultural, and situational differences (Watson, Randolph, & Lyons, 2005). The number of grandchildren living with or being raised by their grandparents has been increasing in the United States because of increases in longevity, divorce, adolescent pregnancy, and parental drug use (Hayslip & Kaminski, 2008). Grandparents who take in grandchildren have better health, higher educational attainment, are younger, and are more likely to work outside the home than grandparents who move in with their children, but those who are full-time caregivers of grandchildren are at a higher risk of depression, stress, and health problems (Silverstein, 2009).

Adolescent Pregnancy

The United States has the highest teen pregnancy and birth rates of any industrialized nation despite marked declines since the early 1990s (CDC, 2003). Adolescent pregnancy and childrearing may have many negative consequences for both mother and child, including increased health risks (pregnancy-induced hypertension, preeclampsia, low birth weight, neurological problems, and child illness), high school dropout, academic difficulties, delinquency, substance abuse, and mental health problems (Oxford, Gilchrist, Gillmore, & Lohr, 2006). Children of teenage mothers are more likely to become teen parents themselves, perpetuating this intergenerational cycle. Adolescent mothers who remain in school and who delay subsequent childbearing fare much better over time than do adolescent mothers who drop out of school or have additional children closely spaced together.

Transition to Parenthood

The average age at which women give birth for the first time increased from about 21 years of age in 2001 to 25.2 in 2005. Advantages of having children in the twenties include more physical energy, fewer medical problems during pregnancy and childbirth, and decreased likelihood of building up expectations for children. Advantages of childbearing in the thirties include parents who have more time to consider career and family goals, maturity, the benefit of their experiences to engage in more competent parenting, and more established careers and higher income for childrearing expenses. In both planned and unplanned pregnancies, prospective parents experience mixed emotions and have romantic illusions about having and raising a child. Parents may find it difficult to manage the various aspects and roles in their lives, including developing a strong attachment with their infant; maintaining existing attachments to spouses, family, and friends; continuing their careers; and continuing to develop as an individual. Many couples report decreases in marital satisfaction after the birth of an infant (Cowan & Cowan, 2000).

School Transitions

The primary aims of education are to provide children with cognitive and social–emotional skills, reinforce cultural traditions, and develop literacy. A successful initial transition to school establishes a foundation for later academic achievements and social–emotional development. Children who enter school with skills such as positive social behaviors (cooperativeness and friendliness) and cognitive and literacy competence (linguistic maturity) tend to perform better in kindergarten (Ladd, Birch, & Buhs, 1999). After kindergarten, the second most important school transition is into middle or junior high school. This transition occurs around the same time as many other changes in an individual's life (puberty, formal operational thought, decreased dependency on parents, and increased independence), and is correlated with students' reported declines in school satisfaction, motivation, and self-esteem, more symptoms of depression, and lower grades and participation in extracurricular activities (Simmons & Blyth, 1987; Hirsch & Rapkin, 1987).

References

Adolph, K. E., & Berger, S. E. (2005). Physical and motor development. In M. H. Bornstein, & M. E. Lamb (Eds.), *Developmental science: An advanced textbook* (pp. 223–282). Mahwah, NJ: Erlbaum.

Ahrons, C. R. (2007). Family ties after divorce: Long-term implications for children. *Family Process, 46,* 53–65.

Ainsworth, M. D. S. (1979). Infant-mother attachment. *American Psychologist, 34,* 932–937.

Allport, G. (1955). *Becoming: Basic considerations for a psychology of personality.* New Haven, CT: Yale University Press.

American Academy of Pediatrics (AAP). (2013). Promoting the well-being of children whose parents are gay or lesbian. *Pediatrics, 131*(4), 827–830.

Austin, M. P., Mitchell, P., & Goodwin, G. M. (2001). Cognitive deficits in depression: Possible implications for functional neuropathy. *British Journal of Psychiatry, 178,* 200–206.

Baltes, P. B. (1987). Theoretical propositions of life-span developmental psychology: On the dynamics between growth and decline. *Developmental Psychology, 23,* 611–626.

Baltes, P. B., & Baltes, M. M. (1990). Psychological perspectives on successful aging: The model of selective optimization with compensation. In P. B. Baltes & M. M. Baltes (Eds.), *Successful aging: Perspectives from the behavioral sciences* (pp. 1–34). New York, NY: Cambridge University Press.

Baltes, P. B., Lindenberger, U., & Staudinger, U. M. (2006). Life-span theory in developmental psychology. In W. Damon & R. M. Lerner (Eds.), *Handbook of child psychology: Vol. 1. Theoretical models of human development* (6th ed., pp. 569–664). Hoboken, NJ: Wiley.

Baltes, P. B., Reese, H. W., & Lipsitt, P. (1980). Life-span developmental psychology. *Annual Review of Psychology, 31,* 65–110.

Bornstein, M. (1989). Sensitive periods in development: Structural characteristics and causal interpretations. *Psychological Bulletin, 105,* 179–197.

Bornstein, M. H., & Lamb, M. E. (2002). *Development in infancy: An introduction.* Mahwah, NJ: Erlbaum.

Borroni, B., Costanzi, C., & Padovani, A. (2010). Genetic susceptibility to behavioural and psychological symptoms in Alzheimer's disease. *Current Alzheimer Research, 7*(2), 158–164.

Bowlby, J. (1969). *Attachment and loss* (Vol. 1). London, UK: Hogarth Press.

Brazelton, T. B., & Nugent, J. K. (1995). *The neonatal behavioral assessment scale.* Cambridge: Mac Keith Press.

Brent, R. L. (2004). Environmental causes of human congenital malformations: The pediatrician's role in dealing with these complex clinical problems caused by a multiplicity of environmental and genetic factors. *Pediatrics,* (113), 957–968.

Bronfenbrenner, U. (1979). *The ecology of human development.* Cambridge, MA: Harvard University Press.

Bronfenbrenner, U. (1986). Ecology of the family as a context for human development: Research perspectives. *Developmental Psychology, 22,* 723–742.

Bronfenbrenner, U., & Morris, P. A. (2006). The bioecological model of human development. In R. M. Lerner & W. Damon (Eds.), *Handbook of child psychology: Vol. 1, Theoretical models of human development* (6th ed., pp. 793–828). Hoboken, NJ: John Wiley.

Campbell, J. D., Trapnell, P. D., Heine, S. J., Katz, I. M., Lavallee, L. F., & Lehman, D. R. (1996). Self-concept clarity: Measurement, personality correlates, and cultural boundaries. *Journal of Personality and Social Psychology, 70,* 141–156.

Case, R. (1987). Neo-Piagetian theory. Retrospect and prospect. *International Journal of Psychology, 22,* 773–791.

Case, R. (1999). Conceptual development in the child and the field: A personal view of the Piagetian legacy. In E. K. Skolnick, K. Nelson, S. A. Gelman, & P. H. Miller (Eds.), *Conceptual development.* Mahwah, NJ: Erlbaum.

Centers for Disease Control and Prevention (CDC). (2003). Births: Final data for 2002. *National Vital Statistics Reports, 52*(10), 1–5.

Centers for Disease Control and Prevention. (2012, August 16). *Fetal alcohol spectrum disorders (FASDs): Data and statistics.* Retrieved from www.cdc.gov /ncbddd/fasd/data.html

Chasnoff, I. J., Wells, A. M., Telford, E., Schmidt, C., & Messer, G. (2010). Neurodevelopmental functioning in children with FAS, pFAS, and ARND. *Journal of Developmental and Behavioral Pediatrics: JDBP, 31*(3), 192–201. doi: 10.1097/DBP.0b013e3181d5a4e2

Cicchetti, D., Rogosch, F. A., Gunnar, M. R., & Toth, S. L. (2010). The differential impacts of early physical and sexual abuse and internalizing problems on daytime cortisol rhythm in school-aged children. *Child Development, 81*(1), 252–269.

Cowan, P. A., & Cowan, C. P. (2000). *When partners become parents: The big life change for couples.* Mahwah, NJ: Erlbaum.

Crick, N. R. (1996). The role of overt aggression, relational aggression, and pro-social behavior in the prediction of children's future social adjustment. *Child Development, 67*(5), 2317–2327.

Davidson, H. A., Dixon, R. A., & Hultsch, D. F. (1991). Memory anxiety and memory performance in adulthood. *Applied Cognitive Psychology, 5,* 423–433.

Duncan, G. J., Dowsett, C. J., Claessens, A., Magnuson K., Huston, A. C., Klebanov, P., … Japel, C. (2007). School readiness and later achievement. *Developmental Psychology, 43*(6), 1428–1446. doi: 10.1037/0012-1649.43.6.1428 and 10.1037/0012-1649.43.6.1428.supp (Supplemental).

Eldar-Avidan, D., Haj-Yahia, M. M., & Greenbaum, C. W. (2009). Divorce is part of my life…resilience, survival, and vulnerability: Young adults' perceptions of the implications of parental divorce. *Journal of Marital and Family Therapy, 35,* 30–46.

Eisenberg, N., Fabes, R. A., Karbon, M., Murphy, B. C., Wosinski, M., Polazzi, L., … Juhnke, C. (1996). The relations of children's dispositional prosocial behavior to emotionality, regulation, and social functioning. *Child Development, 67,* 974–992.

Eisenberg, N., Fabes, R., & Spinrad, T. L. (2006). Prosocial development. In W. Damon, & R. M. Lerner (Series Eds.) & N. Eisenberg (Vol. Ed.), *Handbook of child psychology: Vol. 3. Social, emotional, and personality development* (6th ed., pp. 646–718). Hoboken, NJ: Wiley.

Erikson, E. H. (1968). *Identity: Youth and crisis.* New York, NY: Norton.

Freund, A. M., & Baltes, P. B. (1998). Selection, optimization, and compensation as strategies of life management: Correlations with subjective indicators of successful aging. *Psychology and Aging, 13,* 531–543.

Gottlieb, G. (2007). Probabilistic epigenesis. *Developmental Science, 10*(1), 1–11.

Gottlieb, G., Wahlstein, D., & Lickliter, R. (2006). The significance of biology for human development: A developmental psychobiological systems view. In W. Damon & R. M. Lerner (Series Eds.) & R. Lerner (Vol. Ed.), *Handbook of child psychology: Vol. 1. Theoretical models of human development* (6th ed., pp. 210–257). New York, NY: Wiley.

Greenough, W. T., Black, J. E., & Wallace, C. S. (1987). Experience and brain development. *Child Development, 58,* 539–559.

Grych, J. M. (2002). Marital relationships and parenting. In M. H. Bornstein (Ed.), *Handbook of parenting.* Mahwah, NJ: Erlbaum.

Hart, B., & Risley, T. R. (1995). *Meaningful differences in the everyday experience of young American children.* Baltimore, MD: Paul H. Brookes.

Hayslip, B., & Kaminski, P. L. (Eds.). (2008). *Parenting the custodial grandchild.* New York, NY: Springer Publishing Company.

Hetherington, E. M., & Kelly, J. (2002). *For better or for worse: Divorce reconsidered.* New York, NY: Norton.

Hirsch, B. J., & Rapkin, B. D. (1987). The transition to junior high school: A longitudinal study of self-esteem, psychological symptomology, school life, and social support. *Child Development, 58,* 1235–1243.

Hoelter, L. (2009). Divorce and separation. In D. Carr (Ed.), *Encyclopedia of the life course and human development.* Boston, MA: Gale Cengage.

Hoff, E. (2006). How social contexts support and shape language development. *Developmental Review, 26,* 55–88.

Hyde, J. S. (2005). The gender similarity hypothesis. *American Psychologist, 60,* 581–592.

Hyde, J. S., & DeLamater, J. D. (2008). *Human sexuality* (10th ed.). New York, NY: McGraw-Hill.

Kagan, J. (2002). Behavioral inhibition as a temperamental category. In R. J. Davidson, K. R. Scherer, & H. H. Goldsmith (Eds.), *Handbook of affective sciences.* New York, NY: Oxford University Press.

Kagan, J. (2008a). Fear and weariness. In M. M. Haith, & J. B. Benson (Eds.), *Encyclopedia of infant and early childhood development.* Oxford, UK: Elsevier.

Kagan, J. (2008b). Temperament. In A. Kazdin (Ed.), *Encyclopedia of psychology.* Washington, DC, and New York, NY: American Psychological Association and Oxford University Press.

Kagan, J. (2010). Emotions and temperament. In M. H. Bornstein (Ed.), *Handbook of cultural developmental science.* New York, NY: Psychology Press.

Kazdin, A. E. (2001). *Behavior modification in applied settings* (6th ed.). Belmont, CA: Wadsworth/Thomson Learning.

Kohlberg, L. (1976). Moral stages and moralization. In T. Lickona (Ed.), *Moral development and behavior* (pp. 31–53). New York, NY: Holt, Rinehart, & Winston.

Kudielka, B. M., & Kirschbaum, C. (2005). Sex differences in HPA axis responses to stress: A review. *Biological Psychology, 69*(1), 113–132.

Ladd, G. W., Birch, S. H., & Buhs, E. S. (1999). Children's social and scholastic lives in kindergarten: Related spheres of influence? *Child Development, 70,* 1373–1400.

Lamb, M. E. (2005). Attachments, social networks, and developmental contexts. *Human Development, 48*(1), 108–112.

Lansford, J. E. (2009). Parental divorce and children's adjustment. *Perspectives on Psychological Science, 4,* 140–152.

Lerner, R. M. (1997). The continuity-discontinuity issue. *Concepts and theories of human development* (2nd ed., pp. 183–215). Mahwah, NJ: Erlbaum.

Lewis, M., & Mayes, L. (2012). The role of environments in development: An introduction. In L. Mayes & M. Lewis (Eds.), *The environment of human development: A handbook of theory and measurement* (pp. 1–14). New York, NY: Cambridge University Press.

Main, M. (1996). Introduction to the special section on attachment and psychopathology: 2. Overview of the field of attachment. *Journal of Consulting and Clinical Psychology, 64*(2), 237–243.

Masten, A. S. (2011). Resilience in children threatened by extreme adversity: Frameworks for research, practice, and translational synergy. *Development and Psychopathology, 23*(2), 493–506. doi: 10.1017/s0954579411000198

Nagin, D., & Tremblay, R. (2005). What has been learned from group-based trajectory modeling? Examples from physical aggression and other problem behaviors. *Annals of the American Academy of Political and Social Science, 602,* 82–117.

National Institute of Child Health and Human Development. (2013, March 14). *Child development and behavior branch*. Retrieved from http://www.nichd .nih.gov/about/org/der/branches/cdbb/Pages/overview.aspx

NICHD Early Child Care Research Network. (2002). Early child care and children's development prior to school entry: Results from the NICHD study of early child care. *American Educational Research Journal, 39*(1), 133–164.

Oldehinkel, A. J., Ormel, J., Veenstra, R., De Winter, A., & Verhulst, F. C. (2008). Parental divorce and offspring depressive symptoms: Dutch developmental trends during early adolescence. *Journal of Marriage and Family, 70*, 284–293.

Oxford, M. L., Gilchrist, L. D., Gillmore, M. R., & Lohr, M. J. (2006). Predicting variation in the life course of adolescent mothers as they enter adulthood. *Journal of Adolescent Health, 39*, 20–36.

Patterson, C. J. (2009). Lesbian and gay parents and their children: A social science perspective. *Nebraska Symposium on Motivation, 54*, 147–182.

Pfeifer, M., Goldsmith, H. H., Davidson, R. J., & Rickman, M. (2002). Continuity and change in inhibited and uninhibited children. *Child Development, 73*, 1474–1485.

Piaget, J. (1954). *The construction of reality in the child*. New York, NY: Basic Books.

Pollak, S. D., Klorman, R., Thatcher, J. E., & Cicchetti, D. (2001). P3b reflects maltreated children's reactions to facial displays of emotion. *Psychophysiology, 38*, 267–274.

Rogoff, B. (1990). *Apprenticeship in thinking: Cognitive development in social context*. New York, NY: Oxford University Press.

Rothbart, M. K. (2004). Temperament and the pursuit of an integrated developmental psychology. *Merrill-Palmer Quarterly, 50*, 492–505.

Rothbart, M. K., & Bates, J. (2006). Temperament. In W. Damon & R. M. Lerner (Series Eds.) & N. Eisenberg (Vol. Ed.), *Handbook of child psychology: Vol. 3. Social, emotional, and personality development* (6th ed., pp. 99–166). Hoboken, NJ: Wiley.

Rotterman, M. (2007). Marital breakdown and subsequent depression. *Health Reports, 18*, 33–44.

Ruble, D. N., Martin, C. L., & Berenbaum, S. A. (2006). Gender development. In W. Damon & R. M. Lerner (Series Eds.) & N. Eisenberg (Vol. Ed.), *Handbook of child psychology: Vol. 3. Social, emotional, and personality development* (6th ed., pp. 858–932). Hoboken, NJ: Wiley.

Sameroff, A. (2010). A unified theory of development: A dialectic integration of nature and nurture. *Child Development, 81*(1), 6–22.

Sameroff, A. J., & Chandler, M. (1975). Reproductive risk and the continuum of caretaking casualty. In F. D. Horowitz, M. Hetherington, S. Scarr-Salaptek, & G. Siegel (Eds.), *Review of child development research* (Vol. 4, pp. 187–244). Chicago: University of Chicago Press.

Sameroff, A., & Fiese, B. (2003). Transactional regulation: The developmental ecology of early intervention. In J. Shonkoff & S. Meisels (Eds.), *Handbook of early childhood intervention*. New York, NY: Cambridge University Press.

Samson, J. E., Ojanen, T., & Hollo, A. (2012). Social goals and youth aggression: Meta-analysis of prosocial and antisocial goals. *Social Development, 21*, 645–666.

Sayer, L. C. (2006). Economic aspects of divorce and relationship dissolution. In M. A. Fine & J. H. Harvey (Eds.), *Handbook of divorce and relationship dissolution*. Mahway, NJ: Erlbaum.

Silverstein, M. (2009). Caregiving. In D. Carr (Ed.), *Encyclopedia of the life course and human development*. Boston, MA: Gale Cengage.

Simmons, R. G., & Blyth, D. A. (1987). *Moving into adolescence: The impact of pubertal change and school context*. Hawthorne, NY: Aldine de Gruyter.

Steinberg, L. (2008). A social neuroscience perspective on adolescent risk-taking. *Developmental Review, 28,* 78–106.

Steinberg, L., Vandell, D. L., & Bornstein, M. (2011). *Development: Infancy through adolescence* (1st ed.). Belmont CA: Wadsworth Cengage Learning.

Surén, P., Roth, C., Bresnahan, M., Haugen, M., Hornig, M., Hirtz, D., … Stoltenberg, C. (2013). Association between maternal use of folic acid supplements and risk of autism spectrum disorders in children. *Journal of the American Medical Association, 309*(6), 570–577. doi: 10.1001/jama.2012.155925

Thelen, E., & Smith, L. B. (2006). Dynamic systems theories. In R. M. Lerner & W. Damon (Eds.), *Handbook of child psychology (6th ed.): Vol. 1, Theoretical models of human development* (pp. 258–312). Hoboken, NJ: Wiley.

Thelen, E., & Smith, L. B. (2006). Dynamic development of action and thought. In W. Damon, & R. M. Lerner (Eds.), *Handbook of child psychology* (6th ed.). New York, NY: Wiley.

Thomas, A., & Chess, S. (1977). *Temperament and development*. New York, NY: Brunner/Mazel.

Thomas, A., & Chess, S. (1991). *Temperament in adolescence and its functional significance*. In R. M. Lerner, A. C. Petersen, & J. Brooks-Gunn (Eds.). *Encyclopedia of adolescence* (Vol. 2). New York, NY: Garland.

Torquati, J. C., Raikes, H. H., Huddleston-Casas, C. A., Bovaird, J. A., & Harris, B. A. (2011). Family income, parent education, and perceived constraints as predictors of observed program quality and parent rated program quality. *Early Childhood Research Quarterly, 26*(4), 453–464. doi: 10.1016/j.ecresq.2011.03.004

Tronick, E. Z., & Cohn, J. F. (1989). Infant-mother face-to-face interaction: Age and gender differences in coordination and the occurrence of miscoordination. *Child Development, 60*(1), 85–92.

Vermeer, H. J., & van IJzendoorn, M. H. (2006). Children's elevated cortisol levels at daycare: A review and meta-analysis. *Early Childhood Research Quarterly, 21*(3), 390–401. doi: 10.1016/j.ecresq.2006.07.004

Vygotsky, L. (1978). Tool and symbol in child development & Internalization of higher psychological functions. In M. Cole, V. John-Steiner, S. Scribner, & E. Souberman (Eds.), *L. Vygotsky, Mind in society*. Cambridge, MA: Harvard University Press.

Waite, L. J. (2009). Marriage. In D. Carr (Ed.), *Encyclopedia of the life course and human development*. Boston, MA: Gale Cengage.

Watson, J. A., Randolph, S. M., & Lyons, J. L. (2005). African-American grandmothers as health educators in the family. *International Journal of Aging and Human Development, 60,* 343–356.

World Health Organization (WHO). (2012, September). *Children: Reducing mortality: Fact sheet*. Retrieved from http://www.who.int/mediacentre/factsheets/fs178/en

WHO Multicentre Growth Reference Study Group. (2006). WHO Motor Development Study: Windows of achievement for six growth motor development milestones. *Acta Paediatrica Supplement* (450), 86–95. Retrieved from http://www.who.int/childgrowth/standards/motor_milestones/en/index.html

Zahn-Waxler, C., & Radke-Yarrow, M. (1990). The origins of empathic concern. *Motivation and Emotion, 14,* 107–129.

Zhou, Q., Lengua, L. J., & Wang, Y. (2009). The relations of temperament reactivity and effortful control to children's adjustment problems in the United States and China. *Developmental Psychology, 45,* 724–739.

Review Questions

1. "Development"

    A. Is synonymous with growth
    B. Follows the same invariable sequence for most individuals
    C. Is a variable process of relatively enduring growth and change that makes an individual better adapted to the environment
    D. Is primarily a biological maturational process determined by an individual's genotype
    E. Stops at the end of adolescence/in early adulthood

2. The phenotype is

    A. The set of genes an individual inherits
    B. All the settings with which the individual directly interacts
    C. The observable appearance and characteristics a child develops
    D. Entirely determined by the genotype

3. A sensitive period in an individual's development

    A. Could also be called an "all-or-nothing" period
    B. Is only relevant to sensory processes
    C. Is a stage theory
    D. Is a time of heightened sensitivity to certain environmental stimuli

4. The concept of continuity involves

    A. Sensitivity to the environment engendered by experience
    B. Gradual, continuous process of change
    C. The notion of a developmental stage
    D. Sudden emergence of new forms of thought and behavior

5. *Resilience* refers to the processes of pathways and patterns

    A. Associated with an elevated probability of an undesirable outcome
    B. Of the constant interplay of biology and the environment
    C. Of positive adaptation during or following significant threats or disturbances
    D. Of modeling and observational learning

6. A member of a group in which research has shown an elevated probability of a negative outcome is described as

    A. Resilient
    B. Active
    C. At risk
    D. Polyadic

7. An example of a model of development with a passive child and an active environment is

    A. Piaget's cognitive-developmental theory
    B. Bronfenbrenner's bioecological model
    C. Operant conditioning processes
    D. Transactional processes

8. According to Piaget, through the process of equilibration
    A. Children develop internal structures called schemata
    B. Children use primary circular reactions to learn about the world
    C. Children attempt to create a balance of the processes of assimilation and accommodation
    D. Children form internal mental representations

9. During which of Piaget's cognitive-developmental stages do children understand the concept of conservation?
    A. Sensorimotor
    B. Preoperational
    C. Concrete operational
    D. Formal operational

10. A teacher provides a small amount of assistance to help a child accomplish a task that he would not be able to complete independently. According to Vygotsky,
    A. The teacher is providing instruction within the child's zone of proximal development
    B. The teacher is providing socioemotional but not cognitive support to the child
    C. The child is using assimilation and accommodation to learn a new concept
    D. The child is scaffolding his understanding to please the teacher

11. A child's father recently lost his full-time job and has begun to work the night shift at the local drugstore. The stress has caused her parents to fight more and they can no longer afford her piano lessons. She now sees her father occasionally at breakfast but he is usually so tired from work that he sleeps in. In regard to Bronfenbrenner's ecological systems theory, the father's change in jobs is categorized as a(n) _____ influence on his daughter's development.
    A. Microsystem
    B. Mesosystem
    C. Exosystem
    D. Macrosystem

12. Which of the following statements are true about life span developmental theory?
    A. Early stages of development are emphasized as more important in shaping growth than later stages
    B. Adaptive development is viewed as occurring mainly as a result of early attachment relationships
    C. Change occurs over time at the same rate in various domains
    D. Change is both multidimensional and multidirectional

13. Baltes's selective optimization with compensation theory
    A. Extended Freud's views on the self from a psychoanalytic perspective
    B. Described well-defined stages of growth and change across the life span, from birth to late adulthood
    C. Is based on the assumption that individual change occurs at different rates throughout the life span
    D. Attempts to describe a single path by which most individuals are able to age successfully

4. GROWTH AND LIFE SPAN DEVELOPMENT   151

14. A cell divides into a copy of itself with each resulting cell receiving a full copy of all 46 chromosomes during

   A. Mitosis
   B. Crossing over
   C. Meiosis
   D. Implantation

15. The process of elimination of unused and unnecessary synapses is

   A. Epigenesis
   B. Synaptogenesis
   C. Synaptic pruning
   D. Anoxia

16. When an infant's response to a repeatedly presented stimulus decreases,

   A. Dishabituation has occurred
   B. The infant prefers the stimulus
   C. The infant cannot continue in the study
   D. Habituation has occurred

17. The HPA axis, which regulates the body's stress response system, includes what primary components?

   A. Hypothalamus, pituitary gland, adrenal gland
   B. Hippocampus, pituitary gland, aorta
   C. Heart, pineal gland, amino acids
   D. Hypothalamus, parotid gland, adrenal gland

18. _____ tends to show the greatest age-related decrease in performance.

   A. Episodic memory
   B. Semantic memory
   C. Procedural memory
   D. Phonology

19. Gender constancy

   A. Develops at the same time as the sense of gender identity
   B. Does not develop until adolescence
   C. Is the concept that gender is permanent
   D. Is the ability to discriminate between males and females

20. Secondary emotions

   A. Include joy, surprise, sadness, anger, fear, and disgust
   B. Depend on higher mental capacities
   C. Emerge in the earliest months of life
   D. Appear to be universal and rooted in human biology

21. A 15-month-old child prefers a regular eating and sleeping schedule but quickly adapts to a change in his routine. He is generally in a positive mood throughout the day. According to Thomas and Chess, what temperament style does this child have?

   A. Easy
   B. Difficult
   C. Slow to warm up
   D. Secure

22. School-aged children whose temperament is categorized by low effort control

    A. Are extremely friendly and enjoy being in new and unfamiliar situations
    B. Become easily distressed and often fuss and cry for no apparent reason
    C. Are cautious about their surroundings and appear apprehensive at school
    D. Quickly become intensely emotional and exhibit problematic externalizing behaviors

23. An infant uses his mother as a secure base from which to explore a new environment. While playing, he occasionally glances back to make sure his mother is still there. They appear to have generally positive interactions with each other. This child most likely has which type of attachment to his mother?

    A. Secure
    B. Insecure avoidant
    C. Insecure resistant
    D. Insecure disorganized

24. What is the name of the observational measure Ainsworth developed to investigate differences in the quality of attachment between infants and their caregivers?

    A. The Strange Situation
    B. The Secure Situation
    C. The Attachment Situation
    D. The Separation Situation

25. The Kohlbergian approach to moral development

    A. Grew directly from Piaget's stage theories
    B. Represents a life span developmental approach
    C. Did not account for differences among individuals
    D. Sought to understand individual moral reasoning using the Moral Judgment Interview

26. Sameroff's Transactional Model

    A. Is a developmental learning theory emphasizing the role of modeling peer behavior
    B. Describes the reciprocal interactions between an individual and the environment that shapes development
    C. Is a stage theory of identity development
    D. Is the basis for most DBT (dialectical behavior) therapies

27. Internal Working Models

    A. Are ideas formed by therapists about how their patients will respond to therapy
    B. Are largely formed during parent–child interactions in childhood, and serve as the basis for understanding future relationships
    C. Are typical biological responses to psychopharmaceutical medication
    D. Were first described by Rorschach

28. According to the research of Erik Erikson, identity formation

    A. Concludes in adolescence, when individuals discover their "true selves"

    B. Is a complex process of self-actualization beginning in adolescence

    C. Cannot be empirically studied until children become verbal

    D. Is the product of conflicts that occur in different forms in various stages of life

29. One of the biggest social factors directly and indirectly influencing the interactions among the different subsystems within a family is

    A. Income

    B. Chronic disease

    C. The marital relationship

    D. Mental health disorders

30. What is one of the biggest concerns for many women who have experienced a divorce?

    A. Increased dependence on spirituality

    B. Increased financial difficulties

    C. Decreased educational attainment

    D. Decreased fertility

Answers to Review Questions

1. **C. Is a variable process of relatively enduring growth and change that makes an individual better adapted to the environment**

   Development is relatively enduring growth and change that makes an individual better adapted to the environment by enhancing the individual's ability to engage in, understand, and experience more complex behavior, thinking, and emotions. Simple growth and change are part of development, but development is different. Development is "best described and studied as a variable process in which individual differences in cognitive, social, affective, language, neurobiological maturation, environment and life experiences, and genetics interact in complex ways" (National Institute of Child Health and Human Development, 2013) involving a constant interplay between biology and the environment, occurring in a multi-layered context, accumulating, and continuing throughout life.

2. **C. The observable appearance and characteristics a child develops**

   *The **phenotype**, or the observable appearance and characteristics a child develops, is the result of interaction between genetic and environmental influences over time.*

3. **D. Is a time of heightened sensitivity to certain environmental stimuli**

   ***Sensitive period** means that in an individual's development there are times of heightened sensitivity to certain environmental stimuli, when a particular experience (or lack of it) has a more pronounced effect on the organism than does the experience at another time; this may apply to many developmental processes including sensation, language, attachment, and more.*

4. **B. Gradual, continuous process of change**

   *The concept of **continuity** involves the notion that development is a gradual, continuous process of change, whereas the concept of **discontinuity** involves the notion that development is punctuated by periods of rapid change and sudden emergence of new forms of thought and behavior. Formal developmental theories, which take a discontinuous approach, are also called stage theories.*

5. **C. Of positive adaptation during or following significant threats or disturbances**

   Resilience science in human development refers to the study of the processes of, capacity for, or pathways and patterns of positive adaptation during or following significant threats or disturbances.

6. **C. At risk**

   *An individual described as **at risk** is a member of a group for which research has shown an elevated probability of the negative outcome under consideration.*

7. **C. Operant conditioning processes**

   In a model with a passive child and an active environment, the environment is viewed as controling the child's behavior and development. Operant conditioning processes fall into this view.

8. C. Children attempt to create a balance of the processes of assimilation and accommodation

Through adaptation, children build mental structures, called schemas, to organize knowledge, adapt to the world, and adjust to new environmental demands. In the process of assimilation, individuals incorporate new information or experiences into an existing schema. In the process of accommodation, individuals adjust their schema to take into account new information or experiences. By a mechanism called equilibration, *children attempt to create a balance between assimilation and accommodation. The internal search for equilibrium is the motivation for change and helps to explain children's shift from one stage of thought to the next. As a result of these processes, children undergo cognitive change.*

9. C. Concrete operational

Conservation is the understanding that changing the appearance of an object or substance does not change its basic properties. The beaker test is a task that demonstrates conservation. Conservation develops during the concrete operational stage, when the child is between 7 and 11 years of age.

10. A. The teacher is providing instruction within the child's zone of proximal development

The zone of proximal development (ZPD) encompasses the tasks that are too difficult for a child to complete on his own but can be learned and accomplished with the guidance of an adult or more skilled child. The lower limit of the ZPD is the level of skill a child has while working independently and the upper limit is the level of additional capability with the assistance of an instructor.

11. C. Exosystem

The exosystem includes contexts with which the individual does not directly interact but that have indirect influences on development.

12. D. Change is both multidimensional and multidirectional

Life span developmental theory posits that change over time occurs in a variety of domains (e.g., biological, cognitive, and social) and at various rates. Development thus involves processes of growth and decline as individuals age, with these changes taking place at different rates during different periods of life.

13. C. Is based on the assumption that individual change occurs at different rates throughout the life span

SOC theory describes the substantial variety that is typical across the life span, with early development characterized by considerable growth and gains in the biological, cognitive, and social domains, and late adulthood typically involving loss and decline in these areas.

14. A. Mitosis

During ordinary cell reproduction, or mitosis, a cell divides into a copy of itself. Each resulting cell receives a full copy of all 46 chromosomes.

15. C. Synaptic pruning

Synaptic pruning is the process of elimination of unused and unnecessary synapses.

16. D. Habituation has occurred

Habituation has occurred when the response to a stimulus decreases when the stimulus is repeatedly presented (i.e., the assumption is that habituation is similar to boredom). Dishabituation occurs when the response to a stimulus increases with presentation of a novel change in the stimulus.

17. A. Hypothalamus, pituitary gland, adrenal gland

The hypothalamus, in association with the pituitary and adrenal glands (located in the brain and kidneys, respectively), is the primary system involved in the production of the hormone cortisol in response to stress.

18. A. Episodic memory

Episodic memory tends to show the greatest age-related decreases in performance.

19. C. Is the concept that gender is permanent

Gender identity begins to develop very early with the ability in toddlerhood to discriminate between males and females and then label themselves and others by gender. It is not until age 6 or 7 that children show evidence of a sense of gender constancy, or the concept that gender is permanent and immutable (Ruble et al., 2006). In middle childhood, gender consciousness solidifies, functioning as an organizing framework for children's thoughts about themselves in relation to others, choices of friends and activities, and a guide for behavior.

20. B. Depend on higher mental capacities

Secondary emotions, sometimes called self-conscious or other-conscious emotions, involve evaluation of oneself and increase as the infant becomes self-aware. They do not emerge until the second or third year of life and depend on higher mental capacities, including an objective sense of the self as distinct from others, awareness of standards for behavior, and a sense of responsibility for one's actions.

21. A. Easy

Thomas and Chess classified children into three temperament categories: easy, difficult, and slow to warm up. Easy children are generally in a positive mood, establish regular routines quickly, and adapt easily to new experiences. Difficult children often react negatively and cry frequently, have irregular routines, and are slow to accept change. Slow-to-warm-up children have low activity levels, are somewhat negative, and exhibit low mood intensity.

22. D. Quickly become intensely emotional and exhibit problematic externalizing behaviors

Rothbart and Bates proposed that the structure of temperament can be characterized into three broad dimensions: extraversion/surgency, negative affectivity, and effortful control (self-regulation). Children with high effortful control do not allow their arousal level to become too high and have developed self-soothing strategies. Children with low effortful control have difficultly regulating their arousal and quickly become agitated and intensely emotional. Low effortful control in school-aged children has been correlated with externalizing problems, such as cheating, lying, being disobedient, and aggressiveness.

23. A. Secure

Attachment is an emotional bond between a child and his primary caregivers that endures over the lifetime. A child with a secure attachment uses the caregiver as a secure base from which to explore. The caregiver responds appropriately, promptly, and consistently to child's needs.

24. A. The Strange Situation

Ainsworth operationalized Bowlby's attachment construct by developing the Strange Situation Procedure, a series of eight separations and reunions between a 12- to 18-month-old child and his caregiver, during which the child's amount of exploration, behaviors, and reactions are observed. Ainsworth used the Strange Situation to explore individual differences in patterns of attachment behavior and identified three major attachment types: secure, avoidant, and ambivalent/resistant. A fourth attachment type, disorganized/disoriented, was added by Main.

25. D. Sought to understand individual moral reasoning using the Moral Judgment Interview

Lawrence Kohlberg used the Moral Judgment Interview, a structured qualitative tool, in order to categorize the moral decision making of individuals from childhood through adulthood.

26. B. Describes the reciprocal interactions between an individual and the environment that shape development

The Transactional Model understands development as an ongoing sequence of constant reciprocal interactions between an individual and his or her context, with an equal emphasis on the individual and the environment in contributing to change over time.

27. B. Are largely formed during parent–child interactions in childhood, and serve as the basis for understanding future relationships

As described by Bowlby in relation to attachment theory, internal working models are cognitive schemas first formed by children with their primary caregivers. Over time, children develop expectations, perceptions, and emotions about relationships with others based largely on this attachment relationship. Although a poor attachment relationship may lead to expectations of others as manipulative, untrustworthy, or indifferent, a quality attachment relationship tends to provide the basis for an internal working model of mutually beneficial relationships with others.

28. D. Is the product of conflicts that occur in different forms in various stages of life

For Erikson, each stage of life is characterized by a conflict that must be resolved in order to promote future positive development. Erikson described eight stages of conflict, with those in infancy and early childhood centering on autonomy and relations with caregivers; in later life these conflicts center on the value of one's life and providing guidance and support to future generations.

29. C. The marital relationship

The family is a social system that consists of several subsystems that are defined in terms of generation, gender, and role, as well as division of labor and attachments. Each member of the family is a participant in several subsystems. The family subsystems directly and indirectly influence each other through interactions within the marital relationship, parenting, and child behaviors. Parents who report they are happily married demonstrate more sensitivity, warmth, responsiveness, and affection toward their children than unhappily married parents. Support of the marital relationship and promotion of marital satisfaction through marriage-enhancement programs and interventions that enhance parenting skills increase intimacy, communication, and affection toward children.

30. B. Increased financial difficulties

Due to a decrease from their predivorce income, divorced mothers experience increased workloads and rates of job instability, and residential moves to less desirable neighborhoods with lower quality schools.

5

Assessment and Diagnosis

Megan N. Scott, Cynthia Kane, and Scott J. Hunter

Broad Content Areas

- Psychometrics
- Assessment models and instruments
- Assessment methods for initial status of and change by individuals, couples, families, groups, and organizations/systems

Psychological assessment is a process of gaining information about and an understanding of an individual in order to facilitate informed decision making. The goals of psychological assessment are varied and include screening: measurement of specific characteristics or traits; determination of risk; diagnosis; vocational planning; evaluation of the impact of intervention; and intervention planning, among other possible goals. There are numerous assessment methods that comprise testing, including interview, direct observation, informal assessment procedures, and norm-referenced (standardized) assessment.

Assessment Theories and Models

Broadly, *psychometrics* refers to the study of psychological measurement, and includes the measurement and assessment of intelligence, specific abilities, knowledge in a given area, personality traits, behavior, attitudes, symptoms, and educational or vocational progress. The field of psychometrics focuses primarily on the development and validation of measurement instruments that are employed in the field of psychology, for both research and clinical use. Among the earliest psychometric measures were those developed in the early 1900s for the purpose of intelligence testing. One of the earliest tests was the Binet–Simon Scale, which was first developed by Alfred Binet and Theodore Simon in 1905, to identify children with what we now call intellectual disability, who were enrolled in French schools (Binet & Simon, 1905; Sattler, 2001). This was the first standardized intelligence test, and was administered in a fairly consistent way across test takers. It consisted of 30 items with increasing levels of difficulty. Binet and Simon used this scale to provide what they characterized as an objective diagnosis of the presence and severity of intellectual disability in test takers, and with an implied understanding of age-based development when providing diagnosis.

Since the introduction of intelligence testing with the creation of the Binet–Simon scale, two competing theories of intelligence have developed and have supported the ongoing development and structure of batteries created and put in use to date, a *general-factor (g) theory of intelligence* and a *multiple-factor theory of intelligence* (Sattler, 2001). Current hierarchical models underlying testing view intelligence as consisting of a general intelligence factor that is situated at the top of a hierarchy of skills, with broad abilities comprising the middle, and specific factors or abilities situated at the base. Additionally, more recent views of intelligence highlight the roles of underlying biology and unfolding cognitive and adaptive development as significant influences on intelligence and its representation (Sattler, 2001; Sternberg & Kaufman, 1998). As will be discussed below in greater detail, accompanying these models of how intelligence is best understood and assessed are two primary theories underlying the development of measurement tools used in psychological assessment, including intelligence testing. These are Classical Test Theory (CTT) and Item Response Theory (IRT).

Assessment in Practice

Assessment is a core component of psychological practice and research. Many different specialties within the field of psychology use tests and measures to capture and define domains of interest. As such, the development and use of psychological measures is an important skill that remains pertinent to the identity of a psychologist. Within professional psychology, clinical, counseling, school, developmental, industrial–organizational, vocational, rehabilitation, and social psychologists all commonly use tests and measures. Tests for the characterization and classification of select groups of individuals are particularly used by applied psychologists. A discussion of domains of practice that commonly require the use of standardized measures for their professional practice follows.

Clinical and counseling psychologists typically make use of tests that define and characterize patterns of adaptation and functioning, either to classify an individual or to provide diagnosis. Personality assessment, measurement of mood and behavioral functioning, and assessment of current functioning and adaptive capacity are commonly considered. Measures used are typically referenced to a range of functioning, spanning typical developmental presentation to dysfunction, and capture the degree to which symptoms and traits are present and either influence or interfere with functioning.

School psychologists most typically employ measures that characterize and define how an individual is able to learn. Functioning within the school setting is the primary focus of the school psychologist; measures tapping intelligence, academic skill, language, visual and motor processing, and behavior are among the tools most commonly used by a school psychologist. Monitoring of intervention is also an important component of school psychological practice.

Neuropsychology is a specialty within clinical psychology that incorporates knowledge of brain functioning and the relationship between the brain and behavior (Boake, 2008), and makes use of standardized testing approaches to elucidate and describe these relationships. Neuropsychologists apply this knowledge to understand and characterize an individual's profile of neurocognitive strengths and weaknesses in relation to brain development and abnormal brain functioning. Neuropsychological assessment can provide information to help determine whether dysfunctional behavior is primarily due to a neurological or organic cause, or whether the behavior is more functional in nature. By comparing the pattern of strength and weaknesses to known neurocognitive profiles of specific disorders, neuropsychological evaluations help to clarify the nature and severity of neurological injury or insult and are used to clarify both medical and psychological diagnoses. Neuropsychological evaluations are also frequently used to assess learning disabilities and complex behavioral and emotional conditions.

Vocational and rehabilitation psychologists frequently emphasize how well an individual is able to meet demands for independence across development, with a goal of increasing success at work and learning as a primary focus. Measures used by these professionals typically address such areas as functional skill for meeting specific vocational and educational goals, monitoring of skill development, and adaptations that are required to facilitate adaptive and behavioral functioning. Assessment of underlying capacity and how this may be broadened and refined, as possible, is also considered an important element of practice.

Approaches to Assessment

Behavioral assessment has been defined as "an exploratory hypothesis-testing process in which a range specific procedure is used in order to understand a given child, group, or social ecology and to formulate and evaluate specific intervention strategies" (Ollendick & Hersen, 1984, p. 6). The basis of behavioral assessment lies in the assumption that behavior is a product of an interaction between an individual and his or her environment. Typically, behavioral assessment is used to describe a particular behavior or pattern of behavior, and to understand what leads to and maintains it across time. This information is important in determining a treatment or intervention to address a problematic behavior and to then evaluate the efficacy of the intervention used to alter or change that given behavior. Functional behavioral assessment (FBA) is a specific method of behavioral assessment that operationalizes and then characterizes the presence and impact of a select behavior or group of behaviors. It additionally defines the parameters that influence and underscore the display of the behavior, and guides how to best intervene.

Ecological assessment uses primarily observational methods to examine and understand the physical and psychological variables that impact behavior in a given environment or setting (Sattler & Hoge, 2006). Psychological variables include an individual's relationships with peers, teachers, parents, spouses, co-workers, or other individuals in a given setting, whereas physical variables include the specific physical aspects of the environment such as lighting, noise, spatial arrangement of furniture, or seating. Hiltonsmith and Keller (1983) have described a framework for organizing data collected in ecological (person setting) assessment. Their model consists of three components: "setting appearance and contents," which are observable physical aspects of the setting; "setting operation" or the interaction and communication patterns within an environment and how the setting is being used; and "setting opportunities," which are opportunities contained within the environment that support the development of cognition and language, as well as social–emotional growth.

Assessment Methods

There are a number of different assessment methods used by psychologists. These include standardized administration, self-report, informant report, structured and semi-structured interviews, direct observation, and psychophysiological assessment. In industrial–organizational psychology, important assessment methods include direct observation, assessment centers, and work samples.

Standardized administration in assessment refers to giving a test or measure under consistent, or standard, conditions. This includes the use of the same administration, item content, and scoring criteria across all individuals who are presented with the measure. In test development, *standardization* refers to the process in which a measure is first administered to a representative sample of a given group under consideration for the test, for example, children in the United States who are between 6 and 17 years of age, in order to develop scoring norms. These norms represent the range of performance that can be expected across the measure and serve to define the typical pattern of response the test elicits.

Norm-referenced tests are standardized tests or measures that compare an examinee's performance to the performance of a specified group of participants. The reference population, or the population of participants represented by the measurement norms, is most commonly defined by age, as seen with the example given above. Other characteristics, including grade, clinical presentation, diagnostic group status, gender, and racial or cultural group status, may also be used. The use of norms allows the psychologist to determine a score for the person being tested that is compared to the distribution of scores attained on the measure by the normative sample. This quantifies the examinee's performance on the given measure relative to the reference group. Norm-referenced testing can also allow for evaluation of changes in an individual's performance over time.

A criterion-referenced test is used to assess where an examinee stands on a particular criterion, or domain of skill, status, or functioning. Criterion-referenced tests tend to be used to assess an individual's knowledge or skill in a hierarchical fashion, as would be consistent with expectations for learning. These types of tests are most often used in educational and vocational settings to assess progress or mastery of a given skill or subject matter. Examples of criterion-referenced tests include driving tests, licensing exams, or high school graduation examinations.

Self-report measures are typically symptom-based questionnaires and surveys, or semi-structured and structured interviews (discussed further below). These include both broad-based measures of a range of symptoms across a number of diagnostic categories (e.g., symptom checklists or broad personality inventories, like the Personality Assessment Inventory), and narrow measures of symptoms seen with specific disorders (e.g., the Beck Anxiety Inventory or the Children's Depression Inventory, Second Edition). When working with children and adolescents, informant reports are particularly important. An informant report is a questionnaire, rating, or checklist measure that is most typically completed by a parent or teacher, but, depending on the measure, may be used with a caretaker or spouse. As with self-report measures, informant-report measures may be broad in nature (e.g., Behavioral Assessment System for Children/Adolescents, Second Edition) or specific to the symptoms of a given disorder (e.g., Conners Third Edition, which is used to assess attention deficit hyperactivity disorder (ADHD) related concerns). With the use of self- and informant-report measures, it is important to consider that different informants completing these measures may view an individual quite differently based on the context of the interaction with the person being evaluated, and the opportunities the informant may have for comparison. Therefore, it is often quite helpful to seek information regarding a particular individual being assessed from multiple informants, whenever possible. In addition, it is important to remember that informant ratings are never without some degree of bias, and can be impacted by a range of variables, including the severity of the individual's symptoms; the child's ethnicity, gender, and socioeconomic status; the informant's familiarity with the individual; or his or her tolerance for problematic behavior, among other factors (Sattler & Hoge, 2006).

Clinicians gain critical assessment information through interviews with clients, parents, spouses, teachers, and other informants. Unstructured and semistructured interviews are less formal opportunities to gain information, providing an examinee with the opportunity to provide information about her or himself, outside of a standardized assessment format. Unstructured interviews are typically open-ended interactions with an examiner or clinician, frequently conducted without a standard format or structure, aside from some initial questions of interest. Unstructured interviews allow for flexibility, rapport building, and the ability to further examine information that arises in the context of the interview. However, due to their lack of standardization, there is some concern when unstructured interviews are used as the sole source of information when developing a diagnosis, given the limited reliability and validity inherent in the nonstructured approach. Semistructured and structured interviews, in contrast, have been developed to be administered in a standardized manner and as a result, reduce problems with reliability and validity found in unstructured interviews. There are a number of commonly used semistructured and structured interviews that have good psychometric properties; these include the Schedule for Affective Disorders and Schizophrenia (SADS), the Diagnostic Interview Schedule (DIS), and the Structured Clinical Interview for the *DSM-IV* (SCID), among others. These tools are most commonly used within research settings, but are not uncommon in clinical settings where focused diagnostic procedures are required.

Together, the use of direct observation and behavioral assessment provide useful sources of information about an examinee of interest. By observing an individual in her natural environment, such as the school setting for children, the psychologist is able to gain an understanding of antecedent and consequent responses that may influence learning and behavior. Additionally, direct observation methods provide a snapshot of an individual's behavior within and across a variety of settings, outside of the testing environment. As such, they can be useful when assessing interpersonal and social behavior, contextual learning, and how behavior may differ across environments. The accuracy of informant report of behavior or functioning in a given environment can be evaluated with direct observation. Systematic observations and FBAs further allow the examiner to identify and describe target behaviors, as well as understand the antecedents and consequences of behavior to inform behavioral interventions. These methods can further be used to examine the effectiveness of behavioral and psychological interventions. When conducting systematic or structured observations, individuals are typically observed in a naturalistic environment, such as home, work, or school, and the examiner records objective data about behaviors observed. In FBA, counts of behavior and descriptions of controls and guides are also made.

There are several observational assessments that can be employed by a psychologist. These range from global descriptions of behavior to targeted ratings of the frequency and intensity of specific behaviors. Narrative recording assessments provide a running record of an individual's behavior throughout the observation period, with the examiner noting behaviors of interest. Interval recording methods, also known as time-sampling methods, require target behaviors to be operationally defined in objective, clear, specific terms, in order for the examiner to effectively identify and monitor the behavior during observation. Observation is divided into brief time intervals and the examiner records whether a specific behavior occurs during each interval recorded. The occurrence or absence of the behavior during each interval is then tallied across the entire observation. This type of observational assessment is appropriate when a given behavior occurs frequently, or does not have a clear beginning or ending. With event sampling, the psychologist records the frequency of a target behavior during the observation. With this method, it can be quite challenging to assess behaviors that occur frequently or take place over a long duration; hence, it is more common to use time-sampling methods when addressing a frequent problematic behavior.

Rating recordings allow the examiner to rate a given behavior, in regard to its intensity or duration. These types of ratings are typically made using a 5-point Likert scale (e.g., from not present to present). As just mentioned, these ratings typically assess intensity or severity of a behavior; they are also used to gain broad impressions of behavior. Although this approach allows for the collection of qualitative data about the behavior, the reliability of this approach across raters or examiners varies significantly, due to the difficulty found in objectively and consistently rating target behaviors.

Functional behavioral assessment is a method of behavioral assessment that is most commonly used to evaluate problematic behaviors in order to develop and evaluate the effectiveness of a behavioral intervention plan. The key components of an FBA are to define a problem behavior, determine the antecedents or the events that precede the problem behavior, and outline the consequence of the behavior or the function it serves. This information allows the clinician to develop a hypothesis about why a given behavior is occurring, and supports the systematic assessment of that hypothesis. An intervention plan is then formulated to address the problematic behavior and the intervention is implemented. After the intervention plan has been implemented, the effectiveness of the plan is evaluated (Miller, Tansy, & Hughes, 1998), and changes are made as required, to ensure that problematic behaviors are appropriately diminished or managed. FBA is derived directly from operant conditioning models of behavior.

Direct observation, assessment centers, and work samples are methods of assessment in work settings and are common methods in industrial and organizational psychology. Assessment centers are defined as a setting where "a standardized evaluation of behavior based on multiple inputs" can occur (International Task Force on Assessment Center Guidelines, 2009, p. 244). In an assessment center, "several trained observers and techniques are generally used. Judgments about behavior are made, in major part, from specifically developed assessment simulations" (International Task Force on Assessment Center Guidelines, 2009, p. 245). The raters or observers meet to discuss the results of the behavior observed during the assessment, and ratings of performance are pooled together to evaluate the individual's performance across a number of work-related dimensions. Alternatively, results may be integrated "by a statistical integration process" (International Task Force on Assessment Center Guidelines, 2009, p. 245). There are nine key components for an evaluation process to be considered an assessment measure, including job analysis/competency modeling, behavioral classification, assessment techniques, multiple assessments, simulations, assessor training, recording behavior and scoring, and data integration (International Task Force on Assessment Center Guidelines, 2009).

Assessment centers typically evaluate behaviors and skills that are specific to a job's content, as well as evaluate the types of problems that typically arise on the job. They may include norm-referenced testing to assess cognitive abilities or personality, and criterion-based tests that assess job knowledge. During the assessment process, raters observe and evaluate an individual's performance on the simulation activities. An overall rating is provided at the end of the assessment that integrates the information from the assessment activities. Work samples are most often used to assess job potential. Works samples are constructed activities or exercises meant to simulate on-the-job situations, specifically ones that are important to a given job. These may include giving a presentation, role-playing an interaction with a customer or coworker, or completing a series of in-basket exercises that test the individual's ability to handle administrative tasks required by a position.

Psychometric Theory

Classical Test Theory, Item Response Theory, and Generalizability Theory

Classical Test Theory (CTT) and Item Response Theory (IRT) are the two primary theories that underlie the development of measurement tools used in psychological assessment. CTT is based on the work of Charles Spearman, and was first presented in 1904. It is defined as "a psychometric theory based on the view that an individual's observed score on a test is the sum of a true score component for the test taker, plus an independent measurement error component" (American Educational Research Association [AERA], American Psychological Association [APA], & National Council Measurement in Education [NCME], 1999, p. 172). In other words, an individual's score on any given instrument (i.e., the observed score) is composed of that individual's true score and error, neither of which is individually observable. According to CTT, the true score is conceptualized as the average score an individual would achieve on a specific test, given an infinite number of administrations of that test (Alagumalai & Curtis, 2005; DeVellis, 2006).

The equation for CTT is $S_i = t_i + e_i$, where S_i is the raw score on the test, t_i is the true score, and e_i is the error term. The error term in CTT is assumed to be random error and should not be correlated with either the raw score or the true score according to the assumptions of CTT. As a result, error sources cannot be distinguished or identified.

Generalizability Theory (G Theory) is an extension of CTT. It conceptualizes error in a way that allows for the evaluation of both error and the reliability of measurement procedures (AERA, APA, & NCME, 1999; Gao & Harris, 2012). G Theory identifies sources of measurement error, separates the influence of each source, and then estimates the individual sources of measurement error. In G Theory, an individual's score on a test or measure is conceptualized as a sample from among an infinite number of administrations or possible observations on that measure. Potential sources of error include all of the characteristics of the assessment measure, including test forms, test items, circumstances under which the test is administered, the rater, and other related sources. Reliability of measurement is evaluated by conducting a generalizability study (G study), the purpose of which is to quantify individual sources of measurement error (AERA, APA, & NCME, 1999; Gao & Harris, 2012; Webb, Shavelson, & Haertel, 2006).

IRT focuses on the examination of individual items in test development. In IRT, the relationships between the construct being measured and the individual test responses are examined across multiple levels. Test developers rely on three parameters when examining test item relationships: item difficulty (the percentage of test takers who get a specific item correct), item discrimination (how that item discriminates between those who do well versus those who do poorly on the test as a whole), and the probability that a question is answered correctly by guessing. The item characteristic curve (ICC) or item response function (IRF) is then calculated; the ICC is a mathematical function that is used to illustrate the increasing proportion of correct answers for an item, at higher levels of the ability or trait being measured by a given assessment.

Item and Test Characteristics

When developing an assessment battery or choosing which individual tests to administer, the psychometric properties of the measure under consideration must be taken into account. For a measure to have adequate psychometric properties, it must be both reliable and valid.

Reliability refers to the degree to which test scores are consistent. When referring back to G Theory, reliability will include the degree to which testing is free from measurement error (Gao & Harris, 2012). In CTT, a score on a test is thought to reflect an individual's true score on the ability or trait being assessed as well as error. Therefore, the reliability coefficient is an indicator that reflects the degree of consistency or the degree to which scores are free from error. Reliability coefficients are denoted with the letter *r* and range from 1.00 (indicating perfect reliability) to 0.00 (indicating the absence of reliability).

There are different types of reliability estimates to consider in test development and selection. *Test–retest reliability* refers to the stability of scores over time. The test–retest reliability correlation is obtained by administering a specific test to the same group at two different points in time. The pair of scores for the same people across the two administrations is then correlated. Generally, a closer test–retest interval leads to a higher reliability coefficient. The use of test–retest to assess reliability is appropriate when the trait or ability being measured is thought to be relatively stable over time.

The alternate form reliability coefficient (also known as equivalent or parallel form reliability) is generated by administering two or more interchangeable forms of a given test to the same group and correlating the results across test forms. An example of this is the Woodcock-Johnson Third Edition (WJ-III) Tests of Achievement (2001), which has two comparable forms, A and B. These alternate test forms measure the same constructs, have similar content, and use the same directions. A key factor in the reliability between alternate forms is that the items included with both have the same level of difficulty. An advantage of using parallel or alternate forms of a test is that the practice effect, or memory for content of a previously administered test or measure, is minimized.

Internal consistency reliability is based on the scores obtained by an individual during one administration of a test. It is calculated to determine the consistency of the items within the measure. This internal consistency reliability coefficient allows test developers and users to assess the reliability of a measure without requiring a second administration of the same measure or a parallel form of the measure. There are two types of internal consistency reliability. In split-half reliability, the test is divided into two equivalent halves and correlated. According to Cohen and Swerdlik (2002), there are three steps to computing a split-half reliability coefficient, including dividing the test into two halves (typically odd and even items), calculating the correlation between the two halves, and then adjusting the split-half reliability score using the Spearman–Brown formula. The Spearman–Brown formula is used to estimate the internal consistency of an entire test from the reliability of one half of a test. It is derived from the formula that is used to estimate the reliability of a test that has been shortened or lengthened by a number of test items. The Spearman–Brown formula is:

$$r_{SB} = \frac{nr_{xy}}{1 + (n - 1)r_{xy}},$$

where r_{SB} is the Spearman–Brown adjusted reliability coefficient, r_{xy} is the Pearson r in the original length test, and n is the number of items in the revised version of the test divided by the number of items in the original version of the test.

An internal consistency reliability coefficient can also be estimated by examining interitem consistency, the correlation among all items on a scale. The inter-item consistency coefficient is only useful when test items are homogeneous, and therefore meant to measure a single trait or factor. The Kuder–Richardson formula 20 (KR-20) can be used as an alternative approach for calculating split-half reliability when examining internal consistency of a homogeneous test.

Finally, *inter-rater* or *interscorer reliability* refers to the consistency of the performance or behaviors of a test taker. A high inter-rater reliability coefficient indicates that scores on a test are calculated or derived in a consistent and systematic manner across examiners. It is evaluated using percentage agreement, kappa, the interclass correlation coefficient, or the product-moment correlation coefficient.

Once reliability of a measure is established, validity can be examined. A measure must be reliable in order to be considered valid. *Validity* refers to the extent to which a given test accurately and precisely measures what it is meant to measure. The validity coefficients represent the strength of the relationship between a predictor and a criterion or outcome measure. As with reliability, there are a number of different types of validity to consider when examining the psychometric properties of a test.

Face validity has to do with the examinee's perception of the validity of a test while taking it. Face validity is different than actual validity, as a test may seem valid even when it is not. However, face validity is important because it can impact how an examinee approaches a test and a lack of face validity may lead to a lack of confidence in the effectiveness of the test.

Early on four types of validity were described, including content validity, construct validity, concurrent validity, and predictive validity (The American Psychological Association, American Educational Research Association, and the National Council on Measurement Education, 1954). Concurrent and predictive validity were later combined into criterion validity. This latter model of validity has been referred to as the trinitarian or the three-in-one model of validity. There has been ongoing debate over this model of validity since its identification. Additionally, according to the APA's Standards for Educational and Psychological Testing (1999; with an upcoming revision to be released in 2013), there are five sources of evidence for validity to be considered in test construction and selection, including evidence based on test content, response processes, internal structure, relations to other variables, and the consequences of testing.

Content validity describes how well a test includes the range of information that is needed, across items, to test the construct that is being measured. Content validity is often assessed by independent evaluators or experts in the field, and is usually addressed during test development.

As noted above, criterion validity is composed of both concurrent validity and predictive validity. It provides a judgment about the adequacy with which a test score can estimate an individual's performance on a criterion of interest. For example, the criterion validity of the Beck Depression Inventory, Second Edition (BDI-II; Beck, Steer, & Brown, 1996) refers to the extent to which the test's score estimates an individual's level of depressive symptoms, within a 2-week period. Concurrent validity is calculated by examining the correlation between a new measure and an established measure that is administered at the same time to assess the criterion of interest. Using the same example, if a new measure of depression being developed is well correlated with the BDI-II, when administered to the same sample, that measure is considered to have good concurrent validity. Predictive validity is the extent to which scores on the test predict a specified criterion score established to address the presence or absence of a particular criterion. Therefore, the predictive validity coefficient represents the correlation between obtained test scores and the criterion of interest.

When a test or measure is used to predict classification within a group or to assign a diagnosis, such as using a test to accurately diagnose a disorder like posttraumatic stress disorder (PTSD), sensitivity and specificity are important statistical concepts to consider, particularly when interpreting the results of the test. *Sensitivity* refers to the proportion of people who are accurately identified as possessing a certain trait, attribute, or behavior that is being measured; in our example, that would be the number of people with PTSD who are accurately diagnosed. In turn, *specificity* refers to the proportion of people who are accurately classified as not having the condition or trait, attribute, or behavior being measured, for example, the number of people who do not have PTSD and who are appropriately not given a diagnosis. Sensitivity and specificity are often considered in relationship to Type 1 and Type 2 errors.

Construct validity refers to the extent to which a test is correlated (or associated) with the trait or ability it claims to assess. While criterion-related validity assesses the relationship between a new measure and established measures that assess the same criterion, construct validity refers to the relationship between the new test and the construct itself. This is much harder to measure, but one method for establishing construct validity is the use of a multitrait–multimethod matrix. The multitrait–multimethod matrix (Campbell & Fiske, 1959) compares a new measure with another measure that examines the same trait or condition in a different way, as well as with measures that use the same method for measuring different traits or conditions. This results in a matrix of correlations that determine both convergent validity (the extent to which a measure correlates with other measures designed to assess the same trait or condition) and divergent validity (the extent to which a measure does not correlate with ones with which it should not theoretically correlate). Factor analysis (which is more completely discussed in the statistics chapter) is another means of demonstrating convergent and divergent validity. In test development and psychometric research, factor analysis is typically used to examine the factor or factors being assessed by the items on a given test, and how well the items comprising the measure combine into selected, appropriate domains that are relevant to the condition or trait's identification.

Lastly, test bias and fairness are important considerations when discussing the validity of a test or selecting tests for use in clinical practice. Test bias refers to the presence of a factor or element within a test that causes systematic variation or error leading to impartial measurement across groups. An example of test bias is when a test is found to systematically underpredict the performance or ability of members of a specific group, that is, changes in how school-age youth are identified as eligible for special education placement in California were instituted when test bias was suspected because many youth from lower socioeconomic backgrounds were found to consistently underperform on a standardized test of knowledge acquisition in comparison with same-aged, middle-class peers (*Larry P. v. Riles,* 1979). Test bias can be assessed by examining the regression lines derived from a measure used to predict performance on a criterion, specifically through examination of the slope, intercept, and the error estimate of the regression lines for different groups completing the test.

In contrast to test bias, test fairness refers to the extent to which a test is used fairly, to classify and categorize a specific criterion. According to the Standards for Educational and Psychological Testing (1999) there are four primary ways to consider fairness in relation to psychological testing. These include: "fairness as a lack of bias," "fairness as equitable treatment in the testing process," "fairness as equality in outcomes of testing," and "fairness as opportunity to learn." Each of these is assessed and interpreted through a process of review, typically by a group of experts evaluating the success by which a measure or set of measures supports these standards. Ultimately, fairness is an aspirational goal of testing, which is achieved through rigorous attention to both reliability and validity.

Tests for the Measurement of Characteristics and Behaviors of Individuals

Social, Relational, Emotional, and Behavioral Functioning in Children/Adolescents

A number of measures are available to assess social–emotional, behavioral, and relational functioning across the life span. These can be either broad-based measures of assessment, meaning they assess a number of internalizing and externalizing problems within one behavior rating or checklist, or more circumscribed measures of a particular mood or behavioral pattern. For children and adolescents, self-report, parent-report, and teacher-report questionnaires are typically used to assess functioning across environments. It is important to seek information from multiple informants because each individual will have a different frame of reference, or may interpret an individual's behavior in different ways, based on the demands of the setting in which they observe the child. In addition, demands can vary substantially across environments, so it is important to assess an individual's behavior and social–emotional functioning across the range of environments they participate in, in order to fully appreciate and conceptualize their social, emotional, and behavioral functioning.

The Achenbach System of Empirically Based Assessment (Child Behavior Checklist: Achenbach & Rescorla, 2001; Teacher Report Form: Achenbach & Rescorla, 2001; Youth Self-Report: Achenbach & Rescorla, 2001) generates three primary index scores: Total Problems, Internalizing Problems, and Externalizing Problems. Scores are represented as T-scores and compared with a mean of 50 and a standard deviation of 10. Although the reliability of the attained dimensional scores is adequate, the psychometric properties of some of the syndrome scales are low and should not be used independently for determining diagnosis. The Achenbach System is particularly used in clinical research.

The Behavior Assessment System for Children–Second Edition (BASC-2; Reynolds & Kamphaus, 2004) measures adaptive skills, behavioral symptoms, internalizing problems, externalizing problems, and school problems. There are Parent and Teacher Report forms available for individuals ages 2 to 21 and Self-Report forms for individuals ages 8 to 25. It has reasonable reliability and validity (Sattler & Hoge, 2006). The BASC-2 was principally developed to coordinate with *Diagnostic and Statistical Manual (DSM)*-based (American Psychiatric Association, 2000) diagnostic categories, and as such, holds greater reliability and validity with regard to the characterization of psychopathology seen in youth.

Mood Assessment in Children

To assess specific concerns regarding mood in children, such as anxiety, measures like the Multidimensional Anxiety Scale for Children (Marsh, 1997) and the Revised Children's Manifest Anxiety Scale, Second Edition (2008) can be administered. The Child Depression Inventory, Second Edition (CDI-II) and the Beck Youth Inventories-Second Edition (Beck, Beck, & Jolly, 2005) can both be administered to assess symptoms of depression, with critical items looking at suicidal ideation.

For the assessment of autism spectrum disorder, measures such as the Gilliam Asperger Disorder Scale (GADS; Gilliam, 2001), the Gilliam Autism Rating Scale–Second Edition (GARS-2; Gilliam, 2006), the Social Communication Questionnaire (SCQ; Rutter, LeCouteur, & Lord, 2003), and the Social Responsiveness Scale (Constantino, 2005) are all regularly used with parents and caregivers. These measures assess symptom domains pertinent to diagnosis, including communication, social interaction, repetitive and stereotyped behaviors, and restricted areas of interest.

Assessment of Mood in Adults

With regard to the assessment of mood concerns in adults, the Beck scales are commonly administered brief self-report measures of a client's symptoms of anxiety or depression. The Beck Depression Inventory (BDI) was originally developed in 1961 and was copyrighted in 1978 (Beck et al., 1961; Beck, Rush, Shaw, & Emery, 1979; Beck & Steer, 1993). It emphasized assessing both cognitive and behavioral symptoms of depression, and is consistent with the etiological model of depression developed by Beck and colleagues (1979). The current version, the BDI-II (Beck et al., 1996), is widely used for the assessment of depression in individuals aged 18 and above, and is commonly used with both psychiatric populations as well as to assess levels of depression in nonpsychiatric patients (Groth-Marnat, 2003). It has high test–retest (0.93 over a 1-week interval) and internal consistency reliability (0.89 to 0.94), as well as good content and divergent validity (Beck et al., 1996;

Dozois, Dobson, & Ahnerg, 1998; Groth-Marnat, 2003). The BDI-II has reasonable concurrent validity with other commonly used measures of depression, including the Hamilton Psychiatric Rating Scale for Depression, the Beck Hopelessness Scale, and the Depression Anxiety Stress Scale (Groth-Marnat, 2003). The BDI-II has a two-factor structure, addressing somatic–affective and cognitive symptoms (Beck et al., 1996). This structure has been replicated in other studies (Dozois et al., 1998).

Several other Beck scales are also commonly used with adults, including the Beck Anxiety Inventory (BAI; Beck, 1993a) and the Beck Hopelessness Scale (Beck, 1993b). The BAI can be administered to individuals between 17 and 80 years of age to assess the presence of and interference from anxiety symptoms over a period of one month. Like the BDI-II, the BAI also has a two-factor structure, addressing both cognitive and somatic symptoms, and it is consistent with Beck's cognitive model of anxiety (Beck, 1993a).

The State-Trait Anxiety Inventory (STAI) is one of the older and more commonly researched measures of anxiety (Spielberger, Gorsuch, Lushene, Vagg, & Jacobs, 1983). It has three separate test forms. The purpose of the STAI is to assess current state-associated symptoms of anxiety, including temporary experiences of worry and fear, and what has been termed *trait anxiety*, otherwise known as longstanding personality traits that are consistent with anxiety.

Finally, commonly used clinician ratings of mood include the Hamilton Rating Scale of Depression (HRSD; Hamilton, 1967) and Hamilton Rating Scale of Anxiety (HRSA; Hamilton, 1959). Both of these scales are publicly available, brief, ratings of observed symptoms of depression and anxiety, and are most commonly used in clinical research. Because both the Beck and Hamilton scales are meant to assess current symptoms of depression and anxiety, they can be used to monitor not only present mood status, but also treatment progress.

Cognitive Functioning

Both psychoeducational and neuropsychological assessment involve systematic, standardized testing across multiple domains of cognitive functioning, including general intellectual ability, attention, verbal and language skills, visual perceptual and motor capacities, memory, and executive functioning skills (Sparrow & Davis, 2000). Assessment of general cognitive capability typically involves the use of an intelligence test battery, like the Wechsler scales, whose construction is primarily based on psychological theories of skill and capacity. Many of the most commonly used intellectual batteries are based on or incorporate aspects of the Cattell–Horn–Carroll (CHC) theory of intelligence in their development.

CHC theory refers to the combination of two prominent models of intelligence: the Cattell–Horn Model and Carroll's Three Stratum Model (1993). The Cattell–Horn Model (Horn & Cattell, 1967) postulates two types of intelligence: fluid and crystallized. *Fluid intelligence* refers to nonverbal and primarily non-culturally biased abilities, such as new learning and efficiency on novel tasks (Sattler, 2001). *Crystallized intelligence* refers to an individual's knowledge base or range of acquired skills, which are dependent on exposure to both culture and the specific general information that is valued by a given culture. Carroll's Three Stratum Model, also known as Carroll's Three Stratum Factor Analytic Theory of Cognitive Abilities, was developed following a review of research studies that emphasized the presence of individual differences in cognitive abilities and suggested that the relationship among these individual differences can be captured across three categories: a set of narrow cognitive abilities, such as reading comprehension (Narrow); a set of eight broad factors that include fluid intelligence, crystallized intelligence, general memory and learning, visual perception, auditory perception, retrieval capacity, cognitive speediness, and processing speed (Broad); and a general intelligence factor (commonly referred to as *g*; General; Carroll, 1993). Because there was significant overlap among these theories, the Cattell–Horn–Carroll Integrated Model was proposed.

Historically, the CHC has included nine broad stratum abilities: Crystallized Intelligence (Gc), Fluid Intelligence (Gf), Quantitative Reasoning (Gq), Reading and Writing Ability (Grw), Short-Term Memory (Gsm), Long-Term Storage and Retrieval (Glr), Visual Processing (Gv), Auditory Processing (Ga), and Processing Speed (Gs) (Sattler, 2001). In a review of the factor analysis research on CHC, McGrew (2005) proposed that six additional domains should be added to this structure to improve its capacity for fully representing the range of abilities that ultimately comprise *g*.

Common Intellectual Batteries

The first version of the Stanford-Binet Intelligence Test was published in 1905, and was based on an adaptation of the Binet–Simon Scale. It is currently in its fifth version. The Stanford-Binet Intelligence Scales–Fifth Edition (SB-5) is appropriate for individuals aged 2 to 85 years of age. It generates a Full Scale IQ score, which is a measure of general cognitive abilities, and Nonverbal and Verbal Domain Scores. Cognitive Factor Scores, across verbal and nonverbal demands for information processing, include Fluid Reasoning, Knowledge, Quantitative Reasoning, Visual-Spatial Processing, and Working Memory. The psychometric properties of the SB-5 are quite good, with internal consistency reliability scores between the full scale and domain scores falling above 0.90 and the subtest coefficients ranging from 0.84 to 0.89 (Roid, 2003).

The current Wechsler intelligence scales include the Wechsler Adult Intelligence Scale–Fourth Edition, Wechsler Intelligence Scale for Children–Fourth Edition, and Wechsler Preschool and Primary Scale of Intelligence–Third Edition. The first version of the Wechsler-Bellevue Intelligence Scale was published for use with adults in 1939 and the Wechsler Intelligence Scale for Children was published in 1949. Wechsler defined intelligence as "the capacity to act purposely, think rationally, and to deal effectively with [the] environment" (Wechsler, 1949, p. 3). Each edition of the Wechsler scales is designed to provide an understanding of capability across domains that support this overall model of intellectual functioning.

The Wechsler Adult Intelligence Scale–Fourth Edition (WAIS-IV) is appropriate for use with individuals aged 16 to 89 (Wechsler, 2008). It generates a Full Scale IQ score, consistent with the standing model of a general intellectual factor, as well as factor analytically derived subscales, that reflect separable domains of skill. These four factors are Verbal Comprehension, Perceptual Reasoning, Working Memory, and Processing Speed, and each is represented as a primary index score. The reliability coefficients for the subtests, the index scores, and the Full Scale IQ scores range from 0.88 and 0.98. With the most recent iteration, the WAIS-IV, several new subtests were introduced, based on a move to a more neuropsychologically informed structure for the battery. These include Visual Puzzles, Finger Weights, and Cancellation. Several subtests were no longer found to aggregate within the principal factor structure, and were made optional. With this version, updated norms were developed that relate well with previous versions of the battery.

The Wechsler Intelligence Scale for Children–Fourth Edition (Wechsler, 2003) is appropriate for use with children aged 6 to 16 years of age. This measure generates a Full Scale IQ score as well as Verbal Comprehension, Perceptual Reasoning, Working Memory, and Processing Speed Index scores. The internal consistency coefficients among the index scores and the Full Scale IQ score range from 0.88 and 0.97, with test–retest scores ranging from 0.86 to 0.93. The WISC-IV Technical Manual provides information on score patterns for specific diagnostic groups, including children and adolescents with autism, ADHD, and learning disabilities, as a reference (Psychological Corporation, 2003).

For children aged 2 years, 6 months to 7 years, 3 months, the Wechsler Preschool and Primary Scale of Intelligence–Third Edition (WPPSI-III) can be administered to assess intellectual functioning. The WPPSI-III generates Verbal, Performance, and Full Scale IQ scores as well as a Processing Speed Quotient and General Language Component. The internal consistency scores for the scales ranged from 0.89 and 0.96 and it is reasonably well correlated with the WISC-IV (Psychological Corporation, 2003). Of note, the WPPSI-IV, which covers a slightly broader age group of 2 years, 6 months to 7 years, 7 months, was released in late 2012. It is structured quite differently from the WPPSI-III, following the broad neuropsychological model developed with the WISC-IV and WAIS-IV. It provides for a Full Scale IQ score, and then five subfactors, including a Verbal Comprehension Index (VCI), Visual Spatial Index (VSI), Working Memory Index (WMI), Fluid Reasoning Index (FRI), and Processing Speed Index (PSI). Ancillary measures and indices are also incorporated, to support improved clinical utility.

The Kaufman Assessment Battery for Children-II (KABC-11; 2004a) is an assessment of cognitive abilities for individuals aged 3 through 18. Its development was based on an integration of Cattell–Horn–Carroll theory and Luria's neuropsychological model. The KABC-II produces scores across five scales, including Simultaneous, Sequential, Planning, Learning, and Knowledge domains. It has been favorably compared psychometrically with the Wechsler scales and SB-5

The Woodcock-Johnson III Normative Update (NU) Tests of Cognitive Abilities (WJ-III NU Cog.; Woodcock, McGrew, & Mather, 2007b) is a test of cognitive abilities that is predominantly based on the Cattell–Horn–Carroll theory of cognitive abilities. The WJ-III NU Cog. is administered to individuals from the age of 2 to more than 90 years of age. It is commonly used in educational settings, often in tandem with its partner battery, the WJ-III Tests of Achievement. It has been found to have solid psychometric properties and is considered both reliable and valid.

There are also several nonverbal measures of intelligence that can be administered to individuals who are either unable to effectively use language, do not speak English as a primary language, or who are lower functioning, and hence less linguistically skilled. The Leiter International Performance Scale–Revised (Leiter-R; Roid & Miller, 1997) and the Universal Nonverbal Intelligence Test (UNIT; Bracken & McCullum, 1997) were both developed to be used in situations in which language is an issue. The Leiter-R is meant to be a nonverbal, nonculturally biased test of cognitive abilities. It is administered to individuals 2 to 21 years of age. It does not require verbal comprehension skill, as instructions are provided primarily through pantomime and gestures. The UNIT is another nonverbal measure of intelligence that is appropriate for use in individuals between the ages of 5 and 17. It, as well, requires no language for administration and is considered a useful nonculturally biased measure of cognitive functioning. As noted above, both of these nonverbal intelligence measures are reliable and appropriate for use with individuals who are non-English speakers, come from different cultural backgrounds, or who have language impairment, hearing impairment, or known cognitive delays.

Neuropsychological Functioning

Neuropsychological evaluations typically assess a number of domains of cognitive functioning, including attention and orientation, executive functioning, perceptual abilities, language and verbal abilities, memory, motor function, and visual construction and visual motor integration skills. There is an extensive list of neuropsychological assessment tools that are used during these evaluations; as a result, the most common batteries developed for neuropsychological assessment will be discussed here, from a broad standpoint, and without a focus on any one specific assessment tool. For more extensive information on the variety of specific tests that are available for use by the neuropsychologist, the reader is directed to other references, including detailed texts by Baron (2004), Lezak, Howieson, and Loring (2004), and Strauss, Sherman, and Spreen (2006).

Among the most commonly used fixed-battery approaches to neuropsychology, the Halstead–Reitan Neuropsychological Test Battery was most recently revised in 1993 (Reitan & Wolfson, 1993). In its current version, the Halstead–Reitan is composed of a number of individual measures that when used together, allow the clinician to distinguish patients with neurological insult from those who are healthy. Each of the tests that make up the Halstead–Reitan Battery can also be administered individually as a measure of a particular domain of functioning, and separate tests from the battery are commonly used as parts of more flexible assessment approaches to cognitive and neuropsychological functioning. The subtests include the Category Test, Tactual Performance Test, Speech-Sounds Perception Test, Seashore Rhythm Test, the Finger Tapping Test, and the Trail Making Test. There are also tests of aphasia, lateral dominance, and sensory–perceptual abilities included in the larger battery. The Halstead Impairment Index provides cutoff scores to help determine whether the examinee's performance is consistent with neurological insult.

The Neuropsychological Assessment Battery (Stern & White, 2003) consists of 36 different subtests that examine five areas of neuropsychological functioning, including Attention, Language, Memory, Spatial, and Executive Functioning. It is appropriate for use with individuals between the ages of 18 and 97 years of age. A screening module is available for use. The assessment can be used in its entirety as a full battery or individual subtests can be administered for screening or to address specific questions. There are descriptive statistics for the raw scores available for several specific populations, including individuals with ADHD, dementia, traumatic brain injury, multiple sclerosis, aphasia, HIV/AIDS, and in a rehab setting.

For children and adolescents, there are very few neuropsychological assessment batteries available. There is a children's version of the Halsted–Reitan Battery, which includes downward extensions to some of the subtests. However, norms for these measures are both significantly out of date and comprise very small samples. Additionally, norms for mid-adolescent ages are unavailable.

The NEPSY-II (A Developmental NEuroPSYchological Assessment; Korkman, Kirk, & Kemp, 2007) is a battery designed to evaluate multiple domains of neuropsychological development from preschool through adolescence. The NEPSY-II has two forms available: one for children aged 3 to 4 and the other, for individuals

5 through 16 years of age. It yields six domain scores across 32 subtests. The domains assessed include Attention/Executive Functioning, Language, Memory and Learning, Sensorimotor Functioning, Visual-Spatial Processing, and Social Perception. Like the NAB, the NEPSY-II can be administered in its entirety, or specific subtests can be administered individually to address targeted questions. The NEPSY-II has been co-normed with the WPPSI-3, WPPSI-4, and the WISC-4.

Ability, Aptitude, and Achievement

The term "ability" has been used to describe an individual's capacity to perform a specific skill or task and is thought to encompass both aptitude and achievement. Achievement typically refers to measures of knowledge acquired in specific settings like a classroom. Aptitude is thought to represent an individual's potential to learn a given task.

The Wechsler Individual Achievement Test–Third Edition (WIAT-III; Wechsler, 2009) is used to assess academic achievement in individuals aged 4 through 50 years. It has been co-normed with all other Wechsler intelligence scales and the Differential Ability Scale–Second Edition (DAS-II). Like each of the following measures discussed, the WIAT-III focuses principally on reading, including decoding and comprehension; mathematical operations and problem solving; and written expression. Listening comprehension and oral sharing of knowledge are also assessed.

The Kaufman Test of Educational Achievement, Second Edition (KTEA-II; Kaufman & Kaufman, 2004b) was co-normed with KABC-II. The KTEA-II can be administered to individuals 4 through 25 years of age for the Comprehensive Form and ages 4 through 90 years and older for the Brief Form. It emphasizes core academic skill development.

The Woodcock-Johnson III Normative Update (NU) Tests of Achievement (WJ-III NU Ach.; Woodcock et al., 2007a) assesses academic achievement and oral language. It was co-normed with the WJ-III NU Cog. The WJ-III NU Ach. has two parallel forms, and include both Standard and Extended batteries. Like the WJ-III NU Cog., the WJ-III NU Ach. is appropriate for use with individuals aged 2 through 90 years and older.

There are a number of assessments that focus on specific areas of academic achievement, such as reading (e.g., the Gray Oral Reading Test–5th Edition, the Gray Silent Reading Test, and the Nelson–Denny Reading Test), writing (Test of Written Language–4th Edition), and mathematics (Key Math). Each of these tests taps essential elements of academic skill development and supports data attained from the broader academic batteries.

Curriculum-based measurement is the regular assessment of children with short standardized and validated measures for the purpose of monitoring the development and mastery of academic skills. Performance-based measurement involves the evaluation of an individual's ability to perform a specific skill or produce a specific item or skill. These assessments can be completed through observation and/or ratings, or through use of a psychometric test of performance addressing the specific skill of interest.

Aptitude tests typically include a number of subtests that assess an individual's aptitude or potential to learn and master different skills, and are often used for job placement programs or educational and vocational counseling. There are few tests that assess aptitude purely; instead, most assess both achievement and aptitude.

An example is the Armed Services Vocational Aptitude Battery, which is used to determine both whether an individual is qualified to enroll in the Armed Forces, and to address aptitude for specific jobs or careers within the military.

The General Aptitude Test Battery (Form C & D, [GATB] 1983) was developed by the U.S. Employment Service to assess general intelligence, verbal aptitude, numerical aptitude, spatial aptitude, form perception, clerical perception, motor coordination, finger dexterity, and manual dexterity. The GATB is used for job placement and vocational counseling with high school students and adults. Many of the tasks on the GATB are timed, so individuals with slow processing speed or fine motor impairment may earn scores that are impacted. There has been some concern raised regarding differential validity and prediction across groups by race with this battery (Hartigan & Wigdor, 1989).

The Differential Aptitude Test–Fifth Edition (Bennett & Seashore, 1990) is an aptitude test developed for use with students in grades 7 to 12, as well as into adulthood. It assesses general cognitive abilities, perceptual abilities, and clerical and language skills.

In addition to these aptitude test batteries, there are specific aptitude tests that examine focused domains of potential job performance. Psychomotor ability tests assess fine motor speed, coordination, and dexterity as related to job performance; examples include the Purdue Pegboard test and the Minnesota Rate of Manipulation Tests. Another form of special aptitude measures is mechanical aptitude tests, which assess an examinee's performance on motor dexterity, spatial and perceptual reasoning, mechanical reasoning, and mechanical comprehension. Examples include the Bennett Mechanical Comprehension Test and the Mechanical Reasoning Test.

Personality

Structured personality assessment typically involves the use of self-administered, multiple choice, objective tests of personality and psychopathology. The Personality Assessment Inventory (PAI; Morey, 1991) consists of 344 items, which are written at a fourth-grade reading level. The PAI is appropriate for use with adults aged 18 and above. It was developed using a construct validation approach, in which subscales were first created during the initial design of the test, and the content and discriminant validity of the items included in the test were then examined to determine whether they were appropriate to the domains being measured. Items found nondiscriminant were removed from the test (Morey, 2003). The PAI consists of 22 scales, including 4 validity scales, 11 clinical scales tied to *DSM-IV-TR* (APA, 2000) diagnostic criteria, 5 scales that examine variables related to treatment, and 2 interpersonal functioning scales. Validity is assessed using the Inconsistency, Infrequency, Negative Impression, and Positive Impression scales. A malingering index has been published that provides guidelines for integrating information across a number of scales of the PAI to assess the likelihood of malingering (Morey, 1996). The Clinical Scales include Somatic Complaints, Anxiety, Anxiety-Related Disorders, Depression, Mania, Paranoia, Schizophrenia, Borderline Features, Alcohol Problems, and Drug Problems. The treatment scales include Aggression, Suicidal Ideation, Nonsupport, and Treatment Rejection. The Dominance and Warmth scales comprise the Interpersonal domain. An Adolescent Version of the PAI is available as well, for administration to individuals aged 12 through 18 years.

The Minnesota Multiphasic Personality Inventory was originally developed by Hathaway and McKinley in 1940 as a method for identifying psychiatric diagnoses. An empirical criterion keying strategy was used as the framework for its development. Empirical criterion keying refers to a process of test development in which test items are selected for inclusion and then scored within a scale, based on whether a target clinical population has responded differently from a comparison group. For the MMPI, items that differentiated between a control group and a clinical group comprising patients at the University of Minnesota Hospital who had major psychiatric diagnoses were ultimately included. The second edition of the MMPI (MMPI-2) was published in 1989 and included several important changes, including the addition of new scales, replacement of out-of-date test items, and updated norms (Butcher, Dahlstrom, Grahmam, Tellegen, & Kaemmer, 1989). During the revision process, the content scales were redeveloped using a content analysis approach as opposed to the empirical criterion keying approach. The MMPI-2 is appropriate for administration to adults aged 18 and older. There are 10 Clinical Scales, including Hypochondriasis, Depression, Hysteria, Psychopathic Deviation, Masculinity–Femininity, Paranoia, Psychasthenia, Hypomania, and Social Introversion. It yields validity scales, including the Lie Scale, F (Frequency Scale), K (Correction Scale), ? Scale (Cannot Say), VRIN Scale (Variable Response Inconsistency Scale), TRIN Scale (True Response Inconsistency), and S Scale (Superlative Self-Presentation). On the MMPI-2, raw scores are converted to *T*-scores, with a *T*-Score of 65 (94th percentile) or above being considered clinically significant. There is a Spanish version of the MMPI-2 as well as an adolescent version, the MMPI-A, which can be administered to individuals between 14 and 18 years of age (Butcher et al., 1992). Results obtained from the MMPI-2 are typically used to describe patterns of personality and behavioral difficulty. Review involves profile analysis as opposed to diagnostic assignment, as research has consistently indicated that neither the MMPI-2 nor MMPI-A is effective in facilitating a concrete diagnosis.

The Millon Clinical Multiaxial Inventory–Third Edition (MCMI-III) is a self-report questionnaire developed to assess personality (Millon, 1997). It was originally introduced in 1977 to support diagnosis of Axis II personality disorders. In its original development, both a rational-theory based method and empirical criterion keying were used. In rational-theory based methodology, specific items are selected to assess a construct that is determined a priori; in the case of the MCMI, content items were determined based on an overarching theory of personality and then validated to ensure that they in fact fit with the given theory being used. The MCMI-III can be administered to individuals 18 years and older. It is available in a Spanish version. It yields 28 scales, including four "modifying indices" (Disclosure, Desirability, Debasement, and Validity); 11 clinical personality profiles consistent with both *DSM-IV-TR* and theoretical criteria (Schizoid, Avoidant, Depressive, Dependent, Histrionic, Narcissistic, Antisocial, Aggressive, Compulsive, Passive–Aggressive, and Self-Defeating); three severe forms of personality pathology (Schizotypal, Borderline, and Paranoid); seven clinical syndromes (Anxiety, Somatoform, Bipolar: Manic, Dysthymia, Alcohol Dependence, Drug Dependence, and Post-Traumatic Stress Disorder); and three severe syndromes (Thought Disorder, Major Depression, and Delusional Disorder).

The use of unstructured personality assessments, also known as projective testing, is based on the assumption that determining how an individual responds to ambiguous stimuli can yield useful clinical information and diagnostic clarification. The Rorschach Inkblot Test (or Technique) is one of the most well-known projective assessments. With this procedure, Rorschach developed one of the first empirically based scoring systems to support the clinical interpretation of an examinee's responses to the inkblot stimuli. The Rorschach, as it is commonly referred to, consists of 10 cards containing bilaterally symmetrical inkblots on a white background. Although half of the inkblots are black and grey, three contain pastel colors, and two have portions that are red. The administration of the procedure involves two parts: the initial association phase, during which the examinee is presented with the cards in a predetermined order, and is asked to freely describe what is seen; and the inquiry phase, which involves the examiner collecting additional information from the examinee about the initial responses made through structured questioning.

There are several different scoring systems available for the Rorschach, although Exner's (2003) scoring system is the most widely used at this time. With the Exner System, the examiner scores each of the individual's responses based on a set of criteria, including Location (where on the inkblot the examinee is focused when giving a response), Determinants (the style or characteristics of the blot that led to an examinee's response), Content (either the category under which the examinee's response and description falls, or the quantity perceived in the response), and whether the response offered is Popular (frequently observed in the sample population) or not. A series of Special Scores based on 15 categories that can be used to take into account rare or unusual aspects of responses have been developed. It is noteworthy that significant controversy surrounding the use of the Rorschach continues to date, due mostly to concerns regarding the psychometric properties of the measure. Research has yielded inconsistent findings in terms of validity and reliability; for example, research regarding the sensitivity of the Rorschach Inkblot Test to discriminate psychopaths from nonpsychopaths has been quite inconsistent (Gacono & Meloy, 2009; Wood et al., 2010). Presently, many programs in professional psychology provide limited instruction in the Rorschach, given this ongoing uncertainty about its validity and usefulness apart from other means of clinical information gathering.

Vocational Interest

Assessments of vocational interest have been used in the field of psychology for almost a century. Many of the commonly used vocational interest assessments have been developed from E. K. Strong's early work in the empirical construction of occupation scales and John Holland's theory of vocational interest (Campbell & Borgen, 1999). Holland posits that there are six dimensions of vocational interest that he conceptualized in terms of a hexagon (Holland, 1997). Each dimension is arranged around the hexagon in a clockwise direction starting with what he termed "Realistic." The interest domains identified are denoted as RIASEC, and include: Realistic, Investigative, Artistic, Social, Enterprising, and Conventional.

The Self-Directed Search was originally published in 1979 and most recently revised in 1994. It is a self-report questionnaire that can be both scored and interpreted by the individual taking the test. Scoring allows the examinee to identify a score profile (the top three domain scores) and compare it to an assortment of profiles for different occupations and fields of study.

E. K. Strong first published the Strong Vocational Interest Inventory in 1927. To generate scoring scales and develop norms for this measure, he asked participants from a number of different occupational backgrounds what they were interested in and then compared the results obtained across a diverse group of individuals both employed in and apart from the occupations that were of interest (Campbell & Borgen, 1999). Since its inception, the Strong Vocational Interest Inventory has been revised several times to support its continued use, given occupational changes over time. The most recent version of the Strong Interest Inventory (2012) yields scores across four scales: General Occupational Themes, Basic Interest Scales, Personal Style Scales, and Occupational Scales. The General Occupational Themes scale measures the six categories of occupational interest developed by Holland's work that were mentioned previously (RIASEC). The Basic Interest scale assesses areas of vocational interest, whereas the Personal Style scale assesses work style, learning environment, leadership style, risk taking, and team orientation. Finally the occupational scale assesses the fit between an individual's interests and the interests of people of the same gender in a given occupation or career.

The Kuder Occupational Interest Survey is a self-report measure of vocational interest that was developed by measuring the similarity between an individual's responses and the average interests of people employed in a given occupation. It yields scores across four domains: Occupational scales, College Major scales, Vocational Interest Estimates, and Dependability Indices.

The Campbell Interest and Skill Survey (Campbell, 1992) is the most recent addition to the vocational interest inventories. It was originally published in 1992 and yields scores related to occupational orientation (Orientation scales), which are similar to the range of interests described by Holland's theory. It also includes Basic and Occupational Scales, making it similar to other surveys mentioned previously.

Health Behavior

A growing number of measures have been developed over the latter half of the twentieth century and into the 21st century to assist in understanding emotional and behavioral status in individuals with medical and health concerns. Many of these measures have been developed for use in ongoing research looking at the interface between health and behavior (e.g., health-related quality-of-life inventories, such as the EQ-5D or the PedsQL [Pediatric Quality of Life Inventory]). A small number of measures have been introduced into the clinical realm, given their usefulness in helping characterize specific concerns, such as difficulties with treatment adherence and mood secondary to illness. The majority of these measures are devoted to a particular domain or focus of interest, such as physical activity, risky behaviors, such as drinking or cigarette smoking, or eating patterns. The Youth Risk Behavior Surveillance System (YRBSS) is a self-report measure comprising questions addressing activity level (e.g., television watching) and engagement in risk behaviors (e.g., drinking, substance use, and sexual behaviors), that can be administered to adolescents and early adults. An adult version, the Behavioral Risk Factor Surveillance System (BRFSS), covers similar domains of functioning.

Broad assessments of health behaviors are less available for general clinical use. One example of a broad health measure is the Battery for Health Improvement–Second Edition (BHI-2; Bruns & Disorbio, 2003), which was developed to assess psychological issues that impact evaluation and treatment of medical patients.

The results of the BHI-2 can be used to facilitate the development of a treatment plan to address ongoing concerns, improve quality of life, and potentially improve treatment adherence. The BHI-2 can be administered to individuals 18 through 65 years of age. It generates Validity Scales, Physical Symptom Scales, Affective Scales, Character Scales, and Psychosocial Scales.

Malingering

The question of malingering has received a significant amount of focus in recent years in response to heightened concerns regarding secondary gain and its impact on assessment. As psychologists have become increasingly involved in forensic consultations, questions regarding motivation and investment have become more common, as well. Symptom validity testing refers to the development and use of measures and assessment procedures to try to assess an examinee's level of effort and investment during psychological testing; measures used for this purpose are referred to as SVTs. Malingering or lack of effort can be assessed directly or by examining the validity scales of various assessment measures. Personality assessment instruments, including the PAI, PAI-A, MMPI-2, MMPI-A, and MCMI-III all include validity scales, which should be examined first in order to determine whether an examinee's approach to the completion of the measure was reliable and consistent. The validity scales specifically support the examiner's ability to interpret the results of these assessment measures and to evaluate response biases that may impact profiles obtained. Similarly, many of the self-report and informant-report questionnaires assessing behavior and social–emotional functioning now include validity indices. Objective measures of validity commonly used by neuropsychologists include the Test of Memory Malingering, Rey 15-Item Test, and the Recognition Memory Test; these are the most commonly used SVTs in clinical practice (Slick, Tan, Strauss, & Hultsch, 2004).

Assessment of Competence and Criminal Responsibility

Competency to stand trial refers to a defendant's ability to understand and participate in legal proceedings. This law comes from the ruling set forth in *Dusky v. United States* (1960), in which the U.S. Supreme Court provided that a defendant must have "sufficient present ability to consult with his lawyer with a reasonable degree of rational understanding…[and have a] rational as well as factual understanding of the proceedings against him" (Otto, 2006, p. 83). The role of psychologists in competency evaluations is to assess and describe an individual's ability to both understand and participate in legal proceedings, and identify and describe any psychological disorders, cognitive impairment, or neurological insult that may impact capacity.

Separate from competency to stand trial is the question of whether a "not guilty by reason of insanity" (NGRI) defense is appropriate for use with a specific trial involving a person claiming mental illness as a reason behind her crime. Although this plea is rarely used in court, psychologists are frequently called on to evaluate criminal responsibility (Stafford & Ben-Porath, 2002). The majority of jurisdictions in the United States have adopted the American Law Institute (ALI)

Test (1962) as a standard for determining criminal responsibility. The first paragraphs read:

1. A person is not responsible for criminal conduct if at the time of such conduct as a result of mental disease or defect he lacks substantial capacity either to appreciate the criminality of his conduct or to conform his conduct to the requirements of the law.

2. As noted in the Article, the terms "mental disease or defect" do not include an abnormality manifested by repeated criminal or otherwise antisocial conduct.

Furthermore, in 1984, Congress passed the Insanity Defense Reform Act, which now stands in all federal jurisdictions. This Act adopts the M'Naghten Rule (Stafford & Ben-Porath, 2002), a standard of criminal responsibility, which must prove that, at the time of committing a criminal act, the accused did not know what he or she was doing because of a "severe mental disease or defect," putting the burden of proof on the accused. There are other legal definitions that psychologists should be aware of that apply to the idea of criminal responsibility, specifically the "guilty but mentally ill" plea and a finding of "diminished capacity." Similar to the discussion above regarding the insanity defense, "guilty but mentally ill" is a plea that acknowledges the contribution of a mental illness and its impact on functioning when addressing the defendant's guilt and advises the approach to sentencing, as a result. Diminished capacity is a legal doctrine that allows psychologists to testify as to whether or not a defendant had mental capacity to intend to commit a crime (in legal terms, *mens rea*; Stafford & Ben-Porath, 2002). The Rogers Criminal Responsibility Assessment Scales (Rogers, 1984) have been developed to facilitate this type of evaluation. Guidelines are also available in several texts to assist in this area of practice (Rogers & Shuman, 2000; Stafford & Ben-Porath, 2002).

Risk of Future Violence

There are two types of assessments of aggression that psychologists are commonly asked to undertake: retrospective and prospective assessment of aggression risk. Retrospective assessments involve an attempt to assess or evaluate aggression that has happened in the past in order to explain the ongoing propensity toward such behavior moving forward. This type of assessment is important in treatment planning, because past aggressive acts can inform ongoing understanding of risk for poor behavior, and as a result, help to guide the identification and implementation of appropriate treatment interventions aimed at preventing future aggression (Megargee, 2002).

Prospective evaluations of aggression are risk assessments used to examine "dangerousness." This is a legal term used to describe "an individual's propensity to commit dangerous acts" (Scott & Resnick, 2006, p. 599). With this type of assessment, a psychologist is asked to determine whether aggression will occur in the future, committed either by a person or group, and if it is believed likely to occur, what the aggressive behavior will ultimately look like.

Individual risk assessments attempt to determine whether there is a threat, currently or in the immediate future, that a specific individual will engage in aggressive behavior. Unfortunately, there are no structured psychological measures or interviews currently in use that have demonstrated strong predictive validity for assessing future aggression (Megargee, 2002; Scott & Resnick, 2006).

With regard to risk for violence and aggression, available assessment approaches that are typically used include collecting information about an individual's past from case history; conducting a clinical interview with the individual suspected to be at risk for such behavior; and conducting interviews with that individual's family members, friends, co-workers, and acquaintances. When reviewing the patient's history, attention should be paid to known factors that increase risk for violence, including a history of aggressive behavior and violent acts (Klassen & O'Connor, 1988; MacArthur Foundation, 2001); a history of substance abuse; a history of psychosis, specifically prior to hospitalization or treatment; and a history of psychiatric and personality disorders that have been associated with an increased risk of violence, such as antisocial personality disorder, borderline personality disorder, and personality disorder not otherwise specified (Scott & Resnick, 2006). During an interview with the examinee, a clinician should attend to the individual's affective state and interpersonal style with regard to emotion; it has been found that individuals who are angry or are unable to show empathy for others are at a higher risk for committing a violent act (Menzies, Webster, & Spejak, 1985). Clinicians should assess for and about the experience of emotions that often lead to aggression, such as anger, hostility, rage, and hatred (Megargee, 2002). These can be assessed through direct interview and the use of psychological measures such as the MMPI-2 or MMPI-A, the MCMI-III, the PAI, or the State-Trait Anger Expression Inventory–2 (Spielberger, 1999).

There are several risk assessment instruments that have been developed to be used directly in this context, including the Hare Psychopathy Checklist–Revised (PCL-R; Hare, 1991), the Violence Risk Appraisal Guide (Webster, Harris, & Rice, 1994), and the Historical, Clinical, Risk Management-20 (HCR-20; Webster, Douglas, Eaves, & Hart, 1997). It is important to note that none of these measures should be used in isolation when determining risk; however, each can be useful in conjunction with other clinical data when gathering information regarding risk. Finally, clinicians must also be attentive to and aware of the role secondary gain and extrinsic motivation can play with regard to the risk for and display of aggressive behavior (Magargee, 2002).

Suicide Evaluation

Assessment of suicide risk should be part of any evaluation conducted with a client, either as part of the initial diagnostic evaluation, part of a neuropsychological or psychological evaluation, or integrated into ongoing treatment. Clinicians need to ask patients about the presence of current and/or past suicidal ideation and behaviors. If past ideation and behaviors are endorsed, detailed information about when these past thoughts and behaviors occurred, the content of the ideation, whether a plan was developed, and the details of the behaviors should be openly discussed, including assessing whether the patient exhibited active or passive suicidal behaviors. When assessing current risk, information should be gathered, through an interview with the patient that is either structured or unstructured, about his or her current thoughts and plans. Additionally, a set of psychological measures that address risk of suicide can be administered; see a list of assessment measures later in this section. Information can also be gathered from other informants such as spouses, family members, and friends.

Assessment of suicide risk requires the clinician to examine the seriousness of the threat, the ideation associated with the threat, the motivating factors related to the threat, the presence and viability of the plan, and access to means to complete the suicide plan (Sattler & Hoge, 2006). When conducting an interview, the clinician is advised to keep in mind seven risk factors for suicide that have been identified by Joiner, Walker, Rudd, and Jobes (1999). These include previous suicidal behavior, types of current suicidal ideation and symptoms, precipitant stressors, overall symptom presentation, self-control and impulsivity, predispositions, and protective factors. As noted above, there are specific assessment tools that are available to help assess suicide risk; these include the Beck Depression Inventory–Second Edition (Beck et al., 1996), Beck Hopelessness Scale (BHI; Beck, 1993b), Beck Scale for Suicidal Ideation (BSSI; Beck, 1991), Suicidal Ideation Questionnaire (SIQ; Reynolds, 1987, 1988), and the Suicidal Behavior History Form (Reynolds & Mazza, 1992). For additional information regarding measures of suicidal risk, the reader is referred to Brown's review of suicide evaluation measures available on the National Institute of Mental Health (NIMH) website as well as the chapter written by Stolberg and Bongar (2002).

Issues Associated With Differential Diagnosis

Differential diagnosis refers to the process by which a clinician considers the possible multiple sources behind a patient's symptoms, cognitive deficits, or behavioral difficulties, by assessing which of several possible diagnostic categories, together or independently, best explain or describe a given pattern of concerns. The process of making a differential diagnosis involves generating multiple hypotheses that are based on the presenting patient's current problems, his or her history of difficulty, the information obtained from informants, and the clinical impression that develops, based on interview with the individual (Lezak et al., 2004). These hypotheses regarding possible diagnoses are evaluated systematically by comparing the symptom profile, performance on assessment measures (if administered), and the degree of current impairment in tandem with knowledge about base rates of the disorder. Ultimately, the clinician comes to a decision regarding a likely given diagnosis or diagnoses, in the case of multiple concerns. For example, in clinical neuropsychology, this process references a profile of strengths and weaknesses across neuropsychological testing data, and a resulting comparison of this data with profiles that are empirically developed and described in the literature regarding individuals with neurological, medical, developmental, and/or psychiatric disorders. As data are collected, hypotheses regarding diagnosis are revised and adapted in order to match and fit with criteria consistent with a given psychiatric, medical, or neuropsychological diagnosis (Lezak et al., 2004).

Criteria for Selection and Adaptation of Assessment Methods

One of the primary considerations when selecting an assessment method or tool is the extent to which the measure can be used to answer the referral question. In addressing this decision, the clinician considers her own training, familiarity with a given measure, and the experience and knowledge required to appropriately interpret the data generated by a given assessment. The time and expense required to administer one assessment compared to another are also considered. To support the choice, the psychometric properties of the measure under consideration are reviewed to assist in ensuring that the measure(s) to be administered within an assessment battery are valid and reliable for the questions being asked (Groth-Marnat, 2003).

Special considerations are required when selecting and administering assessment measures with specific populations. For patients with sensory (e.g., vision or hearing) or motor impairment, consideration is given to the disability status of the examinee to ensure that measures used are least likely to be impacted by a given impairment. Additional attention is paid to how test administration materials may be adapted for use with individuals with impairment (e.g., enlarging text for patients with vision impairment or ensuring that test materials are in the appropriate visual field for those patients with a visual field cut). Lezak and colleagues (2004) describe a number of accommodations to consider when assessing individuals with sensory, motor, or severe cognitive impairment.

When working with patients from culturally and linguistically diverse backgrounds, clinicians must be aware of issues related to racial and ethnic identity, acculturation, language, and cultural norms in terms of how they impact and influence behavior. Additionally, expectations about gender roles and family dynamics, religion, socioeconomic status, understanding and acceptance of the field of psychology, and cultural patterns for handling stress or crisis, among other issues, are important factors to consider and address. When conducting standardized assessments with individuals who are from diverse backgrounds, clinicians need to be very cognizant of concerns regarding evaluation bias in assessment; this is specifically the case with regard to intellectual testing. It is best when the examiner is able to choose a test that has been found to have few differences across cultural groups in its understanding and completion. For example, Levav, Mirsky, French, and Bartko (1998) found that reaction-time measures embedded in tests of sustained attention were not significantly impacted by culture or education level, whereas other aspects of attention assessed were significantly different based on both country of origin and education level. For individuals for whom English is not the primary language, there are a number of assessment measures available that require either a nonverbal response, or that are standardized for use with other languages that can be considered. Additionally, use of a translator may be warranted, although there are a number of risks involved in taking that approach. Measures of cognitive abilities that are theoretically culture free and are less likely to be impacted by language difference (e.g., the Leiter-R or UNIT, both discussed previously) are often acceptable options. For additional information on this topic, the reader is referred to the *Handbook of Multicultural Assessment,* Third Edition (Suzuki, Ponterotto, & Meller, 2008).

Diagnostic Classification Systems

International Classification of Diseases

The International Classification of Diseases (ICD) is recognized as the universally accepted classification system used by the medical community. Described by the World Health Organization (WHO) as "the standard diagnostic tool for epidemiology, health management, and clinical purposes" (World Health Organization, 2012), the ICD is used for disease classification and is the core system used in the coding of claims for the purpose of health insurance reimbursement. ICD classifications also enable the collection and storage of diagnostic data for such purposes as determining incidence and prevalence, as well as mortality and morbidity. The ICD, currently in its tenth iteration, has its roots in a diagnostic coding system initiated in Great Britain in 1839. Known as the London Bills of Mortality and later as the International List of Causes of Death, the formal classification of disease came under the direction of the World Health Organization in 1948 in an effort to track trends in disease and international health (Grider, 2012). Interest in using the ICD clinically resulted in a revision of the ICD-9 known as the International Classification of Diseases, 9th Revision, Clinical Modification (ICD-9-CM). The final transition from ICD-9-CM to ICD-10-CM is to be implemented on October 1, 2013, and the development of ICD-11 is under way and expected to be implemented in 2015. The ICD-9 classifies disorders by specifically identifying the area or system of the body that is affected and the nature of the injury or condition. Modifications presented in the ICD-10 will allow for greater specificity. In contrast to the current three- to five-character diagnostic codes, the ICD-10 will allow for codes of three to seven characters in length. These will provide more details in terms of anatomy, injury or condition, and type of intervention.

Diagnostic and Statistical Manual of Mental Disorders

The *Diagnostic and Statistical Manual of Mental Disorders*, Fifth Edition (*DSM-5*) published by the American Psychiatric Association in 2013, provides the criteria required to diagnose mental health disorders in both children and adults. This formal classification of mental disorders was first developed in response to the need for collecting statistical information. The initial documentation of mental illness fell under one category "idiocy/insanity" in the U.S. 1840 census. Disorders were further broken down into seven categories for the 1880 census. In 1917, a formal committee was convened consisting of the Committee on Statistics of the American Psychiatric Association and the National Commission on Mental Hygiene to gather statistics across mental health institutions. The U.S. Army later formed its own system of categorization to address disorders that presented in outpatient settings that were treating veterans and servicemen during World War II. The ICD-6 was released following the war, largely in collaboration with the Veterans Administration, and for the first time included a section addressing mental disorders. The first edition of the *Diagnostic and Statistical Manual of Mental Disorders* (*DSM*) was published in 1952. As with each subsequent revision, the *DSM-I* was developed in coordination with the ICD. With an emphasis on clinical utility, the *DSM-I* contained descriptions of diagnostic categories. The *DSM-II* was published in 1968 and included a greater number of disorders as well as changes in terminology. The seventh printing of the *DSM-II*, published in 1974, removed homosexuality as a diagnostic category. The *DSM-III*, published in 1980, introduced significant changes such as the multiaxial system and explicit diagnostic criteria. Several inconsistencies were found within this new system as well as unclear criteria for several categories. As such, revisions and corrections were made in the publication of the *DSM-III-R*, which was released in 1987.

The *DSM-IV*, published in 1994, was developed using a three-stage empirical process, including comprehensive and systematic literature review, reanalysis of data, and field trials comparing *DSM-III*, *DSM-III-R*, ICD-10, and proposed *DSM-IV* criterion sets across several sites (APA, 2000). A text revision of *DSM-IV* was published in 2000. The *DSM-IV-TR* sought to bridge the gap between the *DSM-IV* and the fifth edition, which was released in 2013. Although no new categories, disorders, or subtypes were introduced in the *DSM-IV-TR*, revisions and additions were included in the text sections to reflect updated empirical findings. This elaboration and clarification in such areas as Diagnostic Features, Associated Features and Disorders, Specific Culture and Gender Features, and Prevalence served to enhance the clinical value of the *DSM-IV*.

The *DSM-IV-TR* organizes disorders into 16 diagnostic classes, with an additional section named Other Conditions That May Be a Focus of Clinical Attention (APA, 2000). Although the *DSM-IV-TR* is organized using a categorical approach, it cannot be assumed that each category of mental disorder is a discrete entity and is mutually exclusive of other diagnostic categories. Additionally, because individuals must meet only subsets of items from a longer list in a polythetic criterion set, there is no singular presentation of diagnosis. Individuals may meet criteria for the same disorder but presentation of symptoms may not be homogeneous. Although this categorical approach presents limitations in terms of boundaries between diagnoses and heterogeneity between cases within classes, it is a stronger choice than a dimensional approach. Although the dimensional approach has the benefit of classifying disorders based on quantification of characteristics, thus allowing for more reliable diagnosis of boundary cases and the reporting of subthreshold cases, dimensional approaches have proven unsuccessful as numerical descriptors do not provide a useful clinical picture of disorders (APA, 2000). Additionally, they are incompatible with settings requiring discrete labeling of disorders. Attempts are being made with the fifth and newest edition of the *DSM* to incorporate a more dimensional format, allowing for symptoms to be considered along diagnostic spectrums and allowing for consideration of severity (Widiger et al., 2005).

DSM-IV-TR diagnoses are made with the following multiaxial assessment format:

Axis I   Clinical Disorders
             Other Conditions That May Be a Focus of Clinical Attention

Axis II   Personality Disorders
             Mental Retardation

Axis III   General Medical Conditions

Axis IV   Psychosocial and Environmental Problems

Axis V   Global Assessment of Functioning

When more than one Axis I diagnosis is present, the principal diagnosis is listed first. Personality disorders are listed on Axis II. Relevant general medical conditions are listed on Axis III, except in such cases that the mental disorder is the direct result of the medical condition. In those instances, the clinical disorder is listed on Axis I with the notation that it is due to the related medical disorder. The relevant medical disorder is then noted on Axis III. For example, Dementia Due to a General Medical Condition would be listed on Axis I, whereas the medical condition (e.g., Parkinson's Disease or HIV) would be listed on Axis III. Psychosocial and environmental problems are notated on Axis IV and may include problems with primary support group, problems related to social environment, educational problems, occupational problems, housing problems, economic problems, problems with access to health care services, problems related to interaction with the legal system/crime, or other psychosocial and environmental problems (e.g., exposure to disaster, war, etc.). The Global Assessment of Functioning (GAF) reported on Axis V is a rating of the individual's current overall psychological, social, and occupational functioning. The GAF has a range of 0 to 100, with 100 being the highest level of functioning. Symptom severity and level of functioning are both taken into account with the determination of functioning being based on the worse of the two.

In such cases, where full criteria are not met for a diagnosis, but clinical presentation is positive for significant symptomology, several qualifiers may be used to indicate diagnostic uncertainty. A provisional diagnosis may be made when information is lacking to make a firm diagnosis but there is ample evidence that full criteria for the disorder will be met once this information is obtained. This may occur when additional history must be gathered or the information provided is incomplete or lacking in detail. A provisional diagnosis is also warranted when symptoms are present and do not appear to be remitting imminently, but have not met the minimum time requirement for a specific disorder. The descriptor of Not Otherwise Specified is applied when symptoms are below the diagnostic threshold for a particular disorder, but are still consistent with the prescribed clinical presentation of the disorder. It is also applicable when etiology is uncertain, when data collection is incomplete but presentation fits within a particular diagnostic class, or when symptoms do not meet diagnostic criteria but cause significant distress or impairment. Diagnosis is deferred when inadequate information is provided for diagnostic judgment.

Factors Influencing Interpretation of Data and Decision Making

Once data are collected, whether through interview, observation, assessment, or collateral report, interpretations are made. Psychologists ideally follow an evidence-based approach to diagnosis. Evidence-based decisions are made by integrating empirical research, clinician training, and comprehensive data collection, typically garnered through the use of standardized, norm-referenced measures. This model limits the use of the clinician's intuitive judgment and does not allow for heuristics such as trial and error, rules of thumb, or educated guesses, all of which may contribute to error or bias. Clinicians and researchers such as Paul Meehl and Sir Karl Popper supported the use of algorithmic analysis of data as opposed to subjective inference in interpreting and predicting behavior. Meehl's research supported the use of "mechanical data" over clinical prediction (Meehl, 1978). Cultural and group differences may (and often do) exist, and these are important to acknowledge and address; however, these differences must be evident in data rather than being formulated as a result of the clinician's own standards and perceptions, which may reflect cultural biases rather than actual differences. Examination of base rates provides a context for the interpretation of information. Rather than focusing solely on observable qualities, base rates provide important statistical information that guides diagnostic judgments by addressing directly the quantity of a population that will likely meet specific criteria, thus providing a perspective in terms of population characteristics and expectations.

Methods for the Measurement of Individual, Couples, Family, Group, and Organizational Change

Once an intervention has been put in place, adherence to that intervention is critical in the evaluation of the efficacy of that treatment. Additionally, in cases of empirically proven interventions, adherence to a treatment plan is of the utmost importance for positive outcomes. Participants must comply with treatment plans in order to fully benefit from the intervention. There are several methods of monitoring treatment compliance and efficacy. Continuous monitoring of behavior can be accomplished through continuous observation. This may be conducted by an outside observer or the subject and recorded in writing, through video recording, or computerized documentation. Examiners focus on the count or number of occurrences of the behavior, the rate or frequency of the behavior per unit of time, how that rate changes over time, and the duration of the behavior.

Behavioral analysis refers to the observation and measurement of a specific behavior. The target behavior should be measured prior to intervention and then continually monitored throughout the course of intervention to observe change. Ideally, the behavior is observed across environments. Examiners note antecedents to the behavior as well as consequences of the behavior. Observers may also note the subject's responses to the behavioral consequences. Knowledge on the part of the participant that the behavior is being observed may actually serve to impact the target behavior. This is known as the *observer effect*.

Organizations monitor behavior in an attempt to promote best practices. This process, known as benchmarking, follows the same general methodology of identifying a target behavior, observing and recording the frequency of the behavior, and developing an intervention to alter, eliminate, or replace the behavior. Organizations encourage behaviors that fit into their model of best practice and focus on behaviors that interfere with efficiency, productivity, and growth within the organization.

Response to intervention (RTI) uses frequent progress measurement to determine the efficacy of treatment planning and services. RTI employs short-term, as well as long-term, discrete measureable goals that can be assessed at predetermined points in time. RTI is most frequently used in schools to address learning and behavior difficulties. As with other forms of intervention monitoring, RTI serves to encourage accountability, both on the part of the student participating in the intervention, as well as those providing services.

In the case of treatment, and in RTI, relapse or failure to meet goals is defined by the continuation or return to the maladaptive behavior or unsatisfactory level of performance. Once relapse has been determined, care providers must then reassess the original treatment plan, revise interventions, and resume the monitoring of patient adherence. Several factors will affect treatment compliance. These include the patient's readiness and willingness to change, feasibility of intervention, and external support.

Use of Computers, the Internet, and Related Technology in Assessment and Evaluation

As technology has progressed over the last several decades, the field of psychology has sought to adjust to and benefit from these advances. The use of computers, the Internet, and related technology has had an impact on how assessments and diagnostic evaluations are conducted and scored, how therapeutic needs are met, and how issues of confidentiality are addressed. There have been many advantages resulting from the use of technological strides, including greater ease of record keeping and access, better coordination of care, quick and accurate computer scoring programs, statistical programs, and research accessibility (Strecher, 2007).

Although there appear to be many benefits inherent in these innovations, they also present questions related to such issues as validity, efficiency, ethics, and confidentiality. Examples of current research into these areas include the potential for compromised validity in computer-administered measures, patient resistance to computerized interface, threats to protected health information, and misuse of the Internet in terms of self-diagnosis and information gathering. Early findings suggest positive responses to such innovations as computer-based intervention (Marks & Cavanagh, 2009).

References

Achenbach, T. M., & Rescorla, L. A. (2001). *Manual for the ASEBA school-age forms & profiles*. Burlington, VT: University of Vermont, Research Center for Children, Youth, & Families.

Alagumalai, S., & Curtis, D. D. (2005). Classical test theory. In S. Alagumalai, D. D. Curtis, & N. Hungi (Eds.), *Applied Rasch measurement: A book of exemplars* (pp. 1–14). Dordrecht, Netherlands: Springer.

American Educational Research Association (AERA), American Psychological Association (APA), & National Council Measurement in Education (NCME). (1999). *Standards for educational and psychological testing*. Washington, DC: American Educational Research Association.

American Law Institute. (1962). *Model penal code. Section 4.01*. Philadelphia, PA: Author.

American Psychiatric Association. (1952). *Diagnostic and statistical manual of mental disorders*. Washington, DC: Americn Psychiatric Press.

American Psychiatric Association. (1974). *Diagnostic and statistical manual of mental disorders* (2nd ed.). Washington, DC: American Psychiatric Press.

American Psychiatric Association. (1980). *Diagnostic and statistical manual of mental disorders* (3rd ed.). Washington, DC: American Psychiatric Press.

American Psychiatric Association. (1987). *Diagnostic and statistical manual of mental disorders* (3rd ed., rev.). Washington, DC: American Psychiatric Press.

American Psychiatric Association. (1994). *Diagnostic and statistical manual of mental disorders* (4th ed.). Washington, DC: American Psychiatric Press.

American Psychiatric Association. (2000). *Diagnostic and statistical manual of mental disorders* (4th ed., text rev.). Washington, DC: American Psychiatric Press.

American Psychiatric Association. (2013). *Diagnostic and statistical manual of mental disorders* (5th ed.). Washington, DC: American Psychiatric Press.

American Psychological Association, American Educational Research Association, & National Council on Measurement Education. (1954). *Technical recommendations for psychological tests and diagnostic techniques*. Washington, DC: American Psychological Association.

Baron, I. S. (2004). *Neuropsychological evaluation of the child (Baron, Neuropsychological evaluation of the child)*. Oxford, UK: Oxford University Press.

Beck, A. T. (1991). *Beck Scale for Suicidal Ideation*. Upper Saddle River, NJ: Pearson Education.

Beck, A. T. (1993a). *Beck Anxiety Inventory*. Upper Saddle River, NJ: Pearson Education.

Beck, A. T. (1993b). *Beck Hopelessness Scale*. Upper Saddle River, NJ: Pearson Education.

Beck, A. T., & Steer, R. A. (1993). *Beck Depression Inventory*. San Antonio, TX: Psychological Corporation.

Beck, A. T., Steer, R. A., & Brown, G. K. (1996). *Beck Depression Inventory–II*. Upper Saddle River, NJ: Pearson Education.

Beck, A. T., Rush, A. J., Shaw, B. F., & Emery, G. (1979). *Cognitive therapy for depression*. New York, NY: Guilford Press.

Beck, A. T., Ward, C. H., Mendelson, M., Mock, J., & Erbaugh, J. (1961). An inventory for measuring depression. *Archives of General Psychiatry, 4*, 561–571.

Beck, J. S., Beck, A. T., & Jolly, J. B. (2005). *Beck Youth Inventories* (2nd ed.). Upper Saddle River, NJ: Pearson Education.

Bennett, H. G., & Seashore, A. G. (1990). *Differential Aptitude Test–5th edition (DAT-5)*. Upper Saddle River, NJ: Pearson Education.

Binet, A., & Simon, T. (1905). Methodes nouvelles pour le diagnostic du niveau intellectuel des anormaux. [A new method for the diagnosis of the intellectual level of abnormal persons]. *L'Annee Psychologique, 11*, 191–244.

Boake, C. (2008). Clinical neuropsychology. *Professional Psychology: Research and Practice, 39(2)*, 234–239.

Bracken, B. A., & McCullum, S. M. (1997). *Universal nonverbal intelligence test*. Austin, TX: Pro-Ed.

Brown, G. K. (2002). *A review of suicide assessment measures for intervention research with adults and older adults*. Rockville, MD: National Institute of Mental Health.

Bruns, D., & Disorbio, J. M. (2003). *Battery for health improvement-2*. Upper Saddle River, NJ: Pearson Education.

Butcher, J. N., Dahlstrom, W. G., Grahmam, J. R., Tellegen, A. M., & Kaemmer, B. (1989). *Minnesota multiphasic personality inventory–2 (MMPI-2): Manual for administration, scoring, and interpretation*. Minneapolis, MN: University of Minnesota Press.

Butcher, J. N., Williams, C. L., Graham, J. R., Archer, R. P., Tellegen, A., Ben-Porath, Y. S., & Kaemmer, B. (1992). *MMPI-A (Minnesota multiphasic personality inventory-adolescent): Manual for administration, scoring, and interpretation*. Minneapolis, MN: University of Minnesota Press.

Campbell, D. P. (1992). *Campbell interest and skill survey*. Minneapolis, MN: National Computer Systems.

Campbell, D. P., & Borgen, F. H. (1999). Holland's theory and the development of interest inventories. *Journal of Vocational Behavior, 55*, 86–101.

Campbell, D. T., & Fiske, D. W. (1959). Convergent and discriminant validation by the multitrait-multimethod matrix. *Psychological Bulletin, 56*, 81–105.

Carroll, J. B. (1993). *Human cognitive abilities: A survey of factor-analytic studies*. Cambridge, UK: Cambridge University Press.

Cohen, R. J., & Swerdlik, M. (2002). *Psychological testing and assessment: An introduction to tests and measurements*. New York, NY: McGraw-Hill.

Constantino, J. N. (2005). *Social responsiveness scale*. Los Angeles, CA: Western Psychological Services.

DeVellis, R. F. (2006). Classical test theory. *Medical Care, 44,* S50–S59.

Dozois, D. J. A., Dobson, K. S., & Ahnberg, J. L. (1998). A psychometric evaluation of the Beck Depression Inventory–II. *Psychological Assessment, 10,* 83–89.

Dusky v. United States. (1960). 362 US 402.

Exner, J. E. (2003). *The Rorschach: A comprehensive system. Volume 1: Basic foundations* (4th ed.). New York, NY: Wiley.

Gacono, C. B., & Meloy, J. R. (2009). Assessing antisocial and psychopathic personalities. In J. N. Butcher (Ed.), *Oxford handbook of personality assessment* (pp. 567–581). New York, NY: Oxford University Press.

Gao, X., & Harris, D. J. (2012). Generalizability theory. In H. Cooper (Ed.), *APA handbook of research methods in psychology, Vol. 1. Foundations, planning, measures, and psychometrics* (pp. 661–681). Washington, DC: American Psychological Association.

Gilliam, J. E. (2001). *Gilliam Asperger's disorder scale.* Austin, TX: Pro-Ed.

Gilliam, J. E. (2006). *Gilliam autism rating scale* (2nd ed.). Austin, TX: Pro-Ed.

Grider, D. J. (2012). *Principles of ICD-10-coding.* American Medical Association. New York, NY: Random House.

Groth-Marnat, G. (2003). *Handbook of psychological assessment* (4 Eds.). Hoboken, NJ: Wiley.

Hamilton, M. (1959). The assessment of anxiety states by rating. *British Journal of Medical Psychology, 32,* 50–55.

Hamilton, M. (1967). Development of a rating scale for primary depressive illness. *British Journal of Medical Psychology, 6,* 278–296.

Hare, R. D. (1991). *The Hare Psychopathy Checklist* (revised). Toronto, Ontario: Multi-Health Systems.

Hartigan, J. A., & Wigdor, A. K. (Eds.). (1989). *Fairness in employment testing: Validity generalization, minority issues, and the general aptitude test battery.* Washington, DC: National Academy Press.

Herk, N. A., & Thompson, R. C. (2012). *Strong interest inventory manual supplement: Occupational scales update 2012.* Mountain View, CA: CPP, Inc.

Hiltonsmith, R. W., & Keller, H. R. (1983). What happened to the setting in person-setting assessment? *Professional Psychology: Research and Practice, 14,* 419–434.

Holland, J. L. (1979). *Professional manual for the self-directed search.* Palo Alto, CA: Consulting Psychologists Press.

Holland, J. L. (1994). *The self-directed search.* Odessa, FL: Psychological Assessment Resources.

Holland, J. L. (1997). *Making vocational choices* (3rd ed.). Odessa, FL: Psychological Assessment Resources.

Horn, J. L., & Cattell, R. B. (1967). Age differences in fluid and crystallized intelligence. *Acta Psychologica, 26,* 107–129.

International Task Force on Assessment Center Guidelines. (2009). Guidelines and ethical considerations for assessment center operations. *International Journal of Selection and Assessment, 17,* 243–253.

Joiner, T. E., Walker, R. L., Rudd, M. D., & Jobes, D. A. (1999). Scientizing and routinizing the assessment of suicidality in outpatient practice. *Professional Psychology: Research and Practice, 30*(5), 447–453.

Kaufman, A. S., & Kaufman, N. L. (2004a). *Kaufman Assessment Battery for Children–Technical manual* (2nd ed.). Circle Pines, MN: American Guidance Service.

Kaufman, A. S., & Kaufman, N. L. (2004b). *Kaufman test of educational achievement* (2nd ed.). Circle Pines, MN: American Guidance Service.

Klassen, D., & O'Connor, W. A. (1988). A prospective study of predictors of violence in adult male mental health admissions. *Law and Human Behavior, 12,* 143–158.

Korkman, M., Kirk, U., & Kemp, S. (2007). *NEPSY-II, second edition: Clinical and interpretive manual.* Bloomington, MN: NCS Pearson.

Kovacs, M. (2011). *Children's Depression Inventory–I.* North Tonawanda, NY: Multi-Health Systems.

Larry P. v. Riles, 495 F. Supp. 926. (N.D. Ca. 1979).

Levav, M., Mirsky, A. F., French, L. M., & Bartko, J. J. (1998). Multinational neuropsychological testing: Performance of children and adults. *Journal of Clinical and Experimental Neuropsychology, 20,* 658–6772.

Lezak, M. D., Howieson, D. B., & Loring, D. W. (2004). *Neuropsychological assessment* (4th ed.). Oxford, UK: Oxford University Press.

MacAruthur Foundation. (2001). *The MacArthur violence risk assessment study executive summary.* Retrieved August 11, 2002, from http://macarthur.virginia.edu/risk.html

Marks, I., & Cavanagh, K. (2009). Computer-aided psychological treatments: Evolving issues. *Annual Review of Clinical Psychology, 5,* 121–141.

Marsh, J. S. (1997). *Multidimensional anxiety scale for children (MASC).* North Tonawanda, NY: Multi-Health Systems, Inc.

McGrew, K. S. (2005). *The Cattell–Horn–Carroll theory of cognitive abilities: Past, present, and future.* In D. P. Flanagan, J. L. Genshaft, & P. L. Harrison (Eds.), *Contemporary intellectual assessment: Theories, tests, and issues* (pp. 136–182). New York, NY: Guilford Press.

Meehl, P. E. (1978). Theoretical risks and tabular asterisks: Sir Karl, Sir Ronald, and the slow progress of soft psychology. *Journal of Consulting and Clinical Psychology, 46,* 806–834.

Megargee, E. I. (2002). Assessing the risk of aggression and violence. In J. N. Butcher (Eds.), *Clinical personality assessment: Practical approaches* (2nd ed., pp. 435–451). New York, NY: Oxford University Press.

Menzies, R. J., Webster, C. D., & Sepejak, D. S. (1985). The dimensions of dangerousness: Evaluating the accuracy of psychometric predictions of violence among forensic patients. *Law and Human Behavior, 9,* 49–70.

Miller, J. A., Tansy, M., & Hughes, T. L. (1998). Functional behavioral assessment: The link between problem behavior and effective intervention in schools. *Current Issues in Education, 1*(5). Retrieved December 10, 2012, from http://cie.asu.edu/volume1/number5/

Millon, T. (1997). *Millon clinical multiaxial inventory-III manual* (2nd ed.). Minneapolis, MN: National Computer Systems.

Morey, L. C. (1991). *The personality assessment inventory professional manual.* Odessa, FL: Psychological Assessment Resources.

Morey, L. C. (1996). *An interpretive guide to the personality assessment inventory.* Odessa, FL: Psychological Assessment Resources.

Morey, L. C. (2003). *Essentials of PAI assessment.* Hoboken, NJ: Wiley.

Morey, L. C. (2007). *The personality assessment inventory professional manual.* Lutz, FL: Psychological Assessment Resources.

National Center for Health. (n.d.). *About the international classification of diseases, 10th revision, clinical modification ICD-10-CM.* Available from http://www.cdc.gov/nchs/about/otheract/icd9/icd10cm.htm

Ollendick, T. H., & Hersen, M. (1984). An overview of child behavioral assessment. In T. H. Ollendick & M. Hersen (Eds.), *Handbook of child and adolescent assessment: Principles and procedures.* New York, NY: Allyn & Bacon.

Otto, R. K. (2006). Competency to stand trial. *Applied Psychology in Criminal Justice, 2,* 83–113.

Reitan, R. M., & Wolfson, D. (1993). *Halstead-Reitan neuropsychological test battery: Theory and clinical interpretation* (2nd ed.). Tucson, AZ: Neuropsychology Press.

Reynolds, W. M. (1987). *Suicidal ideation questionnaire.* Odessa, FL: Psychological Assessment Resources.

Reynolds, W. M. (1988). *Suicidal ideation questionnaire: Professional manual.* Odessa, FL: Psychological Assessment Resources.

Reynolds, C. R., & Kamphaus, R. W. (2004). BASC-2: *Behavior assessment system for children* (2nd ed.). Upper Saddle River, NJ: Pearson Education.

Reynolds, W. M., & Mazza, J. J. (1992). *Suicide behavior form: Clinician's guide.* Odessa, FL: Psychological Assessment Resources.

Reynolds, C. R., & Richmond, B. O. (2008). *Revised children's manifest anxiety scale: Second edition (RCMAS-2).* Western Psychological Services.

Rogers, R. (1984). *Rogers criminal responsibility assessment scales (R-CRAS) and test manual.* Odessa, FL: Psychological Assessment Resources.

Rogers, R., & Shuman, D. W. (2000). *Conducting insanity evaluations* (2nd ed.). New York, NY: Guilford Press.

Roid, G. H. (2003). *Stanford Binet Intelligence Scales–Fifth edition: Technical manual.* Itasca, IL: Riverside.

Roid, G. H., & Miller, L. J. (1995, 1997). *Leiter International Performance Scale–Revised.* Wood Dale, IL: Stoelting CO.

Rutter, M., LeCouteur, A., & Lord, C. (2003). *Social Communication Questionnaire.* Los Angeles, CA: Western Psychological Services.

Sattler, J. M. (2001). *Assessment of children: Cognitive applications* (4th ed.). San Diego, CA: Jerome M. Sattler.

Sattler, J. M., & Hoge, R. D. (2006). *Assessment of children: Behavioral, social, and clinical foundations* (5th ed.). San Diego, CA: Jerome M. Sattler.

Scott, C. L., & Resnick, P. J. (2006). Violence risk assessment in persons with mental illness. *Aggression and Violent Behavior, 11,* 598–611.

Slick, D. J., Tan, J. E., Strauss, E. H., & Hultsch, D. F. (2004). Detecting malingering: A survey of experts' practices. *Archives of Clinical Neuropsychology, 19,* 465–473.

Sparrow, S. S., & Davis, S. M. (2000). Recent advances in the assessment of intelligence and cognition. *Journal of Child Psychology and Psychiatry, 41,* 117–131.

Spearman, C. (1904). General intelligence, objectively determined and measured. *American Journal of Psychology, 15,* 201–293.

Speilberger, C. D. (1999). *State–Trait Anger Expression Inventory-2.* Lutz, FL: PAR, Inc.

Spielberger, C. D., Gorsuch, R. L., Lushene, R., Vagg, P. R., & Jacobs, G. A. (1983). *Manual for the State–Trait Anxiety Inventory.* Palo Alto, CA: Consulting Psychologists Press.

Stafford, K. P., & Ben-Porath, Y. S. (2002). Assessing clinical responsibility. In J. N. Butcher (Eds.), *Clinical personality assessment: Practical approaches* (2nd ed., pp. 452–465). New York, NY: Oxford University Press.

Stern, R. A., & White, T. (2003). *Neuropsychological assessment battery.* Lutz, FL: Psychological Assessment Resources.

Sternberg, R. J., & Kaufman, J. C. (1998). Human abilities. *Annual Review of Psychology, 49,* 479–502.

Stolberg, R., & Bongar, B. (2002). Assessment of suicide risk. In J. N. Butcher (Eds.), *Clinical personality assessment: Practical approaches* (2nd ed., pp. 435–451). New York, NY: Oxford University Press.

Strauss, E., Sherman, E. M. S., & Spreen, O. (2006). *A compendium of neuropsychological tests: Administration, norms, and commentary.* New York, NY: Oxford University Press.

Strecher, V. (2007). Internet methods for delivering behavioral and health-related interventions (eHealth). *Annual Review of Clinical Psychology, 3,* 53–76.

Strong, E. K., Jr. (1927). A vocational interest test. *Educational Record, 8,* 107–121.

Suzuki, L. A., Ponterotto, J. G., & Meller, P. J. (2008). *Handbook of multicultural assessment* (3rd ed.). San Francisco, CA: Wiley.

Webb, N. M., Shavelson, R. J., & Haertel, E. H. (2006). Reliability coefficients and generalizability theory. In C. R. Rao & S. Sinharay (Eds.), *Handbook of statistics* (Vol. 26, pp. 81–124). Amsterdam: Elsevier B. V.

Webster, C. D., Douglas, K. S., Eaves, D., & Hart, S. D. (1997). *HCR-20: Assessing the risk for violence (version 2).* Vancouver, British Columbia: Mental Health, Law, and Policy Institute, Simon Fraser University.

Webster, C. D., Harris, G. T., & Rice, M. E. (1994). *The violence prediction scheme: Assessing dangerousness in high risk men.* Toronto, Ontario: Centre of Criminology, University of Toronto.

Wechsler, D. (1949). *Manual for the Wechsler Intelligence Scale for Children.* San Antonio, TX: Psychological Corporation.

Wechsler, D. (2002). *Wechsler Preschool and Primary Scale of Intelligence–Third edition (WPPSI-III) administration and scoring manual.* San Antonio, TX: Psychological Corporation.

Wechsler, D. (2003). *Wechsler Intelligence Scale for Children–Fourth edition (WISC-IV) administration and scoring manual.* San Antonio, TX: Psychological Corporation.

Wechsler, D. (2008). *Wechsler Adult Intelligence Scale–Fourth edition (WAIS-IV): Technical and interpretive manual.* San Antonio, TX: Pearson.

Wechsler, D. (2009). *Wechsler Individual Achievement Test–Third edition (WIAT-III).* San Antonio, TX: Pearson.

Widiger, T. A., & Simonsen, E. (2005). Alternative dimensional models of personality disorder: Finding a common ground. *Journal of Personality Disorders, 19,* 110–130

Wood, J. M., Lilienfield, S. O., Nezworski, M. T., Garb, H. N., Allen, K. H., & Wildermuth, J. L. (2010). Validity of Rorschach Inkblot scores for discriminating psychopaths from nonpsychopaths in forensic populations: A meta-analysis. *Personality Assessment, 22*(2) 336–349.

Woodcock, R. W., McGrew, K. S., & Mather, N. (2001). *Woodcock-Johnson III tests of achievement.* Itasca, IL: Riverside Publishing.

Woodcock, R. W., McGrew, K. S., & Mather, N. (2007a). *The Woodcock-Johnson III normative update (NU) tests of achievement.* Itasca, IL: Riverside Publishing.

Woodcock, R. W., McGrew, K. S., & Mather, N. (2007b). *Woodcock-Johnson III normative update (NU), tests of cognitive abilities.* Itasca, IL: Riverside Publishing.

World Health Organization. (2012). International classification of diseases (ICD). Retrieved from http://www.who.int/classifications/icd/en

Review Questions

1. This domain of practice is typically focused on understanding the relationship between brain and behavior through assessment:
   A. Clinical psychology
   B. Industrial–organizational psychology
   C. Neuropsychology
   D. School psychology

2. Hiltonsmith and Keller's (1983) framework for organizing data from an ecological assessment include all of the following except:
   A. Setting operation
   B. Setting foundation
   C. Setting opportunities
   D. Setting appearance and contents

3. Which of the following is an example of a criterion-referenced test?
   A. Driving exam
   B. MMPI-2
   C. GRE
   D. WAIS-IV

4. The process of defining a target behavior, determining the antecedents of the behavior, and describing the consequence or function of the target behavior is referred to as:
   A. Direct observation
   B. Event sampling
   C. Narrative recording
   D. Functional behavioral assessment

5. A psychologist is attempting to gather more information regarding the severity and frequency of a patient's target behavior problems of hitting peers through a school observation. What is the most appropriate observation method to use?
   A. Event sampling
   B. Direct observation
   C. Interval recording
   D. Narrative recording

6. It is helpful to gain information from multiple informants regarding an examinee because informant ratings may be influenced by:
   A. Ethnicity
   B. Socioeconomic status
   C. Familiarity with the individual
   D. All of the above

7. Which of the following is not a key component of an assessment center?
   A. Job analysis
   B. Single assessor evaluation
   C. Simulations
   D. Assessor training

8. In Item Response Theory, item discrimination refers to:
   A. The percentage of test takers who get the answer correct
   B. How well the item distinguishes who scores high versus low on a test
   C. Probability of getting an item correct by chance
   D. The proportion of test takers who fail the item

9. According to Generalizability Theory, which of the following constitutes potential sources of error in test measurement?
   A. Test items
   B. Rater/examiner
   C. Time of day test was administered
   D. All of the above

10. Which of the following is not true about reliability and validity?
    A. Validity of a measure indicates the extent to which it measures what it is supposed to measure
    B. In order for a measure to be reliable it must be valid
    C. The reliability coefficient reflects the degree of consistency of a measure
    D. In order for a measure to be valid it must be reliable

11. Which of the following is not true about test–retest reliability?
    A. It refers to the stability of a test over time
    B. It is appropriate to use when the trait or ability is thought to be variable across time
    C. The interval between test and retest can impact the reliability coefficient
    D. It is assessed by administering the measure to the same group at two time points

12. The Kuder–Richardson formula (20) is used to measure:
    A. Inter-rater reliability
    B. Parallel form reliability
    C. Internal consistency reliability
    D. Test–retest reliability

13. Kappa measures:
    A. Inter-rater reliability
    B. Test–retest reliability
    C. Content validity
    D. Criterion validity

14. The trinitarian model of validity includes all of the following except:
    A. Construct validity
    B. Concurrent validity
    C. Content validity
    D. Criterion validity

15. This type of validity refers to the extent to which a measure or test is associated with the trait or ability it is intended to measure:

    A. Construct validity
    B. Concurrent validity
    C. Criterion validity
    D. Content validity

16. A decrease in Type II error leads to:

    A. An increase in sensitivity
    B. An increase in specificity
    C. An decrease in Type I error
    D. None of the above

17. Which of the following would be appropriate to use as a broad-based measure of social–emotional and behavioral functioning in an assessment with a 10-year-old?

    A. Beck Anxiety Inventory
    B. Child Depression Inventory–II
    C. Social Responsiveness Scale
    D. Behavior Assessment System for Children–2

18. The Cattell–Horn–Carroll (CHC) theory of intelligence has historically included nine broad stratum abilities, including all of the following except:

    A. Fine Motor Ability
    B. Quantitative Reasoning
    C. Long-Term Storage and Retrieval
    D. Writing Ability

19. According to the Cattell–Horn Model, what were the two types of intelligence?

    A. Quantitative Reasoning and Perceptual Reasoning
    B. Fluid Intelligence and Crystallized Intelligence
    C. Crystallized Intelligence and Perceptual Reasoning
    D. Perceptual Reasoning and Emotional Intelligence

20. Which of the following is considered an unstructured personality assessment?

    A. Minnesota Multiphasic Personality Inventory–2
    B. Personality Assessment Inventory–Adolescent
    C. Millon Clinical Multiaxial Inventory–Third Edition
    D. Rorschach Inkblot Test

21. In Holland's theory of vocational interest, which of the following dimensions are listed in the order expected on the hexagon?

    A. Realistic, Artistic
    B. Conventional, Realistic
    C. Investigative, Enterprising
    D. Social, Conventional

22. Which of the following is not true of symptom validity testing (SVT)?

  A. It should be used when there is a question of secondary gain
  B. It assesses the number and severity of symptoms a patient presents with
  C. It is a necessary component of forensic work
  D. SVT can include use of the Rey 15-Item Test and the Recognition Memory Test

23. Which of the following is appropriate for a defense when a trial involves a patient who claims metal illness as a reason behind the crime?

  A. Not guilty by reason of insanity
  B. Guilty but mentally ill
  C. Mens rea
  D. Diminished capacity

24. In evaluating risk for future violence, which of the following historical factors should be considered in terms of their likelihood of increasing the risk for future violence?

  A. History of substance abuse
  B. History of aggressive behavior
  C. History of school failure
  D. A and B

25. According to Joiner and colleagues' work (1999), which of the following risk factors should be assessed when evaluating suicide risk?

  A. Precipitant stressors
  B. Protective factors
  C. Predispositions
  D. All of the above

26. Which of the following is not an axis included on the *DSM-IV-TR?*

  A. Social and Occupational Functioning Assessment Scale
  B. General Medical Conditions
  C. Psychosocial and Environmental Problems
  D. Global Assessment of Relational Functioning Scale

27. Continuous monitoring is used to monitor:

  A. All of the subject's target behaviors during an interval
  B. A subject's behaviors at given intervals
  C. The number of occurrences of a specific behavior during an interval
  D. Whether or not a subject engages in specific behavior

28. The *DSM-IV* uses a _____ approach to diagnosis:

  A. Homogeneous
  B. Global
  C. Continuous
  D. Polythetic

29. This is the extent to which a test measures what it is meant to measure:
   A. Reliability
   B. Item Response Theory
   C. Validity
   D. Generalizability Theory

30. According to the *DSM-IV-TR* multiaxial assessment format, Axis II captures:
   A. General Medical Conditions
   B. Personality Disorders
   C. Clinical Disorders
   D. Psychosocial and Environmental Problems

Answers to Review Questions

1. **C. Neuropsychology**

   Neuropsychology is the study of the relationship between the brain and behavior. Clinically neuropsychologist use standardized assessments to examine an individual's profile of neurocognitive strengths and weaknesses. This profile is then compared to known profiles of specific disorders to help clarify the nature and severity of neurological insult.

2. **B. Setting foundation**

   The three components of the model are setting appearance and contents, setting operation, and setting opportunities.

3. **A. Driving exam**

   A criterion-referenced test is used to assess where an examinee stands on a particular criterion, or domain of skill, status, or functioning. A driving exam assesses a specific acquired or learned skill.

4. **D. Functional behavioral assessment**

   FBA is a method of behavioral assessment in which observation is used to determine the antecedent and consequence or function of a target behavior. The data collected through the FBA are then used to develop and implement a behavioral intervention.

5. **A. Event sampling**

   Event sampling is appropriate when the target behavior has a clear beginning and ending and does not occur at a very high frequency. With event sampling, the observer rates the frequency of the behavior during a set period of time.

6. **D. All of the above**

   Informant ratings can be impacted by a range of variables, including the severity of the individual's symptoms; the child's ethnicity, gender, and socioeconomic status; the informant's familiarity with the individual; informant's tolerance for problematic behavior; among other factors.

7. **B. Single assessor evaluation**

   By definition, for a process to be considered an assessment center it requires that multiple assessors observe and rate each examinee's performance. Because the process relies on ratings from multiple assessors, it is important for assessors to have appropriate training. A job analysis is used to determine the skills or competencies vital to success in a given job. The assessment includes job-simulation activities to observe the examinee's performance on these tasks.

8. **B. How well the item distinguishes who scores high versus low on a test**

   There are three key parameters when examining test item relationships: item difficulty (the percentage of test takers who get a specific item correct), item discrimination (how that item discriminates between those who do well versus those who do poorly on the test as a whole), and the probability that a question is answered correctly by guessing.

9. **D. All of the above**

In Generalizability Theory, sources of measurement error can include aspects of the measurement itself as well as the circumstances under which a test was administered.

10. **B. In order for a measure to be reliable it must be valid**

A test can be reliable and not valid. It can consistently measure the same construct even if it is not measuring the construct it is supposed to measure.

11. **B. It is appropriate to use when the trait or ability is thought to be variable across time**

The use of test–retest reliability is appropriate when the trait or ability being measured is thought to be relatively stable over time.

12. **C. Internal consistency reliability**

The Kuder–Richardson formula (20) (KR-20) is a formula used to calculate split-half reliability, which is one of several approaches to assessing internal consistency reliability.

13. **A. Inter-rater reliability**

Kappa is a measure of inter-rater reliability, which estimates the reliability between two raters. Kappa takes the inter-rater agreement that occurs by chance into account when estimating reliability.

14. **B. Concurrent validity**

The trinitarian model of validity posits that there are three primary components of validity that should be considered: construct validity, content validity, and criterion validity.

15. **A. Construct validity**

Content validity describes how well a test includes the range of information that is needed to test the construct being assessed. Concurrent validity examines the correlation between a new measure and other measures known to assess the construct of interest. Finally, criterion validity refers to the adequacy with which a test or measure estimates an individual's performance on a construct of interest.

16. **A. An increase in sensitivity**

A decrease in Type II error would lead to a decrease in the false negative rate, which would improve sensitivity or the proportion of people who are accurately identified as possessing a certain trait, attribute, or behavior that is being measured.

17. **D. Behavior Assessment System for Children–2**

The BAI and CDI-II are specific measures of anxiety and mood symptoms. The SRS is used to assess social skills and social responsiveness when considering a diagnosis of an autism spectrum disorder. The BASC-2 is a broad measure of social–emotional and behavioral functioning. There are parent, teacher, and self-report forms of the BASC-2.

18. A. Fine Motor Ability

The CHC has included nine broad stratum abilities: Crystallized Intelligence (Gc), Fluid Intelligence (Gf), Quantitative Reasoning (Gq), Reading and Writing Ability (Grw), Short-Term Memory (Gsm), Long-Term Storage and Retrieval (Glr), Visual Processing (Gv), Auditory Processing (Ga), and Processing Speed (Gs).

19. B. Fluid Intelligence and Crystallized Intelligence

The Cattell–Horn Model (Horn & Cattell, 1967) postulates two types of intelligence, fluid and crystallized.

20. D. Rorschach Inkblot Test

The MMPI-2, PAI-A, and MCMI–III are considered structured personality assessment measures. In contrast, the Rorschach Inkblot Test is a projective test, which is often considered to be an unstructured measure of personality.

21. B. Conventional, Realistic

In Holland's theory of vocational interest, each dimension is arranged around the hexagon in a clockwise direction starting with what he termed "Realistic." The interest domains identified are denoted as RIASEC, and include Realistic, Investigative, Artistic, Social, Enterprising, and Conventional.

22. B. It assesses the number and severity of symptoms a patient presents with

Symptom validity testing refers to the development and use of measures and assessment procedures to try to assess an examinee's level of effort and investment during psychological testing; measures used for this purpose are referred to as SVTs. Assessments of examinee effort should always be included in forensic testing.

23. A. Not guilty by reason of insanity

"Not guilty by reason of insanity" is the defense used in cases in which mental illness is examined as a factor being considered when evaluating criminal responsibility. In contrast, guilty but mentally ill indicates criminal responsibility while taking mental illness into account when addressing the individual's guilt and advising sentencing. Diminished capacity refers to whether the individual had the capacity to form the intention to commit a crime or mens rea.

24. D. History of substance abuse and history of aggressive behavior

Attention should be paid to known factors that increase risk for violence, including a history of aggressive behavior and violent acts; a history of substance abuse; a history of psychosis, specifically prior to hospitalization or treatment; and a history of psychiatric and personality disorders that have been associated with an increased risk of violence, such as antisocial personality disorder, borderline personality disorder, and personality disorder not otherwise specified (Scott & Resnick, 2006).

25. D. All of the above

The seven risk factors for suicide that have been identified by Joiner and colleagues (1999) include previous suicidal behavior, types of current suicidal ideation and symptoms, precipitant stressors, overall symptom presentation, self-control and impulsivity, predispositions, and protective factors.

26. A. Social and Occupational Functioning Assessment Scale

The Social and Occupational Functioning Assessment Scale (SOFAS) is not currently included as an axis on the DSM-IV. Although similar to the GAF, it differs in that it focuses exclusively on overall severity of symptoms and takes general medical conditions into account when formulating ratings.

27. A. All of a target subject's behaviors during an interval

This question addresses the different methods of recording behavior. In addition to the correct answer referring to the recording of all of a subject's behaviors during an interval, interval recording refers to monitoring in which a subject is observed at given intervals and it is noted whether or not the subject is engaging in the target behavior during that specified interval. Frequency recording tracks the number of times a behavior occurs.

28. D. Polythetic

A polythetic system requires an individual to meet a subset of criteria from a list of diagnostic criteria. In a homogeneous system, each individual meeting criteria for the same disorder would present with identical symptoms. There are no global or continuous approaches to diagnosis.

29. C. Validity

Generalizability Theory and Item Response Theory are psychometric theories. Reliability refers to the degree to which test scores are consistent. As discussed above, validity *refers to the extent to which an assessment measures what it is meant to measure.*

30. B. Personality Disorders

Axis II captures Personality Disorders and Intellectual Disability (Mental Retardation).

6

Treatment, Intervention, Prevention, and Supervision

Sonia Suchday, Miriam Frankel, Carlos Marquez, and Cheryl Seifert

Broad Content Areas

- Individual, couple, family, group, organizational, or community interventions for specific problems/disorders in diverse populations
- Intervention and prevention theories
- Best practices and practice guidelines
- Consultation and supervision models
- Evidence supporting efficacy and effectiveness of interventions

This chapter provides a brief overview on the topics of treatment, intervention, prevention, and supervision. Specifically, the chapter covers how these topics can be tailored to relate to different populations as it is imperative to adjust a treatment approach to the variations that exist among the individual, couple, family, group, organization, community, and more diverse populations. In addition, current theories on intervention and prevention are discussed. These are presented with accompanying evidence supporting the efficacy of these interventions and prevention techniques. An overview of consultation, counseling, and supervision models is given, as well as best practice guidelines for emergent therapeutic areas such as technology, performance enhancement, and adjunctive interventions. Finally, health care systems and their effect on treatment are discussed.

Treatment Decision Making

Matching Treatment to Diagnosis

Growth of research on effective treatments for various mental health issues has made it possible to identify and tailor interventions for disorders and individuals. Specific treatments are effective for specific disorders, and elements of the treatment can be tailored to individuals' diagnoses, lifestyle, characteristics, preferences, and culture.

Matching Characteristics of Client to Therapist

Rapport is established easily in the therapeutic environment when clients perceive similarities between themselves and the therapist, such as gender and ethnicity. These similarities are hypothesized to enable bonding and understanding in the therapeutic dyad and can encourage self-disclosure and therapeutic gains. However, results on gender and ethnicity matching are mixed and more extensive research is needed (Bryan, Dersch, Shumway, & Arredondo, 2004).

Cost and Benefit Analysis

Psychotherapy has been demonstrated to be effective in reducing the overall financial cost of mental illness in communities (Lazar, 2010). On an individual level, however, some treatments appear to be effective but may present the client with either immense costs, or potential damage. Ethically, therapists are required to do no harm, and therefore must consider whether the benefit of experimental or costly treatments is advantageous when accounting for the risk involved (Koocher & Keith-Spiegel, 2008).

Assessing Readiness to Change

The Transtheoretical Model is based on the idea that behavior change is more successful when it is based on individuals' preparedness for change, which occurs in stages (Prochaska, DiClemente, & Norcross, 1992). Individual treatments need to be tailored to the client's stage of change. The benefit will be an overall reduction of cost, as treatments the client is not ready for will not be employed (Miller & Rollnick, 2002). For example, an individual in the precontemplation stage will not benefit from a smoking-cessation intervention if he or she does not believe he or she needs to stop smoking.

Prochaska and DiClemente posed a model of change that describes the levels of ambivalence and readiness to change an individual might go through: precontemplation, contemplation, preparation, action, and maintenance (Prochaska et al., 1992). A person in the precontemplation phase might not recognize his or her behavior or issue as being problematic and that change has not occurred to them. When an individual enters the contemplation stage, he or she might have some ambivalence toward change but recognizes that a problem exists. Following this, a person enters the decision-making stage. The individual makes the commitment to change, and then enters the action stage where the person actively changes behavior that has been deemed problematic. In the final phase, the person continues in the maintenance change where the change has been established and ongoing effort is made to progress and avoid relapse (Littell & Girvin, 2002).

Contemporary Theories/Models of Treatment/ Intervention and Their Evidence Base

Psychoanalysis/Psychodynamic Theory

Psychoanalysis is a model of treatment based on ideology proposed by Sigmund Freud. The foundation of psychoanalysis is that thoughts, beliefs, and awareness work in levels: conscious, preconscious, and unconscious (Wood & Wood, 2008). According to psychoanalytic theory, behavior and mental health are largely influenced by childhood experience and progression through stages of development. Freud's conceptualization about development included the idea that the ego develops from the id and the id exerts ongoing influence on the ego (Blass, 2012). Reactions to stress, according to this theory, are determined by prior experiences and unconscious drives, and are referred to as defense mechanisms. Displacement, rationalization, projection, reaction formation, regression, sublimation, and repression are all defense mechanisms (Wood & Wood, 2008).

Defense mechanisms are methods that manifest into actions that are meant to protect the individual from incoming threats. Displacement is when an individual is not afforded a platform for his or her aggression toward the direct stimuli and therefore releases that energy by targeting another (Irving, 1962). A person who uses rationalization tries to adopt a more acceptable motive than an otherwise unacceptable one, akin to intellectualization. Projection is a defense that happens when a person who finds certain motives that he or she possesses unacceptable, places them on others. Reaction formation is used as an expression of repressed desires in contrast to those desires (Irving, 1962). Regression is a response to frustration and is used to reduce tension by reverting the ego to an earlier stage of development. Sublimation is a defense mechanism that allows unacceptable impulses or thoughts to transform into socially acceptable expressions. One might employ the repression defense when experiencing trauma, thus, one would build psychic blocks removing them from consciousness. Repression is a defense that is supported by other defenses in response to threatening stimuli (Irving, 1962).

Treatment of physical and mental health symptoms in psychoanalysis involves exploration of past experiences as the present is determined by the past. In treatment, psychoanalysts allow the client to engage in free association, in which the client is allowed to talk uninhibitedly with the belief that through free speech, the patient and psychoanalyst will uncover problems and internal conflicts that the patient may be unaware of and enable the patient to gain control of his or her full self (Corsini & Wedding, 2008). Psychoanalysts also consider transference (i.e., the client's relationship with the therapist) a powerful therapeutic tool. Dream interpretation is another tool that serves many purposes, including examination of the patient's thoughts and reactions toward the psychoanalyst (Eerola, 2010). The process of psychotherapy involves three phases: the opening phase, which involves identifying the presenting problem and severity; the middle phase, which entails therapeutic treatment; and the final phase, termination (Corsini & Wedding, 2008). Psychoanalysis has been most effective in treating dramatic and eccentric clusters of personality disorders (Wood & Wood, 2008).

Adlerian Psychotherapy

Adlerian psychotherapy, also referred to as individual psychotherapy, is a model of treatment that views dreams, thoughts, emotions, and physical health as working together holistically as opposed to working as distinct entities (Wood & Wood, 2008). Healthy living is governed by the way one connects to others, including family, community, and/or society in general. Adler emphasized the child's perception of his or her role in family dynamics (Corsini & Wedding, 2008). Adler postulated that mental health was contingent on how a child perceives his self and ideal self. When not synchronized, the individual would develop an inferiority complex, whereas in healthy individuals, these feelings would be managed using adequate coping mechanisms (Corsini & Wedding, 2008). In treatment, Adlerian psychotherapists use future-oriented strategies that emphasize how goals determine individuals' course of life (Wood & Wood, 2008). Psychotherapy consists of four specific aims: establishing and maintaining a healthy relationship with the patient; discovering the patient's way of life, including reactions to stimuli, relationships, and goals, and their effects on life; building insight through therapy; and reorientation of the individual (Corsini & Wedding, 2008). During treatment, the therapist's role is to provide an ideal persona of a healthy person for the patient to imitate and model to enable change and growth (Corsini & Wedding, 2008).

Analytical Psychotherapy

Analytical psychotherapy, also known as Jungian psychotherapy, considers the patient–therapist relationship as a prototype of the general structure of the patient's relationship pattern (Wood & Wood, 2008). Jung based analytical psychotherapy on four tenets: the self-regulating psyche, or soul; the unconscious, which was considered compensatory and elaborate; the relationship with the patient, which facilitates awareness and health; and several stages to self-improvement (Corsini & Wedding, 2008). According to Jung, society shares a collective unconscious that influences various aspects of life and certain archetypes that govern personality are adopted from it (Wood & Wood, 2008). Symptoms, such as neuroses, in analytical therapy are considered a product of the whole personality; hence, in treatment the whole personality is considered, rather than the symptom alone (Corsini & Wedding, 2008). Treatment emphasizes the creation of healthy balance between internal opposites and different aspects of people's lives, focusing on present and future goals (Wood & Wood, 2008). Some basic therapeutic techniques include confession (recalling personal experiences), elucidation (insight into internal processes), education (improvement of personal/health behavior), and transformation (process of self-actualization) (Corsini & Wedding, 2008).

Client-Centered Therapy

Developed by Carl Rogers, client-centered therapy focuses on the client as the expert on his or her experiences and emphasizes trust between the patient and therapist as critical to successful treatment (Wood & Wood, 2008). According to Rogers, negative views of the self and the world delay development and growth, leading to mental health problems. These problems can be reversed through a positive and nurturing environment provided by the therapist in treatment (Wood & Wood, 2008). Conditions for healing to occur include the creation of a nurturing and nonthreatening environment, genuineness, unconditional positive regard, and empathy. The creation of these therapeutic conditions may lead to increased self-esteem, internal locus of control, and enhanced openness to new experience and coping (Corsini & Wedding, 2008). Conditions for change include maintaining a nondirective attitude, respect, and a partnership with the patient (Corsini & Wedding, 2008).

Existential Psychotherapy

Existential psychotherapy is influenced by early European philosophy that focused on observing human existence, perspectives on life, and the world attained from this observation (Wood & Wood, 2008). The foundation of existential psychotherapy relies on the notion that individuals' perceptions of the world differ, and therapeutic issues need to be viewed within an individual's worldview (Wood & Wood, 2008). The existential tenet of life is that everyone experiences emotions, and existential theory does not label certain emotions as pathological (Hoffman & Cleare-Hoffman, 2011). Emotions are defined as being pathological based on their situational and cultural context. Threats such as death, seclusion, and loss of liberty may challenge individuals' coping abilities and existential treatment enables individuals to accept responsibility for adapting to and growing from these experiences (Wood & Wood, 2008). The therapist serves as a guide, demonstrating possibilities the patient can achieve. A healthy alliance between therapist and patient is crucial in order for the patient to transcend and achieve meaning despite adversity (Corsini & Wedding, 2008).

Gestalt Therapy

Gestalt psychologists believe that individuals are defined by their environment, social networks, family, and memories. The interaction of these factors may contribute to the whole person, but the individual is more than simply the sum of these aspects of themselves. The therapeutic process encompasses an understanding of the interactions among these aspects of life and experience (Corsini & Wedding, 2008; Wood & Wood, 2008). Dysfunction results from a failure to learn from experience and engaging in repetitive patterns of behavior (Corsini & Wedding, 2008). Rapport and trust form the basis of an interactive treatment approach in Gestalt therapy (Wood & Wood, 2008). The goal of therapy is to achieve homeostasis, an internal balance between physical and internal mechanisms Techniques used to achieve homeostasis include imagining reactions to real-life events, writing and expressing emotions to a significant person without actually sending it, and then writing a response based on what you believe that person might say, and increasing the patient's awareness of his or her reactions, both psychological and physical, to a specific situation (Wood & Wood, 2008).

Behavioral Therapy

Behavior theorists believe that poor mental health is a product of learned dysfunctional behavior (Wood & Wood, 2008). In treatment, techniques used may be grouped into three categories: applied behavior analysis, neobehavioristic mediation stimulus response, and social cognitive theory (Corsini & Wedding, 2008). Behavioral therapy was the first therapeutic perspective based on the scientific method. According to behavior therapists, abnormal behavior is nonpathological, and is acquired and maintained through the same processes and principles as normal behavior. Treatment strategies associated with behavioral therapy include assessing antecedents (current and historical), behavior, consequences, and behavioral reconstruction; treatment is tailored to an individual's unique presentation and focuses on observed behavior (Corsini & Wedding, 2008). Behavioral therapy has evolved since its conception and is manifested in integrative couple therapy, acceptance and commitment therapy, functional analytic psychotherapy, and dialectical behavioral therapy (DBT). Some of these therapies emphasize acceptance as a therapeutic tool (Cordova, 2001). There is empirical evidence for the efficacy of behavioral therapy in treating depression, autism, childhood developmental disorders, etc. (Wood & Wood, 2008).

Cognitive Therapy

According to cognitive thinkers and therapists, stress response entails an interaction among cognitive, affective, motivational, and behavioral responses that are based on experience and learning (Corsini & Wedding, 2008). Individuals view the information from the external and internal environment through the lens of personal experience, history, and learning to respond to the world around them (Corsini & Wedding, 2008). Physiology and emotion moderate these responses and these become maladaptive when one perceives incoming stimuli based on personal biases. These maladaptive responses result from inaccurate perceptions of internal or external cues and rigid responses that do not change regardless of environmental cues, external or internal (Corsini & Wedding, 2008). Perceptions form schemas, or core beliefs specific to an individual, that comprise the cognitive, affective, behavioral, and motivational systems, as well as personality, and are influenced by core beliefs, also known as cognitive vulnerabilities, as well as affect modes. In treatment, therapists attempt to correct biases by engaging the patient in testing his or her core beliefs against reality. Additional therapeutic techniques include skills training, implementation and practice, and various behavioral techniques (Corsini & Wedding, 2008).

Family Therapy

Family therapy defines a family as a system of individuals and sheds light on how the members influence each other and how they, themselves, are influenced—a concept known as reciprocal causality (Corsini & Wedding, 2008). Family therapy focuses on the relationship network among families, between spouses, and, if warranted, identifies one specific member in the network who has caused a rift in the network and helps ameliorate it (Wood & Wood, 2008). Family therapists do not follow a single theory, but believe that individuals are products of their social connections, symptoms are maintained through family systems, and treatment goals should help modify maladaptive patterns of interaction between family members to allow each member to adopt a more functional outlook of him or herself as a member of the family (Corsini & Wedding, 2008).

Historically, family therapy has been conceptualized by Murray Bowen (Guerin, 1997). Structural family therapy is an approach devised by Minuchin that places an emphasis on the family as a system rather than focusing on the individual member as being problematic (Kim, 2003). Jay Haley and Cloé Madanes devised an approach to family therapy that attempts to identify a problem, most often the child's, within the framework of the family in order to ameliorate conflict, called strategic family therapy (Stone, 2012).

Contemplative Therapies

Contemplative therapies, specifically yoga and meditation, and more recently, breathing techniques, are becoming increasingly popular in the United States (Wardle, Lui, & Adams, 2012). These therapies focus on the creation of psychological, physical, spiritual balance, and harmony to enhance well-being (Corsini & Wedding, 2008). Therapeutic techniques combine physical postures, mental exercises, and breathing techniques to achieve a harmonious integration of mind, body, and soul. Contemplative therapists believe that dysfunction and psychological suffering arise because the mind is uncontrolled; suffering may also be a product of shared dysfunction, cultural beliefs, and defenses (Corsini & Wedding, 2008). Psychological and spiritual and even physical suffering can be alleviated by training the mind. Methods used to train the mind include enhanced attention and awareness and calming the mind (Corsini & Wedding, 2008). Such therapies have relied highly on a qualitative rather than a quantitative empirical approach for their support and therefore have received criticism on their efficacy (Wardle et al., 2012).

Integrative Therapies

Rivalries among different schools of thought led to the development of the integrative approach to psychotherapy. This approach focuses on the uniqueness of the individual patient and tailors treatment to patients' needs (Corsini & Wedding, 2008). The basic concepts of integrative therapy are as follows: technical eclecticism, which enables mental health professionals to choose the best treatment approach for a particular person and problem, and theoretical integration, in which at least two modes of therapy are combined. Combining modes of therapy is based on the idea that a combination of modes is more effective at explaining and resolving issues compared to any single mode; identification and utilization of common factors that reflect underlying principles of different therapies to create an efficacious treatment; and assimilative integration, which entails firmly rooting oneself in one mode of therapy with an openness to incorporate methods outside of one's orientation (Corsini & Wedding, 2008). Integrative therapies emphasize the creation of a strong therapeutic relationship between the patient and therapist, use a variety of techniques to guide assessment, treatment planning, and identify and tailor treatment strategies and modalities for their patients without being limited by theoretical boundaries (Corsini & Wedding, 2008). Integrative approaches are beneficial in cases where known treatments are insufficient (Strachan, Gros, Ruggiero, Lejuez, & Acierno, 2012). For example, among combat-exposed veterans unresponsive to exposure therapies, behavioral activation has been effective in alleviating depression, anxiety, and other symptoms of posttraumatic stress disorder (PTSD; Strachan et al., 2012).

Comparative Analysis of Treatment for Disorders

Depression

Lifetime prevalence rates for major depressive disorders are estimated as high as 16.5% for adults in the United States (Kessler, Berglund, Demler, Jin, & Walters,

2005). In addition, there are significant gender differences, with women demonstrating rates of depression that are double that of men (National Survey on Drug Use and Health [NSDUH], 2008). According to the *Diagnostic and Statistical Manual of Mental Disorders* (4th ed., text rev.; *DSM-IV-TR*; American Psychiatric Association, 2000), a diagnosis of major depressive disorder requires a history of one or more major depressive episodes. A depressive episode is characterized by at least 2 weeks of depressed mood and/or anhedonia, plus four more of the following symptoms: significant weight loss or gain, sleep disturbance, psychomotor agitation or retardation, fatigue or reduced energy, feelings of worthlessness or guilt, difficulty in concentration, and thoughts of death or suicide (American Psychiatric Association, 2000). In addition, there must be significant distress or impairment in functioning in important life areas (e.g., occupation, social life, etc.).

Numerous psychotherapies have been developed and empirically validated as effective treatments for depression. One example, and the psychotherapy with the most research support as a treatment for depression, is cognitive therapy (Young, Rygh, Weinberger, & Beck, 2008). Cognitive therapy combined with psychopharmacological treatments of depression has also been consistently found to reduce rates of relapse to depression significantly more than psychopharmacological treatments alone (Young et al., 2008). In addition to cognitive therapy, interpersonal psychotherapy and behavioral activation are also empirically supported treatments for depression. Some research has attempted to compare the efficacy of different forms of psychotherapy for depression and has produced mixed results. For example, one study demonstrated that interpersonal psychotherapy was slightly more efficacious than cognitive behavioral therapy (CBT), nondirective supportive treatment, behavioral activation treatment, psychodynamic treatment, problem-solving therapy, and social skills training (Cuijpers, van Straten, Andersson, & van Oppen, 2008). Other research has shown these therapies to be equally effective.

Bipolar Disorders

Bipolar disorders are characterized by the presence of periods of elevated and/or depressed mood and are classified into two types: bipolar I and bipolar II. According to the *Diagnostic and Statistical Manual of Mental Disorders* (American Psychiatric Association, 2000), a diagnosis of bipolar I requires the occurrence of at least one manic episode in a person's lifetime. A manic episode is defined by at least 1 week of elevated or irritable mood that accompanies at least three of the following symptoms: inflated self-esteem, decreased need for sleep, more talkative than usual or pressured speech, flight of ideas or racing thoughts, distractibility, increase in goal-directed activity, excessive involvement in pleasurable activities that may result in negative outcomes. Depressive episodes will also typically occur, although they are not required for this diagnosis. In contrast, an individual with a bipolar II diagnosis will experience at least one major depressive episode as well as at least one hypomanic episode. A hypomanic episode is distinguished from a full manic episode on the basis of duration of symptoms (i.e., lasting at least 4 days versus a full week) and whether impairment in functioning is caused by these symptoms. However, a marked impairment in functioning is required as a result of the overall disorder for both bipolar I and bipolar II (American Psychiatric Association, 2000). About 4% of the population of the United States is estimated to have some form of bipolar disorder diagnoses in their lifetime (Kessler et al., 2005).

Medications have traditionally been viewed as the treatment of choice for bipolar disorder, and there is little deniability that pharmacotherapy can be effective for symptom reduction. However, there is also evidence that nonpharmacological treatment approaches for bipolar disorders have significant benefit (Scott, 2007). A recent meta-analysis found an overall medium effect size for the efficacy of CBT as a treatment for bipolar disorder (Hofman, Asnaani, Vonk, Sawyer, & Fang, 2012). In addition, the Systematic Treatment Enhancement Program for Bipolar Disorder (STEP-BD) study was a randomized clinical trial that compared pharmacological treatment of bipolar disorder alone with medication and psychotherapy combined (Miklowitz et al., 2007). The researchers included several different types of psychotherapy, including CBT and family-focused therapy. Overall, STEP-BD participants benefited most from the combination of therapy and medication (Miklowitz et al., 2007), although there was not an obvious advantage of one type of psychotherapy over any other.

Eating Disorders

Eating disorders are most commonly, although not exclusively, diagnosed in women. The two eating disorders described in the *DSM-IV-TR* are anorexia nervosa, with a lifetime prevalence rate of 0.3%, and bulimia nervosa, with lifetime prevalence rates estimated at 1% (Hoek, 2006). A diagnosis of anorexia nervosa requires the presence of four criteria: (1) refusal to maintain a normal weight; (2) fear of gaining weight; (3) disturbance in one's experience of weight, or undue influence of weight on self-evaluation or denial of the seriousness of low body weight; and (4) amenorrhea (i.e., absence of at least three consecutive menstrual cycles; American Psychiatric Association, 2000). Anorexia nervosa can be characterized as binge eating/purging type or restricting type. The second disorder classified in the *DSM-IV-TR* is bulimia nervosa, which is characterized by recurrent binge eating and compensatory behavior (e.g., vomiting, fasting, excessive exercise, etc.) at least twice a week for 3 months. In addition, the person perceives her self-image to be directly linked to her weight. Bulimia nervosa can be further classified as either: purging type or nonpurging type (American Psychiatric Association, 2000).

Cognitive behavioral therapy is the current standard of psychosocial treatment for eating disorders (Wilson, Grilo, & Vitousek, 2007). Several adaptations of CBT have been developed specifically for the treatment of eating disorders. These treatments include cognitive behavioral therapy for bulimia nervosa (CBT-BN; Fairburn, Cooper, Shafran, & Wilson, 2008) and enhanced cognitive behavioral therapy (CBT-E; Fairburn, Cooper, & Shafran, 2003). Family therapy has also been widely researched and a significant amount of empirical evidence exists that supports the use of family therapy, particularly the "Maudsley model" of family therapy, for treatment of anorexia nervosa (Wilson et al., 2007).

Anxiety Disorders

Generalized anxiety disorder (GAD), panic disorder, phobias, obsessive-compulsive disorder (OCD), and posttraumatic stress disorder (PTSD) are all classified as anxiety disorders in the *DSM-IV-TR*.

Generalized Anxiety Disorder

GAD is characterized by excessive worry that is difficult to control. The worry occurs most days and lasts for more than 6 months. As much as 5% of the population is estimated to suffer from GAD at some point in their lifetime (American Psychiatric Association, 2000). In addition, GAD has been shown to be more common in women than men (Brown, O'Leary, & Barlow, 2001). In a review of 22 studies comparing psychodynamic, supportive, and cognitive behavioral therapies, cognitive behavioral therapy had better treatment outcomes for anxiety symptoms among those patients diagnosed with GAD (Hunot, Churchill, Teixeira, & de Lima, 2010).

Panic Disorder

An individual with panic disorder experiences unexpected and recurrent panic attacks, as well as a month of at least one of the following: concern about additional attacks, worry about what the attack means (i.e., am I having heart attack?), or a change in behavior due to the panic attacks (American Psychiatric Association, 2000). Panic attacks are defined in the *DSM-IV-TR* as "discrete period of intense fear or discomfort that develops suddenly and peaks within 10 minutes. Usually involves physiological arousal and stress response." Cognitive behavioral treatments for panic disorder have been shown to have some efficacy, specifically: psychoeducation and skills training (coping skills) improve therapy outcomes (Meuret, Wolitzky-Taylor, Twohiq, & Craske, 2012).

Phobias

A specific phobia is an excessive or unreasonable fear of an object or situation, and exposure to the feared stimulus causes intense anxiety (American Psychiatric Association, 2000). The person will attempt to avoid the stimulus despite awareness that the fear is excessive. Phobias have been treated effectively with methods such as *in vivo exposure*, virtual reality, and cognitive therapy. Relapse is a problem in specific phobias, occurring regularly within a year post-follow up (Choy, Fyer, & Lipsitz, 2007). Another type of phobia, social phobia, also known as social anxiety disorder, is a fear of social or performance situations (American Psychiatric Association, 2000). Cognitive behavioral therapy is known to be an effective treatment for social anxiety disorder.

Obsessive-Compulsive Disorder

Obsessive-compulsive disorder (OCD) is characterized by the presence of either obsessions or compulsions, or in the majority of cases both. Obsessions are recurrent thoughts that an individual finds difficult to control. Compulsions are repetitive behaviors or mental acts that occur in response to an obsession and the goal of which is to reduce distress. A common example of this relationship is an obsession about germs leading to washing one's hands repeatedly in order to prevent contamination. Lifetime prevalence rates of OCD are estimated at about 1.6% of the population of the United States (Kessler et al., 2005). Exposure and ritual prevention is an evidence-based psychotherapy for treatment of OCD (Franklin & Foa, 2008). Serotonergic antidepressant medications have also been shown to effectively reduce OCD symptoms. Some evidence suggests that exposure and response prevention is as good alone as the therapy combined with medications. In other words, medication does not necessarily contribute additional benefit above and beyond those of psychotherapy (Franklin & Foa, 2008).

Posttraumatic Stress Disorder

Posttraumatic stress disorder may occur after an individual is exposed to a trauma that involves threat to his or her own personal safety, or the safety of another, and results in the experience of fear, helplessness, or horror (American Psychiatric Association, 2000). Symptoms of PTSD are classified into three categories: re-experiencing symptoms (e.g., nightmares and flashbacks), avoidance and numbing symptoms (e.g., avoiding reminders of trauma and detachment from others), and physiological hyperarousal (e.g., sleep problems, irritability, and hypervigilance). For a diagnosis of PTSD, symptoms must persist for at least 1 month. The prevalence rates of lifetime PTSD are estimated at 6.8%, and rates of PTSD are almost three times as high in women, compared to men (Kessler et al., 2005). Evidence-based treatments for PTSD include prolonged exposure (McLean & Foa, 2011 [for review]), cognitive processing therapy (e.g., Chard, Schuster, & Resick, 2012 [for review]; Forbes et al., 2012), eye movement desensitization and reprocessing (EMDR), and pharmacological treatments.

Psychotic Disorders

The *DSM-IV-TR* defines *psychotic* as "delusions or prominent hallucinations, with the hallucinations occurring in the absence of insight into their pathological nature." The psychotic disorders include schizophrenia, which is characterized by two or more of the following symptoms: delusions, hallucinations, disorganized speech, disorganized or catatonic behavior, and negative symptoms. The individual must experience social or occupational impairment and demonstrate at least 6 months of some traits of the disorder. Psychotic disorders are primarily treated with antipsychotic medication. However, there is evidence that individuals with psychotic disorders may also benefit from psychotherapy, particularly when combined with pharmacological treatments (Hofman et al., 2012). Patients with schizophrenia experiencing positive symptoms have benefited from CBT and those suffering acute episodes of psychosis have also benefited from CBT supplemented by pharmacotherapy (Hofman et al., 2012).

Addictions

The *DSM-IV-TR* categorizes substance use disorders as either abuse or dependence. For an individual to be diagnosed with substance abuse, he or she must experience significant negative consequences of his or her substance use. Examples include problems in relationships (e.g., arguments, physical fights, etc.) and problems related to work (e.g., lateness, intoxicated while working, etc.). In addition to negative consequences of substance use, substance dependence also includes the presence of tolerance and/or withdrawal. There are a wide range of treatments available for substance use disorders. Twelve-step, self-help programs such as Alcoholics Anonymous have been demonstrated to be useful and provide ongoing social support for those trying to stop using substances. There are also cognitive behavioral treatments developed for substance use that are targeted at helping individuals identify triggers and cope with urges to use substances. Generally these treatments are adapted and applied for specific substances, for example,

CBT for cocaine use (Carroll et al., 1994). Other empirically supported treatments for substance use disorders include contingency management, motivational interviewing, and behavioral couple therapy (Carroll & Onken, 2005).

Personality Disorders

Personality refers to persistent and pervasive patterns of behaviors. A disorder of personality occurs when a personality "deviates significantly from an individual's cultural expectations" and begins to create negative consequences for the person (e.g., problems in relationships, occupational functioning, etc.; American Psychiatric Association, 2000). Personality disorders in the *DSM-IV-TR* are divided into three clusters: A (odd or eccentric disorders), B (emotional disorders), and C (disorders of anxiety). The specific disorders included in cluster A are paranoid, schizoid, and schizotypal personalities. Cluster B includes antisocial, borderline and histrionic personality disorders; and cluster C comprises avoidant, dependent, and obsessive-compulsive personality disorders. Traditionally, personality disorders have been treated with long-term, psychodynamic therapies. However, more recently therapies based on cognitive behavioral theory and aimed at specific personality disorders have been developed. For example, dialectical behavioral therapy (DBT) is the leading empirically supported treatment for borderline personality disorder (BPD). About 1.6% of the population of United States has been diagnosed with BPD. DBT integrates CBT, dialectics, and Eastern philosophies (e.g., meditation) and has demonstrated efficacy for improvements in symptoms of DBT (e.g., decreases in suicide attempts and nonsuicidal self-injury; Linehan & Dexter-Mazza, 2008).

Pervasive Developmental Disorders

Autistic Disorder
Autistic disorders are characterized by deficits in social functioning and communication and may manifest as abnormalities related to spoken language (American Psychiatric Association, 2000). Children with this disorder also present with repetitive or stereotyped movements such as rocking behaviors or hand flapping. Rates of this disorder are estimated at 5 cases per 10,000 and onset occurs prior to 3 years of age (American Psychiatric Association, 2000). Asperger's disorder is similar to autistic disorder sans delays in language and cognitive functioning. In addition, individuals with Asperger's disorder in general present with rigid fixations on specific topics that may appear obsessional in nature (American Psychiatric Association, 2000).

Rett's Disorder
A child with Rett's disorder demonstrates normal development prenatally, at birth, and at least 5 months post birth. This period of normal development is then followed by a slowing of normal development or decline in functioning (American Psychiatric Association, 2000). The child may demonstrate the following symptoms: slowing of head growth, loss of hand skills, loss of social engagement, poorly coordinated movements and impaired language development (American Psychiatric Association, 2000). Rett's disorder is less common than autistic disorders.

Treatment for Pervasive Developmental Disorders

Treatment of pervasive developmental disorders (PDDs) typically involves behavioral interventions that may rely on strategies based on learning theory, such as use of positive reinforcement to shape behavior. The goals of therapy are generally improvement of desirable behaviors, such as use of language and social skills. One example of this type of treatment is functional communication training (Durand & Carr, 1991). This treatment begins with an analysis of behavior in order to identify the target for change, and then uses principles of reinforcement to increase the desired behaviors. Another well-known treatment for PDDs is TEACCH, which stands for Treatment and Education of Autistic and related Communication-handicapped Children (Schopler, 1997). TEACCH is a classroom-based program that provides highly individualized treatment to children with PDDs.

Attention-Deficit and Disruptive Behavior Disorders

Attention Deficit Hyperactivity

According to the *DSM-IV-TR*, a diagnosis of attention deficit hyperactivity disorder (ADHD) requires the presence of six symptoms of inattention (difficulty with attention, listening, following through with instructions and tasks, etc.) or six symptoms of hyperactivity–impulsivity (e.g., difficulty sitting still, excessive movement, excessive talking, etc.) that have lasted at least 6 months and began before the age of 7. The treatment of choice for this disorder is a combination of stimulant medications and behavioral interventions (Wicks-Nelson & Israel, 2006). Parent training is also supported as a treatment for ADHD, and the primary goal of this treatment is to teach parents skills to support their child and manage the disorder (Schachar & Tannock, 2002).

Disruptive Behavior Disorders

Conduct disorder is the developmental precursor to antisocial personality disorder. Children diagnosed with conduct disorder are generally unconcerned with the rights and well-being of others and are generally not compliant with the rules of society. Criteria for the disorder include three or more of the following symptoms: aggression to people and animals, destruction of property, deceitfulness or theft, and serious violations of rules (American Psychiatric Association, 2000). Oppositional defiant disorder (ODD) is also a behavior characterized by negative externalizing behaviors (i.e., "acting out") and negative social interactions on the part of the child. However, this disorder is considered to be at a level less severe than conduct disorder. In fact, if criteria for conduct disorder are met, ODD is not diagnosed. ODD is characterized by four or more of the following: often loses temper, argues with adults, defies adult requests; deliberately annoys people; blames others for mistakes or misbehavior; easily annoyed by others; angry and resentful; spiteful or vindictive (American Psychiatric Association, 2000). Parent training is also used for the treatment of disruptive behavior disorders. In addition, cognitive problem-solving skills training is another supported therapy aimed at teaching prosocial behavior to children with these disorders (Wicks-Nelson & Israel, 2006).

Prevention and Intervention With Special Populations

Prevention is defined as an action or method aimed at the general population, or at segments of the population with varying levels of risk for any health-related problem. The goal of prevention is to enhance protective factors and reduce risk. Prevention encompasses three tiers of action: primary, secondary, and tertiary (Doyle, 2006). Primary prevention strategies rely on education, motivational encouragement, social support, law and policy, and environment to inform the public of risk factors that lead to disease (Gullotta & Bloom, 2003). Risk is determined at the social, psychological, and biological levels (World Health Organization [WHO], 2004). Primary prevention is universal and may involve campaigns that target the general population or groups that are not necessarily at immediate risk and equip these groups with knowledge they may apply to future risks (Doyle, 2006). For example, a universal prevention strategy is integrated curricula in schools and colleges that focus on the enhancement of general, social, and cognitive skills to promote and protect mental health (Opler, Sodhi, Zaveri, & Madhusoodanan, 2010). Selective prevention targets high-risk groups within a population to prevent the development of disease and disability. *Indicated prevention* refers to strategies toward target groups that exhibit symptoms indicative of illness but that do not meet full criteria (Brenner, Madhusoodanan, Puttichanda, & Chandra, 2010).

Secondary prevention refers to efforts aimed to reduce prevalence and impact of disease (WHO, 2004) by promoting the adoption of behaviors that protect and improve health. An example of secondary prevention is smoking cessation and increased physical activity in individuals with depression following a myocardial infarction (Myers, Gerber, Benyamini, Goldbourt, & Drory, 2012).

Tertiary methods of prevention reduce the negative impact of disease by restoring function and reducing disease-related complication. Goals of tertiary prevention include the reduction of disability, improvement of function, enhancing rehabilitation efforts and impact, and relapse prevention (WHO, 2004).

Prevention in Special Populations

Victims of Trauma

There are special populations that appear to be particularly vulnerable to psychiatric illness due to circumstances out of their control, such as life events, biology, and social/cultural factors. For instance, victims of natural disaster are prone to develop PTSD, depression, and anxiety (Sajatovic, Sanders, Alexeenko, & Madhusoodanan, 2010). Rape crisis centers are an example of an indicated prevention method and a primary preventive measure for women who have been victimized (Sajatovic, Sanders, Alexeenko, & Madhusoodanan, 2010).

Immigrants/Minorities

Annually, there are over 250,000 immigrants arriving to the United States. The immigration experience is usually accompanied by stress, which makes this population vulnerable to mental illness (Sanders & Alexeenko, 2010). To reduce immigration-related stress, primary prevention methods include the provision of resources to ameliorate the challenges encountered by immigrants, including language training, promotion of general health, and education. Among immigrant youth, such as students from and/or of Mexican descent who are at high risk, a secondary prevention program targeting substance use may include education about pressures and dangers resulting in alcohol and drug use (Marsiglia, Ayers, Gance-Cleveland, Mettler, & Booth, 2012).

Military

Military personnel experience trauma that places them at a significant risk for PTSD and a proportion of the military return from combat with clinical manifestation of PTSD or subthreshold symptoms. The National Vietnam Veterans Readjustment Study reported that the prevalence of PTSD in returning military personnel was 9% to 15%, whereas subthreshold symptomology of PTSD was present in 8% to 11% (Gros et al., 2010). Current preventive approaches for PTSD in military personnel include exposure strategies coupled with education and stress management skills training (Hourani, Council, Hubal, & Strange, 2011).

Enhancing Growth and Performance

Athletic Performance

A psychologist's ability to improve athletic performance is based on several theories. For example, the psychological skills training theory uses cognitive techniques such as imagery and self-talk to improve self-confidence and lower anxiety (Birrer & Morgan, 2010). Recently there has been a trend toward mindfulness and acceptance and commitment techniques in order to increase athletes' awareness of their psychological state (Moore, 2009). It is widely believed that mental strength is a key element in determining variations in athletic performance; however, such research is limited by lack of accurate definitions and psychometric measurement of mental strength (Crust, 2007). Psychologists involved in improving athletic performance must tailor their approach to the specific sport as well as individual characteristics of the client, including cognitive and emotional strengths and weaknesses. More empirical research is needed in many areas related to athletic performance (Martin, Vause, & Schwartzman, 2005).

Coaching

Although there are many different ways of defining coaching and diverse techniques that are included under it, generally the term encompasses all efforts to improve performance. In a recent review, coaching strategies such as client's readiness to change or coach's clarification of goals had a significant impact on outcomes; however, results were not consistent or expected (Grief, 2007). In professional organizations, coaching has become common; however, activities that comprise coaching may not differ significantly from activities and goals of human resource development (Hamlin, Ellinger, & Beattie, 2008).

Effects of Burnout

Current research on the effects of burnout in the workplace emphasizes multiple factors that increase the likelihood of burnout. These include: work overload, insufficient reward, breakdown of community, absence of fairness, lack of control, and conflicting values (Angerer, 2003). Recent research has also begun to investigate the constructs that are protective of the individual in the workplace such as maintaining a positive environment and value of his or her work (Freeney & Tiernan, 2006).

Organizational Development

Organizational development (OD) refers to the act of enhancing performance of organizations by promoting change of individuals and systems. The common aspects of OD include using an individual to facilitate change, focusing on relationships within the organization; support from management of the organization, and perceiving change as an ongoing process (Grieves, 2000). OD strives to improve the organization's capacity to benefit all parties involved, including financially, quality of life, and work performance (Taute & Taute, 2012). Behavior-influenced primary interventions, such as setting goals and reward implementation, are used to enhance organization effectiveness. This field of science derives its strategy from social, industrial, organizational behavior, sociology, and psychotherapy (Taute & Taute, 2012). There are three phases in conducting OD: identifying the problem through consultation with managing officials and the entity that requested OD implementation; diagnostics through information gathering and interviews in order to interpret and address the issues; intervention in which the plan of action to diminish the problem is implemented, otherwise known as the joint action planning (JAP); and the evaluation process to assess the effectiveness of the intervention (Taute & Taute, 2012).

Human Resource Management

The primary function of Human Resources (HR) in organizations is to maintain and improve performance in that institution (Boselie, Dietz, & Boon, 2005). One method HR uses to improve performance is targeting customer satisfaction. Socialization tactics improve communication skills and through skills building, the employee becomes better attuned to customer needs and satisfaction (Cantarello, Filippini, & Nosella, 2012). Cross-training activities implemented by HR have improved product quality, employee competency, and problem solving within the employee framework. Research has demonstrated that the use of HR increases company profits and lowers employee turnover (Guest, Michie, Conway, & Sheehan, 2003). However, there are many management and organizational theories and techniques with little consensus on impact of these theories and techniques on performance (Boselie et al., 2005).

Career Performance

Psychologists use both objective and subjective measures to assess current employees as well as to predict a potential employee's future performance. Objective measures include validated tests used to evaluate a potential employee's projected performance, such as cognitive and personality tests. Subjective measures include interview ratings (Kwaske, 2004). Measures used will vary depending on the training of the professional. Specifically, professionals may be trained in clinical psychology, industrial and organizational (I/O) psychology, or may be an HR professional or recruiter, with little psychological training (Kwaske, 2004).

Consultation

Consultation is defined as an interaction between a professional psychologist or a *consultant* and a *consultee* who may be a client, group of colleagues, or a system.

This interaction is generated for a specific problem, person, or program. The consulting psychologist applies his or her area of expertise in response to needs and objectives of the consultee (Arredondo, Shealy, Neale, & Winfrey, 2004). Consultation differs from supervision, in that there is no significant ongoing relationship and the dynamics are not necessarily hierarchical.

Current Models

Current models of consultation include client-centered case consultation, consultee-centered case consultation, program-centered administrative consultation, and consultee-centered administrative consultation (Caplan & Caplan, 1993). Client-centered case consultation is focused on problem resolution, whereas consultee-centered consultation (CCC) is concerned with improving the clients' skills, confidence, and professional objectivity in addition to problem resolution (Caplan, Caplan, & Erchul, 1994). Consultants often use the interaction between the consultee and consultant to gauge the challenges of the situation (Hylander, 2012). Consultee-centered administrative consultation entails assessing professional performance in unfamiliar situations, whereas program-centered administrative consultation is used to create a plan of action that suits and improves the mental health affinity of a community (Knotek, 2006). In these models, consultants are able to tailor their approach based on the population and their specific needs. In addition, behavioral consultation has been widely used in school settings (Knotek & Sandoval, 2003). It involves identifying problematic behaviors and using problem-solving techniques (Snyder, Quirk, & Dematteo, 2011).

Adapting Models to Multiple Populations

It is important to adapt the current consultation models to the population being dealt with. Couples will most likely be defined as client centered, whereas organizations will likely require understanding the larger structure and dynamics involved in organizational consultation. Families may be client or consultee centered (Caplan & Caplan, 1993; Knotek & Sandoval, 2003).

Career Counseling

Literature indicates that career counseling is an effective individual intervention with short-term career counseling being the most heavily researched (Perdrix, Stauffer, Masdonati, Massoudi, & Rossier, 2012). Theoretical approaches that influence career counseling include constructivism theory, systems theory, action theory, and paradoxical theory (Amundson, 2005). Modern approaches to career counseling have seen an increase in the use of the narrative approach in which the individual is engaged as an active agent in a story of his or her career development (McMahon, Watson, Chetty, & Hoelson, 2012).

Constructivism Theory

Within the constructivist framework, career is conceptualized by internal locus of control and the subjective experience of the client (Amundson, 2005). This approach allows people to shape their work lives through active participation and decision making, enabling them to discriminate between alternatives and construct their personal career goals. Within this model, counselors are able to work with individuals' interpretation of issues in their work lives, adaptation to rapid changes in their environment, and their interpretation of career success to enhance career development (Amundson, 2005).

Systems Theory

In systems theory, career development is viewed as a result of the involvement between the individual and contextual variables (Amundson, 2005). Individual systems encompass gender, interest, and personality. Contextual systems include social and environmental contexts; interaction between these systems changes over time. The counselor views this as a dynamic process and works with the individual to help him or her adapt and change with their environment (Amundson, 2005).

Action Theory and Paradoxical Theory

Action theory connects action and career with action being individual, social, and all other goal-oriented activities (Amundson, 2005). Social aspects refer to the importance of social networks in the development of careers. The main idea in the paradoxical theory is to explain and enhance concise career decisions with confidence and a realistic view (Amundson, 2005). A phenomenon described in paradoxical theory is "planned happenstance," which describes career development arising from random events; however, the probability of these random events occurring is influenced by certain traits such as curiosity, optimism, and risk taking.

Narrative Career Counseling

Narrative career counseling is a constructivist approach to career counseling that has been increasingly used over the last decade (McMahon et al., 2012). Critical to narrative counseling is listening to the client's accounts; the counselors' role is to engage the client as a personal agent in his career development. Moreover, counselors place the client in stories with real-life scenarios to help them gain a holistic picture of the client's life and reactions to a variety of career-involved experiences (McMahon et al., 2012).

Career Assessments

Several assessments are used and are important to career counseling, including both quantitative and qualitative assessments. In conjunction with the action theory, a qualitative assessment may consist of interviewing the family in order to gauge the client's interest and aptitude in career development (Schultheiss, 2005). Formal quantitative measures used in career development are the Strong Interest Inventory to measure interest and the Skills Confidence Inventory, which measures the relationship between self-assurance and career choice (Whiston, Lindeman, Rahardja, & Reed, 2005).

Adjunctive Interventions

Although traditional talk therapy and pharmacotherapy have been demonstrated as first-line treatments for many mental illnesses, recent research has indicated that many additional techniques may be beneficial to implement in order to maximize health and wellness.

Support Groups

Support groups have been demonstrated to be effective in improving mental health outcomes in populations with anxiety, depression, chronic mental illness, and those suffering from bereavement (Pistrang, Barker, & Humphreys, 2008). Specifically, these groups can foster a sense of community, and reduce the isolative impact of mental illness. Currently, research is lacking in well-designed empirical studies on effectiveness of support groups and the results of existing studies have been mixed (Pistrang et al., 2008).

Individual Self-Help

There has been a mushrooming of self-help materials in web-based, electronic, and print media over the past decade. There are many benefits of self-help materials, including self-empowerment, anonymity, and reduction of costs. In addition, utilization of self-help materials sought out by individuals has been demonstrated to be effective for relief in some psychiatric symptoms, specifically for anxiety disorders and assertiveness (Papworth, 2006). However, therapist-assisted self-help was found to be a more effective treatment than self-help alone (Coull & Morris, 2011).

Indigenous Support Systems

There are many aspects of an individual that contribute to wellness. One of the most important is the quality and quantity of social support from families, friends, and the larger community. Research has demonstrated the need for effective social support as an adjunct to traditional treatments and it is imperative for enhanced quality of life (Hansson, 2006).

Spirituality

Incorporating spirituality into evidence-based treatments is an effective treatment strategy in many populations (Post & Wade, 2009). Although traditionally thought to be exclusively for religious individuals, using spirituality in a broader sense has been effective for many nonreligious individuals. In addition, evidence shows that spirituality is protective against disease (Brawer, Handal, Fabricatore, Roberts, & Wajda-Johnston, 2002).

Complementary and Alternative Medicine

The use of techniques such as yoga, meditation, mindfulness, acupuncture, and many others has become a very effective treatment for those with pain, dealing with chronic disease, and those who may be averse to traditional intervention techniques such as talk therapy and pharmacotherapy (Barnes, Bloom, & Nahin, 2008).

Technology

Psychological Assessment

Using the Internet for psychological assessment has become a popular choice for professionals due to ease of use and convenience. Specifically, materials can be easily made available and accessed by many more individuals compared to non-web-based tools (Naglieri et al., 2004). In addition, newer test versions can be made available more easily. However, caution must be exercised, as a complete evaluation and integration of scores is difficult when completed over the Internet (Naglieri et al., 2004). Additionally, most assessment is enhanced by behavioral observation, which is not possible over the Internet. Use of the Internet limits the ability to assess populations that do not have access to the Internet either for geographical or economic and social reasons (Naglieri et al., 2004).

Intervention

Evidence indicates that computer-based interventions may be effective for anxiety and depressive disorders; however, there are currently multiple limitations to this treatment. Specifically, adherence and attrition are more difficult to monitor via computers, and evidence for efficacy is limited for use with severe presentations (Newman, Szkodny, Llera, & Przeworski, 2010). Evidence indicates that computer-based exposure techniques such as virtual reality and social networking may be effective interventions. Internet interventions may provide individuals in remote locations to access; however, this remote access may lead to fewer therapists being present in these areas and also presents ethical issues (Koocher & Keith-Spiegel, 2008). Use of Internet-based interventions, similar to the use of Internet-based assessments, disadvantages the poor who may not have easy access or may not be comfortable with the Internet.

Research

Using computers and the Internet to collect data has become an efficient and cost-effective mechanism for accessing large amounts of data. More individuals can be accessed via the Internet, and large amounts of consumer data are readily available (Kraut et al., 2004). However, there are limitations and disadvantages of collecting data online such as biased samples, inability to monitor whether individuals are answering truthfully, and protection of data. These and other challenges must be addressed when conducting research online (Kraut et al., 2004).

Documentation

The current American Psychological Association guidelines for management of electronic records involve ensuring appropriate documentation storage and privacy (APA, 2007). It is noted that communicating through e-mail with clients may impose unintended risks to privacy and professionals need to be aware of the risks involved as well as their ability to safeguard client information.

Health Care Systems, Structures, and Economics, and How These Impact Intervention Choice

Health Care Systems

Health care systems are networks of people and institutions that work together to provide health care services and resources to the public in conjunction with policies that regulate these services. The goals of health care include provision of high-quality care for the populations they serve, to improve health and promote well-being (Gruskin et al., 2012).

The American health care system is composed of both public and private sectors, with the private sectors dominating the system (Chua, 2006). The Veterans Affairs (VA) health care system is a network that typically assists personnel who have fulfilled their duty to the American military.

Structures

Three models of health care based on financing have been identified: Beveridge model, Bismarck model, and the private insurance model (Lameire, Joffe, & Wiedemann, 1999). The Beveridge model is often referred to as the public model, which is primarily funded through taxation; budgets compete with spending priorities within its system (Lameire et al., 1999). The Bismarck model is referred to as the mixed model and is funded through a combination of premiums and social/mandatory insurance. Countries such as Germany and Switzerland use this model (Lameire et al., 1999). The United States uses a model known as the private insurance model, in which funding is based on premiums through private insurance companies, with the exception of public social care such as Medicare and Medicaid, which is publicly funded (Lameire et al., 1999). Within the private insurance model, health maintenance organizations (HMOs) and preferred provider organizations (PPOs) are some of the networks that are offered through employers (Xu & Jensen, 2006). HMOs generally require enrollees to see physicians within their network for all health care needs and do not cover care from specialists. PPOs allow one to choose a medical provider of his or her choice. HMOs tend to be less expensive and provide a modest copay, whereas PPOs require a higher out-of-pocket expense (Xu & Jensen, 2006).

Health Economics

Over the last decade, health care reforms have impacted costs and affordability of treatment to those who have depleted resources, despite health insurance. Public funding by the government and private funding by private insurance companies provide the financial basis of U.S. health care (Chua, 2006). Individuals and businesses both pay income taxes that provide funding for Medicare.

Moreover, businesses also provide most of the premiums for insurance they delegate through private insurers. The government provides programs such as Medicare, Medicaid, S-CHIP (State Children's Health Insurance Program), and the VA through taxation. Private insurers provide services for individuals, businesses, and government and accept premiums, and in return, the private insurers reimburse providers with private insurance (Chua, 2006).

Cost/Benefit Consideration

Helping the client/patient make a decision on treatment based on cost–benefit analysis is a critical function of health care providers (Cassel & Guest, 2012). Roughly 80% of health care spending is at the recommendation of physicians and at times not all physicians are current in their knowledge of efficient and newer treatments (Cassel & Guest, 2012). Spending on mental health services has increased significantly since the introduction of a variety of medications for mood disorders in the 1980s (Frank, Goldman, & McGuire, 2009). Insurance and payment organizations tend to favor the use of medication over traditional mental health treatments such as psychotherapy. Under public and private insurance, health care management designates costs of service in inpatient and outpatient settings, often favoring the least expensive solution (Frank et al., 2009). Deciding what treatment a patient receives is usually based on clinical information, but cost to the patient should also be considered (Gibson et al., 2012). The utilization and cost of medication have increased, and many with limited resources are forced to consider affordable treatment alternatives (Gibson et al., 2012).

Health and Wellness

In order to enhance health, one must consider multiple factors in addition to physical and mental well-being, such as job satisfaction, resilience, self-esteem, and social skills (Doyle, 2006). Furthermore, promoting health includes addressing risk factors among high-risk groups.

Health Promotion

Health promotion involves approaches that encourage healthy behaviors within a population and target a range of behaviors, including wearing your seat belt in a moving vehicle, promoting physical activity in order to combat childhood obesity, and family planning to prevent teen pregnancy (Randolph, Whitaker, & Arellano, 2012). Strategies such as community organizing, entertainment education, distribution of health-related devices, Internet-based education, mass media advertising, education provider, and policy change and enforcement all constitute methods of health promotion. An example of mass media advertising includes public service announcements through television or radio broadcasts promoting the cessation of smoking by exposing the consequences (Randolph, Whitaker, & Arellano, 2012). The goal behind this method is to provide a conceptual link between certain risk behaviors and images of consequences.

Risk Reduction

Reducing risk, whether in a universal or target population, involves identifying risks that could lead to health issues without the implementation of prevention or intervention programs (Manthorpe & Iliffe, 2012). Early intervention has been found to be important in risk reduction especially for issues that include an early developmental trajectory (Nation et al., 2003). Risk reduction includes the identification and acknowledgment of risk factors and protective factors across diverse settings such as community, family, school, and social networks. For example, risk reduction in older adults attempting suicide may include identifying factors that increase vulnerability to suicide such as poor health, poor social integration, or chronic pain, and implementing secondary prevention interventions that target these risks and help the individual manage them in a way that is both beneficial and productive (Manthorpe & Iliffe, 2012).

Resilience and Wellness

Resilience can be described as the psychological capacity to cope with challenges, including trauma, stress, and other hardships (Froehlich-Gildhoff & Roennau-Boese, 2012). Generally, resilience develops through individuals' life experiences, with childhood events having a greater impact. The salient effects of early childhood experiences on the development of resilience point to the importance of preventive promotion in early years of life; important preventive strategies in early childhood include the development of self-esteem, self-efficacy, self-control, social competence, and problem-solving skills (Froehlich-Gildhoff & Roennau-Boese, 2010). Learning to be positive and optimistic during stressful situations can have beneficial effects such as enhanced well-being and the development of resilience (Tugade & Frederickson, 2007). For example, education about dementia and provision of support to dementia health care workers are methods that have been found to increase resilience to stress and decrease turnover rates in the workforce (Elliot, Scott, Stirling, Martin, & Robinson, 2012).

Contemporary Models of Supervision

Supervision is defined as a one-to-one relationship between a senior and a junior member of the psychology profession, during which the senior member provides ongoing monitoring of issues in practice and skills, enhances professional functioning, and helps the supervisee meet standards of the profession (Pettifor, Schoepp, McCarron, Stark, & Stewart, 2011). Many current researchers have found that effective supervision consists of a positive working relationship, continual assessment of student's skills and needs, and constructive criticism as well as praise (Westefeld, 2009). In a study investigating the evidence base for supervision, researchers found that three tools were used consistently for supervision: giving feedback, using educational role play, and modeling (Milne, Sheikh, Pattison, & Wilkinson, 2011). Although conventional and professional wisdom considers supervision essential to the development of young professionals in the mental health field, there has been little evidence to support the techniques used in the field and very little research on effectiveness (Milne et al., 2011). Supervision is sometimes viewed as a purely clinical event, but in fact, needs to be incorporated into mentoring research, teaching, and administration skills. Specifically, a supervisor can be essential in providing assistance in the areas of conducting and implementing research effectively, while adhering to the specific institution's ethical and administrative requirements (Pettifor et al., 2011). Unfortunately, the current state of clinical psychology has not provided a structure for supervision training, and counseling centers are currently most proficient at providing training in clinical supervision compared to all other types of training sites (Scott, Ingram, Vitanza, & Smith, 2000). However, there are a handful of supervision models with empirical support and an evidence base. These include the developmental model, CBT model, and dynamic model.

Developmental Model

Using the developmental model of supervision is based on the understanding that learning clinical skills occurs in stages. An individual will need different levels of support from a supervisor depending on his or her stage of learning (Smith, 2009).

Cognitive Behavioral Therapy Model

In the absence of a significant evidence base for supervision, using a standard learning model such as CBT, which includes many evidence-based techniques, may be an effective strategy (Milne et al., 2011). CBT supervision consists of many tools that are used in a CBT therapy session, such as setting an agenda and assigning homework.

Psychodynamic Model

The dynamic model of supervision varies depending on the desires of the supervisor. Dynamic supervision can be content or process oriented, and can involve the relationship between supervisor and supervisee, or can focus solely on the dynamic themes of the patient being discussed (Smith, 2009).

In addition to imparting therapeutic techniques to students, it is imperative that supervision encompasses teaching appropriate skills such as documentation and knowledge of current ethical, legal, and multicultural issues. Specifically, supervisors must focus on dealing with multiple relationships, guidelines to prevent malpractice, and fostering multicultural competence (Westefeld, 2009).

References

American Psychiatric Association. (2000). *Diagnostic and statistical manual of mental disorders* (4th ed., text rev.). Washington, DC: American Psychiatric Press.

American Psychological Association (APA). (2007). Record keeping guidelines. *American Psychologist, 62*(9), 993–1004.

Amundson, N. E. (2005). The potential impact of global changes in work for career theory and practice. *International Journal for Educational and Vocational Guidance, 5*, 91–99.

Angerer, J. M. (2003). Job burnout. *Journal of Employment Counseling, 40*(3), 98–107.

Arredondo, P., Shealy, C., Neale, M., & Winfrey, L. L. (2004). Consultation and interprofessional collaboration: Modeling for the future. *Journal of Clinical Psychology, 60*(7), 787–800.

Barnes, P. M., Bloom, B., & Nahin, R. L. (2008). Complementary and alternative medicine use among adults and children: United States, 2007. *National Health Statistics Reports, 12*, 1–24.

Birrer, D., & Morgan, G. (2010). Psychological skills training as a way to enhance an athlete's performance in high-intensity sports. *Scandinavian Journal of Medicine and Science in Sports, 20*(2), 78–87.

Blass, R. B. (2012). The ego according to Klein: Return to Freud and beyond. *International Journal of Psychoanalysis, 93*, 151–166.

Boselie, P., Dietz, G., & Boon, C. (2005). Commonalities and contradictions in HRM and performance research. *Human Resource Management Journal, 15*(3), 67–94.

Brawer, P. A., Handal, P. J., Fabricatore, A. N., Roberts, R., & Wajda-Johnston, V. A. (2002). Training and education in religion/spirituality within APA-accredited clinical psychology programs. *Professional Psychology: Research and Practice, 33*(2), 203–206.

Brener, R., Madhusoodanan, S., Puttichanda, S., & Chandra, P. (2010). Primary prevention in psychiatry—adult populations. *Annals of Clinical Psychiatry, 22*, 239–248.

Bryan, L. A., Dersch, C., Shumway, S., & Arredondo, R. (2004): Therapy outcomes: Client perception and similarity with therapist view. *American Journal of Family Therapy, 32*(1), 11–26.

Cantarello, S., Filippini, R., & Nosella, A. (2012). Linking human resource management practices and customer satisfaction on product quality. *International Journal of Human Resource Management, 23*, 3906–3924.

Caplan, G., & Caplan, R. B. (1993). *Mental health consultation and collaboration*. San Francisco, CA: Jossey-Bass.

Caplan, G., Caplan, R. B., & Erchul, W. P. (1994). Caplanian mental health consultation: Historical background and current status. *Consulting Psychology Journal: Practice and Research, 46*, 2–12.

Carroll, K., & Onken, L. (2005). Behavioral therapies for drug abuse. *American Journal of Psychiatry, 162*, 1452–1460.

Carroll, K., Rounsavill, B., Nich, C., Gordon, L., Wirtz, P., & Gawin, F. (1994). One-year follow-up of psychotherapy and pharmacotherapy for cocaine dependence: Delayed emergence of psychotherapy effects. *Archives of General Psychiatry, 51*, 989–997.

Cassel, C. K., & Guest, J. A. (2012). Choosing wisely: Helping physicians and patients make smart decisions about their care. *Journal of the American Medical Association, 307*, 1801–1802.

Chard, K., Schuster, J., & Resick, P. (2012). Empirically supported psychological treatment: Cognitive processing therapy. In J. Beck & D. Sloan (Eds.), *The Oxford handbook of post-traumatic stress disorders* (pp. 439–448). New York, NY: Oxford University Press.

Choy, Y., Fyer, A. J., & Lipsitz, J. D. (2007). Treatment of specific phobia in adults. *Clinical Psychology Review, 27*, 266–286.

Chua, K. (2006). *Overview of the U.S. healthcare system*. http://www.amsa.org/uhc/HealthCareSystemOverview.pdf (Accessed May 27, 2008). American Medical Student Association Online.

Codrova, J. V. (2001). Acceptance in behavior therapy: Understanding the process of change. *Behavior Analyst, 24*, 213–226.

Corsini, J. R., & Wedding, D. (2008). *Current psychotherapies* (8th ed.). Belmont, CA: Thomson Higher Education.

Coull, G., & Morris, P. G. (2011). The clinical effectiveness of CBT-based guided self-help interventions for anxiety and depressive disorders: A systematic review. *Psychological Medicine, 41*, 2239–2252.

Crust, L. (2007). Mental toughness in sport: A review. *International Journal of Sport and Exercise Psychology, 5*(3), 270–290.

Cuijpers, P., van Straten, A., Andersson, G., & van Oppen, P. (2008). Psychotherapy for depression in adults: A meta-analysis of comparative outcome studies. *Journal of Consulting and Clinical Psychology, 76*, 909–922.

Doyle, J. (2006). *Prevention and early intervention, Issue I addendum: Definitions.* Retrieved from: http://www.emqff.org/press/docs/Prevention%20and%20Early%20Intervention%20Issue%201%20Addendum%2003-07-06.pdf

Durand, V., & Carr, E. (1991). Functional communication training to reduce challenging behavior: Maintenance and application in new settings. *Journal of Applied Behavior Analysis, 24*, 251–264.

Eerola, K. (2010). The first dream in psychoanalysis. *Scandinavian Psychoanalytic Review, 33*, 113–121.

Elliot, K. J., Scott, J. L., Stirling, C., Martin, A. J., & Robinson, A. (2012). Building capacity and resilience in the dementia care workforce: A systematic review of interventions targeting worker and organization outcomes. *International Psychogeriatrics, 24*, 882–894.

Fairburn, C. G., Cooper, Z., & Shafran, R. (2003). Cognitive behavior therapy for eating disorders: A "transdiagnostic" theory and treatment. *Behavior Research and Therapy, 41*, 509–528.

Fairburn, C. G., Cooper, Z., Shafran, R., & Wilson, G. (2008). Eating disorders: A transdiagnostic protocol. In D. Barlow (Ed.), *Clinical handbook of psychological disorders: A step by step treatment manual* (pp. 578–614). New York, NY: Guilford Press.

Forbes, D., Lloyd, D., Nixon, R. D., Elliot, P., Varker, T., Perry, D., … Creamer, M. (2012). Multisite randomized controlled effectiveness trial of cognitive processing therapy for military-related posttraumatic stress disorder. *Journal of Anxiety Disorders, 26*(3), 442–452.

Frank, R. G., Goldman, H. H., & McGuire, T. G. (2009). Trends in mental health cost growth: An expanded role for management? *Health Affairs, 28*, 649–659.

Franklin, M., & Foa, E. (2008). Obsessive-compulsive disorder. In D. Barlow (Ed.), *Clinical handbook of psychological disorders: A step by step treatment manual* (pp. 179–230). New York, NY: Guilford Press.

Freeney, Y., & Tiernan, J. (2006). Employee engagement: An overview of the literature on the proposed antithesis to burnout. *Irish Journal of Psychology, 27*(3–4), 130–141.

Froehlich-Gildhoff, K., & Roennau-Boese, M. (2012). Prevention of exclusion: The promotion of resilience in early childhood institutions in disadvantaged areas. *Journal of Public Health, 20*, 131–139.

Gibson, T. B., Jing, Y., bagalman, J. E., Cao, Z., bates, J. A., Hebden, T., … Doshi, J. A. (2012). Impact of cost-sharing on treatment augmentation in patients with depression. *American Journal of Managed Care, 18*, 15–22.

Grief, S. (2007). Advances in research on coaching outcomes. *International Coaching Psychology Review, 2*(3), 222–249.

Grieves, J. (2000). Images of change: The new organizational development. *Journal of Management Development, 19*(5), 345–447.

Gros, D. F., Strachan, M., Ruggiero, K. J., Knapp, R. G., Frueh, B. C., Egede, L. E., … Acierno, R. (2010). Innovative service delivery for secondary prevention of PTSD in at-risk OIF-OEF service men and women. *Contemporary Clinical Trials, 32*, 122–128.

Gruskin, S., Ahmed, S., Bogecho, D., Ferguson, L., Hanefeld, J., Maccarthy, S., … Steiner, R. (2012). Human rights in health systems frameworks: What is there, what is missing and why does it matter. *Global Public Health: An International Journal for Research, Policy and Practice, 7*, 337–351.

Guerin, P. J., Jr., & Chabot, D. R. (1997). Development of family systems theory. In P. L. Wachtel & S. B. Messer (Eds.), *Theories of psychotherapy: Origins and evolution* (pp. 181–225). Washington, DC: American Psychological Association.

Guest, D. E., Michie, J., Conway, N., & Sheehan, M. (2003). Human resource management and corporate performance in the UK. *British Journal of Industrial Relations, 41*(2), 291–314.

Gulotta, T. P., & Bloom, M. (Eds.). (2003). *Encyclopedia of primary prevention and health promotion*. New York, NY: Kluwer Academic/Plenum Press.

Hamlin, R. G., Ellinger, A. D., & Beattie, R. S. (2008). The emergent 'coaching industry': A wake-up call for HRD professionals. *Human Resource Development International, 11*(3), 287–305.

Hansson, L. (2006). Determinants of quality of life in people with severe mental illness. *Acta Psychiatrica Scandinavica, 113*(429), 46–50.

Hoek, H. W. (2006). Incidence, prevalence and mortality of anorexia nervosa and other eating disorders. *Current Opinion in Psychiatry, 19*(4), 389–394.

Hofman, S. G., Asnaani, A., Vonk, I. J. J., Sawyer, A. T., & Fang, A. (2012). The efficacy of cognitive behavioral therapy: A review of meta-analysis. *Cognitive Therapy and Research, 36*, 427–440.

Hoffman, L., & Cleare-Hoffman, H. (2011). Existential therapy and emotions: Lessons from cross-cultural exchange. *Humanistic Psychologist, 39*, 261–267.

Hourani, L. L., Council, C. L., Hubal, R. C., & Strange, L. B. (2011). Approaches to the primary prevention of posttraumatic stress disorder in the military: A review of the stress control literature. *Military Medicine, 176*, 721–730.

Hunot, V., Churchill, R., Teixeira, V., & de Lima, M. S. (2010). Psychological therapies for generalised anxiety disorder. *Cochrane Database of Systematic Reviews, 2007*, 1.

Hylander, I. (2012). Conceptual change through consultee-centered consultation: A theoretical model. *Consulting Psychology Journal, 64*, 29–45.

Irving, S. (1962). *Personality dynamics and development*. Hoboken, NJ: John Wiley.

Kessler, R., Berglund, P., Demler, O., Jin, R., & Walters, E. (2005). Lifetime prevalence and age-of-onset distributions of *DSM-IV* disorders in the National Comorbidity Survey Replication (NCS-R). *Archives of General Psychiatry, 62*(6), 593–602.

Kim, M. J. (2003). Structural family therapy and its implication for the Asian American family. *Family Journal, 11*, 388–392.

Knotek, S. (2006). Administrative crisis consultation after 9/11: A university's systems response. *Consulting Psychology Journal: Practice and Research, 58*, 162–173.

Knotek, S. E., & Sandoval, J. (2003). Current research in consultee-centered consultation, *Journal of Educational and Psychological Consultation, 14*(3–4), 243–250.

Koocher, G. P., & Keith-Spiegel, P. (2008). *Ethics in psychology and the mental health professions: Standards and cases* (3rd ed.). New York, NY: Oxford University Press.

Kraut, R., Olson, J., Banaji, M., Bruckman, M., Cohen, J., & Couper, M. (2004). Psychological research online. *American Psychologist, 59*(2), 105–117.

Kwaske, I. H. (2004). Individual assessments for personnel selection: An update on a rarely researched but avidly practiced practice. *Consulting Psychology Journal: Practice and Research, 56*(3), 186–195.

Lameire, N., Joffe, P., & Wiedemann, M. (1999). Healthcare systems—An international review: An overview. *Nephrology Dialysis Transplantation, 14*, 3–9.

Lazar, S. G. (Ed.). (2010). *Psychotherapy is worth it: A comprehensive review of its cost-effectiveness.* Arlington, VA: American Psychiatric Press.

Linehan, M., & Dexter-Mazza, E. (2008). Dialectical behavior therapy for borderline personality disorder. In D. Barlow (Ed.), *Clinical handbook of psychological disorders: A step by step treatment manual* (pp. 250–305). New York, NY: Guilford Press.

Littell, J. H., & Girvin, H. (2002). Stages of change: A critique. *Behavioral Modification, 26*, 223–273.

Manthorpe, J., & Iliffe, S. (2011). Social work with older people—Reducing suicide risk: A critical review of practice and prevention. *British Journal of Social Work, 41*, 131–147.

Marsiglia, F. F., Ayers, S., Gance-Cleveland, B., Mettler, K., & Booth, J. (2012). Beyond primary prevention of alcohol use: A culturally specific secondary prevention program for Mexican heritage adolescents. *Prevention Science, 13*, 241–251.

Martin, G. L., Vause, T., & Schwartzman, L. (2005). Experimental studies of psychological interventions with athletes in competitions: Why so few? *Behavior Modification, 29*(4), 616–641.

McLean, C., & Foa, E. (2011). Prolonged exposure therapy for post-traumatic stress disorder: A review of evidence and dissemination. *Expert Review of Neurotherapeutics, 11*(8), 1151–1163.

McMahon, M., Watson, M., Chetty, C., & Hoelson, C. H. (2012). Examining process constructs of narrative career counseling: An exploratory case study. *British Journal of Guidance & Counseling, 40*, 127–141.

Meuret, A. E., Wolitzky-Taylor, K. B., Twohiq, M. P., & Craske, M. G. (2012). Coping skills and exposure therapy in panic disorder and agoraphobia: Latest advances and future directions. *Behavior Therapy, 43*, 271–284.

Miklowitz, D., Otto, M., Frank, E., Reilly-Harrington, V., Wisniewski, S., Kogan, J. N., … Sachs, G. S. (2007). Psychosocial treatments for bipolar depression: A 1 year randomized trial from the Systematic Treatment Enhancement Program. *Archives of General Psychiatry, 64*, 419–427.

Miller, W. R., & Rollnick, S. (2002). *Motivational interviewing: Preparing people for change* (2nd ed.). New York, NY: Guilford Press.

Milne, D. L., Sheikh, A. I., Pattison, S., & Wilkinson, A. (2011). Evidence-based training for clinical supervisors: A systematic review of 11 controlled studies. *The Clinical Supervisor, 30*(1), 53–71.

Moore, Z. E. (2009). Theoretical and empirical developments of the mindfulness-acceptance-commitment (MAC) approach to performance enhancement. *Journal of Clinical Sports Psychology, 4*, 291–302.

Myers, V., Gerber, Y., Benyamini, Y., Goldbourt, U., & Drory, Y. (2012). Post-myocardial infarction depression: Increased hospital admission and reduced adoption of secondary prevention measures—A longitudinal study. *Journal of Psychosomatic Research, 72*, 5–10.

Naglieri, J. A., Drasgow, F., Schmit, M., Handler, L., Prifitera, A., Margolis, A., et al. (2004). Psychological testing on the internet. *American Psychologist, 59*(3), 150–162.

Nation, M., Crusto, C., Wandersman, A., Kumpfer, K. L., Seybolt, D., Morrissey-Kane, E., & Davino, K. (2003). What works in prevention. Principles of effective prevention programs. *American Psychologist, 58*, 449–456.

Newman, M. G., Szkodny, L. E., Llera, S. J., & Przeworski, A. (2010). A review of technology-assisted self-help and minimal contact therapies for anxiety and depression: Is human contact necessary for therapeutic efficacy. *Clinical Psychology Review, 31*, 89–103.

Opler, M., Sodhi, D., Zaveri, D., & Madhusoodanan, S. (2010). Primary psychiatric prevention in children and adolescents. *Annals of Clinical Psychiatry, 22*, 220–234.

Papworth, M. (2006). Issues and outcomes associated with adult mental health self-help materials: A "second order" review or "qualitative meta-review." *Journal of Mental Health, 15*(4), 387–409.

Perdrix, S., Stauffer, S., Masdonati, J., Massoudi, K., & Rossier, J. (2012). Effectiveness of career counseling: A one-year follow-up. *Journal of Vocational Behavior, 80*, 565–578.

Pettifor, J., Schoepp, G., McCarron, M. C. E., Stark, C., & Stewart, D. (2011). Ethical supervision in teaching, research, practice, and administration. *Canadian Psychology, 52*(3), 198–205.

Pistrang, N., Barker, C., & Humphreys, K. (2008). Mutual help groups for mental health problems: A review of effectiveness studies. *American Journal of Community Psychology, 42*, 110–121.

Post, B. C., & Wade, N. G. (2009). Religion and spirituality in psychotherapy: A practice-friendly review of research. *Journal of Clinical Psychology, 65*, 131–146.

Prochaska, J. O., DiClemente, C. C., & Norcross, J. C. (1992). In search of how people change. Applications to addictive behaviors. *American Psychologist, 47*, 1102–1114.

Randolph, K. A., Whitaker, P., & Arellano, A. (2012). The unique effects of environmental strategies in health promotion campaigns: A review. *Evaluation and Program Planning, 35*, 344–353.

Sajatovic, M., Sanders, R., Alexeenko, L., & Madhusoodanan, S. (2010). Primary prevention of psychiatric illness in special populations. *Annals of Clinical Psychiatry, 22*, 262–273.

Schachar, R., & Tannock, R. (2002). Syndromes of hyperactivity and attention deficit. In M. Rutter & E. Taylor (Eds.), *Child and adolescent psychiatry*. Oxford, UK: Blackwell Publishing.

Schopler, E. (1997). Implementation of TEACCH philosophy. In D. J. Cohen & F. R. Volkmar (Eds.), *Handbook of autism and pervasive developmental disorders*. New York, NY: John Wiley.

Schultheiss, D. E. P. (2005). Qualitative relational career assessment: A constructivist paradigm. *Journal of Career Assessment, 13*, 381–394.

Scott, J. (2007). Cognitive theory and therapy of bipolar disorders. *Tidsskrift for Norsk Psykologforening, 44*, 647–657.

Scott, K. J., Ingram, K. M., Vitanza, S. A., & Smith, N. G. (2000). Training in supervision: A survey of current practices. *The Counseling Psychologist, 28*(3), 403–422.

Smith, K. L. (2009). *A brief summary of supervision models.* Retrieved from http://www.gallaudet.edu/documents/academic/cou_supervisionmodels[1].pdf

Snyder, E. P., Quirk, K., & Dematteo, F. (2011). Consulting with families, schools, and communities. In T. M. Lionetti, E. P. Snyder, & R. W. Christner (Eds.), *A practical guide to developing competencies in school psychology* (pp. 69–81). Boston, MA: Springer.

Stone, G. (2012). Strategic family therapy as an alternative to antipsychotics. In S. Olfman & B. D. Robbins (Eds.), *Drugging our children: How profiteers are pushing antipsychotics on our youngest, and what we can do to stop it* (pp. 139–152). Santa Barbara, CA: Praeger/ABC-CLIO.

Strachan, M., Gros, D. F., Ruggiero, K. J., Lejuez, C. W., & Acierno, R. (2012). An integrated approach to delivering exposure-based treatment for symptoms of PTSD and depression in OIF/OEF veterans: Preliminary findings. *Behavior Therapy, 43,* 560–569.

Substance Abuse and Mental Health Services Administration. (2009). Results from the 2008 National Survey on Drug Use and Health: National Findings (Office of Applied Studies, NSDUH Series H-36, HHS Publication No. SMA 09-4434). Rockville, MD.

Taute, W., & Taute, F. (2012). Organizational development: A supplement for the effective organization. *Journal of Workplace Behavioral Health, 27,* 63–78.

Tugade, M. M., & Frederickson, B. L. (2007). Regulation of positive emotions: Emotion regulation strategies that promote resilience. *Journal of Happiness Studies, 8,* 311–333.

Wardle, J., Lui, C., & Adams, J. (2012). Complementary and alternative medicine in rural communities: Current research and future directions. *The Journal of Rural Health, 28,* 101–112.

Westefeld, J. S. (2009). Supervision of psychotherapy: Models, issues, and recommendations. *The Counseling Psychologist, 37*(2), 296–316.

Whiston, S. C., Lindeman, D., Rahardja, D., & Reed, J. H. (2005). Career counseling process: A qualitative analysis of experts' cases. *Journal of Career Assessment, 13,* 169–187.

Wicks-Nelson, R., & Israel, A. (2006). *Behavior disorders of childhood* (6th ed.). New Jersey: Pearson Education.

Wilson, G. T., Grilo, C. M., & Vitousek, K. M. (2007). Psychological treatment of eating disorders. *American Psychologist, 62,* 199–216.

Wood, J. C., & Wood, M. (2008). *Therapy 101: A brief look at modern psychotherapy techniques & how they can help.* Oakland, CA: New Harbinger Publications.

World Health Organization (WHO). (2004). *Prevention of mental disorders: Effective intervention and policy options.* Summary Report. Geneva, Switzerland: Author.

Xu, X., & Jensen, G. A. (2006). Health effects of managed care among the near-elderly. *Journal of Aging and Health, 18,* 507–533.

Young, J. E., Rygh, J. L., Weinberger, A. D., & Beck, A. T. (2008). Cognitive therapy for depression. In D. Barlow (Ed.), *Clinical handbook of psychological disorders: A step by step treatment manual* (pp. 265–320). New York, NY: Guilford Press.

Review Questions

1. The use of self-help materials sought out by individuals has been demonstrated to be effective for relief in some psychiatric symptoms, specifically for:
   A. Assertiveness
   B. Anxiety disorders
   C. Mood disorders
   D. Both assertiveness and anxiety disorders

2. What does the research show on the widely known belief that similarities between client and therapist, such as gender and ethnicity, can help promptly develop and nurture a strong and trusting rapport?
   A. The research supports the benefit of client/therapist similarities
   B. The research shows that similarities benefit client/therapist rapport but hinder therapeutic gains
   C. There is no support in the research
   D. The research shows mixed results and this topic needs to be further investigated

3. Which treatment has been well researched and shows good results for treating anorexia nervosa?
   A. Behavioral activation treatment
   B. Nondirective supportive treatment
   C. Family therapy
   D. Cognitive behavioral therapy

4. What is the primary reason for increased spending on mental health care?
   A. Introduction of medications for mood disorder
   B. Government-funded programs
   C. Health care reform
   D. Studies establishing the efficacy of psychotherapy

5. Which contemporary theory relies on empirical support for its evidence base?
   A. Psychoanalysis
   B. Existential psychotherapy
   C. Analytical psychotherapy
   D. Behavioral therapy

6. Which of the following is a limitation when using the Internet to conduct therapy?
   A. There is no evidence that it is an effective treatment
   B. Social networking is not an effective intervention
   C. It raises ethical dilemmas
   D. It has only been shown to be effective for anxiety disorders

7. According to the CBT model of supervision, which is most likely?

   A. A supervisor identifies a supervisee's level of skills and implements assignments each week in order to gauge the supervisee's improvement
   B. A supervisor listens to a supervisee's issues with clients and sympathizes with him or her in order to make them feel more comfortable
   C. A supervisor conducts assessments on the supervisee in order to be certain he or she is psychologically adequate to manage a certain patient
   D. A supervisor conducts cognitive behavioral therapy on a supervisee about his or her own problem areas in life

8. Which of the following is true?

   A. Support groups have been demonstrated to be effective in improving mental health outcomes in populations with anxiety, depression, and chronic mental illness
   B. In addition to offering an economical alternative, the benefits of using self-help materials include self-empowerment and anonymity
   C. Imperative for enhanced quality of life, research has suggested the need for effective social support as an adjunct to traditional treatments
   D. All of the above

9. One of the most important aspects contributing to an individual's wellness is:

   A. The degree to which an individual is able to access self-help materials
   B. The quality and quantity of social support from families, friends, and the larger community
   C. The amount of time afforded to an individual where he can be alone, without interruption, in a quiet space
   D. None of the above

10. When considering the overall cost of mental illness, a therapist is ethically required to:

    A. Pick the method of treatment that would best suit the diagnosis regardless of cost
    B. Carefully weigh the risks versus benefits of all treatments
    C. Try to reduce overall financial cost to the client
    D. Inform the patient of all risks and benefits but leave the final decision up to the client

11. Which is NOT a benefit of the Transtheoretical Model?

    A. The model allows the therapist to identify and discard treatments the client is not yet ready for
    B. The model allows for reduction of overall therapeutic cost
    C. The model allows the therapist to introduce treatments the client might not be ready for, and therefore speed up therapeutic recovery
    D. The model clearly identifies behavior change according to stages

12. What is the standard treatment for bulimia nervosa?

    A. Family therapy
    B. Cognitive behavioral therapy
    C. Social skills training
    D. Behavioral activation treatment

13. The Bismarck model of financing is funded through:

    A. Taxation of citizens

    B. Private insurance companies

    C. Premium-financed mandatory insurance

    D. Public social care programs

14. What determines behavior according to psychoanalysis?

    A. Unconscious desires averred in dreams

    B. Childhood trauma and object relations

    C. Childhood experience and developmental progression

    D. Libidinal urges

15. Why is using the Internet for psychological assessment a good idea?

    A. It does a better job of integrating scores efficiently

    B. It is not susceptible to human error

    C. Everyone in the world has access to the Internet

    D. Updated versions of assessments can be easily accessed

16. Which of these is NOT an important consideration when collecting data online?

    A. Data storage and privacy

    B. Comparing cost

    C. Distance from the researcher

    D. Monitoring the accuracy of responses

17. In victims of trauma, what is an indicated approach to victims of rape?

    A. The use of rape crisis centers

    B. Advocating against violence using media networks

    C. Implementing research on rape and its psychological effects

    D. Reporting a rape offender to the police

18. Which theory in athletic performance uses imagery and self-talk to improve confidence and decrease anxiety?

    A. Psychoanalytic skills training theory

    B. Contemplative skills building theory

    C. Psychological skills training theory

    D. None of the above

19. According to the constructivism theory, what is the main focus of career development?

    A. The subjective experience of the client and personal agency

    B. The career counselor's clinical opinion

    C. The prospective employers

    D. The results of the client's aptitude and achievement assessments

20. Which most likely resembles the narrative approach to career counseling?

    A. A counselor asks a client what he wants to do with his life

    B. A counselor asks a client to engage in a story related to life events and in career settings

    C. A counselor tells a client a story about a friend who got hired at a dream job

    D. A counselor advises a client on career opportunities in the area

21. In academic settings, what consultation approach is often implanted and what does it entail?

   A. Behavioral consultation involving identifying problem behavior and implementing problem-solving methods
   B. Behavioral consultation involving identifying problem areas in academics and implementing cognitive remediation
   C. Cognitive consultation involving identifying cognitive schemas and implementing cognitive behavioral therapy
   D. Family consultation and implementing the help of the family in order to help the client boost his self-esteem

22. In health and wellness, what does risk reduction involve?

   A. Identifying risks, given that preventative methods have been implemented
   B. Identifying existing problems, given that primary preventative methods have been implemented
   C. Identifying risks that have accelerated potential, given no prevention has been implemented
   D. Implementing prevention to a target group

23. According to research, what has been supported as being effective in supervision?

   A. Unconditional positive regard, constructive criticism, and empathy
   B. Relating to the supervisee by sharing experiences with clients
   C. Giving incentives for good work, using assessments to identify and criticize a supervisee, and empathy
   D. Positive working relationship, continual assessment of student's skills/needs, and constructive criticism and praise

24. Which treatment approach is most often associated with unconditional positive regard?

   A. Existential psychotherapy
   B. Behavioral therapy
   C. Gestalt therapy
   D. Client-centered therapy

25. Which treatment implementation would be most beneficial in treating patients with psychotic disorders?

   A. Psychotropic medication and cognitive behavioral therapy
   B. Psychotropic medication alone
   C. Mindfulness-based treatment
   D. Psychotropic medication and mindfulness-based treatment

26. Which preventative method's goal is to reduce disability, improve function, and enhance rehabilitative efforts and employ relapse prevention?

   A. Primary prevention
   B. Secondary prevention
   C. Tertiary prevention
   D. Quaternary prevention

27. A therapist who often employs a variety of techniques in treatment individualized to the patient would consider himself or herself what kind of therapist?

   A. Gestalt therapist
   B. Inclusive therapist
   C. Eclectic therapist
   D. Integrative therapist

28. Which treatment for depression is the most effective for symptom reduction?

   A. Cognitive therapy
   B. Pharmacotherapy
   C. Behavioral activation
   D. Combination of cognitive therapy and pharmacotherapy

29. As a treatment for psychotic disorders, CBT has shown the most benefit for:

   A. Positive symptoms
   B. Disorganized speech
   C. Catatonic behaviors
   D. Negative symptoms

30. Children who receive interventions that enhance self-esteem, self-efficacy, self-
   control, and problem-solving skills will, according to the literature, improve
   what?

   A. Resilience
   B. Academic performance
   C. Popularity
   D. Cognitive function

Answers to Review Questions

1. D. Both assertiveness and anxiety disorders

Self-help materials are effective in relieving psychiatric symptoms; however, according to Papworth (2006), there is more evidence for its efficacy with assertiveness and anxiety disorders.

2. D. The research shows mixed results and this topic needs to be further investigated

Evidence does suggest that gender and ethnicity similarities prompt self-disclosure and rapport; however, literature is scarce and not generalizable. For this, further investigation is warranted.

3. C. Family therapy

A variety of treatment approaches for eating disorders have been investigated. Cognitive behavioral therapy may be the gold standard for eating disorders; however, family therapy, for anorexia nervosa specifically, has been found more efficacious than individual therapy in most treatment studies. More research comparing treatments for eating disorders is needed, though.

4. A. Introduction of medications for mood disorder

Medication use for mental health treatment has increased exponentially within the past two decades. Though other factors have increased spending for mental health care, medication is expensive and its use is highly popular for its temporal efficacy and accessibility.

5. D. Behavioral therapy

Though all treatment approaches may rely on some investigative evidence, behavioral therapy relies primarily on theory supported by evidence provided by research investigation.

6. C. It raises ethical dilemmas

The sharing of private health information in Internet-based treatment poses a threat to its security and consequently presents an ethical concern especially under the Health Insurance Portability and Accountability Act (HIPAA).

7. A. A supervisor identifies a supervisee's level of skills and implements assignments each week in order to gauge the supervisee's improvement

The CBT model in general is a structured approach that incorporates assignments with the goal to teach and enhance one's skills. In supervision, the approach is the same with the agenda of improving the student's clinical skills.

8. D. All of the above

All of these are adjunctive interventions that are beneficial and have some support in improving mental health and wellness compared to more traditional approaches to therapy, such as individual therapy and pharmacotherapy.

9. B. The quality and quantity of social support from families, friends, and the larger community

Hansson (2006) suggests that social support supplements treatment outcomes in terms of individual wellness. Generally, social support is supported as a factor that improves health overall.

10. D. Inform the patient of all risks and benefits but leave the final decision up to the client

Ethically, therapists are responsible for informing the patients of any risk involved in treatment. They are also required to discuss costs both as a fiduciary duty to the patient and for nonmaleficence, ultimately providing the patient with sufficient data to make an informed decision toward treatment.

11. C. The model allows the therapist to introduce treatments the client might not be ready for, and therefore speed up therapeutic recovery

The Transtheoretical Model does not employ treatments that the client is not prepared for. Treatment is geared more toward matching the level of preparedness for change the client is in.

12. B. Cognitive behavioral therapy

The gold standard for bulimia nervosa and binge eating disorder treatment is cognitive behavioral therapy. Its efficacy has been supported in the literature above other approaches. CBT generally has the most evidence for its efficacy for treatment with many mental health disorders.

13. C. Premium-financed mandatory insurance

The Bismarck model is funded through compulsory payroll taxes and is a premium-financed mandatory insurance program. It is currently used in Germany and Switzerland. The Beveridge model or socialized medicine model is funded by the government through taxation. England and Spain use the Beveridge model as does the U.S. Veterans Health Administration. Private insurance companies are financed privately and typically through employers or community organizations and adjust price based on perceived risk. Public social care programs include Medicare and Medicaid, which are national social insurance programs.

14. C. Childhood experience and developmental progression

Both childhood experience and developmental progression influence how defense mechanisms are employed throughout the life span, incidentally influencing behavior.

15. D. Updated versions of assessments can be easily accessed

Among the benefits of using psychological assessments online such as easy access, convenience, and cost-effectiveness, versions of assessments can be easily updated according to the latest research. There are drawbacks to conducting assessments via the Internet, however.

16. C. Distance from the researcher

Collecting data online is a cheap, convenient, and accessible way to conduct research. The researcher must consider a variety of factors, including inability to monitor truthful answering, behavioral observations, and privacy of information. However, distance from the researcher is not important to consider.

17. A. The use of rape crisis centers

Indicated prevention targets groups exhibiting symptoms that implicate illness or disorders, which does not qualify as a full-blown diagnosis. Rape crisis centers target a population that has experienced rape (trauma), a population that exhibits a plethora of symptoms akin to trauma.

18. C. Psychological skills training theory

Psychological skills training theory uses cognitive techniques to enhance mental strength through anxiety reduction and to increase confidence. Mental strength is thought to determine variation in athletic performance.

19. A. The subjective experience of the client and personal agency

In the constructivist approach to career development, the client assumes the responsibility of creating career goals. The counselor uses a collaborative approach incorporating the client's interpretation of conflict and success to guide and enhance career development.

20. B. A counselor asks a client to engage in a story related to life events and in career settings

Narrative career counseling involves listening to the client's experience in order to improve the client's sense of autonomy in his or her career development. Counselors may use this to place the client in a hypothetical scenario in order to enhance conflict resolution and gain a broader perspective on career-related events.

21. A. Behavioral consultation involving identifying problem behavior and implementing problem-solving methods

Consultants tailor their approach as per the population. In the academic setting, a behavioral consultant would identify problematic behavior of a student(s) and use a problem-solving approach. This would be favored over the remaining options.

22. C. Identifying risks that have accelerated potential, given no prevention has been implemented

Early intervention is pivotal in order to minimize risk. Therefore risk reduction will involve assessment of risks and protective factors in their element and employ preventative measures to avoid escalation.

23. D. Positive working relationship, continual assessment of student's skills/needs, and constructive criticism and praise

Positive working relationship, continual assessment of a student's skills/needs, and constructive criticism and praise are valuable toward the development of mental health of trainees according to Westefeld (2009). However, more research in clinical supervision is needed to further assess the efficacy of a variety of methods.

24. D. Client-centered therapy

Carl Rogers emphasized the use of genuineness, empathy, and unconditional positive regard as central for healing in treatment. These conditions coupled with a nurturing and secure environment lead to a greater treatment outcome. Existential psychotherapy proposes life perspective and human existence as fundamental for treatment. Behavioral therapy uses behavior techniques that are heavily researched, and Gestalt therapy is defined by social networks, family, and memories.

25. A. Psychotropic medication and cognitive behavioral therapy

Though mindfulness-based approaches have some empirical support in treating psychotic disorders, the literature suggests that medication coupled with cognitive behavioral approaches to treatment are the most efficacious.

26. C. Tertiary prevention

Primary and secondary prevention efforts involve the beginning stages of disease involving risk reduction and health promotions to reduce prevalence, whereas tertiary methods involve already employed preventative efforts and aim to reduce impact of disease. Tertiary approaches aim to minimize long-term effects of disease.

27. D. Integrative therapist

The integrative approach does not adhere to one theory of psychotherapy and instead individualizes treatment according to the patient's needs and the presenting problem.

28. D. Combination of cognitive therapy and pharmacotherapy

The combination of therapy and psychopharmacological interventions has been shown to be most effective for treatment of depression.

29. A. Positive symptoms

CBT has been shown to help individuals manage positive symptoms, such as hallucinations and delusions.

30. A. Resilience

As part of resilience and wellness, preventative measures toward younger populations that build self-esteem, self-efficacy, problem solving, etc. will improve resilience. Early childhood experience is crucial to the development of health and wellness, and resilience.

7

Research Methods and Statistics

*Christian DeLucia, Jessica M. Valenzuela, Amy E. Ellis,
and Danette Beitra*

Broad Content Areas

- Research design, methodology, and program evaluation (PE)
- Instrument selection and validation
- Statistical models, assumptions, and procedures
- Dissemination methods

This chapter focuses on four broad content areas: (a) research design, methodology, and program evaluation (PE); (b) instrument selection and validation (topics covered under the more general topic of measurement); (c) statistical models, assumptions, and procedures; and (d) dissemination methods.

We use several levels of headings to provide a sufficient chapter road map. When necessary, the text is supplemented with several figures and a table. The statistics content is purposefully non-mathematical. Consequently, we present relatively few equations.

Many of the topics described in this chapter are covered in full-semester courses in doctoral programs in clinical psychology (e.g., the analysis of variance). We attempted to take such vast topics and present them in a manner that would balance breadth and depth.

Research Methodology

Science can be described as a systematic approach to knowledge acquisition. This continuum of knowledge acquisition is vast and ranges from simple observation/description to more sophisticated causal investigations. Research methods are the tools scientists use to acquire knowledge.

Theory and Hypotheses

A theory is an organized set of beliefs about a phenomenon. For example, a theory of alcohol use disorder etiology might posit several inter-related yet distinct developmental pathways to problematic alcohol use involving a broad spectrum of genetic, family environment, and broader social influences. According to Popper (2002), scientific theories must result in a set of propositions, or hypotheses, that can be refuted or disconfirmed. Hypotheses are predictions about association between/among variables that often derive from a larger theoretical framework. Examples of hypotheses are (a) inconsistent discipline is associated with behavior problems in children and (b) cigarette smoking causes lung cancer.

Campbell's Validity Typology

Internal Validity

Internal validity is the extent to which the association between x and y is *causal* in nature. For example, one might examine whether psychotherapy (x) is causally related to a reduction in depression (y). A valid causal inference requires satisfaction of three criteria: (a) statistical association, (b) temporal precedence, and (c) nonspuriousness. Statistical association occurs when the hypothesized cause and its effect covary (e.g., exposure to psychotherapy is associated with lower levels of depression, relative to no treatment). Temporal precedence occurs when the putative cause precedes its effect in time (e.g., symptom remission could not predate exposure to psychotherapy if psychotherapy is its cause). The third criterion, nonspuriousness, occurs when the hypothesized cause—and not some other factor—is responsible for the effect. Spurious causes are referred to by Campbell and his colleagues as threats to internal validity.

External Validity

External validity is the extent to which the causal association can be *generalized to* or *across* variations in study instances (e.g., individuals, treatments, outcomes, settings, and times).

Statistical Conclusion Validity

Statistical conclusion validity examines whether there is a statistical association between x and y and the magnitude of this association. Many statistical conclusion validity issues—including statistical significance, effect size estimation, and statistical power—are discussed in the statistics section of this chapter.

Construct Validity

Construct validity is the extent to which inferences can be made from particular study instances (e.g., individuals) to the higher-order constructs from which they presumably derive. For example, researchers sometimes use inadequate labels to describe study instances (e.g., label a treatment "progressive relaxation" when the treatment has many additional therapeutic components).

Study Design

In the ideal scenario, the primary research question proactively drives all decisions regarding participant sampling, study design, measurement of key study constructs, and analyses. In this next section, several study designs are described.

Group-Based Randomized Experiments

Randomized experiments are considered the gold standard for assessing causality. In a randomized experiment, participants might be randomly assigned to either brief dynamic psychotherapy for depression or a no-treatment control condition. In a basic two time-point (pretest–posttest) design, individuals who meet eligibility criteria are typically assessed at baseline, randomly assigned to a condition, exposed to treatment (or not, depending on condition), and then assessed at posttest. In this hypothetical study, the effect of primary interest is whether exposure to brief dynamic treatment *causes* a reduction in depression, relative to receiving no treatment.

Random assignment of participants to treatments uses a chance process (similar to a lottery drawing) to determine which participants are exposed to treatment and which are not. The use of random assignment precludes systematic pretest group differences because the groups are probabilistically equated on all measured and unmeasured characteristics. Consequently, the randomized control condition generates an important *hypothetical counterfactual* regarding what would have happened to individuals had they not been exposed to brief dynamic treatment. Note that the benefits of random assignment can be undone once the study commences (e.g., by differential attrition).

Efficacy Trials
In efficacy trials, an intervention's effects are examined under ideal circumstances, particularly with respect to treatment implementation. Efficacy trials often feature substantial clinician training and supervision and close monitoring of treatment adherence (often to a manual).

Effectiveness Trials
In effectiveness trials, an intervention's effects are examined under real-world conditions. Such trials often take place outside of academic settings (e.g., community mental health centers). Training and supervision will be less intensive relative to what is typically observed in efficacy trials and clients will often be less homogeneous diagnostically (e.g., more severe cases or comorbid cases may be included).

Intent-to-Treat Analyses
Intent-to-treat analyses were designed to analyze outcome data from randomized experiments involving participant attrition. In intent-to-treat analyses, researchers analyze outcome data from participants as a function of their original group assignment, regardless of their level of exposure to treatment. The analysis is intended to provide a conservative (and real-world) estimate of the treatment effect because it is based on cases exposed to varying levels of treatment. Unfortunately, when individuals drop out of treatment, they usually fail to provide additional outcome data, creating *missing data* problems in the analysis. When outcome data are collected on all participants, regardless of their exposure to treatment, intent-to-treat analyses achieve their intended purpose. These analyses are complicated greatly by the presence of missing data, however.

Single-Case Experiments

As with group-based experiments, single-case experiments are often designed to increase internal validity—that is, assess the causal influence of an intervention on an outcome. (Our discussion of single-case experiments follows that presented by Kazdin, 2003.) Common features of single-case experiments include intensive assessment before, during, and after intervention. Prolonged baseline assessment provides information about the pattern of changes in the outcome in the absence of the intervention.

ABAB Designs

The ABAB design is a single-case design that alternates the baseline (A) phase (intervention absent) with an intervention (B) phase (intervention present). The outcome of interest is assessed on multiple occasions within each phase. For example, in studying a child with frequent tantrums, a clinician might collect baseline tantrum data during days 1 through 4 (i.e., the first A phase), tantrum data during days 5 through 8 in which parents are implementing time-out in response to all tantrums (i.e., the first B phase). This 8-day sequence would then be repeated one more time to observe the outcome under the second A and B phases. The idea is that the frequency of tantrums will be higher in the absence of the intervention (during the A phases; see Figure 7.1 for a hypothetical outcome plot).

Multiple Baseline Designs

In multiple baseline designs, replication of an effect is sought over multiple baselines, which can reflect different behaviors, settings, and/or children (just to name a few). In Figure 7.2, results from a hypothetical multiple baseline design, with measurements of tantrums, aggressive acts toward siblings, and foul language (for a single child) are provided. Solid lines represent the frequency of the relevant behavior in the absence of the intervention (i.e., during a baseline phase). Dashed lines represent the frequency of the relevant behavior once the intervention is implemented for the given behavior (e.g., time-out implemented following each aggressive act directed toward a sibling). Figure 7.2 shows that the baseline for aggressive acts toward siblings lasted 4 days (i.e., measurement was conducted and no intervention applied), the baseline for tantrums lasted 7 days, and the

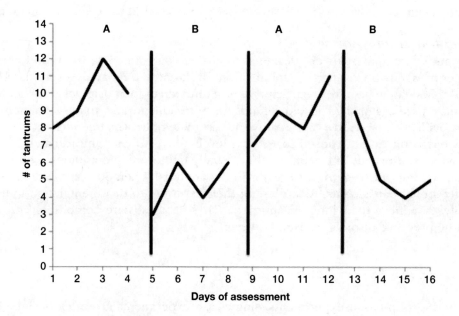

FIGURE 7.1 Data from an ABAB design.

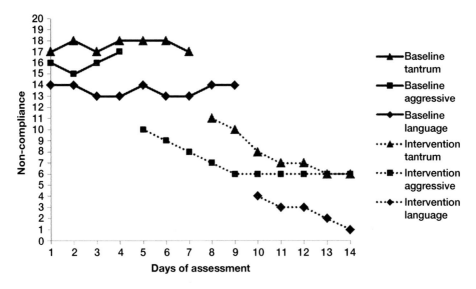

FIGURE 7.2   Results from a hypothetical multiple baseline design.

baseline for foul language lasted 9 days. The results suggest that each behavior occurred less often once the intervention was introduced for that particular behavior—consistent with an intervention effect.

Evaluating Results in Single-Case Experiments

Although inferential statistical procedures can be used to analyze data from single-case experiments, it is more common for clinicians to rely on visual inspection of the data. Visual inspection is often supplemented with descriptive statistics. For example, clinicians can examine *mean changes* by comparing the average frequency of the outcome across different phases of the experiment (e.g., during the A vs. B phases). Clinicians can also examine *level shifts* in which they compare the last data point in an immediately prior phase to the first data point in an immediately subsequent phase. If the latency of response is hypothesized to be immediate (e.g., the behavior will reduce dramatically as soon as the intervention is implemented), one might predict dramatic level changes between adjacent (baseline-intervention) phases. Clinicians can also examine *slope* (or functional form) *changes* by examining the rate of behavior change in different phases. For example, the behavior might increase in a fairly linear (i.e., constant) manner during the initial A phase and become fairly stable during the initial B phase. Such a change can be described as a change in slope—with the slope being positive in the A phase and flat (i.e., near zero) in the B phase.

Quasi-Experimental Studies

Quasi-experimental studies are experiments that lack random assignment of units to conditions. Similar to randomized experiments, a subset of units is typically exposed to an intervention. Two common quasi-experiments in clinical psychology result when participants self-select into treatment conditions and when various intact groups (e.g., clients at different community mental health clinics) are differentially exposed to treatment conditions. When assignment is nonrandom, the burden is on the researcher to identify and render implausible alternative explanations for an apparent intervention effect (i.e., the researcher must rule out various threats to internal validity).

Correlational Studies

Correlational studies (also called passive observational studies) are conducted when the researcher is not actively manipulating anything (like exposure to an intervention). Passive observational studies are often used to gain insight into the emergence of a relevant phenomenon (e.g., externalizing problems).

Case–Control Designs

Case–control designs compare a group of participants who possess a certain characteristic (e.g., diagnosis of attention deficit hyperactivity disorder [ADHD]) with a group of participants who do not possess the characteristic. The former group comprises the *case* group and the latter group, the *control* group. For example, a researcher might be interested in examining whether children with ADHD differ from controls (without ADHD) on peer relations.

Cohort Designs

In cohort designs, an intact group (i.e., cohort) is followed over time to examine the emergence of—and/or change—in some outcome of interest. These designs are classified as longitudinal (also known as prospective) because individuals are assessed on at least two occasions. In some instances, a single cohort of individuals is followed. For example, researchers interested in the possible effects of neighborhood-level variables on substance use might follow a cohort of preschoolers in a given neighborhood for several years to examine associations among variables of interest. Multiple cohorts might also be followed. For example, one might be interested in following adolescents at high risk versus low risk for eventual alcohol use disorders. Multiple cohort studies are distinguished from case–control studies because in case–control studies, the groups differ on a central characteristic (e.g., diagnosis of ADHD) whereas in multiple cohort studies, the groups differ on exposure to some factor (e.g., poverty). If the multiple cohorts also differ in their age or some other salient developmental marker at the study's inception, the study is called a cross-sequential design. Such designs allow for the study of a longer developmental period over fewer years of data collection because several developmental cohorts (e.g., toddlers, pre-schoolers, and school-aged children) are embedded in the study.

Uncontrolled Case Studies

Case studies—in which one or a few cases are studied intensively—can also be subsumed under correlational research (if the researcher's status is passive, as described above). The prototypical uncontrolled case study follows a single individual over time in the hope of understanding the case in a more comprehensive and nuanced manner.

Critical Appraisal and Application of Research Findings

Not all studies are created equally. Moreover, the conclusions reached by authors are not always consistent with the contents of their research reports. Consequently, readers must play active roles in critically appraising research.

In Figures 7.3 through 7.5, results from three hypothetical studies designed to examine the effects of brief dynamic psychotherapy on depression are presented. The data in Figure 7.3 derive from a design in which a single group of individuals was assessed at pretest, exposed to brief dynamic psychotherapy, and then assessed at posttest and two subsequent follow-ups. In such plots, average symptom levels (in this case, depression) are plotted as a function of treatment group and time point. Assuming the change depicted in Figure 7.3 is clinically meaningful, these data are *consistent* with an intervention effect. Although heartening, these data raise the question, "Did the treatment cause the observed reductions in depression?" Unfortunately, given the study's design, it is difficult to answer this causal question unambiguously.

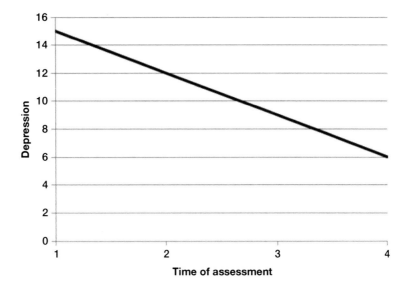

FIGURE 7.3   Hypothetical outcome plot from a single-group design. The bold line represents treated participants.

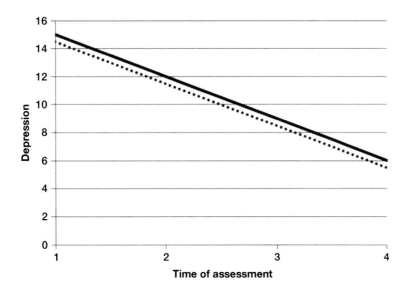

FIGURE 7.4   Hypothetical outcome plot from a randomized controlled trial. Results are not consistent with an intervention effect. The bold line represents treated participants and the dotted line, controls.

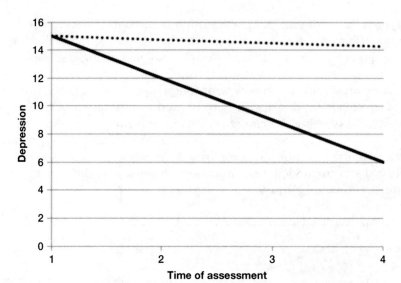

FIGURE 7.5   Hypothetical outcome plot from a randomized controlled trial. Results are consistent with an intervention effect. The bold line represents treated participants and the dotted line, controls.

The data in Figures 7.4 and 7.5 derive from two different randomized controlled trials in which brief dynamic psychotherapy was compared to a no-treatment control condition. The results in Figure 7.4 are *not consistent* with an intervention effect because the reductions in depression exhibited by individuals exposed to brief dynamic treatment are identical to reductions exhibited by no-treatment control participants. Both groups improved at the same rate over time.

The results in Figure 7.5 are *consistent* with an intervention effect because individuals exposed to brief dynamic treatment reported greater reductions in depression relative to no-treatment control participants. We assume that the data depicted in Figure 7.5 represent a true treatment effect, given the presence of a randomized no-treatment control group and the assumed absence of plausible alternative explanations. In all three plots, the average change in depression among treated participants is identical. The juxtaposition of the plots (e.g., Figures 7.4 and 7.5, relative to Figure 7.3) reinforces the importance of design features (e.g., random assignment) that bolster confidence in inferences (e.g., improve internal validity).

Below, several common threats to internal validity that can be particularly salient in studies that resemble the one-group pretest–posttest design are discussed. These threats—if deemed plausible in a given study—can help explain how results like those in Figure 7.3 could be mistaken for an intervention effect.

Threats to Internal Validity

Maturation
Maturation is a threat to validity when naturally occurring changes are mistaken for an intervention effect—when symptoms remit because of the passage of time rather than the effects of an intervention.

History
History is a threat to validity when some event (or constellation of events) occurs during the study and impacts the results in a manner mistaken for an intervention

effect. For example, individuals who seek treatment for depression might make several other concomitant life changes (e.g., exercise more regularly and read self-help books) that can help depression symptoms remit. These historical influences—and not the intervention—might be responsible for observed lower levels of depression following treatment.

Statistical Regression

Statistical regression—also known as regression to the mean—occurs when extreme scores tend to revert back to the mean on a subsequent evaluation. Statistical regression is more plausible in single-group studies in which *extreme performers* (e.g., severely depressed individuals) comprise the study sample.

Attrition

Attrition is a threat to validity when the pattern of participant drop-out impacts the results in a way interpreted as an intervention effect. In a single cohort study, if individuals who either remained stable in their symptoms or worsened, dropped out of the study, it would leave mostly participants who improved. An outcome analysis based solely on the improvers might be mistaken for an intervention effect.

Testing

Testing is a threat to validity when exposing individuals to the pretest changes them in ways that might be mistaken for an intervention effect. For example, a pretest that asks detailed questions about the personal and social consequences of one's alcohol use might inspire individuals to lower their consumption.

Instrumentation

Instrumentation is a threat to validity when the measurement tool changes and impacts the results in a manner mistaken for an intervention effect. For example, if a more restrictive operationalization of "alcohol-related emergency room visits" were used following a media campaign designed to reduce alcohol-related injuries, an ostensible reduction in such visits might be mistaken for an effect of the media campaign.

Selection and Interactions With Selection

Selection occurs in multiple-group studies when systematic differences among intervention groups can be mistaken for an intervention effect. In multiple-group studies, these threats are often labeled interactions with selection. An example is provided below.

Evaluating the Potential Impact of Internal Validity Threats

In single-group studies, a threat has to be *capable* of producing the pattern of results that were observed (e.g., in one group receiving a treatment for depression, other behaviors, like reading self-help books, could account for improved outcomes following treatment). In multiple-group studies, a threat has to be both *capable* of producing the pattern of observed results *and* it has to *vary systematically by group*. In other words, the threat has to be more prevalent in one of the groups. For example, in a two-group study, if the intervention group is more likely to naturally experience symptom remission relative to the control group, this differential maturation pattern could be mistaken for an intervention effect. This threat would be labeled a selection by maturation threat because the two groups are systematically different (i.e., selection) in their maturation. In multiple-group studies, all internal validity threats are considered interactions with selection because any threat (e.g., statistical regression) must vary systematically by group.

External Validity Issues

Thus far, our discussion of critical appraisal has focused on internal validity issues. Clinicians and researchers are also interested in the generalizability of causal inferences (e.g., whether an intervention supported in university-based clinics would work in community clinics). The following questions are relevant to external validity. Would the intervention be effective for men and women? Would the intervention be effective if delivered by paraprofessionals rather than clinical psychologists? Would the effects of the intervention persist over a longer follow-up? Would the intervention—developed with Caucasian families of European descent—produce similar results in Latino families of Cuban descent? To test such questions empirically, one must test statistical interactions between the primary predictor (e.g., intervention) and the external validity characteristic of interest (e.g., participant sex). Consequently, threats to external validity are often framed as "interactions of the causal effect with...." Answers to these questions help establish possible boundaries of an intervention's effects and are often quite useful to researchers and clinicians.

Construct Validity Issues Related to Clinical Interventions

Internal validity asks, "Does the intervention work?" whereas external validity asks, "Under what conditions does it work?" Another valuable question is "How does the intervention work?" This last question involves establishing the construct validity of a given intervention in which the primary mechanisms of change are elucidated (e.g., Are decreases in social isolation and increases in positive cognitions leading to improvements in depressive symptoms following treatment?). Given the comprehensive nature of many psychological interventions, it is rare that participants are randomly assigned to interventions targeting a single mechanism. As such, attempts to elucidate mechanisms often involve statistical mediation analyses in which hypotheses about putative mechanisms are tested explicitly. An example of mediation is provided in the statistics section.

Therapeutic attention is a classic construct validity threat in randomized controlled trials in which an active intervention is compared to a no-treatment control. Intervention effects might result from *therapeutic attention* rather than from the mechanisms targeted by the intervention (e.g., reduced depressive cognitions). Measuring client change on the mechanisms (i.e., mediators) and conducting mediation analyses can help clarify issues of construct validity.

Levels of Evidence

The current discussion of levels of evidence is modeled after Mudford, McNeill, Walton, and Phillips (2012). As knowledge in an area accumulates, discussions of ordering *evidence sources* along a continuum from low to high become more prominent. Often, for example, results from studies that tend to produce stronger internal validity inferences (e.g., well-conducted randomized controlled trials) are categorized as providing higher levels of evidence. Results from studies that tend to produce weaker internal validity inferences (e.g., single-group pretest–posttest designs) are categorized as providing lower levels of evidence. In addition to considering internal validity, external validity might be considered in levels of evidence. For example, replication of findings across multiple research groups and/or client populations would further strengthen a relatively higher level of evidence. Results from smaller-scale uncontrolled studies (e.g., case study and qualitative study) would be rated the lowest level of evidence among empirical studies. Expert opinions that are not data-based are considered the lowest level of evidence overall.

Researchers use various forms of research synthesis to integrate several studies on a related topic. Historically, these syntheses were narrative reviews of the literature in which researchers organized "box counts" of significant, nonsignificant, and counter findings. In the more recent past, researchers have relied on meta-analytic techniques to conduct formal quantitative syntheses of the literature. In meta-analysis, researchers seek to explain variability in study effect sizes (e.g., the magnitude of the treatment–outcome association) as a function of study characteristics (e.g., methodological features and types of interventions). As such, meta-analysis can be a powerful tool in the accumulation of knowledge.

Measurement

The next section covers topics related to constructs of interest discussed throughout the chapter (e.g., depression), their measurement, and their inter-relations with other constructs. This section was informed primarily by the following sources: Clark and Watson (1995), West and Finch (1997), John and Bennet-Martinez (2000), and Messick (1995).

Latent Constructs and Observable Measures

Observable study measures (i.e., tests) are considered fallible representations of the latent (unobserved) constructs of interest (e.g., depression). For example, a measure of depression might capture several sources of variance—including systematic variance related to depression, systematic variance related to other constructs (e.g., anxiety), systematic method variance related to its measurement format (e.g., self-report), and random error. Psychologists study these and other related issues by theorizing about a nomological network (Cronbach & Meehl, 1955)—the relations among observed measures, relations between observed measures and latent constructs, and relations among latent constructs. Predictions derived from a relevant nomological network can be examined empirically by accruing evidence regarding a measure's reliability and validity.

Classical Test Theory and Reliability

Classical Test Theory assumes that the variance of an observed measure comprises two additive sources—true score variance and random error variance. True score variance reflects the construct of interest (e.g., depression). Random error variance reflects all other factors that vary randomly over testing occasions to impact an individual's score (e.g., fatigue). As such, the reliability of a measure is viewed as the ratio of true score variance to total variance. (True score variance is consistent with *consistency* or *dependability*, concepts that are often invoked in discussions of reliability.) Because it is impossible to know an individual's true score on a psychological attribute, in order to estimate reliability, classical test theorists assume that two psychological tests can be constructed in a parallel manner. Tests are considered parallel if (a) the tests measure the same psychological construct (also known as "tau equivalence"), and (b) the tests have the same level of error variance. These assumptions allow one to estimate reliability using respondents' observed scores through various methods—including internal consistency, test–retest, alternate or parallel forms, and inter-rater or interobserver.

Internal Consistency
Internal consistency is used to measure reliability on a single testing occasion by examining the degree of inter-item correlation in multiple item tests. Cronbach's alpha is a common index of internal consistency and is a function of the number of test items and the degree of inter-item correlation. Other measures of internal consistency reliability include (a) Kuder–Richardson Formula 20—often abbreviated KR-20—which can be used when the items are dichotomous, and (b) split-half reliability—based on sorting the items on a psychological test into two parallel subtests of equal size. Note that measures of internal consistency are often erroneously interpreted as evidence of a scale's unidimensionality—suggesting that the multiple items reflect a single construct.

Test–Retest
Test–retest reliability is used to measure the reliability of a measure over time. The test–retest approach is heavily dependent on the assumption that true scores remain stable across the test–retest interval. Consequently, test–retest reliability coefficients are often referred to as stability coefficients. Pearson's correlation and the intraclass correlation coefficient are common indices of test–retest reliability.

Alternate or Parallel Forms
Alternate-forms reliability is assessed by correlating two tests meant to measure the same construct. The tests are of alternate or parallel forms because the items on each test—although distinct—are thought to represent the same underlying construct. Pearson's correlation and the intraclass correlation coefficient are common indices of alternate-forms reliability.

Inter-Rater Reliability
Sometimes, raters or coders are used to code observational data. An example might involve asking a parent–child dyad to participate in a puzzle-completion task that is videotaped. The tape can later be coded for various constructs (e.g., cooperation). If at least two raters are used, inter-rater reliability can be computed by one of several indices (e.g., Cohen's kappa and the intraclass correlation).

Validity

Historically, validity has been framed with the following question, "Does the test measure what it purports to measure?" In the past two decades, this fairly *simple* question has been expanded. In a recent publication of measurement standards in psychology and education, the American Psychological Association, the American Education Research Association, and the National Council on Measurement in Education agreed that construct validity is an organizing framework that should include evidence from five primary domains: (a) test content, (b) response processes, (c) internal structure, (d) relations with other variables, and (e) consequences of use (1999). Below, we describe several of these elements and how they relate to the forms of validity commonly discussed in textbooks (e.g., content validity).

Face Validity

As the name implies, face validity is the extent to which items appear to measure the construct of interest. Face validity has implications for how individuals respond to items; as such, it can be conceptualized as an element of response processes.

Content Validity

Content validity examines whether test items adequately represent the content domains for the relevant construct. In measurement design, content validity is often examined empirically by asking experts to rate the adequacy of items in relation to the relevant content domains (e.g., for the construct of depression, experts might require the inclusion of items rating hopelessness, vegetative symptoms, suicidal ideation, etc.).

Structural Validity

Structural validity—also known as internal structure—is the extent to which the structure of the *measure* is consistent with the theorized factor structure of the *construct*. Structural validity questions can be assessed empirically using exploratory and/or confirmatory factor-analytic procedures (see below). For example, the Big Five Inventory is a measure theorized to capture five broad personality factors— extraversion, agreeableness, conscientiousness, neuroticism, and openness—and its factor structure is consistent with these five factors (e.g., John, 1990).

Criterion Validity

The measure should correlate with other measures (i.e., criterion variables) in a manner consistent with a priori hypotheses. For example, a measure of deviance proneness should correlate with measures believed to reflect deviance (e.g., early onset of illicit drug use). When these associations are contemporaneous, concurrent criterion validity is examined. When the criterion is measured at a subsequent time point, predictive criterion validity is examined. Criterion validity can also be evaluated by seeing whether relevant groups vary on the characteristic of interest (e.g., youth with juvenile justice involvement should be higher on deviance proneness relative to youth without juvenile justice involvement).

Convergent and Discriminant Validity

Theory regarding associations among constructs—that is, a piece of the nomological network described above—can be used to predict how measures of constructs *converge* with either measures of similar constructs or different measures of the same construct, and *diverge* from measures of dissimilar constructs. A multitrait–multimethod matrix can be used to evaluate convergent and discriminant validity. For example, a researcher might predict that two measures of depression (e.g., one based on self-report and one based on partner report) should correlate more highly with one another than with two measures of anxiety. Such a pattern would be consistent with convergent and discriminant validity.

Extensions of Classical Test Theory and Statistical Tools Used in Measurement

Generalizability Theory

Generalizability Theory assumes that in addition to true score variance, there are additional possible sources of *systematic* variance (i.e., facets) that contribute to an individual's score on a test. Researchers can vary these facets and see whether they account for significant variance in an individual's score. For example, a researcher could examine whether person (e.g., sex and age) or setting (e.g., classroom, playground, and home) variables impact observer agreement on aggression ratings.

Item Response Theory

Item Response Theory (IRT) extends Classical Test Theory by taking into account that an individual's response is influenced by qualities of both the individual and the test item. In the classic single-parameter (Rasch) model for dichotomous items, the probability of a correct response is viewed as a function of (a) item difficulty, and (b) respondent's level on the trait. For example, the vast majority of respondents with an average level of the trait (e.g., intelligence) might respond correctly to an easy item, but incorrectly to a hard item. Furthermore, in a two-parameter model, items also vary in their level of *discrimination*. Items that are high on discrimination are better able to differentiate individuals on the trait of interest (e.g., can distinguish those with low vs. high intelligence).

Exploratory and Confirmatory Factor Analysis

Exploratory factor analysis (EFA) and confirmatory factor analysis (CFA) are statistical procedures used to examine factor structure. Underlying both approaches is the notion that the latent (i.e., unobserved) constructs account for common variance in the observed items. EFA is used when developing/refining a measure or when researchers are less certain about the measure/construct's factor structure. CFA is used when existing theory makes specific predictions about a measure/construct's factor structure. Both procedures quantify factor loadings (i.e., the association between an item and its factor) and correlations among factors. Also, both procedures require the user to make many analytical decisions. In EFA, three primary decisions involve (a) choosing a method of factor extraction, (b) choosing a method of factor rotation, and (c) deciding on the number of factors to retain. Factor rotation methods—which impact factor loadings and correlations among factors—are either orthogonal or oblique. In orthogonal rotations, the factors are assumed to be uncorrelated. In oblique rotations, the factors are assumed to be correlated—often the case in psychology. In practice, determining the number of factors to retain is frequently accomplished by visual inspection of the scree plot and by the "eigenvalues greater than 1" criterion. Both approaches attempt to differentiate between factors that account for meaningful variance and those that do not. A more sophisticated approach to determining the number of factors is based on parallel analysis in which factors are retained when their eigenvalues are greater than *parallel* eigenvalues based on randomly generated data.

In CFA, the researcher chooses an estimation routine and typically chooses a means of comparing competing models for relative fit (e.g., comparing a three-factor solution with a two-factor solution). Several fit indices can help with this last decision—including the chi-square test, root mean square error of approximation (RMSEA), and standardized root mean square residual (SRMR). All fit indices quantify (albeit in slightly different ways) how well the model-implied covariance matrix reproduces the estimated population covariance matrix of the analysis variables.

Measurement Error

For a set of depression measures, one can capture the shared depression-related variance across the measures in the form of a latent variable by using CFA. This latent variable is theoretically free from measurement error because the non-depression-related variance has been removed. One of the advantages of conducting statistical analyses on latent variables (as in the case of structural equation modeling, described below), is the gain in statistical power that results when measurement error is removed from the constructs of interest.

Measure Development, Selection, and Use With Heterogeneous Participant Populations

The topics discussed above are also relevant for measure development and selection. The nomological network surrounding a particular construct and its dimensions (i.e., factors) can be used to develop a measure. Such a process often begins by reading the relevant literature to refine one's understanding of the construct, its potential factors, and its possible boundaries (how it is different from other related constructs). From there, the researcher can begin to develop a broad item pool covering the content dimensions (i.e., factors) that map his or her current theoretical understanding. Items should be well written and easily understood by the target population. Items that are hard to understand (e.g., use double negatives) and items that create possible response conflicts (e.g., by posing a compound question) should be avoided. Experts in the area can help the scale developer assess whether the construct content is adequately captured by the item pool. Once the initial item pool is finalized, different samples of respondents are typically asked to complete the measure. Early in the process, respondents might be asked to give qualitative feedback (e.g., feedback on item readability, understandability, and language usage). Later, statistical analyses (e.g., EFA, CFA, and IRT) may be used to make decisions about final items to retain. The initial process concludes when the desired psychometric properties (e.g., reliability) have been achieved and preliminary construct validation efforts suggest the measure is operating in a way consistent with theory. The process of construct validation, however, is iterative and subject to revision as the relevant nomological network is augmented by additional research.

In selecting a measure, the type of data of primary interest should be considered. John and Bennet-Martinez (2000) categorize data sources into four categories: LOTS. The L is for life events data; O for observational data; T for testing—including standardized measures of performance, motivation, and/or achievement; and S for self-report data. Researchers will often collect data from at least two data sources for a more comprehensive view of a construct. For example, clinicians who work with parents of children with disruptive behaviors might ask parents to report on parenting practices. Researchers might also videotape parent–child interactions and ask independent judges to objectively rate parenting practices. In this case, parents' self-report of parenting practices (S) can be corroborated by observational ratings of parenting practices (O). At the minimum, measures should meet two criteria: (a) the measures should fit the researcher's conceptualization of the construct, and (b) the existing psychometric data should suggest that the measure is reliable and valid.

These criteria are more easily satisfied when the researcher is studying individuals similar to those on whom the original measure was developed. If the researcher is studying individuals who have not been represented in existing theory and research, the researcher should examine whether the measure "behaves the same way" in the novel sample. This can be accomplished by examining whether there is adequate reliability and a similar factor structure (structural validity) in the novel sample. Also, various forms of criterion validity can be examined. For example, researchers can examine whether the construct predicts subsequent outcomes in a similar manner in the novel sample. Note that these strategies are based on the assumption that the construct's nomological network is similar for the original and novel samples. If the nomological network is different in the novel sample (e.g., because the construct has a different factor structure and/or the construct has a different pattern of criterion validity), results obtained in that sample can be misleading. In such a situation, researchers should work to develop a measure that captures the richness of the construct in the novel sample. This would require following the steps noted above in measure development and validation.

Statistical Methods

Statistical methods are organized around two broad categories—descriptive and inferential. Inferential statistics are often further divided into parametric and nonparametric methods. Prior to discussing these various classes of statistics, levels of measurement are discussed.

Levels of Measurement

Characteristics of interest to psychologists (e.g., depression, IQ, and extraversion) are measured using many different response scales. There are four common levels of measurement: nominal, ordinal, interval, and ratio.

Nominal
A nominal scale is used to categorize qualitative variables that cannot be ordered along a quantitative dimension (e.g., sex). Nominal scales allow researchers to specify differences in *kind*, but not differences in amount.

Ordinal
An ordinal scale allows researchers to arrange responses according to order or relative rank. Although response options can be judged *greater than* or *less than* one another, the magnitude of such differences is unknown. Many variables in psychology are measured by a Likert response scale, such as 1 (strongly disagree), 2 (disagree), 3 (neither disagree nor agree), 4 (agree), and 5 (strongly agree).

Interval

An interval scale of measurement allows one to order and examine magnitude differences among responses. Magnitude differences can be examined because every unit of measurement is equal to every other unit along the entire range of responses. An interval scale lacks a true zero point (suggesting the complete absence of the characteristic). The Fahrenheit temperature scale is an example of interval data.

Ratio

Variables measured on a ratio scale have both equal intervals and a true zero point. Although it is hard to imagine psychological variables with a true zero point (e.g., someone with no extraversion), many physical variables are measured on ratio scales (e.g., height).

Descriptive Statistics

Descriptive statistics are used to organize, describe, and simplify data. Descriptives include measures of central tendency and variability. Researchers often use tabular and/or graphical displays to examine descriptive statistics. For example, Figure 7.6 is a histogram, which plots responses (aggregated into columns or pillars) along the *x*-axis (i.e., the horizontal axis) and the frequency of occurrence along the *y*-axis (i.e., the vertical axis).

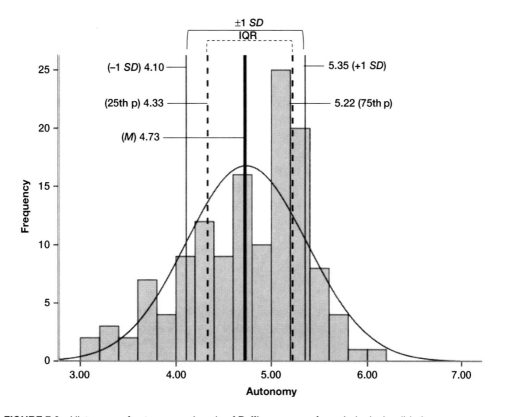

FIGURE 7.6   Histogram of autonomy subscale of Ryff's measure of psychological well-being.

Central Tendency

Measures of central tendency are used to identify the center of a distribution of scores. The mean is the arithmetic average and is computed by adding up the scores and dividing by the number of scores. The mean is used for interval or ratio scales when the distributions are not highly skewed. The median is the score that corresponds to the 50th percentile. It cuts the distribution of scores in half. The median is used when (a) data are ordinal, or (b) when data are interval or ratio, but the distribution is highly skewed (the median is less affected by skewness). The mode is the most commonly occurring score. The mode is used when data are nominal.

In symmetrical distributions, the mean and median are identical. In symmetrical distributions with a single mode, the mean, median, and mode are identical. In real-world data, in which some departure from symmetry is typical, these values will vary somewhat. Adding/subtracting constants (e.g., subtracting the number 10) from all scores will have the same impact on the mean (e.g., the new mean equals the original mean minus 10). The same is true for multiplying or dividing all scores by a constant.

The data presented in Figure 7.6 are based on a measure of autonomy (Ryff, 1989) assessed by nine items (e.g., *my decisions are not usually influenced by what everyone else is doing*) on a six-point Likert response scale ranging from 1 (*strongly disagree*) to 6 (*strongly agree*). In this case, each individual's score ($N = 133$) is based on a mean of the nine items. In Figure 7.6, the overall sample mean (M), represented by the thicker solid black line, is 4.73. Although not presented in the histogram, the median and mode are 4.89 and 5.00, respectively.

Variability

Measures of variability describe the scatter or dispersion of scores in a distribution. The range is computed by subtracting the minimum from the maximum observed value. The interquartile range captures the middle 50% of the distribution and is computed by subtracting the 25th percentile (first quartile) from the 75th percentile (third quartile). The standard deviation (SD) captures the average distance of scores from the mean; its computation involves a series of steps (see below). The variance is the square of the standard deviation. In Figure 7.6, two dashed vertical lines denote the 25th (4.33) and 75th percentiles (5.22). Consequently, the interquartile range is 0.89. The standard deviation for this subscale is 0.62. The thinner solid vertical lines denote −1 SD (4.10) and +1 SD (5.35).

In general, the variance and standard deviation are preferred measures of variability, given that they are derived from all scores and are involved in the computation of many parametric statistics. The definitional formula for the sample standard deviation is as follows:

$$SD = \sqrt{\frac{\sum(x - M)^2}{N - 1}}.$$

If the square root symbol were removed, the resulting quantity would be the variance. The numerator of the fraction is commonly called the sum of squares (SS) and is short for sum of squared deviations (i.e., the mean is subtracted from each score, squared, and the resulting numbers are added). The denominator of the fraction, sometimes called the finite sample correction, is equal to degrees of freedom (df). Dividing the SS by a smaller number ($N - 1$, rather than N) makes the standard deviation larger to correct for the fact that samples tend to be less variable than the populations from which they derive. Unlike the mean, adding/subtracting constants from a set of scores does not alter the standard deviation (the standard deviation of the new variable will equal that of the original variable). Similar to the mean, multiplying/dividing by a constant has the same impact on the standard deviation.

The Normal Distribution and z Scores

An examination of Figure 7.6 suggests that the shape of the distribution of autonomy responses is *approximately* normal (characterized by a distinct peak in the center and symmetrical halves). Many physical and psychological characteristics follow a normal distribution, but are measured by different scales (e.g., inches for height and pounds for weight) with different means and standard deviations. It is sometimes helpful to place these characteristics on a common scale. z scores provide a common scale and as such, the z distribution is often referred to as the standard normal distribution. Because the standard normal distribution plays a prominent role in statistics, it is worth looking closely at some of its properties.

z Score Conversion   Values for any variable believed to follow a normal distribution can be converted to z scores with the following formula:

$$z = \frac{x - M}{SD}.$$

(These are sample statistics, quantities based on samples of observations. If one had all scores from the entire population, they would report population parameters instead of statistics. Population parameters are represented by Greek symbols: M would be replaced by μ and SD would be replaced by σ.)

Properties of the Normal z Distribution   When a z-score conversion is used, the resulting z distribution has the following properties: (a) the mean is 0; (b) the standard deviation is 1; and (c) each z score represents the position of the score in relation to the mean, in standard deviation units. In other words, a z score of −1.27 denotes a score exactly 1.27 standard deviations *below* the mean.

Probability and the Normal z Distribution   Figure 7.7 contains the standard normal distribution for IQ. The x-axis displays values of original scores, z scores, and T-scores. Vertical lines denote the mean and ± 1, 2, and 3 standard deviations. A percentile suggests that a certain proportion of scores fall at or below the score

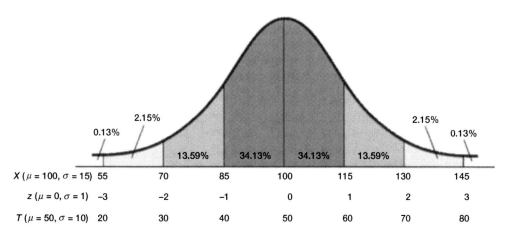

FIGURE 7.7   The standard normal z distribution based on IQ (with raw scores, z scores, and T-scores depicted on x-axis).

in question. For example, the percentile associated with a z score of 1.96 is 0.975 (suggesting that 97.5% of scores are less than or equal to a z score of 1.96). This also suggests that the proportion of z scores falling above 1.96 is 0.025 (or 2.5%), because these two proportions have to sum to 1.0. The percentages of scores in each area of the standard normal distribution are also displayed.

Note that in addition to using a z-score standardization, researchers sometimes use a T-score standardization. The T-score standardization sets the new mean at 50 and the new standard deviation at 10. As such, a score of 60 falls 1 SD above the mean and a score of 40 falls 1 SD below the mean. Relevant percentiles can be computed by conversion of T to z: $(T - 50)/10$.

Distribution Shape and Departures From Normality

One can see that Figure 7.6—based on real-world data for the autonomy subscale of psychological well-being—and the depiction of the standard normal (z) distribution in Figure 7.7 are different. Although Figure 7.7 is perfectly symmetrical (equal right and left halves), Figure 7.6 is skewed. Skewness measures departures from symmetry in which there is a piling of cases on the lower (positive skew) or higher end (negative skew). Figure 7.6 data are negatively skewed (skewness = −0.57). When variables are negatively skewed, the mean, median, and mode are typically ordered from lowest to highest (the opposite is true of positively skewed data). Kurtosis measures the relative peakedness of the distribution. Leptokurtic distributions (positive kurtosis values) are more peaked than the normal curve, whereas platykurtic distributions (negative kurtosis values) are flatter. Kurtosis for Figure 7.6 is −0.24. Note that if a distribution is skewed (as in Figure 7.6), converting the original scores to z scores will not alter the shape of the distribution (skew and kurtosis values will remain unchanged).

Inferential Statistics

Parametric and Nonparametric Approaches

Inferential statistics are often divided into two broad classes—parametric and nonparametric. Compared to nonparametric statistics, parametric statistics (a) make more distributional assumptions (e.g., that the distribution is normal), (b) assume data are measured on an interval or ratio scale, (c) are conducted on actual data (as opposed to on ranks derived from data), and (d) allow researchers to test more specific hypotheses about the populations from which they are drawn. Nonparametric statistics are typically used when assumptions of parametric approaches are (seriously) violated and/or when the data cannot be used to compute necessary quantities for parametric statistics. If the assumptions of parametric statistics are met, they result in more powerful statistical tests.

Given that parametric statistics are more commonly used in psychology, this general analytical approach is described extensively and examples are provided.

Null Hypothesis Significance Testing

Null hypothesis significance testing (NHST) is the most commonly encountered hypothesis testing method in psychology. In NHST, the researcher specifies two mutually exclusive hypotheses (null and alternative) regarding the population parameter of interest. The typical null hypothesis posits no effect in the population. For example, in a study examining the effects of psychotherapy on depression in a group that received treatment and a control group, the null hypothesis specifies that the two population means are equal ($\mu_t = \mu_c$). The alternative hypothesis— sometimes labeled the researcher hypothesis—subsumes all other possible outcomes (in this case, that the two population means are not equal).

Statistical Significance and Probability   Once sample data are collected and analyzed using an appropriate test statistic, the researcher makes a decision to declare results as statistically significant (i.e., rejecting the null hypothesis) or nonsignificant (i.e., failing to reject the null hypothesis). When the sample data would occur relatively infrequently assuming the null hypothesis (e.g., the data would occur less than 5% of the time if the null hypothesis were true—$p < .05$), the results are considered statistically significant and the null hypothesis is rejected.

Correct and Incorrect Researcher Decisions   Type I errors occur when a *true* null hypothesis *is* incorrectly rejected (i.e., results are declared statistically significant even though the null hypothesis is true). The probability of type I errors is equal to the alpha (α) or the a priori criterion set for statistical significance (usually 0.05 or 5%). Type II errors occur when a *false* null hypothesis *is not* rejected (i.e., results are not declared statistically significant even though the null hypothesis is false). The long range probability of type II errors is beta (β).

Statistical Power   Statistical power is the probability of correctly rejecting a false null hypothesis (i.e., finding an effect when one exists in the population) and it is calculated as $1 - \beta$. If the probability of a type II error (β) in a given study was 0.20, then statistical power would be equal to 0.80 (i.e., $1 - \beta = 1 - 0.20 = 0.80$). Several factors can influence power, including sample size (as N increases, power increases), alpha (as alpha increases, power increases), directional versus non-directional hypothesis tests (directional tests are more powerful; see below), the magnitude of the effect (larger effects result in more power), and the reliability of the measures used (more reliable measures result in more power).

Supplementing Information Regarding Statistical Significance   Statistical significance is influenced by sample size in problematic ways (e.g., larger, meaningful effects might not reach statistical significance in smaller samples, but smaller, less meaningful effects might reach statistical significance in larger samples). Therefore, statistical significance information should be supplemented with effect size estimates that describe the magnitude or strength of the effect under consideration (discussed below). Confidence intervals construct an interval around a given population parameter (e.g., a correlation coefficient). These intervals provide information regarding statistical significance and provide lower- and upper-bound estimates of the parameter—based on a certain level of confidence (e.g., 95%). For example, a correlation of 0.47 with a 95% confidence interval ranging from 0.20 to 0.69 suggests that one can be 95% confident that this specific interval contains the population parameter. In this example, because the interval does not contain zero (the typical population parameter assumed under the null), the results will be regarded as statistically significant (at $\alpha = 0.05$).

Clinical significance, like effect size, goes beyond statistical significance to describe the clinical importance of an effect. Clinical significance can be quantified in several ways. For example, in a study examining the effects of cognitive-behavioral treatment on women with body dysmorphic disorder, Rosen, Reiter, and Orosan (1995) showed that following treatment, 81.5% of treated participants were classified as clinically improved versus 7.4% in the control group. Clinically significant improvement was operationalized as (a) no longer meeting diagnostic criteria and (b) scoring two standard errors below a pretest score on one of the primary study outcomes. Based on these data, the odds of reaching this threshold of clinically significant improvement were 55 times higher in the treated group relative to the control group!

The One-Sample z Test

The one-sample z test can be used to compare a single sample mean to a population mean, when the population standard deviation is known. Let us assume that a researcher was interested in testing whether a sample of college students ($N = 20$) scored significantly different than average (100) on a standard intelligence (i.e., IQ) test. We will also assume a population standard deviation of 15. The null hypothesis in this situation would be $\mu = 100$ and the alternative hypothesis would be $\mu \neq 100$. Assume that the average IQ in the sample is 110. On the face of it, this sample statistic appears different than the population parameter under the null hypothesis (100). Remember that hypothesis testing examines the probability of the data, given the null. In this instance, it would be important to know the probability of obtaining a sample mean of 110, given a population mean of 100. If it is determined that this sample mean would occur relatively infrequently (e.g., less than 5% of the time) under the null, the null hypothesis would be rejected. Probability theory helps inform this decision.

The Sampling Distribution of the Mean   If data are collected from all possible random samples of size 20 (the current sample size) from a population with a mean IQ of 100 (the value assumed under our null hypothesis), many of these sample means will be close to the population mean (e.g., 99, 98, 101, 102) and fewer sample means will be farther away (e.g., 80, 81, 120, 121). If a histogram is used to plot all of these sample means (i.e., create a sampling distribution of the mean), three important facts are observed: (a) the mean of all sample means will equal the population mean; (b) the standard deviation of the sampling distribution (also called the standard error of the mean) will equal the population standard deviation divided by the square root of sample size (in this case, $15/\sqrt{20} = 3.35$); and (c) the sampling distribution will be normal. The standard error of the mean and other standard errors quantify the average distance of sample statistics from relevant population parameters. With these pieces of information, the probability of observing the particular sample statistic ($M = 110$) based on a population parameter of 100 can be quantified. This is where the one-sample z test becomes relevant.

Computations for the One-Sample z Test   The formula for the one-sample z test is as follows:

$$z = \frac{M - \mu}{\sigma_M}.$$

The numerator is the difference between the sample mean ($M = 110$) and the population mean ($\mu = 100$). The denominator is the standard error of the mean (3.35, computed above). If z is solved, the answer is 2.98. Although this was not stated explicitly above, the hypothesis test in this instance is two-tailed or nondirectional (leaving open the possibility that the sample mean will be *larger* or *smaller* than the population mean of 100). This lack of specificity (regarding the difference between the sample statistic and the population parameter) results in a two-tailed or nondirectional hypothesis test. Because it is known that the sampling distribution of the mean follows a normal distribution, the standard normal table can be used to quantify the probability of our sample data—given the population mean assumed under the null.

Determining Statistical Significance If the percentile associated with the z test statistic of 2.98 in the standard normal table (presented in most statistics texts) is looked up, 0.9986 is found, which suggests that 99.86% of z test statistics fall at or below the observed value of 2.98. Therefore, the proportion of z scores falling above the value is 0.0014 (i.e., $1 - 0.9986$) or 0.14%. In a nondirectional hypothesis test, this value of 0.0014 needs to be smaller than 0.025 (i.e., $\alpha/2 = 0.05/2 = 0.025$), which it clearly is. z scores of -1.96 and $+1.96$ separate the middle 95% of z scores from the extreme 5% (2.5% in each of the two tails of the distribution). These special z values are called critical z values when a two-tailed hypothesis test is conducted and $\alpha = 0.05$. Under a one-tailed or directional hypothesis test, the critical z value would be $|1.65|$ because its percentile is approximately 0.95, suggesting that 5% (i.e., 0.05) of z test statistics fall in the relevant distribution tail.

The One-Sample t-Test
Researchers use the one-sample t-test instead of the one-sample z test if the population standard deviation is unknown (a more typical scenario). The sample standard deviation would be used in the formula in lieu of the population standard deviation and the t-test would be assessed for statistical significance by computing the probability of the observed t statistic based on a t distribution on $N - 1$ degrees of freedom.

The Independent Samples t-Test

Uses The independent samples t-test (i.e., student's t-test) is used to test mean differences between two populations on a continuous measure. (The term *continuous* is generally used to refer to responses measured on an interval or ratio scale. In psychology, Likert response scales are usually treated as interval-level scales.) For example, one might want to test whether men and women differ significantly in their average level of need for emotional support. The relevant populations are men and women and the outcome is need for emotional support. Sample data will be used to examine the null (e.g., $\mu_{Female} = \mu_{Male}$) and alternative (e.g., $\mu_{Female} \neq \mu_{Male}$) hypotheses.

Assumptions and Technical Information Assumptions include (a) an interval- or ratio-level dependent variable (e.g., emotional support); (b) the observations in each sample are independent of one another (i.e., the independence assumption), (c) the dependent variable is normally distributed in each population (i.e., the normality assumption), and (d) the population variances of the dependent variables are equal (i.e., homogeneity of variance assumption). The test statistic forms a ratio of the mean difference between the two samples to its standard error. Degrees of freedom (df) = $N - 2$ (where N is the total sample size). A relevant effect size is Cohen's d, which is a standardized mean difference and is computed as the ratio of the difference between the two sample means to the pooled standard deviation. Because ds can take on positive or negative values, strength is interpreted in absolute value (i.e., ds of -0.3 and $+0.3$ denote the same magnitude). (Interpretive guidelines for Cohen's d are small, $|.20|$; moderate, $|.50|$; and large, $|.80|$.)

Hypothetical Example   The results of an independent samples t-test revealed that on average women reported a significantly higher need for emotional support than did men, $t(98) = 2.50$, $p = .014$, $d = 0.50$. The technical statistical information is as follows: (a) t is the name of the test statistic used; (b) $98 = df$; (c) 2.50 is the independent samples t-value; (d) $p = .014$ is the exact probability value from a two-tailed hypothesis test; and (e) $d = 0.50$ is the effect size estimate based on Cohen's d, which denotes a moderate effect size.

The Paired Samples or Related Samples t-Test

In the independent samples t-test, each participant contributes a single data point to the analysis (e.g., a single score on depression). These data are assumed to be independent across the various individuals in the study. In the paired samples t-test, each "participant" contributes a pair of data points to the analysis, which are assumed to be dependent (i.e., correlated). The pair of data points can include one's report of the same construct (e.g., pretest and posttest depression), one's report of two constructs (e.g., anxiety and depression), or two judges of the same construct (e.g., mother and father report of a child's anxiety). The paired samples t-test examines mean differences across the observation pairs.

The Analysis of Variance and Related Models

General Structure   The analysis of variance (ANOVA) model is often used when predictor variables can be coded as finite categorical variables (e.g., with two, three, or more categories) and the outcome is at the interval or ratio level. Predictor variables are referred to as independent variables or factors. Factor categories are referred to as levels and the outcome is referred to as the dependent variable.

One-way ANOVA models include one factor, whereas factorial ANOVAs include two or more factors. ANOVAs can also be categorized as (a) between-subjects (in which all groups comprising the various factor levels are independent), (b) within-subjects (in which the same individuals are exposed to all levels of all factors), and (c) mixed (in which at least one between- and one within-subjects factor is included).

General Assumptions and Technical Information   Assumptions include (a) an interval- or ratio-level dependent variable; (b) the independence assumption; (c) the normality assumption; and (d) homogeneity of variance. As the name ANOVA implies, the ultimate analysis focuses on ratios of variance estimates. Note that a variance is a "sum of squares" (SS) quantity divided by a relevant degree of freedom (df) quantity. (The variance estimates are typically referred to as mean squares.) The test statistic is the F test (named after Fisher, who invented ANOVA).

In a simple one-way between-subjects ANOVA, the F test is computed as follows:

$$F = \frac{SS_b/df_b}{SS_w/df_w}.$$

The numerator quantities are often referred to as *between-group* quantities ($_b$) and capture variability due to treatment and error. The denominator quantities are *within-group* quantities ($_w$) and capture variability only due to error. Numerator degrees of freedom (df_b) are equal to G − 1 (where G is the number of factor levels). Denominator degrees of freedom (df_w) are equal to N − G (where N is the overall sample size). A number of effect sizes could be used with ANOVA models.

The various indices—like omega squared, ω^2—reflect the proportion of variance in the outcome that is explained by the factors. Interpretive guidelines for omega squared are small = 0.01, medium = 0.06, and large = 0.15.

Note that a one-way between-group ANOVA with two factor levels has the same structure as the independent samples t-test. In such instances, the test statistics are related as follows: $t^2 = F$.

Main Effects and Interactions   In a two-way ANOVA examining the effects of stress (high and low levels) and support (high and low levels) on test performance, the full-factorial design (i.e., a design in which all possible main and interaction effects are estimated) yields a main effect of stress, a main effect of support, and a stress-by-support interaction. In general, main effects examine the unique effect of an independent variable on an outcome. In the present example, a main effect of stress might suggest that test performance is significantly lower in the high-stress condition relative to the low-stress condition. In general, interactions examine whether the effects of one predictor on an outcome vary significantly as a function of another predictor. In the present example, a stress-by-support interaction might indicate that the effects of stress depend on the level of support. For example, the difference in test performance in the low and high stress conditions might be attenuated in the high-support condition and exacerbated in the low-support condition—suggesting that the effects of stress on performance vary significantly by support. (When interactions are significant, main effects are usually not interpreted.)

Omnibus Tests of Significance and Post Hoc Contrasts   In models for which there are three or more levels of a factor (e.g., low, medium, and high levels of stress), the test of the factor's main effect is an omnibus statistical test. When significant, the researcher can reject the null that all population means are equal. Differences between two specific groups (e.g., low and high stress levels) are not revealed by this omnibus statistical test. Instead, omnibus tests are typically followed by a series of additional tests (e.g., comparing each pairs of means). These more focused contrasts are often referred to as post hoc tests. Conducting multiple statistical tests raises the familywise type I error rate associated with the full set of analyses (beyond the desired 0.05 level). Consequently, researchers typically use an alpha adjustment procedure to limit the familywise error rate. Perhaps the simplest of these methods is the Bonferroni correction, which takes the original alpha level (say 0.05) and divides it by the number of post hoc tests performed. The resulting quantity becomes the criterion for statistical significance for all post hoc tests.

One-Way Between-Subjects   A one-way between-subjects ANOVA can be used to contrast two or more treatment groups (e.g., CBT, interpersonal therapy [IPT], and control).

One-Way Within-Subjects   A one-way within-subjects ANOVA can be used to examine a single cohort's symptom levels over two or more assessments (e.g., pretest, posttest, and follow-up measures for individuals exposed to a single intervention). In within-subjects designs that include three or more levels of a (quantitative) factor, researchers can examine trend analyses to see whether the average trend is linear (the means can be plotted along a straight line), quadratic (the shape of the plot of means has one distinct bend), or some other higher-order form. An additional assumption of these kinds of repeated-measures designs is the sphericity or circularity assumption, which assumes that the *variances of the differences* of the various factor levels are equal. (The sphericity assumption extends the typical homogeneity of variance assumption to these difference scores.) If the same individuals are exposed to different interventions (e.g., three interventions to improve basic math skills), the order of exposure might have an impact on the outcome. In such instances, researchers might incorporate counterbalancing as a design feature (e.g., through the use of a Latin square design). Such design features allow researchers to examine the possible effects of treatment ordering on the outcome.

Two-Way Between-Subjects   A two-way between-subjects ANOVA evaluates the effect of two independent variables on a dependent variable. For example, one might be interested in examining whether ADHD diagnosis (present or absent) and testing environment (quiet or noisy room) have an impact on performance. The full-factorial two-by-two design yields (a) a main effect of ADHD diagnosis, (b) a main effect of testing environment, and (c) the diagnosis-by-testing environment interaction.

Two-Way Within-Subjects   A two-way within-subjects ANOVA could be built by exposing a group of children with ADHD to two levels of a psychostimulant drug-dose factor (e.g., 5 and 10 mg) crossed with two levels of a testing-environment factor (e.g., quiet and noisy rooms). In other words, all children would be observed under all four study conditions (e.g., 10 mg, quiet room) and performance would be the dependent variable. This design yields (a) a main effect of psychostimulant dose, (b) a main effect of testing environment, and (c) the psychostimulant dose-by-testing environment interaction.

Two-Way Mixed Design (One Between-Subjects Factor and One Within-Subjects Factor)   The two-group, pretest–posttest treatment outcome study is an example of a two-way mixed design. The between-subjects factor is treatment group (e.g., treatment vs. control) and the within-subjects factor can be labeled time of assessment (e.g., pretest vs. posttest). Similar to other designs we discussed, this design yields (a) a main effect of treatment, (b) a main effect of time of assessment, and (c) a treatment-by-time-of-assessment interaction. In this type of design, the interaction is typically the effect of primary interest because it suggests that the pretest to posttest change varies significantly as a function of treatment group (e.g., the treatment group declines in symptoms while the control group remains stable).

Higher-Order Designs   All of the designs discussed above can be extended to include additional factors—for example, a two (treatment vs. control) by two (male vs. female) by two (pretest vs. posttest) design. Although ANOVA designs can include many factors, it is worth noting that psychologists rarely predict and/or probe interactions involving more than three factors.

Analysis of Covariance   Any of the designs described above can be changed from an ANOVA model to an ANCOVA (analysis of covariance) model by adding one or more covariates. A covariate is a variable whose influence the researcher hopes to *control* while examining the effect of the variable of primary theoretical interest. ANCOVAs are used in two primary manners: (a) to increase statistical power in randomized experiments (when the covariate is uncorrelated with intervention conditions, but correlated with the dependent variable); and (b) to *control* for possible confounding influences (i.e., controlling for variables associated with both intervention conditions and the dependent variable) in nonrandomized designs.

When researchers use ANCOVA, they often present group comparisons of adjusted means (i.e., means adjusted for the effects of the covariates) on the dependent variable of interest. Assumptions of the ANCOVA model include (a) the covariates are measured without error and (b) the effects of the covariates on the outcome are constant over levels of the independent variable. (Although not necessarily intuitive, this last assumption precludes the presence of covariate–independent variable interactions, and is also known as the homogeneity of regression lines assumption.) If important covariates are omitted, statistical control will not be optimal.

Multivariate Analysis of Variance   Many of the ANOVA models described above are referred to as univariate ANOVA models because the analysis focuses on a single dependent variable. In contrast, the multivariate ANOVA model (i.e., MANOVA model) allows for multiple dependent variables to be analyzed in a single model. In MANOVA, the actual analysis is performed on an *optimized linear combination* of the multiple dependent variables (one that maximizes between-group differences while minimizing within-group differences). A number of test statistics are generated by MANOVA (Pillais's trace, Wilk's lambda, Hotelling's trace, and Roy's largest root).

In the discussion of inferential statistics thus far, the focus has mostly been on comparisons among means. Below, statistical associations typically described in the context of correlation and regression are explored.

The Pearson Product-Moment Correlation (r)

Uses   Assume that a researcher was interested in examining the relationship between achievement motivation and grade point average in a sample of college students. The association between these two variables could be quantified by the Pearson product-moment correlation (i.e., r), which measures linear associations between two continuous variables. The null hypothesis in this situation is typically $\rho = 0$ and the alternative hypothesis would be $\rho \neq 0$ (where ρ is the symbol for the population correlation).

Assumptions and Technical Information   Assumptions include (a) both variables are interval or ratio level, (b) bivariate normality (i.e., the joint distribution is normal), and (c) the variability in one of the variables is relatively constant across values of the other variable (i.e., homoscedasticity). Proper interpretation requires a linear association between the two variables. Correlations range from −1 to +1, with larger absolute values suggesting stronger associations. Positive correlations result when cases above the mean on one variable tend to be above the mean on the other variable (e.g., study time and performance). Negative correlations result when cases above the mean on one variable tend to be below the mean on the other variable (e.g., illicit drug use and academic performance in high school). Correlations near zero result when an individual's score on one variable conveys little information about his or her score on the other variable. Effect size is estimated by computing the square of the correlation (i.e., the coefficient of determination), which is the proportion of shared variance between the two variables. Common interpretative guidelines for r^2 are as follows: small = .01, medium = .09, and large = .25. Several factors can influence the magnitude of a correlation, including the shape of the two distributions (as distributions diverge, the correlation diminishes), the reliability of measures (less reliable measures limit the maximum possible correlation), and restricted range (homogeneous responses on one or both variables diminish the correlation).

Other Correlations

Although less widely used in psychology, alternatives to Pearson's r exist and are generally used with ordinal data or when the assumptions of the Pearson's r are not satisfied. The point-biserial correlation is used when one variable is dichotomous (i.e., sex) and the other is continuous. The tetrachoric correlation is used when both variables are dichotomous. The polychoric correlation, which is a generalization of the tetrachoric correlation, is used when both variables are ordinal and comprise a relatively finite number of categories (say three to five). Spearman's rank correlation coefficient and Kendall's tau coefficient are both nonparametric tests that are used when responses on the two variables are rank ordered.

Ordinary Least Squares Regression

Uses   Ordinary least squares (OLS) regression allows for the prediction of a single continuous outcome (often referred to as the criterion) from one or more predictor variables (which can be nominal, ordinal, interval, or ratio). The multiple regression model (i.e., a model with multiple predictors) can be specified as follows: $Y_i = a + b_1(x_{1i}) + b_2(x_{2i}) + \cdots + b_k(x_{ki}) + e_i$. Terms that carry the subscript i are free to vary by individual. As such, Y_i is individual i's value on the outcome. The a is the y-intercept (i.e., the predicted value of Y when all predictors are equal to zero). The bs represent the unstandardized linear regression coefficients. Each quantifies the linear association between the relevant predictor and the outcome and has the following interpretation: for every one-unit increase in x, Y changes by b units. There are k predictors in all (i.e., in a three-predictor model, $k = 3$). The e_i (i.e., the residual) is the error in prediction associated with the model for each individual: $e_i = Y_i - \hat{Y}_i$ (where $\hat{Y}_i$ is the predicted value of the outcome for the individual in question). The regression constants (a and bs) are determined by minimizing the error in prediction associated with the model.

Assumptions and Technical Information   Assumptions include (a) the predictors are fixed variables (suggesting that the same values are sampled over studies), (b) the predictors are measured without error, (c) the predictor–outcome associations are linear, (d) the means of the errors "balance out" (i.e., are assumed to be zero over many replications), (e) errors are independent of one another, (f) the residuals have constant variance for all predictor values (homoscedasticity; heteroscedasticity results if this assumption is violated), and (g) the residual is uncorrelated with the predictor variables (can be ensured through randomization of treatments in experiments). Multicollinearity results when predictors are redundant (i.e., highly correlated in a pairwise or generalized manner). Regression diagnostics can be used to assess for violations of these various assumptions.

In practice, significance tests are examined for the full model (which tests whether the full set of predictors accounts for significant variance in the outcome) and for the individual predictors. The test of an individual predictor examines whether the predictor in question accounts for significant incremental variance in the outcome, above all other predictors in the model. It is often desirable to examine the incremental variance associated with various subsets of predictors. This last approach is referred to as hierarchical regression analysis, which results when the full model is built by adding predictors to the model sequentially. (Hierarchical regression analysis is sometimes confused with stepwise regression analysis, which is an atheoretical approach to predictor entry used more often in exploratory analyses.)

Example   Table 7.1 presented output from a hierarchical regression model in which the criterion—positive relations with others (a facet of Ryff's 1989 conceptualization of psychological well-being)—was predicted from six predictors organized into three subsets or blocks (i.e., demographics, other covariates, and

TABLE 7.1   A Hierarchical Regression Model Predicting Positive Relations With Others From Demographics, Other Covariates, and Recovery-Related Practices

	b	se	p	f^2
Block 1: Demographics:				
$F(2, 130) = 3.90, p = .023, R^2 = .057$				
Age	.001	.006	.863	< .001
Sex (0 = female, 1 = male)	−.157	.109	.150	.012
Block 2: Other covariates:				
$\Delta F(2, 128) = 26.44, p < .001, \Delta R^2 = .276$				
Substance use severity	−.161	.071	.024	.041
Neuroticism	−.304	.056	< .001	.235
Block 3: Recovery-related predictors:				
$\Delta F(2, 126) = 8.42, p < .001, \Delta R^2 = .079$				
Home group comfort	.197	.053	< .001	.110
Abstinence duration	.015	.008	.056	.029

Note: Full model was statistically significant, $F(6, 126) = 14.66, p < .001, R^2 = .41$.
All coefficients are from final model.

recovery-related predictors). (As mentioned above, these data were part of a larger study examining recovery-related correlates of psychological well-being in Narcotics Anonymous members; DeLucia et al., 2012.) The full model was statistically significant, $F(6, 126) = 14.66, p < .001, R^2 = .41$, suggesting that the complete set of six predictors accounted for significant variance in the outcome. (F tests are generally reported for overall model results or for testing the incremental variance associated with predictor subsets. t-tests are generally reported for assessing the effects of the individual predictors.)

The incremental variance associated with the addition of each predictor block was as follows: (a) the demographic predictors accounted for significant variance in positive relations with others, $F(2, 130) = 3.90, p = .023, R^2 = .057$; (b) when entered second, the other covariates accounted for significant incremental variance in positive relations with others (over the demographic predictors), $\Delta F(2, 128) = 26.44, p < .001, \Delta R^2 = .276$; and (c) when entered last, the recovery-related predictors accounted for significant incremental variance in the outcome (over the demographics and person-level covariates), $\Delta F(2, 126) = 8.42, p < .001, \Delta R^2 = .079$. (The delta symbols, Δ, are used in place of the words "change in.")

The entries in the b column of Table 7.1 are the unstandardized partial regression coefficients for all six predictors from the final model (when all predictors are included). In the example, the regression coefficient for neuroticism is statistically significant, b = −0.304, SE = 0.056, p < .001, which suggests a one-unit gain in neuroticism is associated with a 0.304 unit *decrease* in positive relations with others (i.e., the outcome or criterion variable). The strength of association between individual predictors and the outcome can be quantified by computing Cohen's f^2 values, which are computed as the square of the partial correlation (between the predictor in question and the outcome) divided by 1—the square of the partial correlation. The f^2 values are presented in Table 7.1. Interpretive guidelines are as follows: small = 0.02, medium = 0.15, and large = 0.35. Standardized regression coefficients can also be used to quantify the effect of a single predictor. Although not presented in Table 7.1, the standardized regression coefficient for neuroticism is −0.41, suggesting that a one (standard deviation) unit increase in neuroticism is associated with a 0.41 (standard deviation unit) *decrease* in positive relations with others.

Testing Interactions   In the six-predictor regression model described above, no interactions between or among predictor variables were estimated. Models that do not include interaction effects are referred to as additive effects models. In regression, an interaction between two predictors can be included in the analysis by creating a cross-product of the two predictors (by multiplying them together) and entering this additional variable in the analysis. The significance test for the cross-product predictor is the test of the interaction.

Testing Nonlinear Effects   In the same way trend analyses can be conducted in ANOVA models, tests of nonlinear effects of various predictors can be estimated in regression models. In practice, testing nonlinear effects is accomplished by raising the predictor in question to various powers—where 1 = linear, 2 = quadratic, 3 = cubic, etc. If a researcher was interested in testing the possible quadratic effect of abstinence duration in the model described above, the researcher would square the predictor in question and add the new predictor to the model. The test of its coefficient would be the test of the quadratic effect.

Extensions of the OLS Regression Model

Logistic Regression   Logistic regression is used when the outcome variable comprises ordered (e.g., symptom severity: low, medium, or high) or unordered (e.g., political affiliation: democrat, independent, or republican) categories. Substantive interpretations of the effects of predictors in logistic regression models often involve discussion of relevant odds ratios. For example, a researcher might be interested in predicting alcohol use disorders in young adulthood (0 = no disorder, 1 = disorder) from two predictors (parent alcoholism: 0 = neither parent, 1 = at least one parent; and sex: 0 = female, 1 = male). Assume that both predictors are associated with significantly higher rates of diagnoses and the odds ratios are as follows: parent alcoholism, 4.22; and sex, 2.48. These data suggest that the odds of diagnosis are 4.22 times higher for young adults with alcoholic parents relative to young adults without alcoholic parents. The combined odds of diagnosis for having an alcoholic parent and being male would be 4.22 * 2.48 or 10.46 times higher relative to females without alcoholic parents.

Path Analysis   Although the OLS regression model is extremely flexible in that the predictors can take on myriad forms, it is limited in that the effects of the predictors do not reflect a strong *causal ordering*. In path analysis, models can be structured to reflect a stronger causal ordering. (This class of models is sometimes referred to as causal models.) In Figure 7.8, a path diagram modeled after an analysis conducted by Newcomb and Bentler is presented (1988, p. 80). The authors were interested in examining the possible prospective associations between adolescent drug use and social conformity and the same constructs assessed in young adulthood. Such an analysis provides several useful pieces of information—including (a) the cross-sectional association between the constructs during each developmental period (see "a" and "f" in figure); (b) the degree of stability in each of the constructs across the developmental periods (see "b" and "c" in figure); and (c) the prospective (cross-lagged) associations between the constructs (see "d" and

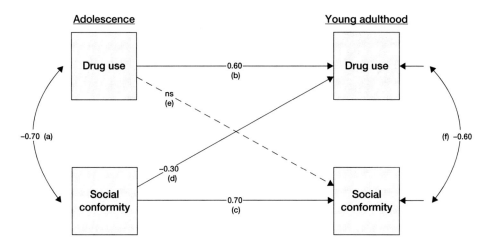

FIGURE 7.8 A path diagram examining prospective cross-lagged associations between drug use and social conformity.

"e" in figure). In the figure, these prospective paths indicate that social conformity in adolescence is a significant prospective predictor of changes in drug use from adolescence to young adulthood. Drug use in adolescence is not a significant prospective predictor of changes in social conformity from adolescence to young adulthood. Consequently, these data suggest a stronger causal ordering from social conformity to drug use, not the other way around.

Structural Equation Modeling Structural equation modeling further extends path analysis to include path analysis with *latent variables*. Latent variables are described above in the context of measurement theory. The classic structural equation model is often discussed as comprising two inter-related parts— the measurement model (in which relations between latent variables and their observed indicators are modeled) and the structural model (in which relations between/among latent variables are modeled). In the Newcomb and Bentler (1988) example discussed above, the constructs were actually latent variables (although our figure did not depict them as such). For example, the latent construct of drug use had three observed indicators: (a) alcohol frequency, (b) cannabis frequency, and (c) hard-drug frequency. Similarly, the latent construct of social conformity had three observed indicators: (a) law abidance, (b) liberalism, and (c) religious commitment. The primary advantage of structural equation modeling over path analysis involves gains in statistical power that result when measurement error associated with predictors and outcomes is reduced.

Nonparametric Statistical Tests
As discussed previously, nonparametric statistical tests often make few if any assumptions about the underlying relevant population distributions. As such, they are sometimes referred to as distribution-free methods. Below, the chi-square test, which is a nonparametric statistical test commonly used in psychology, is discussed. In addition, nonparametric alternatives to some of the more commonly used parametric tests described above are covered.

Chi-Square Test Chi-square tests are used in two primary manners in psychology. Chi-square tests of independence are commonly used to test whether two categorical variables are associated. For example, if a researcher were interested in examining whether men had higher rates of alcohol use disorders than did women, a chi-square test of independence could be computed. If sex and alcoholism status were not associated, the researcher would expect the rate of alcohol use disorders to be similar for men and women (and the chi-square test to be nonsignificant). Chi-square tests of goodness of fit are commonly used in path analysis, CFA, and structural equation modeling to test whether the model-implied variance/covariance matrix fits the estimated population variance/covariance matrix. In these instances, researchers are hoping for nonsignificant chi-squares, which suggest little discrepancy between the two matrices (suggesting that the specified model fits the data well).

Nonparametric Alternatives to Commonly Used Parametric Tests   The Mann–Whitney Test (also called the Mann–Whitney–Wilcoxon Test) is a nonparametric alternative to the independent samples *t*-test and is used when data that can be rank ordered are collected from two different samples of individuals. The Kruskal–Wallis Test is a nonparametric alternative to the between-group ANOVA. Similar to the Mann–Whitney Test, data from three or more samples can be rank-ordered to determine whether the samples are similar, or at least one sample is different from the remaining samples. The Wilcoxon Signed Ranks Test is a nonparametric alternative to the paired samples *t*-test. This test statistic is used when a sample of individuals contributes a pair of data points to the analysis (and the paired differences can be rank-ordered in absolute value). The Friedman Test can be used as a nonparametric alternative to the within-subjects ANOVA with three or more levels. In this analysis, the repeated observations for the various participants are rank-ordered within participants and then summed within factor levels. These sums are analyzed to see whether rankings appear similar or different.

Other Topics in Statistics

Sensitivity and Specificity

Sensitivity and specificity and related topics are often discussed in the context of screening tests. Assume a clinician is using a screening test to differentiate individuals with psychosis from individuals without psychosis. If the clinician examines the test's performance in a sample of individuals who have been evaluated for psychosis by a panel of expert psychologists, the test's sensitivity and specificity can be computed. In this example, the consensus diagnosis conferred by the panel as the *true state of affairs* is being used (e.g., if the expert panel diagnosed as psychotic, the individuals are categorized as psychotic individuals).

Figure 7.9 presents the number of cases in each of the four table cells that result when crossing the two possible outcomes from the screener (not psychotic, psychotic) with the two possible outcomes from the panel's consensus diagnosis (not psychotic, psychotic). The cell labeled "A" includes the number of true positives (i.e., psychotic individuals the test *correctly* classified as psychotic). The cell labeled "B" includes the number of false positives (i.e., nonpsychotic individuals the test *incorrectly* classified as psychotic). The cell labeled "C" includes the false negatives (i.e., psychotic individuals the test *incorrectly* classified as nonpsychotic). The cell labeled "D" includes the true negatives (i.e., nonpsychotic individuals the test *correctly* classified as nonpsychotic). In the present example, sensitivity is the proportion of psychotic individuals correctly classified as

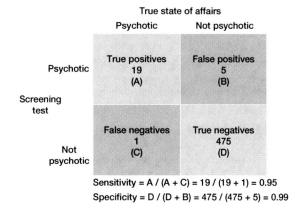

FIGURE 7.9   Sensitivity and specificity based on hypothetical data for a screening test for psychosis.

psychotic by the test. It can be computed as $A/(A + C) = 19/(19 + 1) = 0.95$. In general, sensitivity is the probability of a positive test result, given the presence of the condition. In the present example, specificity is the proportion of nonpsychotic individuals the test correctly classified as nonpsychotic. It can be computed as $D/(B + D) = 475/(5 + 475) = 0.99$. In general, specificity is the probability of a negative test result, given the absence of the condition. In this example, the test does a very good job of correctly classifying individuals with the condition (sensitivity) and individuals without the condition (specificity).

Moderation and Mediation

Moderators are variables that alter the association between another variable and an outcome. Testing for moderation is the same as testing for a statistical interaction between a predictor and a moderator. For example, a researcher might test whether an intervention effect is moderated by participant sex to see whether the effects of the intervention on the outcome are stronger for men or women. A mediator is the mechanism through which a distal predictor operates in influencing an outcome. For example, the salutary impact of a cognitive behavioral treatment for depression might result in lower levels of depression by reducing patients' cognitive distortions. In this scenario, the distal predictor is treatment, the mediator is cognitive distortion, and the outcome is depression. Mediated effects can be tested in many different ways—all of which center on examining whether the indirect effect (of the distal predictor on the outcome through the mediator) is significant.

Qualitative Research

Qualitative research seeks to describe and understand problems using interviews, focus groups, observations, review of naturalistic documents, and other non-numerical data as the basis of analysis and interpretation. It is associated with inductive processes (i.e., moving from specific observations to broader generalizations) and uses methods that enable a pattern to be identified from data that are more abstract in nature. Theoretical and purposeful sampling (aimed at selecting the data that will most serve the researcher's purpose, such as specifically select-ing extreme cases) is often used in qualitative research (in contrast with represen-tative sampling). Although quantitative research methods typically involve theory testing, qualitative methods are often used to generate hypotheses, theory, or a rich understanding of a group's experiences, perspectives, and context.

Types of Qualitative Inquiry

Over 25 approaches to qualitative inquiry have been identified. Approaches vary in terms of the epistemology (philosophy of science) they are most associated with, the disciplines they are associated with, and how systematically they are defined in the literature. Two common approaches are phenomenology and grounded theory.

Phenomenology
Phenomenology centers on understanding participants' lived experiences and emphasizes subjective experience (e.g., understanding personal knowledge, moti-vations, and perspectives).

Grounded Theory
The ultimate goal of grounded theory is to develop a theory ("grounded" in data) about a concept of interest. This approach is used when current theory is lack-ing, nonexistent, or incomplete. An iterative process of collecting and coding data about a phenomenon of interest occurs until a theoretical understanding of the phenomenon and its processes and relationships to other concepts emerges.

Thematic Analysis in Qualitative Research

Across the multiple approaches to qualitative research, data are often analyzed using thematic analysis, a process of identifying and analyzing patterns or themes within data. This can occur either deductively (i.e., starting from a particular the-ory or hypothesis) or inductively (i.e., as in grounded theory above). Braun and Clarke (2006) outline six phases: transcribing and reading through data, generat-ing initial codes or points of interest in the data, searching for themes where codes may be combined, creating a "thematic map" that indicates how themes are inter-connected, defining and naming the themes, and producing a report that relates the thematic map to the original research question and reviews the literature.

Reliability/Validity Issues in Qualitative Research

There are different means of increasing "trustworthiness" or credibility of findings from qualitative research. Data collection in qualitative research often occurs until saturation (point at which data are consistently redundant and provide no new information). In addition, the following techniques are used: triangulation (the use of multiple, varied sources of data, methods, and researchers in order to corrobo-rate results), audits (the use of an external consultant to complete an independent analysis), and member checking (having participants in the study review and pro-vide feedback on the credibility of findings).

Program Evaluation Strategies and Techniques

Although the focus throughout this chapter has been primarily on traditional research and nonevaluative empirical investigations, researchers and clinicians in psychology often work together to use data to make determinations about the value of interventions and programs that exist in the community. PE examines how an intervention or service works, for whom, and under what conditions. In both standard research and PE, the design is intended to be rigorous, systematic, and may even use some of the same methods (e.g., surveys and focus groups). However, there are key differences between the two: PE is often applied to specific programs (traditional research focuses on generalization of knowledge and theory), PE often aims to facilitate decision making and improve programs (as opposed to testing theories/hypotheses), PE questions are often derived from stakeholders and program staff (not researchers), and PE almost always occurs in natural settings (as opposed to controlled settings).

The first step in PE is to identify and engage stakeholders (e.g., administrators, staff, clients, etc.). Next, a needs assessment might be conducted to assess the relative priority of the needs, or "problems," of a specific population in order to determine where resources should be allocated. Needs assessments can include an analysis of existing data as well as collection of new data through quantitative or qualitative means. Evaluators often assess the extent to which services are already available to meet the identified needs, usage rates for existing services, and the potential for needs to be in conflict with one another (e.g., situations where addressing one need might create/exacerbate another need). Needs assessment is one type of formative evaluation (provide information that will result in changes that can improve the effectiveness of that program).

Several evaluation strategies may be used later on in the program's implementation. Process or implementation evaluation strategies are used to determine how program activities are delivered and whether the program is being implemented as planned. Summative evaluations are used to determine whether or not programs have been effective at reaching desired outcomes. They can include a comparison with alternative programs. Formative and summative evaluations may use the same measures and methods, but with *different goals*. Formative evaluations provide information to make needed changes early on, whereas summative evaluations determine a program's success once delivered.

In addition to summative evaluation, cost–benefit analysis (CBA) can also be used to measure the impact of a program. CBA examines the balance of resources/costs spent on a program compared to the benefits to answer the question "have resources been well spent on this program?" This results in a benefit/cost ratio, the worth of a program's outcomes divided by the program's costs, which can then be compared to alternative programs. CBA is controversial in part because it assigns monetary values to the benefits arising from a program.

Participant Sampling and Recruitment

Early on in the research process, researchers must define the population of interest and consider sampling and recruitment strategies. Two primary goals in the recruitment of research participants are to achieve adequate representation of a target population and obtain a sufficient sample size to achieve adequate levels of statistical power for planned analyses. Representativeness is important because a primary research goal is to generalize findings to a target population.

Sample Selection

Samples can be categorized into representative samples (probability sampling) and nonrepresentative samples (nonprobability sampling). In probability sampling, researchers ensure that all individuals in the population of interest have an opportunity to be selected. There are two main kinds of representative samples. In simple random samples, all individuals in the population have an equal likelihood of being selected. In stratified random samples, the researcher creates classes or strata, and then a percentage of the overall sample is selected randomly from each stratum. Note that the terms *random selection* and *random assignment* are often confused. Random selection is how individuals from the population are *selected* for the study. Random assignment, which necessarily occurs after random selection, is how individuals already in the study are *assigned* to various study conditions.

Given the resource requirements of probability sampling, the use of nonprobability sampling is more common. A convenience sample, one kind of nonprobability sample, is collected when participants are recruited because of the researcher's ease of access (e.g., students are asked to volunteer for a study). Purposive sampling is when researchers collect data from individuals with specific characteristics. Snowball sampling, a type of purposive sampling, involves participants inviting others to participate in the study. Respondent-driven sampling uses incentives to overcome possible biases that result from snowball and other chain-referral sampling methods.

The law of large numbers suggests that larger samples tend to be more representative of their populations. Consequently, sampling error (i.e., the difference between the sample and population) is inversely related to sample size (i.e., error increases as sample size decreases). The sampling error that results from probability sampling is random or free from systematic bias. In nonprobability samples, sampling error can reflect systematic bias (e.g., individuals with particular characteristics are systematically under- or overrepresented). Nonparticipation can create a biased sample (regardless of sampling strategy) because individuals who refuse participation are often different from those who participate. Therefore, it is very important to understand barriers to recruitment.

Barriers to Recruitment

Several barriers exist in the recruitment of a representative sample. Participant barriers can include language barriers, transportation barriers, interference with work and family responsibilities, fear/distrust of research, aversion to treatment assignment, and stigma associated with study concepts (e.g., stigma associated with mental health). Investigator barriers may include a lack of knowledge about the target population, limited cultural competence, and research staff members who are not representative of the diversity in the community of interest. Both barriers disproportionately affect racial/ethnic minority individuals and may lead to an underrepresentation of these minorities in research, requiring additional outreach efforts to recruit and retain such individuals. The National Institutes of Health has mandated inclusion of women and racial/ethnic minorities in its sponsored clinical research since 1993.

Outreach Strategies

Several strategies are used by researchers in trying to engage potential research participants. These are often tested in pilot studies examining the feasibility of the research, especially the researcher's recruitment plan. Recruitment outreach can take the form of advertising or communicating with potential participants about the study through the mail, phone, Internet, or in person. Maximizing the representativeness of a sample often involves building trust and relationships with community members of interest, aligning the research question and design with the goals and needs of the community, addressing barriers to participation, ensuring that materials are designed with community members in mind (e.g., literacy level, language preference, and relatable images), and recruiting a diverse research staff.

Community Partnerships

Community-Based Participatory Research (CBPR) is an approach that emphasizes the engagement of community members in research endeavors. CPBR has three objectives: (a) equitable involvement of researchers and community members, (b) incorporation of the unique strengths of both community members (e.g., lived experiences, values, and attitudes) and researchers (e.g., technical knowledge) in research, and (c) outcomes that include new knowledge and direct benefits to the community.

Community Advisory Boards

In order to achieve these objectives, CBPR researchers establish close partnerships with community stakeholders. Stakeholders are individuals or agencies in the community who are directly involved or affected by the work of interest to the researcher. Community representatives are particularly important partners when working with vulnerable populations, because they (e.g., parents, community clinicians, criminal justice officials, etc.) may serve a "gatekeeping" role, mediating researchers' access to these communities.

Partnerships between key community stakeholders and researchers may be formalized through an organizational structure called a Community Advisory Board (CAB), which facilitates ongoing communication between researchers and community members. CABs can have a number of roles and responsibilities, including providing guidance to the researcher on community perspectives and participating in important decisions about sampling, study design, survey wording, interpretation of findings, and how best to use the results for community benefit.

Benefits of Community Partnership

Developing partnerships with community members can require substantial time and resources (e.g., formative work often needs to be done in order to increase community readiness to participate and to build trust in the researcher/research institution). However, partnerships such as these may have several important benefits for both researchers and community members such as recruitment of a broader population, culturally sensitive research methods, and development of more sustainable and effective intervention efforts.

Dissemination and Presentation of Research Findings

One of the final phases of the research cycle is the dissemination of research findings. Traditional dissemination to the academic community occurs in peer-reviewed formats (e.g., journal publications and conference presentations) and includes a clear description of the relevant literature, the significance of the research and its aims (introduction); description of the study design, procedures and analysis (method); a report of the findings (results); and a discussion of the major findings, limitations of the research, and implications (discussion).

Less traditional research dissemination efforts (i.e., outside of academia) can also be considered in order to increase the likelihood that communities can access research and that research findings have the potential to result in community benefit. In developing a nontraditional dissemination plan, it is important to consider the source of the message (what is the perceived credibility of the researcher for the stakeholders?), the message content (how useful and relevant is the research to the stakeholders?), the dissemination method (how to clearly communicate the benefits of the intervention to the stakeholders?), and the intended user of the information (do stakeholders have the resources, skills, and support to benefit from the research?). Nontraditional dissemination efforts can include communication of research findings through local community meetings, media outlets, and policy reports.

References

American Educational Research Association, American Psychological Association, and National Council on Measurement in Education. (1999). *Standards for educational and psychological testing.* Washington, DC: American Educational Research Association.

Braun, V., & Clarke, V. (2006). Using thematic analysis in psychology. *Qualitative Research in Psychology, 3*(2), 77–101. doi: 10.1191/1478088706qp063oa

Clark, L. A., & Watson, D. (1995). Constructing validity: Basic issues in objective scale development. *Psychological Assessment, 7*(3), 309–319. doi: 10.1037/1040-3590.7.3.309

*Cohen, J., Cohen, P., West, S., & Aiken, L. (2003). *Applied multiple regression/correlation analysis for the behavioral sciences* (3rd ed.). Hillsdale: Erlbaum.

Cronbach, L. J., & Meehl, P. E. (1955). Construct validity in psychological tests. *Psychological Bulletin, 52*(4), 281–302. doi: 10.1037/h0040957

DeLucia, C., Bergman, B., Heinowitz, A., Beitra, D., Seibert, S., Howrey, H., & Mizrachi, J. (2012). Recovery-related predictors of psychological well-being among Narcotics Anonymous members. *Alcoholism: Clinical and Experimental Research, 36*(Suppl. 1), 1A–398A. Abstract retrieved from *Special Issue: 35th Annual Scientific Meeting of the Research Society on Alcoholism,* June 23–27, San Francisco, CA. doi: 10.1111/j.1530-0277.2012.01803.x

*Gravetter, F. J., & Wallnau, L. B. (2007). *Statistics for the behavioral sciences* (7th ed.). Belmont, CA: Thomson Wadsworth.

---

*Citations preceded by an asterisk were used as source materials but were not cited in the text.

Information for candidates: The examination for professional practice in psychology. Retrieved from Association of State and Provincial Psychology Boards Web Site: http://www.asppb.net/files/public/IFC.pdf

John, O. P. (1990). The Big Five factor taxonomy: Dimensions of personality in the natural language and in questionnaires. In L. A. Pervin (Ed.), *Handbook of personality: Theory and research* (pp. 66–100). New York, NY: Guilford Press.

John, O. P., & Benet-Martínez, V. (2000). Measurement, scale construction, and reliability. In H. T. Reis & C. M. Judd (Eds.), *Handbook of research methods in social and personality psychology* (pp. 339–369). New York, NY: Cambridge University Press.

Kazdin, A. E. (2003). *Research design in clinical psychology* (4th ed.). Needham Heights, MA: Allyn & Bacon.

*Keppel, G. (1991). *Design and analysis: A researcher's handbook* (3rd ed.). Englewood Cliffs, NJ: Prentice Hall.

Messick, S. (1995). Validity of psychological assessment: Validation of inferences from persons' responses and performances as scientific inquiry into score meaning. *American Psychologist, 50*(9), 741–749. doi: 10.1037/0003-066X.50.9.741

Mudford, O. C., McNeill, R., Walton, L., & Phillips, K. J. (2012). Rationale and standards of evidence in evidence-based practice. In P. Sturmey, & M. Hersen (Eds.), *Handbook of evidence-based practice in clinical psychology* (pp. 3–26). Hoboken, NJ: Wiley.

Newcomb, M. D., & Bentler, P. M. (1988). *Consequences of adolescent drug use: Impact on the lives of young adults*. Newbury Park, CA: Sage.

Popper, K. (2002). Science: Conjectures and refutations. In *Conjectures and refutations: The growth of scientific knowledge* (pp. 43–55). London, UK: Routledge Classics (Original work published 1963).

Rosen, J. C., Reiter, J., & Orosan, P. (1995). Cognitive-behavioral body image therapy for body dysmorphic disorder. *Journal of Consulting and Clinical Psychology, 63*(2), 263–269. doi: 10.1037/0022-006X.63.3.437

Ryff, C. D. (1989). Happiness is everything, or is it? Explorations on the meaning of psychological well-being. *Journal of Personality and Social Psychology, 57*(6), 1069–1081. doi: 10.1037/0022-3514.57.6.1069

*Salkind, N. J. (Ed.). (2010). *Encyclopedia of research design*. Thousand Oaks, CA: Sage.

*Shadish, W. R., Cook, T. D., & Campbell, D. T. (2002). *Experimental and quasi-experimental designs for generalized causal inference*. Boston, MA: Houghton Mifflin.

West, S. G., & Finch, J. (1997). Personality measurement: Reliability and validity issues. In R. Hogan, J. Johnson, & S. Briggs (Eds.), *Handbook of personality psychology* (pp. 143–164). San Diego, CA: Academic Press.

Review Questions

1. Under null hypothesis significance testing, when a test statistic is deemed statistically significant, it indicates that:

   A. The findings are clinically important
   B. The measures used to test study hypotheses were highly reliable
   C. The null hypothesis must be false in reality
   D. The data would occur relatively infrequently, given the specified null hypothesis and alpha level

2. If one could confirm the presence of an internal validity threat, it would suggest:

   A. A limit to the generality of the relevant cause–effect relationship
   B. An alternative explanation for the active ingredients of an intervention
   C. The original study was a quasi-experiment
   D. An alternative explanation for the relevant cause–effect relationship

3. Final grades in a class with grade inflation would result in a distribution with _____, whereas assessing the frequency of daily alcohol use in a sample of fifth graders would result in a distribution with _____.

   A. Negative skew, positive skew
   B. Negative kurtosis, positive kurtosis
   C. Positive skew, negative skew
   D. Heavier tails, lighter tails

4. In a symmetrical distribution of exam scores with a single mode, which set of statistics would result in a higher percentile for an exam score of 87?

   A. $M = 90$, $SD = 3$
   B. $M = 91$, $SD = 8.5$
   C. $M = 95$, $SD = 5$
   D. $M = 89$, $SD = 4$

5. A subscale on a new measure that was developed is found to have a Cronbach's alpha of 0.92. This indicates:

   A. The subscale items load onto a single factor
   B. A subscale score based on the items would demonstrate adequate criterion validity
   C. The items adequately capture the content domain of the relevant construct
   D. The relevant items are intercorrelated

6. _____ factor analysis is used to test a priori hypotheses regarding a construct's _____.

   A. Exploratory, internal consistency
   B. Confirmatory, dimensionality
   C. Confirmatory, principal components
   D. Confirmatory, content validity

7. Which of the following statements are always true?

   A. The standard deviation must be less than the range
   B. There must be a single mode
   C. A z-score of zero must correspond to the median
   D. A and C

8. All of the following study features would increase the chances of finding an intervention effect if one exists in the population, EXCEPT:

A. Recruiting a larger sample of participants
B. Using a more stringent alpha level
C. Increasing the strength of the intervention
D. Conducting statistical analyses using latent variables

9. The standard error of the mean:

A. Is the average distance between all sample means and the population mean, for all random samples of a given size
B. Always equals the population standard deviation
C. Will increase as sample size increases
D. Will decrease as sample size decreases

10. The use of a directional hypothesis test would be most appropriate if:

A. Researchers contrasted two active treatments to see if they could be differentiated
B. Researchers contrasted a novel treatment with a no-treatment control condition
C. Researchers believed they had created a treatment that would result in significant benefit over an existing treatment
D. Researchers were interested in comparing the relative efficacy of two treatments in community-based clinical settings. In prior research, the two treatments had demonstrated comparable benefits when delivered in university-based clinics

11. Which sampling strategy is more likely to violate the independence assumption of standard parametric statistical tests?

A. Individuals are randomly sampled from neighborhoods (one individual per neighborhood)
B. Individuals are sampled from community mental health clinics (one person per clinic)
C. Students are sampled from hundreds of school districts across the United States (one student per district)
D. Clusters of students from various schools across the United States (50 students per school) were sampled

12. In a mixed model ANOVA examining the effects of sex (men vs. women), time of assessment (pretest vs. posttest), and the sex-by-time-of-assessment interaction on depression, all of the following are true, EXCEPT:

A. A sex-by-time-of-assessment interaction would indicate that the pretest to posttest change for men is different than the pretest to posttest change for women
B. A main effect of time would indicate that, on average, participants changed from pretest to posttest
C. A simple sex effect at posttest would indicate that men and women differ in their posttest depression levels
D. A simple time effect for men would indicate that men and women reported different levels of pretest depression

13. A clinician interested in examining whether average self-report of life satisfaction increased for a sample of 15 clients between the intake and termination sessions (i.e., the only two sessions at which life satisfaction was assessed), could use a:

   A. One-way between-subjects ANOVA
   B. One-way within-subjects ANOVA
   C. A paired samples t-test
   D. B and C

14. A full-factorial ANOVA model based on a study examining two treatments (cognitive behavioral vs. interpersonal) delivered in two doses (6-week vs. 12-week), with participants assessed at both pretest and posttest, would yield _____ effects?

   A. 4
   B. 3
   C. 7
   D. 6

15. A researcher is interested in testing an intervention effect (parent management training vs. play therapy) on posttest ADHD symptoms in a sample of middle school students, while statistically controlling for parent motivation to seek treatment. What would satisfaction of the homogeneity of regression lines assumption indicate?

   A. An ANCOVA test would not be an appropriate analysis
   B. The three-way intervention-group-by-parent-motivation-to-seek-treatment by-ADHD-symptoms interaction would be significant
   C. The effect of parent motivation to seek treatment on posttest ADHD symptoms is similar in the parent management training and play therapy intervention groups
   D. There is a significant interaction between intervention group and parent motivation to seek treatment in predicting posttest ADHD symptoms

16. A researcher examining a residual plot from a regression analysis in which alcohol use is predicted from age, which ranges from 12 to 19, notices that the residuals are more tightly clustered for ages 12 through 15 relative to ages 16 through 19. These data suggest the residuals

   A. Are homoscedastic
   B. Are heteroscedastic
   C. Violate the independence assumption
   D. A and C

17. The following statements reflect statistical interactions, EXCEPT:

   A. Cognitive distortions and hopelessness are unique predictors of depression
   B. The effects of stress on anxiety vary as a function of participant sex
   C. The effect of alcohol use escalation during adolescence on alcohol use disorders in young adulthood depends on family history of alcoholism
   D. Academic self-efficacy is more strongly related to undergraduate GPA in lower-income students relative to higher-income students

18. If a researcher estimated a hierarchical regression model predicting substance use frequency in late adolescence from three predictor blocks capturing five predictors (entered in this order): (1) demographics—age and sex; (2) symptoms—internalizing and externalizing; and (3) deviant peer association:

   A. The researcher could test whether the unique effects of age and sex were significant in a model including no additional predictors
   B. The researcher could test whether the demographic predictor block accounted for significant incremental variance over and above the symptom predictor block
   C. The researcher could test whether the internalizing by externalizing interaction is significant
   D. A and B

19. If a researcher was interested in examining whether an intervention produced lower levels of problematic alcohol use for clients with a higher level of baseline motivation, motivation would be a _____.

   A. Moderator
   B. Mediator
   C. Covariate
   D. Construct validity threat

20. A developmental psychopathologist interested in predicting oppositional defiant disorder diagnoses (0 = no diagnosis, 1 = diagnosis) from (a) child temperament, (b) parent antisociality, and (c) parent–child conflict, should use:

   A. An ordinary least squares multiple regression model
   B. A three-factor ANOVA model
   C. A logistic regression model
   D. A three-factor MANOVA model

21. Assume that a researcher is interested in studying parent–child conflict in low-income Spanish-speaking Mexican families living in U.S. towns along the California/Mexican border. He properly translates an instrument developed on middle-class American families of European descent. In his first study, he demonstrates that the scale's internal consistency is similar to that reported in prior studies on middle-class American families:

   A. Although internal consistency is similar to prior work, the measure might fail to capture relevant dimensions of parent–child conflict in low-income Mexican families
   B. The measure might have a different pattern of criterion validity in the low-income Mexican families
   C. The measure might sufficiently capture the construct in low-income Mexican families
   D. All of the above

22. Which of the following designs would likely result in the best relative balance between internal and external validity?

   A. An efficacy trial with a homogeneous participant pool
   B. A quasi-experiment with a homogeneous participant pool
   C. A randomized experiment conducted in a real-world setting with a diverse participant pool
   D. A quasi-experiment conducted in a real-world setting

23. Quasi-experiments:

   A. Can never be used to support a causal connection between an intervention and an outcome

   B. Are generally more vulnerable to external validity threats than are well-conducted randomized experiments

   C. Lack random assignment of units to conditions

   D. A and C

24. A researcher is interested in examining the possible causal influence of sensation seeking on risky sexual behavior in a sample of residential university students. She conducts a cross-sectional survey in which sensation seeking, risky sexual behavior, and other psychosocial outcomes are assessed ($N = 200$). She finds a strong positive association between sensation seeking and risky sexual behavior ($r^2 = .27$). Which issue(s) limits a valid causal inference?

   A. Ambiguous temporal precedence

   B. A possible spurious association between sensation seeking and risky sexual behavior

   C. Lack of random selection

   D. A and B

25. A researcher is interested in developing a theory that better accounts for how online members of a mental health website relate with one another. The current theory that is available is not easily generalized to smaller populations. She decides to observe the website without administering psychological or self-report measures. What research method should she use to help develop her theory?

   A. Quantitative design—experimental method

   B. Quantitative design—quasi-experimental method

   C. Qualitative design—phenomenological method

   D. Qualitative design—grounded theory method

26. The process of identifying and analyzing patterns within qualitative data is known as:

   A. Thematic analysis

   B. Meta-analysis

   C. Content analysis

   D. Trend analysis

27. Dr. Smith is interested in evaluating an existing program aimed at preventing teen pregnancy. The agency she works with has been funding this program for the past year and is interested in determining whether or not the program should continue to be funded next year, and whether it has been effective at achieving desired outcomes. Her evaluation includes pre- and postintervention data on variables such as teen self-esteem, knowledge of high-risk behaviors, and perceived peer pressure. What type of evaluation research will Dr. Smith carry out with these data?

   A. Formative evaluation

   B. Cost–benefit analysis

   C. Summative evaluation

   D. Needs assessment

28. Dr. Velez is studying a difficult-to-reach population, intravenous drug users at high risk for HIV infection. Which of the following sampling types is feasible and might be helpful to her in accessing this population?

A. A purposive sampling method
B. A chain-referral sampling method
C. A simple random sample of the population
D. A stratified random sample of the population

29. Researchers interested in establishing the past year prevalence of major depressive disorder among U.S. high school students would likely implement which of the following design features?

A. Simple random sampling
B. Convenience sampling
C. Simple random assignment
D. Pilot studies

30. Research that encourages the engagement of community members, Community-Based Participatory Research, often includes all of the following, EXCEPT:

A. Researchers first approaching community members following completion of a research study for feedback on next steps
B. Inclusion of community stakeholders in important study decisions (e.g., design, methods, etc.)
C. Development of objectives that include direct benefit to the community from ongoing research activities
D. Development of an equitable partnership between researchers and community members

Answers to Review Questions

1. **D. The data would occur relatively infrequently, given the specified null hypothesis and alpha level**

   A significant test statistic indicates that the data would occur relatively infrequently under the specified null hypothesis and the alpha level (which is usually set to 0.05).

2. **D. An alternative explanation for the relevant cause–effect relationship**

   Internal validity threats provide alternative explanations for the cause–effect relationship under investigation. A is related to external validity and B is related to construct validity.

3. **A. Negative skew, positive skew**

   Negative skew results when scores are piled on the high end of the scale and positive skew results when scores are piled on the low end of the scale.

4. **B. $M = 91$, $SD = 8.5$**

   The solution requires a z-score conversion. The largest z value—in this case, the one closest to zero—will have the highest associated percentile.

5. **D. The relevant items are intercorrelated**

   Cronbach's alpha is a function of scale length and inter-item correlation. A is a common misperception regarding unidimensionality, and B and C are related to validity, as opposed to reliability.

6. **B. Confirmatory, dimensionality**

   Confirmatory factor analysis is used to examine a construct's factor structure. Dimensionality is often used as a synonym for factor structure. Principal-components analysis is commonly considered a type of exploratory factor analysis, although it is a different statistical model.

7. **A. The standard deviation must be less than the range**

   The range is the maximum distance between two scores and the standard deviation is the average distance among scores. Distributions can have more than one mode, and a z-score of 0 will always equal the mean, but will not always equal the median.

8. **B. Using a more stringent alpha level**

   The question is relevant to statistical power—that is, the probability of finding an intervention effect if one exists in the population. Larger samples yield more powerful statistical tests. Increasing the strength of the intervention will increase the magnitude of the effect—also resulting in more power. Conducting analyses using latent variables reduced measurement error—also resulting in more power. A more stringent alpha decreases power.

9. **A. Is the average distance between all sample means and the population mean, for all random samples of a given size**

The correct answer is an appropriate description. B is true when the population standard deviation is known and N = 1. C and D are false because standard errors decrease as sample sizes increase.

10. **C. Researchers believed they had created a treatment that would result in significant benefit over an existing treatment**

Directional hypothesis tests are used when researchers have specific ideas about the relative benefits of treatments. C is the only response in which this specificity is explicit.

11. **D. Clusters of students from various schools across the United States (50 students per school) were sampled**

This strategy is more likely to violate the independence assumption because students are clustered or nested within schools, which typically results in correlated observations among students sampled from the same schools.

12. **D. A simple time effect for men would indicate that men and women reported different levels of pretest depression**

This question taps information related to main effects and interactions. A is a way of describing an interaction, B describes a main effect of time, C describes the simple sex effect at posttest, and D describes a simple sex effect at pretest.

13. **D. B and C**

The scenario suggests examining mean differences on a pair of observations from a single group of participants, which could be analyzed by either a paired samples t-test or a one-way within-subjects ANOVA. The between-subjects ANOVA suggests two distinct groups of participants.

14. **C. 7**

Full-factorial designs estimate all main and interaction effects. In the present scenario, there are 3 main effects, 3 two-way interactions, and 1 three-way interaction.

15. **C. The effect of parent motivation to seek treatment on posttest ADHD symptoms is similar in the parent management training and play therapy intervention groups**

C is another way of stating that the covariate does not interact with the primary independent variable (i.e., intervention group). Satisfaction of the homogeneity of regression lines assumption rules this interaction out. B is incorrect because it includes the dependent variable in an interaction; only independent variables can interact.

16. **B. Are heteroscedastic**

Heteroscedasticity results when the variance of the residuals is not constant across the range of x values.

17. **A. Cognitive distortions and hopelessness are unique predictors of depression**

    In A, the two effects are independent (and additive). In the remaining scenarios, two predictors interact in predicting the outcome.

18. **A. The researcher could test whether the unique effects of age and sex were significant in a model including no additional predictors**

    The test of age and sex in isolation is given by the regression coefficients relevant to the first predictor block (before the model is augmented by the remaining predictors).

19. **A. Moderator**

    Moderators are variables that interact with other variables in predicting an outcome. In this scenario, exposure to the intervention is the primary predictor variable, motivation is the moderator, and depression is the dependent variable.

20. **C. A logistic regression model**

    In this analysis, the outcome variable is dichotomous. Of the modeling options, logistic regression is the only appropriate one.

21. **D. All of the above**

    Although a single data point showing a similar level of internal consistency is a start to empirically examining the measure and construct in the novel sample (i.e., low-income Mexican families), much additional work is needed to better understand the construct and its relation to other constructs in the novel sample.

22. **C. A randomized experiment conducted in a real-world setting with a diverse participant pool**

    Elements of efficacy and effectiveness trials are combined to provide a hybrid design that offers a balance between internal and external validity.

23. **C. Lack random assignment of units to conditions**

    Some quasi-experiments produce valid causal inferences, which rules out A. B would be true if "external" were replaced with "internal."

24. **D. A and B**

    The cross-sectional study fails to establish temporal precedence between sensation seeking and risky sexual behavior. It is also possible that the observed positive association is driven by a common cause (e.g., a broader personality characteristic).

25. **D. Qualitative design—grounded theory method**

    Grounded theory is a qualitative research design that aims to generate a new theory that explains people's experiences and behaviors. It is used when the current theory is lacking, incomplete, or nonexistent. Phenomenological methods C are used when examining individual participant's lived experiences to capture the "essence" of their lives.

26. A. Thematic analysis

Thematic analysis is a method of qualitative analysis that seeks to identify and analyze patterns (or themes) as they emerge within qualitative data. Content analysis, often confused with thematic analysis, counts the number of times a particular concept occurs allowing it to be captured quantitatively.

27. C. Summative evaluation

A summative evaluation can be used to determine whether a program has achieved desired outcomes, whereas formative evaluations, A, are aimed at examining ongoing outcomes in order to develop a new program or improve the effectiveness of an existing program.

28. B. A chain-referral sampling method

A chain-referral sampling method, such as snowball or respondent-driven sampling, will help Dr. Velez access a difficult-to-reach population, because participants will invite other eligible members of their community to participate.

29. A. Simple random sampling

Of the sampling options listed, simple random sampling will provide the best base rate estimated. Although not a response option, stratified random sampling could have been proposed with year in school or age used to form the strata.

30. A. Researchers approaching community members following completion of a research study for feedback on next steps

Researchers in CBPR engage community members in partnerships prior to engaging in research, so that they can develop an equitable partnership (D), ensure benefits to the community from the research (C), and include stakeholders in important study decisions right from the onset (B).

8

Ethical/Legal/Professional Issues

Wayne G. Siegel and John Beauvais

Broad Content Areas

- Codes of ethics
- Professional standards for practice
- Legal mandates and restrictions
- Guidelines for ethical decision making
- Professional training and supervision

The ethical, legal, and professional issues portion of the EPPP is a demanding section that requires the applicant to understand broad and general principals and then apply that knowledge to specific situations. When reading this chapter, one might reason that many of the dilemmas are unlikely to be encountered in someone's specific practice setting. Although that may be true, the expectation is that licensed psychologists understand the rules and ideals described below as they apply to all of psychology. Also, unlike many of the other chapters in this book that have very specific content that is covered, this domain area is ever changing with the times, is often debated, and often ends in no definitive "right or wrong" answer. Most recently, for example, the *American Psychologist* dedicated the majority of an issue to updating ethical guidelines and standards for practice in health care delivery systems, forensic psychology, and in conducting psychological evaluations in child protection matters (American Psychological Association [APA], 2013a, 2013b, 2013c). To better prepare for the EPPP, one must develop a working knowledge of ethical issues so that the best option can be made from available answer choices.

In this chapter, topics that will be highlighted include the APA Ethical Principles of Psychologists and Code of Ethics, professional standards for practice, legal expectations, guidelines for ethical decision making, and professional training and supervision. The information contained in this chapter should not be considered exhaustive. It represents our best effort to raise awareness of the issues and what we believe to be important to the practice of professional psychology.

Ethics Codes and Professional Conduct

The section of the EPPP pertaining to ethical principles and codes of psychologists typically consist of items requiring application of the American Psychological Association's (APA) Ethical Principles of Psychologists and Code of Conduct (APA, 2002a, 2010b) or the Canadian Psychological Association's (CPA) Canadian Code of Ethics for Psychologists (CPA, 2000) to real-life scenarios and dilemmas. Test items regarding ethics are written and selected on the basis of whether or not they can be answered correctly by studying either the APA or CPA codes of ethics, so there is no need to study both the APA and CPA codes (ASPPB Website, 2012).

The American Psychological Association's (APA, 2002a) ethical code features two distinct sections: General Principles and Ethical Standards. Each of these sections guides one toward ethical behavior in a different way. The General Principles are more general and aspirational; they describe an ideal level of ethical behavior toward which psychologists should strive.

Beneficence and Nonmaleficence—Do good; avoid harm. For example, a psychologist should not provide services that are inappropriate or proven to be ineffective such as conversion therapy for gay, lesbian, bisexual, or transgender clients.

Fidelity and Responsibility—Develop trust; accept responsibility of work; uphold professional standards of conduct. For example, in all their interactions, psychologists should engage in behavior that fosters trust and confidence in the profession. This includes but is not limited to behaving ethically and taking appropriate actions when they are aware that other psychologists are not behaving in an ethical manner.

Integrity—Maximize benefits and minimize harm through accuracy and honesty. For example, a psychologist should not misrepresent his or her services to the public or effectiveness of those services. If one enters into an agreement to teach a class, one would not back out of that commitment unless there were highly unusual or unforeseeable circumstances.

Justice—Exercise competence and reasonable judgment. For example, a psychologist may choose to engage in pro bono work or reduce fees for certain clients or groups in order to make effective psychological services available to individuals who might otherwise not have access to such services. Another example would be that when working with a sex offender, the psychologist should acknowledge feelings about the individual criminal behavior but not let that interfere with the individual's right to effective psychological services.

Respect for People's Rights and Dignity—Respect autonomy; maintain professional boundaries; preserve confidentiality and privacy. For instance, in the example above, the psychologist recognized that an individual convicted of a sexual offence, like all individuals, possesses basic human rights and is entitled to effective services.

In contrast to the General Principles section, the Ethical Standards section includes more specific enforceable rules. They are more specific than the General Principles but are broad enough to cover the great range of activities in which psychologists engage. The Standards consist of 89 individual standards within the following 10 categories: In preparation for the EPPP, it is important that the student study these standards closely and identify hypothetical scenarios in which they may apply in real-world practice.

Standard 1: Resolving Ethical Issues
1.01 Misuse of Psychologists' Work
1.02 Conflicts between Ethics and Law, Regulations, or Other Governing Legal Authority
1.03 Conflicts between Ethics and Organizational Demands
1.04 Informal Resolution of Ethical Violations
1.05 Cooperating with Ethics Committees
1.06 Improper Complaints
1.07 Unfair Discrimination Against Complainants and Respondents

Standard 2: Competence
2.01 Boundaries of Competence
2.02 Maintaining Competence
2.03 Bases for Scientific and Professional Judgments
2.04 Delegation of Work to Others
2.05 Personal Problems and Conflicts

Standard 3: Human Relations
3.01 Unfair Discrimination
3.02 Sexual Harassment
3.03 Other Harassment
3.04 Avoiding Harm
3.05 Conflict of Interest
3.06 Third-Party Requests for Services
3.07 Exploitative Relationships
3.08 Cooperation with Other Professionals
3.09 Psychological Services Delivered to or Through Organizations
3.10 Interruption of Psychological Services

Standard 4: Privacy and Confidentiality
4.01 Maintaining Confidentiality
4.02 Discussing the Limits of Confidentiality
4.03 Recording
4.04 Disclosures
4.05 Consultations
4.06 Use of Confidential Information for Didactic or Other Purposes

Standard 5: Advertising and Other Public Statements
5.01 Avoidance of False or Deceptive Statements
5.02 Descriptions of Workshops and Non-Degree-Granting Educational Programs
5.03 Media Presentations
5.04 Testimonials
5.05 In-Person Solicitation

Standard 6: Record Keeping and Fees
6.01 Documentation of Professional and Scientific Work and Maintenance of Records
6.02 Maintenance, Dissemination, and Disposal of Confidential Records of Professional and Scientific Work

6.03 Withholding Records for Nonpayment
6.04 Fees and Financial Arrangements
6.05 Barter with Clients/Patients
6.06 Accuracy in Reports to Payors and Funding Sources
6.07 Referrals and Fees

Standard 7: Education and Training
7.01 Design of Education and Training Programs
7.02 Descriptions of Education and Training Programs
7.03 Student Disclosure of Personal Information
7.04 Mandatory Individual or Group Therapy
7.05 Assessing Student and Supervisee Performance
7.06 Sexual Relationships with Students and Supervisees

Standard 8: Research and Publication
8.01 Institutional Approval
8.02 Informed Consent for Recording Voices and Images in Research
8.03 Client/Patient, Student, and Subordinate Research Participants
8.04 Dispensing with Informed Consent for Research
8.05 Offering Inducements for Research Participation
8.06 Deception in Research
8.07 Humane Care and Use of Animals in Research
8.08 Reporting Research Results
8.09 Plagiarism
8.10 Publication Credit
8.11 Duplicate Publication of Data
8.12 Reviewers

Standard 9: Assessment
9.01 Bases for Assessments
9.02 Use of Assessments
9.03 Release of Test Data
9.04 Test Construction
9.05 Interpreting Assessment Results
9.06 Assessment by Unqualified Persons
9.07 Obsolete Tests and Outdated Test Results
9.08 Test Scoring and Interpretation Services
9.09 Maintaining Test Security

Standard 10: Therapy
10.01 Informed Consent to Therapy
10.02 Therapy Involving Couples or Families
10.03 Group Therapy
10.04 Providing Therapy to Those Served by Others
10.05 Sexual Intimacies with Current Therapy Clients/Patients
10.06 Sexual Intimacies with Relatives or Significant Others of Current Therapy Clients/Patients
10.07 Therapy with Former Sexual Partners
10.08 Sexual Intimacies with Former Therapy Clients/Patients
10.09 Interruption of Therapy
10.10 Terminating Therapy

The Canadian Psychological Association's (CPA, 2000) Canadian Code of Ethics for Psychologists addresses many of the same issues as the APA Code but it is structured differently. It is categorized into four main principles:

Principle I: Respect for the Dignity of Persons. This principle, with its emphasis on moral rights, generally should be given the highest weight, except in circumstances in which there is a clear and imminent danger to the physical safety of any person.

Principle II: Responsible Caring. This principle generally should be given the second highest weight. Responsible caring requires competence and should be carried out only in ways that respect the dignity of persons.

Principle III: Integrity in Relationships. This principle generally should be given the third highest weight. Psychologists are expected to demonstrate the highest integrity in all of their relationships. However, in rare circumstances, values such as openness and straightforwardness might need to be subordinated to the values contained in the Principles of Respect for the Dignity of Persons and Responsible Caring.

Principle IV: Responsibility to Society. This principle generally should be given the lowest weight of the four principles when it conflicts with one or more of them. Although it is necessary and important to consider responsibility to society in every ethical decision, adherence to this principle must be subject to and guided by Respect for the Dignity of Persons, Responsible Caring, and Integrity in Relationships. When a person's welfare appears to conflict with benefits to society, it is often possible to find ways of working for the benefit of society that do not violate respect and responsible caring for the person. However, if this is not possible, the dignity and well-being of a person should not be sacrificed to a vision of the greater good of society, and greater weight must be given to respect and responsible caring for the person.

The Association of State and Provincial Psychology Boards has also developed the ASPPB Code of Conduct (ASPPB, 2005). ASPPB indicates its code differs from the APA and CPA codes in that it represents the profession's own standards and guidelines to its members and is intended to protect the public welfare and promote the integrity of the profession. The ASPPB Code is less specific yet still addresses aspirational issues, enforceable issues, professional matters, and regulatory matters. In the end, it covers areas similar to both the APA and CPA codes. Knowledge specific to the ASPPB Code is not required in order to be successful on the EPPP. The ASPPB Code of Conduct is structured as follows:

   I. Introduction
  II. Definitions
 III. Rules of Conduct
     A. Competence
     B. Multiple Relationships
     C. Impairment
     D. Client Welfare
     E. Welfare of Supervisees, Research Participants and Students
     F. Protecting Confidentiality of Clients

G. Representation of Services

H. Fees and Statements

I. Assessment Procedures

J. Violations of Law

K. Aiding Unauthorized Practice

L. Reporting Suspected Violations

Again, to be successful on the Ethics Codes and Professional Conduct portion of the EPPP, one should have a strong working knowledge of the Code(s) and how to apply them to a range of situations and scenarios. It may be of further benefit to approach these items within the context of 10 common pitfalls identified by Smith (2003)—Understand Multiple Relationships, Protect Confidentiality, Respect Autonomy, Know Supervisory Responsibilities, Identify Client and Role, Document, Practice in Area of Expertise, Abandonment vs. Termination, Stick to the Evidence, and be Accurate in Billing.

Professional Standards for the Practice of Psychology

One might expect that this domain is relatively straightforward; in essence, be competent in what you do and do not practice outside those areas of expertise. However, with ever-changing state laws and regulations it is important for both the novice and seasoned practitioner to be apprised of the expectations that govern ethical, professional practice, as there are increasing amounts of questions and fewer clear-cut answers. The Health Insurance Portability and Accountability Act of 1996 (HIPAA) regulations, third-party observer effects, friending patients or trainees on social media, disclosure of test data, and evidence-based practice are only a few of the domains in which professionals encounter important practice decisions.

Competence

When and how does one obtain competence? During graduate school training, programs consistently monitor whether or not students are making progress toward broad-based, professional competencies in the practice of psychology. A similar process is expected at the internship level, whereas greater specificity is common at the postgraduate level. If the continuum of programs described above is accredited by APA's Commission on Accreditation (CoA), when a person graduates from such a program, many states will use this information as a proxy for competency to determine whether a person is appropriate for licensure. States may also require additional information ranging from identifying specific courses taken, supervision documentation, completion of a jurisprudence exam, and of course, to successful passing of the EPPP! Additionally, many hospitals have further expectations of one's ability to demonstrate competency before issuing either practice or research privileges. Further, specialty areas have developed guidelines for advanced levels of practice. Almost all state and provincial psychology boards have requirements for ongoing continuing-education requirements intended to maintain a level of competence. Data specific to each state can be found on the ASPPB website.

Although the Ethical Principles explain that the boundaries of competency encompass one's "education, training, supervised experience, consulting, or professional experience," both colleagues and employers alike will impose beliefs and expectations about what this means in everyday practice. Questions that may arise include: how much training in neuropsychology is expected for someone to independently administer and interpret tests; what competencies are expected if someone calls himself or herself a clinical health psychologist; how does one incorporate culture into his or her professional practice at the level of providing services; and if a psychologist wants to practice in an area that is previously unfamiliar to him or her, how does he or she obtain the requisite training and experience to be deemed competent? The opinions and resources available to answer these questions can be daunting; however, the process of researching and evaluating the merits of each position (discussed later in this chapter), will help the practitioner determine what answer is in the best interest of his or her client, trainee, and/or research.

(When) To Be or Not To Be a Psychologist?

It is not always clear when psychologists are in positions of responsibility. In several states, psychologists have an obligation to intervene as mandated reporters even when they are not functioning in their practitioner role (Behnke, 2007). For example, in some states if you learn that a child is being abused while not in your professional role, say, at a local sporting event, one would have the same obligation to report as if the information was acquired in your office or another professional context. In other states, the duty to act is more ambiguous. In emergent situations, where the clinician may have less expertise, the APA Ethics Code suggests that clinical help can be offered "to ensure that services are not denied... but are discontinued as soon as the emergency has ended or appropriate service is available." In other types of situations and training settings, psychologists possess the ability to delegate responsibilities to others (e.g., students and research assistants), provided they make sure they take responsibility for the work being performed under their authority. This provision of the Ethics Code suggests that psychologists ensure the competency of the individuals delegated to perform the tasks, provide supervision as appropriate, and avoid dual relationships. Also, a psychologist should be aware of how his or her job potentially influences his or her private life and vice versa. If a psychologist experiences a reduction in his or her capacity to effectively perform his or her job (e.g., medically), he or she has an ethical responsibility to seek help and to determine whether he or she is fit to continue with work-related activities.

Testing

The competent administration and interpretation of educational, psychological, and neuropsychological instruments is a skill that can take many years of study and practice to develop, under appropriate supervision. Practitioners debate the amount and type of training that is sufficient to meet this threshold; yet all practitioners should be aware of the boundaries of their expertise and the ethics of providing appropriate assessments to the populations they serve. First, clinicians need to ensure that tests and normative data are appropriate for each person they evaluate (e.g., whether they are current or obsolete) and that copyright laws on each test measure are followed. Second, informed consent should cover multiple areas such as the purpose of the evaluation, limits of confidentiality, payment structure, supervisory relationships (if trainees or a staff person are involved with clients), how the data will be stored and protected, interpretation considerations (e.g., how is culture incorporated into the findings), how the results will be disseminated, and so forth. Although standard administration settings are the goal, it is not uncommon for the psychologist to amend administration protocols on occasion, but in doing so, should recognize and describe the potential influence on the validity and reliability of the evaluation. For example, some argue that it is not acceptable for a spouse, psychiatry resident, or attorney to be in the room for an evaluation as the bias it may create outweighs the potential benefits (American Academy of Clinical Neuropsychology, 2001).

The Standards for Educational and Psychological Testing (AERA, APA, and National Council on Measurement in Education [NCME], 1999) incorporate the principles noted above as well as provide a comprehensive overview of standards related to the use of psychological tests. Although the standards are currently being revised, one should be familiar with them to be successful on the EPPP. Persons taking the EPPP should also be aware that questions on these topics may cross the boundary between the "Ethics/Professional Issues" domain and other sections. An outline of the current standards is listed below:

> Part I: Test Construction, Evaluation, and Documentation
> Validity
> Reliability and Errors of Measurement
> Test Development and Revision
> Scales, Norms, and Score Comparability
> Test Administration, Scoring, and Reporting
> Supporting Documentation for Tests
>
> Part II: Fairness in Testing
> Fairness in Testing and Test Use
> The Rights and Responsibilities of Test Takers
> Testing Individuals of Diverse Linguistic Backgrounds
> Testing Individuals with Disabilities
>
> Part III: Testing Applications
> The Responsibilities of Test Users
> Psychological Testing and Assessment
> Educational Testing and Assessment
> Testing in Employment and Credentialing
> Testing in Program Evaluation and Public Policy

Guidelines and Standards

As mentioned in the first paragraph, APA recently came out with three documents updating the expectations for the practice of psychology that are largely aspirational in intent and complement the more thorough listing of guidelines and standards listed at the end of this chapter. In the first article, which focuses on practice in health care delivery systems, the authors highlight the expanding role of psychology in health care and especially in multidisciplinary settings (APA, 2013a). The guidelines highlight many tenets, including: provide services within the boundaries of their competence, provide informed consent about the treatment setting and system expectations, pursue appropriate staff appointments and privileges, seek continuing education (CE), and be collaborative with other disciplines. In the second article, focusing on guidelines for forensic psychologists, major highlights for the clinician to be aware of include: be accurate, honest and unbiased; avoid conflicts of interest; be competent; do not provide formal legal advice; be specific in defining the therapeutic versus forensic role; describe limits to confidentiality; strive to avoid contingency fees (minimizing potential bias) and provide some level of pro bono service; provide full informed consent, and so forth (APA, 2013b). Although these and many other points are discussed in detail, the article also offers sage advice on how to handle conflicts with other providers about an ethical issue. Specifically, a first attempt should be made to resolve the issue by speaking with the provider for an informal resolution (if the action does not violate any rights), as opposed to immediately making a report to a third party. The third article (APA, 2013c) focuses on conducting psychological evaluations in child protection matters; it again highlights that, like the others, they are aspirational in intent. Content covered in this document includes: be impartial and competent (otherwise refer out or gain appropriate supervision/consultation); avoid multiple relationships; apply appropriate methods to respond to the referral question; provide informed consent; and define limits to confidentiality, data, and evaluation procedures. As in the second article, strong advice is peppered throughout, such as the recommendation to refrain from providing specific opinions of "fit" between a parent and child if the parties involved were not all personally evaluated by the clinician.

Laws, Statutes, and Judicial Decisions That Affect Psychological Practice

The section of the EPPP pertaining to federal, state, and provincial laws/statutes and/or jurisdiction decisions that affect practice does not require knowledge of specific laws, statutes or decisions. It would be impossible to have specific knowledge of each state's or province's regulations (as an example, the student may want to review the laws of the state in which he or she plans to get licensed). Therefore, EPPP items in this area tend to be more generic and relate to how one applies the laws, statutes, and decisions to real-life clinical and professional situations, and how they may be consistent or in conflict with ethical codes. Items likely reflect what one would do in a particular situation or scenario. For example, if you are working with a client who threatens suicide, this can compete with the APA Code Section 4.01 Maintaining Confidentiality. This section indicates, "Psychologists have a primary obligation and take reasonable precautions to protect confidential information." However, Principle A: Beneficence and Nonmaleficence, suggests we should not take actions that may harm others while also trying to benefit others. In the current scenario, a psychologist may need to violate confidentiality in order to benefit and prevent harm to his or her client. In each specific situation, the psychologist needs to determine which ethical principle or standard should take precedence. In some situations, the correct decision may be obvious but this is not always the case. Consultation is strongly advised when possible.

Sometimes, individuals or bodies that develop laws, statutes, and rules are often not well versed in codes of ethics, and it is not possible for them to anticipate every situation that may arise. It is important to be able to balance what is required by a specific law or statute and what is ethical according to the profession's code. The answer may not always be obvious and requires one to think through the process. It is this process that EPPP items are attempting to assess.

The APA Ethical Principles of Psychologists and Code of Ethics (2002), has a section dedicated specifically to such situations. "Conflicts Between Ethics and Law, Regulations, or Other Governing Legal Authority" states, "If psychologists' ethical responsibilities conflict with law, regulations, or other governing legal authority, psychologists clarify the nature of the conflict, make known their commitment to the Ethics Code, and take reasonable steps to resolve the conflict consistent with the General Principles and Ethical Standards of the Ethics Code. Under no circumstances may this standard be used to justify or defend violating human rights." For example, if a psychologist is subpoenaed to testify against his or her client, he or she would be violating APA Code Section 4.01 Maintaining Confidentiality. By law, the psychologist must show up in court but should assert his or her obligation to maintain confidentiality. In most situations, the judge will order the psychologist to answer the question(s). The psychologist must comply under these circumstances but should be direct and try to not go beyond answering the question(s) that are asked. Questions on the EPPP attempt to tap the knowledge and judgment the test takers need so that they can adhere to laws, statutes, and rules as well as their ability to balance this requirement with the ethical code.

Potential Ethical Dilemmas Associated With Specific Areas of Practice

An ethical dilemma can be defined as "a situation that often involves an apparent conflict between moral imperatives, in which to obey one would result in transgressing another." Regarding the practice of psychology, this may involve conflict between the ethical code of conduct and state or federal statutes or regulations. It may also involve conflict between state or federal statutes or regulations and what you may believe to be in your client's best interest. In relation to the EPPP, ASPPB references the following areas where potential ethical dilemmas may arise: practice management, supervision, multiple relationships (group and family counseling), and ethical issues associated with specific areas of practice (e.g., forensic, law enforcement, psychopharmacology, and dealing with third-party payors). However, given the broad scope that the practice of psychology can take, the potential for conflicts or competing demands is endless.

Given the diversity and complexities of the practice of psychology, it is not possible to develop prescriptive policies or guidelines to address all potential conflicts. In most situations, one must weigh two rights or the lesser of two negatives. The Ethical Principles of Psychologists and Code of Conduct provide some vague guidance. In the Code's introduction, it states:

> In the process of making decisions regarding their professional behavior, psychologists must consider this Ethics code in addition to applicable laws and psychology board regulations. In applying the Ethics code to their professional work, psychologists may consider other materials and guidelines that have been adopted or endorsed by scientific and professional psychological organizations and the dictates of their own conscience, as well as consult with others within the field. If this Ethics code establishes a higher standard of conduct than is required by law, psychologists must meet the higher ethical standard. If psychologists' ethical responsibilities conflict with law, regulations, or other governing legal authority,

psychologists make known their commitment to this Ethics code and take steps to resolve the conflict in a responsible manner in keeping with basic principles of human rights. Section I of the Code, Resolving Ethical Issues, addresses the Misuse of Psychologists' Work (1.01), Conflicts Between Ethics and Law, Regulations, or Other Governing Legal Authority (1.02), and Conflicts Between Ethics and Organizational Demands (1.03). For most matters, the code suggests reasonable steps be taken to resolve the conflict that are consistent with the code and under no circumstances may the codes be used to defend violating human rights. (APA, 2010, p. 4)

Models of Ethical Decision-Making Process

Many students and professional psychologists have not had formal coursework in ethics and even fewer consider themselves to be ethicists. However, what clinicians should possess is a framework for recognizing and conceptualizing issues in order to properly handle an ethical conflict. In medicine, courses and books are frequently used to help understand moral foundations, principles, theories, and methodologies (e.g., Beauchamp & Childress, 2009). In clinical psychology, graduate programs vary in the depth that decision making in ethics is taught, but ultimately, is essential for day-to-day practice of professional psychology. In considering your background in ethics, take a moment and think about what issues have come up in graduate school or in your practice; undoubtedly, you have already experienced different levels of ethical dilemmas. Some of the issues that often come to mind are straightforward and clearly "against the rules" (e.g., maintain professional boundaries with clients). Other issues may be more subtle, and your internal compass tells you that something does not seem right and that you feel a need for clarification and resolution. In these moments, it is helpful to have a process to engage in when evaluating the situation.

Ethical theory revolves around four basic concepts: respect for autonomy, nonmaleficence, beneficence, and justice. Autonomy is the right to make decisions about one's own life and body without coercion by others; nonmaleficence is essentially, "do no harm"; beneficence is the attempt to "do good," and justice calls for people to be treated fairly and similarly. Although variations in meaning are frequently applied to these concepts, it is the application into everyday settings that sets the stage for ethical or nonethical practice. For example, should a psychologist be able to barter for service with some of his or her clients? Should a clinician be able to talk a client out of certain behaviors as this might be interfering with his or her autonomy? When a clinician practices outside of his or her area of expertise, is this maleficence? In the first two questions, it depends on the context. That is, for example, a psychologist can barter if it is not contraindicated to treatment and is not considered exploitative. In the third question, the decision is seemingly clear: only practice in those areas you are competent in. However, a clinician should be aware of alternative solutions to manage the situation in ethical ways (i.e., a clinician can take courses or receive supervision in order to expand the boundaries of his or her competency area).

In considering ethical decision making, multiple perspectives of ethical theory can be employed to help understand how to consider and apply the values contained in the General Principles and Ethical Standards. For a hypothetical example, if someone wants to set up a rural practice where there is a scarceness of resources in the community, he or she may view the ethical code differently depending on his or her perspective of justice, that is, if he or she follows a utilitarian perspective, he or she may try to maximize his or her practice for the common good (i.e., help as many people as he or she can); a libertarian perspective may encourage a practice that helps protect his or her personal rights and property, whereas an egalitarian perspective of justice may influence a clinician to focus on helping those who have the most significant need (Beauchamp & Childress, 1999). As a second example, what should a clinician do if his or her patient asks him or her to fill out a form documenting a disability when there is little evidence the patient has the condition in question, but does believe the patient could use some support? Should the psychologist go ahead with filling it out? From a utilitarian perspective, a psychologist might view his or her role as one that helps all his or her patients as best he or she can and therefore may decide to complete the form. From an egalitarian perspective, the psychologist might feel that filling out the form may deprive others who are more deserving or who have the greatest need. For many, this can be a difficult choice. However, the true process of ethical practice starts with an understanding of the basic principles and then applying them to a situation, which leads to one or more ethically justifiable decisions. Yet, as stated above, when something just does not feel right, it is important to try to understand and define both the ethical conflict and the values that underlie the conflict. One should also gather relevant information in deciding what to do by talking with trusted colleagues, by reviewing the General Principles and Ethical Standards, by searching the web, by calling APA and/or your state ethics board, and even by consulting with your insurer or attorney. Not all ethical conflicts will be addressed and/or answered by these resources, but it is the psychologist's responsibility to seek help when and where needed.

Models and Approaches for Professional Development

Throughout graduate school, the sequence of focus and clinical experiences allows a student to develop basic skills as a professional psychologist. On internship and postdoctoral training, more advanced broad and general skills are developed under close supervision within the context of an organized program. The question is how does one continue to build these skills and know the limits of his or her competencies once a licensed professional? Alternatively, how does the client know you have the skills to help him or her?

Training programs are geared toward meeting expectations put forth by the American Psychological Association's Commission on Accreditation (CoA) and ultimately, state and provincial licensing boards. These groups are interested in making sure that by completing courses and experiences, defined goals and requirements are met. In accredited graduate psychology doctoral programs, all class content is supposed to be up to date and accurate.

Learning and professional development do not stop once the doctoral degree is obtained and licensure occurs. The APA Code Section 2.03 necessitates that psychologists undertake ongoing efforts even when states do not have explicit requirements for CE. However, most states require psychologists to present proof every 2 years that they have attended ongoing CE and there is usually a specific hour requirement every 1 or 2 years. Some states and provinces require ongoing education in specific areas such as in ethics and supervision. Regardless of licensure requirements, the APA Code requires that psychologists stay up to date on the effectiveness of treatments and not use outdated tests; they also need to stay current with regard to research on treatment and interventions. Some may do this in formal ways: through classes, seminars, and other continuing-education activities. Others may make do by reading journals and attending conferences. Sometimes, obtaining the required CE credits and staying current with new treatments, assessment techniques, and course content materials can be quite challenging for those in solo or small group practices. Conversely, it is often easier for those in large group practices or institutional settings to stay compliant with CE requirements as they may have frequent contact with other psychologists and may have additional opportunities for invited lectures and rounds. In such settings, there are also multiple opportunities for formal and informal peer consultation.

As one's career progresses, one may find that the focus of his or her career shifts due to new interests or due to the demands of the setting where one works. In such cases, psychologists must seek out the knowledge and/or clinical skills to ensure they are competent in these new areas. Section 2.01 of the APA Code dictates that psychologists provide services, teach, and conduct research with populations and in areas only within the boundaries of their competence; based on their education, training, supervised experience, consultation, study, or professional experience. And, section 2.01.c of the APA Code states that (c) Psychologists planning to provide services, teach, or conduct research involving populations, areas, techniques, or technologies new to them undertake relevant education, training, supervised experience, consultation, or study. Most state and provincial licensure boards, in addition to hospitals, require that psychologists submit or declare areas of competence. Typically, areas of competence are not well defined with specific required criteria. The burden usually rests with the psychologist to demonstrate that he or she has adequate training in a particular area if challenged.

In some areas of practice, psychologists can obtain certification of advanced training. The American Board of Professional Psychology (ABPP) is the most widely known and accepted credentialing group. In a range of specialty areas, including but not limited to neuropsychology, health psychology, and rehabilitation psychology, the respective specialty area has established detailed educational and training criteria and a peer-reviewed examination process to establish certification in a specialty. Specialty certification is more the norm in the profession of medicine but it is becoming more widely accepted and even expected in psychology.

Patient's/Client's Rights

Government and professional agencies have been very active in recent years with regard to ensuring the protection of patient rights. The Health Insurance Portability and Accountability Act of 1996 is likely the most well known of these reforms and its implications are significant for the clinician who works either in a hospital setting or in private practice. From the moment a patient walks into your facility or office, and you start interacting with him or her, multiple regulations come into play. For starters, psychologists have an obligation to obtain consent. APA Code, Section 3.01 dictates that "when psychologists conduct research or provide assessment, therapy, counseling, or consulting services in person or via electronic transmission or other forms of communication, they obtain the informed consent of the individual or individuals using language that is reasonably understandable to that person or persons" (p. 6). Of particular note, the obligation is that the individual understands what he or she is agreeing to and not just signing a piece of paper. Similarly, when working with minors or other individuals who are not capable of providing legal consent, there is an expectation that the psychologist obtains his or her assent to the level at which the individual is capable. The point here is that the individual is to be treated with respect and dignity even though he or she is not capable of providing legal consent.

As important as obtaining consent is protecting client's confidentiality. Principle E and Section 4 of the APA Code address this in detail and highlight that individuals need to be treated with dignity and worth and have their rights to privacy respected. This can be as simple as neither confirming, nor denying, that someone is engaged in treatment with you and can be as complex as going to court in defending the release of information. It is essential that from the onset of the therapist–patient relationship the limits of confidentiality are properly discussed. Questions like, "can you talk to family members about the condition; how will the information about me be shared with other providers within the hospital setting; what information might be released to secure payments from an insurance company and can any communication be accomplished via e-mail?" are all viable possibilities and are likely to be encountered in your everyday practice.

It is important that given the type and nature of your practice that proper procedures are in place so that ethical practice is never compromised and that questions like the ones just presented are reasonably addressed. In many settings, a written informed consent about these practices is completed, and often revisited at points throughout the course of treatment. It is always your patient's prerogative to refuse treatment and clinicians need to be respectful of that decision. If you work with students, not only do you need to explain the supervisory relationship to your patients, but it is also expected that if voice or images are used for supervision, permission be granted by the patients and ideally, include a discussion on how, when, and where the information will be handled and ultimately destroyed. Supervisors must also be careful that, when information is shared from their practice (e.g., a sample report or consultation to another provider), privacy is maintained and the minimal amount of identifying information is relayed. However, although privacy is protected, it is not absolute. In situations in which there is an intent to harm self or others, in cases of abuse, or by court order, psychologists may have an obligation to break confidentiality and report information to the authorities.

There are also scenarios in which a psychologist may need to make decisions contrary to a patient's desire or wishes. For example, when treating a minor, the psychologist often has an agreement with the parent(s) that certain information can remain within the context of the therapeutic relationship. However, certain information may need to be shared, sometimes against the minor's wishes. Similarly, if the psychologist believes his or her client is a risk to self or others, he or she is obligated ethically, as well as by most state and provincial laws, to take action to try and prevent harm to self or others from occurring (and where prevention involves a duty to both warn and protect and may include being hospitalized against the patient's will). In all such situations, the psychologist must be cognizant of the individual's rights and take the least intrusive or restrictive action possible, while still meeting safety and legal obligations.

Ethics in Research

The protection of patients in research is of critical importance as researchers continue to advance the profession by exploring all new avenues of treatment for patients. Research can range from the molecular level to large-scale interventional studies. For any type of research, there are essential safeguards that need to be followed before any work can be initiated.

No matter what your agency calls it, clinicians who participate in research are advised to seek review through their local institutional review board (IRB). In many circumstances, this is a group of people who will look at a proposed study to help ensure that the potential benefits outweigh the potential risks, that safeguards are followed, and in some cases, that the proposed methodological plan is solid. After given much information from an investigator, the IRB will decide how an approved research protocol is going to be conducted. However, "research" is not a term that is always easy to define. In many settings, the routine evaluation of clinic functions for performance improvement may not formally qualify as "research" and may be approved for an expedited review, or possibly, may not necessitate an IRB review at all.

In the APA Ethical Principles of Psychologists and Code of Ethics, Section 8 deals with many essential requirements of research (e.g., when is institutional approval required, how is informed consent acquired, what is included in the informed consent, and when might informed consent be waived) and how to protect human subjects. However, of critical importance in the informed content process is that participation is voluntary and free from coercion. Other issues and questions to be addressed through the informed consent process include: how does the investigator know that an individual with mild dementia understands the consent form, is this person from a population that is vulnerable to coercion (e.g., prisoners, individuals with posttraumatic stress disorder, children, and students), does this person meet the age to consent? Unfortunately, not all questions can be easily answered, but the ethical practice is to try and ensure that the most ethically justifiable action is chosen in deciding on an answer. To help clarify in defining the principles of how to best protect participants involved in research, several government agencies combined efforts to produce the Belmont report (U.S. Department of Health and Human Services, 1979), a document that highlights three ethical principles for research; namely, respect for persons (and protection for those who are considered vulnerable), beneficence, and justice. These principles and their implications are still used today by many IRBs.

In preparing the informed consent for research, there are multiple components that have implications for ethics and professional behavior. For example, an informed consent should include the purpose of the study explained in understandable language, limits to confidentiality and a discussion on how the data will be protected, an explanation of the risk and benefits to the subject, special consents to record voices and images, details as to how debriefing will occur, and how can the investigator be contacted if there are any concerns or questions (to name but a few). To protect individuals, especially those who might be more vulnerable to financial or other incentives, Section 8 of the Ethics Code highlights the need to make sure that volunteers are not unduly pressured to participate (e.g., offering large sums of money to sign up and offering a weekend pass to individuals on psychiatric inpatient units only if they participate). It also highlights that patients should not be deceived about the research being conducted unless the reasons are appropriately justified and handled.

According to Smith (2003), there are five broad principals to follow in research ethics. These include being open and respectful about publication credit (e.g., working with colleagues up front about the publication order, recognizing that a supervisor should not be the principal first author on a publication based on a student's dissertation, and/or that journal reviewers need to protect the rights of an author before an article is published), be conscious of dual relationships, follow your informed consent guidelines, respect privacy and confidentiality, and know the basics of professional research ethics (e.g., the Belmont report).

Ethics in Supervision

Clinical supervision is a specialized area of psychological practice that has its own foundation of knowledge and skills as well as potential ethical issues. The supervisory relationship is highly interactive and both the supervisor and supervisee are responsible for adhering to ethical guidelines in their relationships to ensure a positive learning and training environment. However, the supervisor, because of the higher status, power, and knowledge base, has the greater responsibility, and must recognize that the supervisee is more vulnerable (CPA, 2000).

Although both the APA (2002a, 2010b) and CPA (2000) codes of ethics address issues specifically pertaining to clinical supervision, the following will focus mainly on issues highlighted in the APA Code.

Although the ultimate purpose of clinical supervision is to foster skill acquisition and ensure competence in unlicensed and less experienced clinicians, the most basic ethical principle involves the concept of doing no harm. The APA Code (APA, 2002a, 2010b) states, "Psychologists take reasonable steps to avoid harming their clients/patients, students, supervisees, research participants, organizational clients, and others with whom they work, and to minimize harm where it is foreseeable and unavoidable" (p. 6). Ethical issues pertaining to clinical supervision typically fit into one of two aspects of this principle. Supervisors need to ensure that the clients of supervisees are not being harmed by inappropriate or poorly delivered services. They also need to ensure that supervisees themselves are not being harmed in the context of the supervisory relationship.

All areas of practice must be within a psychologist's area of competence. The APA Code (APA, 2002a, 2010b) 2.01 (a) Boundaries of Competence states: "Psychologists provide services, teach, and conduct research with populations and in areas only within the boundaries of their competence, based on their education, training, supervised experience, consultation, study, or professional experience" (p. 4). Supervisors need to have competence in clinical supervision itself as well as the specific services (e.g., intervention, assessment, or consultation) being supervised. If one does not have competence in a particular skill or therapeutic technique or working with a specific population, then one should not supervise others in that area. Similarly, one needs to have ample training in clinical supervision to provide competent supervision. This protects the client and the supervisee from harm.

Section 7.06 (a) of the APA Code (APA, 2002a, 2010b) Assessing Student and Supervisee Performance, states: "In academic and supervisory relationships, psychologists establish a timely and specific process for providing feedback to students and supervisees. Information regarding the process is provided to the student at the beginning of supervision" (p. 10). To protect the rights of the supervisee, mechanisms of evaluation should be discussed at the onset of the supervisory relationship and areas of concern or in need of improvement should be reviewed at regular intervals.

Perhaps the most challenging interface of clinical supervision and ethics involves the areas of multiple relationships and professional boundaries. Consistent with APA Code (APA, 2002a, 2010b) 3.08 Exploitative Relationships, supervisors should not benefit from the supervisee relationship at the expense of the supervisee. The Code states: "Psychologists do not exploit persons over whom they have supervisory, evaluative, or other authority such as clients/patients, students, supervisees, research participants, and employees" (p. 6). For example, an internship supervisor may ask an intern to teach section(s) of a psychopathology class he or she is teaching at a local college. If this is a paid faculty position, the supervisor may be exploiting the intern for financial gain. In such situations, it would be very difficult for the intern to decline the request given the power differential. Section 3.05 of the APA Code (APA, 2002a, 2010b) defines a multiple relationship as "when a psychologist is in a professional role with a person and, at the same time is in another role with the same person, in a relationship with a person closely associated with or related to the person with whom the psychologist has the professional relationship, or promises to enter into another relationship in the future with the person or a person closely associated with or related to the person" (p. 6). The Code goes on to· state that "A psychologist refrains from entering into a multiple relationship if the multiple relationship could reasonably be expected to impair the psychologist's objectivity, competence, or effectiveness in performing his or her functions as a psychologist, or otherwise risks exploitation or harm to the person with whom the professional relationship exists. Multiple relationships that would not reasonably be expected to cause impairment or risk exploitation or harm are not unethical." For example, an internship training director may also be the postdoctoral training director. If the intern is applying to the postdoctoral training program, in the same faculty, the training director has multiple relationships with the intern, as his or her internship training director and the training director responsible for screening and selecting postdoctoral applicants. These roles certainly have the potential for impairment, exploitation, or harm, but the risk is low as long as the training director and intern are aware of the conflicting roles.

Although multiple relationships are typically avoidable in clinician–client relationships, as in the scenario described in the previous paragraph, they are often inherent in supervisor–supervisee relationships. Supervision in practicum, internship, and postdoctoral settings not only involves guiding skill acquisition and fostering clinical competency, it equally needs to address professional development, which can sometimes blur professional and personal boundaries. Similarly, in such settings, supervisors may also hold management or leadership roles that may conflict with the supervisor role. Recognizing this possibility, the APA Code, Section 3.05 (b) (APA, 2002a, 2010b) states: "If a psychologist finds that, due to unforeseen factors, a potentially harmful multiple relationship has arisen, the psychologist takes reasonable steps to resolve it with due regard for the best interests of the affected person and maximal compliance with the Ethics Code" (p. 6).

Although there are a host of potentially problematic situations, the only direct prohibition involves sexual relationships with supervisees. Section 7.07, Sexual Relationships with Students and Supervisees, of the APA Code (APA, 2002a, 2010b) states: "Psychologists do not engage in sexual relationships with students or supervisees who are in their department, agency, or training center or over whom psychologists have or are likely to have evaluative authority" (p. 10).

Section 10.01 (c) Informed Consent to Therapy addresses when the therapist is a trainee and the legal responsibility for the treatment provided resides with the supervisor. The patient, as part of the informed consent procedure, is informed that the therapist is in training, is being supervised, and is given the name of the supervisor.

Recommended Reading

American Academy of Clinical Neuropsychology (AACN). (2001). Policy statement on the presence of third party observers in neuropsychological assessments. *Clinical Neuropsychologist, 14*, 433–439.

American Psychological Association (APA). (2002b). *Practice parameters: Screening and diagnosis of autism.* Available from http://www.aan.com/professionals /practice/pdfs/gl0063.pdf

American Psychological Association (APA). (2002c). *Guidelines on multicultural education, training, research, practice and organizational change for psychologists.* Available from http://www.apa.org/pi/oema/resources/policy/multicultural -guideline.pdf

American Psychological Association (APA). (2002d). *Guidelines for assessment of and intervention with persons with disabilities.* Available from http://www.apa .org/pi/disability/resources/assessment-disabilities.aspx

American Psychological Association (APA). (2004). *Guidelines for psychological practice with older adults.* Available from http://www.apa.org/practice/guidelines /older-adults.pdf

American Psychological Association (APA). (2007). *Guidelines for psychological practice with girls and women.* Available from http://www.apa.org/practice/guidelines /girls-and-women.pdf

American Psychological Association (APA). (2007b). *Record keeping guidelines.* Available from http://www.apa.org/practice/guidelines/record-keeping.pdf

American Psychological Association (APA). (2010a). *Guidelines for child custody evaluations in family law proceedings.* Available from http://www.apa.org/practice /guidelines/child-custody.pdf

American Psychological Association (APA). (2011). *Practice guidelines regarding psychologists' involvement in pharmacological issues.* Available from http://www .apa.org/practice/guidelines/pharmacological-issues.pdf

American Psychological Association (APA). (2012a). *Testing and assessment.* Available from http://www.apa.org/science/programs/testing

American Psychological Association (APA). (2012b). *Guidelines for the practice of parenting coordination.* Available from http://www.apa.org/practice/guidelines /parenting-coordination.pdf

American Psychological Association (APA). (2012c). *Guidelines for psychological practice with lesbian, gay and bisexual clients.* Available from http://www. apa.org/pi/lgbt/resources/guidelines.aspx

American Psychological Association (APA). (2012d). *Guidelines for the evaluation of dementia and cognitive change.* Available from http://www.apa.org/pi/aging /resources/dementia-guidelines.pdf

Turner, S. M., DeMers, S. T., Fox, H. R., & Reed, G. (2001). APA's guidelines for test user qualifications: An executive summary. *American Psychologist, 56*(12), 1099–1113.

References

American Educational Research Association (AERA), American Psychological Association (APA), & National Council on Measurement (NCME) in Education. (1999). *Standards for educational and psychological testing*. Washington, DC: American Educational Research Association.

American Psychological Association (APA). (2002a). Ethical principles of psychologists and code of conduct. *American Psychologist, 57*, 1060–1073.

American Psychological Association (APA). (2010b). Amendments to the 2002 "Ethical principles of psychologists and code of conduct." *American Psychologist, 65*(5), 493.

American Psychological Association (APA). (2013a). *Guidelines for psychological practice in health care delivery systems*. Available from http://www.apa.org/about/policy/hospital-privileges.pdf

American Psychological Association (APA). (2013b). *Specialty guidelines for forensic psychology*. Available from http://www.apa.org/practice/guidelines/forensic-psychology.aspx

American Psychological Association (APA). (2013c). *Guidelines for psychological evaluations in child protection matters*. Available from http://www.apa.org/practice/guidelines/child-protection.pdf

Association of State and Provincial Psychology Boards Code of Conduct (ASPPB). (2005). Retrieved April 2, 2009, from http://www.asppb.net/i4a/pages/index.cfm?pageid=3353

Beauchamp, T. L., & Childress, J. F. (2009). *Principles of biomedical ethics* (6th ed.). New York, NY: Oxford University Press.

Behnke, S. (2007, September). The work of the APA ethics office: Frequent calls we receive. *APA Monitor, 38*(8), 56.

Canadian Psychological Association (CPA). (2000). *Canadian code of ethics for psychologists*. www.cpa.ca/aboutcpa/committees/ethics/codeofethics

Smith, D. (2003). Five principles for research ethics. *APA Monitor, 34*(1), 56.

U.S. Department of Health and Human Services (USHHS). (1979). *The Belmont report*. Available from http://www.hhs.gov/ohrp/humansubjects/guidance/belmont.html

Review Questions

1. Your friend, a respected psychologist, suffers a mild traumatic brain injury (TBI) following a car accident. You have noticed that he has been a little more forgetful and that at times he appears confused. What should you do?

   A. Nothing, as he has the obligation to monitor his competency
   B. Nothing, as you believe the mild TBI should soon resolve and he will be back to normal
   C. Talk with him regarding your concerns and encourage him to seek guidance
   D. Report him to the State board

2. A psychologist who has been at your facility for many years tells you that she would like to start using cognitive behavioral therapy (CBT) on the psychiatric inpatient unit after reading a compelling article on the topic. She reports that this is something she has never tried before. What advice would you give her in starting this endeavor?

   A. Good luck!
   B. Suggest she apply for specialized privileges prior to starting the group at this facility
   C. Have a student who is familiar with this modality co-lead the group
   D. Encourage her to be appropriately trained and supervised before starting her own group

3. A radiologist asks you to provide her with a copy of some neuropsychological tests to be included in a research protocol looking at the relationships between imaging and cognitive performance in individuals with hepatitis C. Appropriate responses include:

   A. Provide her with instruments as requested
   B. Only give her older instruments that are already in the public domain
   C. Offer to work with her in participating, training, and/or supervising, as appropriate
   D. Only offer to help if you are listed as second author
   E. B and C

4. Which are potentially ethical methods of recruiting new clients?

   A. Soliciting outside of the ballpark after a team loses the World Series
   B. Soliciting as part of a disaster relief effort
   C. Advertising your 100% success rate in the local paper
   D. Asking your clients whether any of their friends may want to initiate therapy with you
   E. B and C

5. Which of the following may be considered a vulnerable population for research?

   A. Students, when mandated as part of a course requirement
   B. Prisoners
   C. Individuals with dementia
   D. All of the above

6. When a person is believed to lack capacity in making clinical decisions the psychologist should:
   A. Ask family members to help them in deciding how to proceed
   B. Check to see whether there is an identified conservator/surrogate decision maker
   C. Continue as planned and check on informed consent later in the day
   D. Presume the person has capacity until proven otherwise

7. Which of the following statements is most true?
   A. Continuing education is required in every state for all psychologists
   B. Psychologists can practice outside of their competency areas
   C. Psychologists don't protect confidentiality with family members
   D. It is important for psychologists to maintain competencies when working with diverse groups

8. Forensic practitioners should not:
   A. Try to avoid conflicts of interest
   B. Provide formal legal advice
   C. Accurately describe their credentials
   D. Limit comments under any circumstance

9. When conducting a child evaluation of parental fit, a clinician should make a custody opinion after:
   A. Reviewing the file, evaluating the child, and interviewing one parent
   B. Reviewing the file, evaluating the child, and interviewing both parents
   C. Reading the file and interviewing the child
   D. Reading the file, evaluating the child, and interviewing one parent if the data are thought to be unbiased and credible

10. Which is not an example of a dual relationship?
    A. Friending a student on Facebook
    B. Buying a car from a client
    C. Friending a client on LinkedIn
    D. Inviting a client to a party
    E. All of the above are potentially dual-relationship examples

11. After _____ years, it is acceptable to have relationships with a former client.
    A. 1 year
    B. 2 years
    C. 5 years
    D. Never, except in the most unusual circumstance

12. Parts of a research informed consent do not include:
    A. Purpose of research
    B. Right to decline
    C. Limits of confidentiality
    D. Names of other participants
    E. All of the above

13. It is acceptable to make multiple photocopies of tests as part of a research protocol:

   A. Always
   B. Never
   C. Only if copyrighted
   D. Only if you paid for the original

14. It is acceptable to terminate therapy when:

   A. Threatened by the client
   B. Service is not needed
   C. Benefit is not being realized
   D. Service is needed, but client won't pay their bill
   E. All of the above are acceptable grounds to terminate

15. The General Principle that is related to establishing a trusting relationship with colleagues is:

   A. Integrity
   B. Justice
   C. Beneficence and nonmaleficence
   D. Fidelity and responsibility

16. A client in the community is interested in receiving service from you but due to the economy, can only pay you in products from his local farm. In this setting, bartering may be acceptable if it:

   A. Is exploitative
   B. Poses a significant dual relationship
   C. Is not contraindicated to treatment
   D. Bartering is never acceptable for services

17. A psychologist who conducts psychological assessments has not updated the test he uses in 15 years. A colleague files a complaint with an ethics committee against this psychologist. What is the general ethical principle or standard underlying this case?

   A. Competence
   B. Fidelity and responsibility
   C. Integrity
   D. Beneficence and nonmaleficence

18. You want to work with a client from an ethnic group you have not worked with before. You should:

   A. Refer the client to another therapist
   B. Read books about the ethnic group while you are working with the client
   C. Seek supervision and/or consultation before taking on the client and continue supervision/consultation over the course of treatment
   D. Rely on your basic skills as a therapist and everything will work out

19. You are providing psychotherapy to a 15-year-old female client who discloses she had recent sexual contact with her father. She begs you not to tell anyone because she believes it will make things worse. Her parents contact you asking how treatment is progressing because they perceive their daughter is getting worse. You should _____.

  A. Notify her parents as your client is a minor and her parents own the client–therapist privilege

  B. Follow your state's procedure for mandatory reporting of sexual abuse

  C. Discuss your concerns with your client and explain your need to tell her parents and report the abuse to the appropriate agency

  D. Discuss your concerns with your client and explain your need to report the abuse to the appropriate agency

20. While you are providing clinical supervision to a psychology intern, he discloses significant depression in a personal relationship and asks for your advice. You should _____.

  A. Assess the extent of the intern's depressive symptoms and intervene as you deem appropriate

  B. Ignore the request for advice and focus exclusively on the clinical cases you are supervising

  C. Explain the boundaries of your relationship and how it is not ethical for you to address his personal difficulties. You offer to make a referral to a clinician outside of the internship program

  D. Explain that reporting such difficulties in the context of clinical supervision is seen as avoiding the intern's deficient clinical skills

21. You are teaching a class for the local university's doctoral program as adjunct paid faculty. Which of the following is the most ethical option?

  A. Have some of your graduate students guest lecture when you are on vacation, given that they are knowledgeable in the respective topic for the days you are gone

  B. Present the option to substitute teach to all of your graduate students

  C. Have some of your graduate students guest lecture when you are on vacation, given that they are knowledgeable in the respective topic for the days you are gone and compensate them based on what you would have earned for teaching those classes

  D. Present the option to substitute teach to all of your graduate students and compensate them based on what you would have earned for teaching those classes

22. The holder of privilege is usually the _____.

  A. Clinician

  B. Client

  C. Courts

  D. Both client and clinician

23. A psychologist who works as a university professor has not updated his lectures in 15 years. His rationale is that he uses classic readings that are timeless. Select the most accurate statement from an ethical perspective.

A. The psychologist's behavior is completely ethical
B. The psychologist's behavior is not ethical
C. The psychologist should update his lectures to only include the most recent scientific literature
D. The psychologist should update his lectures to include some more current literature

24. A psychologist is dating a graduate student in his class who is approximately 15 years older than other students. The psychologist's behavior is _____.

A. Unethical only if he is having sexual relations with the student
B. Unethical because of poor boundaries and being in a multiple-role relationship with significant potential for harm to the student
C. Ethical because they are only dating
D. Ethical because she is consenting to the relationship and she is an older student

25. A new client of yours discloses that she was receiving therapy from another psychologist a few months back but she terminated that relationship because of sexual advances that were made toward her. You should _____.

A. Have your client tell you the name of the other psychologist and report him or her to the state licensure board
B. Inform your client that the other psychologist's behavior was unethical and discuss what action she may want to take
C. Have your client tell you the name of the other psychologist and confront him in person or on the telephone
D. Do nothing since you did not witness any inappropriate behavior yourself

26. In a group therapy situation (choose the best answer) _____.

A. At the outset of therapy, group members must sign a binding contract to maintain confidentiality
B. The psychologist should discuss the benefits of maintaining confidentiality with group members
C. Group members have no obligation to maintain confidentiality
D. Group members are legally obligated to maintain confidentiality

27. A psychology graduate student believes that her research study is causing harm to some of the subjects. Her supervisor for the study indicates there is no reason for concern because the study was approved by the Institutional Review Board. Who is responsible for the apparent ethical violation?

A. The university where the study is being conducted
B. The research supervisor
C. The student since she designed the study
D. Both the student and the advisor

28. A college-student client that you have been seeing for about 10 months asks you to attend his college graduation ceremony. You should (choose the best answer):

A. Attend the ceremony because you might hurt his feelings if you don't attend
B. Consult with your significant other as the current course of action is not entirely clear
C. Refuse to attend because it is a boundary violation and hence unethical
D. Discuss the potential risks and benefits with your client

29. In the APA Ethical Code of Conduct, the General Principles presented at the beginning of the Code:

A. Are prescriptive and describe what behaviors psychologist can follow in a range of circumstances
B. Are often used by licensure boards for imposing sanctions on psychologists
C. Are aspirational in nature
D. Serve as an introduction to the Code and are not very helpful in guiding ethical behavior

30. Which of the following is not true when considering ethics and clinical supervision?

A. Multiple-role relationships are more common in clinical training in clinical supervision than other areas of psychological practice
B. The higher-status power of the supervisor can be problematic when multiple roles and relationships exist
C. The welfare of the client being seen by the trainee should get greater consideration than the welfare of the trainee
D. Clinical supervision is considered a competence that supervisors should possess

Answers to Review Questions

1. **C. Talk with him regarding your concerns and encourage him to seek guidance**

   Under Standard 2.06(b), Personal Problems and Conflicts, when psychologists become aware of problems that may interfere with work, they should take appropriate measures such as seeking consultation or assistance.

2. **D. Encourage her to be appropriately trained and supervised before starting her own group**

   Standard 2.01(a) explains that psychologists only provide services within the boundaries of their competence.

3. **C. Offer to work with her in participating, training, and/or supervising, as appropriate**

   Standard 9.11 explains the expectation of psychologists to make reasonable efforts to maintain the integrity and security of test materials.

4. **B. Soliciting as part of a disaster relief effort**

   According to Standard 5.06, psychologists do not engage in solicitation of business when potential clients, because of their particular circumstance, are vulnerable to influence (with an exception allowed for providing disaster outreach). To rule out option C, Standard 5.01 addresses false or misleading statements.

5. **D. All of the above**

   Under Standard 8.06, when psychologists offer incentives for participation, they should avoid offering excessive or other reinforcements that are likely to coerce participation.

6. **B. Check to see whether there is an identified conservator/surrogate decision maker**

   Standard 3.10 highlights that when working with people who are not conserved, psychologists take reasonable steps to protect their rights and welfare. Additional obligations are required when a person is conserved.

7. **D. It is important for psychologists to maintain competencies when working with diverse groups**

   Standard 2.03 expects psychologists to maintain their competence and Standard 2.01 explains how factors related to diversity are essential elements in providing services.

8. **B. Provide formal legal advice**

   Special practice guidelines for forensic psychology clarify that practitioners should avoid conflicts of interest (1.03) and should not provide formal legal advice (2.04).

9. B. Reviewing the file, evaluating the child, and interviewing both parents

According to the Guidelines for Psychological Evaluations in Child Protection Matters, Guideline 8 suggests that the psychologist should decline to make opinions beyond the scope of their assessment (i.e., refrain from offering opinions if either a parent or child was not evaluated).

10. E. All of the above are potentially dual-relationship examples

All of the examples could be potentially construed as a multiple relationship as defined by Standard 3.05.

11. D. Never, except in the most unusual circumstance

Standard 10.08 explains that even after 2 years following cessation of therapy, psychologists should not engage in sexual relationships with former clients. If they do, there is a high burden of demonstrating the lack of exploitation.

12. D. Names of other participants

Definition of informed consent, Standard 8.02.

13. B. Never

This answer is based on both Standard 9.11 (maintaining test security) and copyright laws.

14. E. All of the above are acceptable grounds to terminate

Standard 10.10 allows for options A, B, and C. According to both standards 3.12 and 10.09, psychologists must make reasonable resolutions for care in the event that financial limitations become an issue.

15. D. Fidelity and responsibility

The General Principle that is related to establishing a trusting relationship with colleagues is fidelity and responsibility, which is one of the five General Principles.

16. C. Is not contraindicated to treatment

Section 6.05 of the Ethical Code states that barter is acceptable if it is not clinically contraindicated.

17. A. Competence

The psychologist's competence is in question because he is using outdated/obsolete assessment practices (APA Code 9.080).

18. C. Seek supervision and/or consultation before taking on the client and continue supervision/consultation over the course of treatment

The APA Code Section 2.01 indicates psychologists provide services, teach, and conduct research with populations and areas only within the boundaries of their competence, based on their education, training, supervised experience, consultation, study, or personal experience. Seeking the required knowledge and receiving ongoing supervision/consultation would be the most ethical course of action.

19. **D. Discuss your concerns with your client and explain your need to report the abuse to the appropriate agency**

    Although the client is a minor and her parents owned the privilege, it would not be ethical to disclose the session content to them. Because the information was acquired firsthand, you are required to report the sexual contact to the appropriate agency.

20. **C. Explain the boundaries of your relationship and how it is not ethical for you to address his personal difficulties. You offer to make a referral to a clinician outside of the internship program**

    Offering psychotherapy and clinical supervision would constitute a multiple relationship that risks exploitation or potential harm to the intern. The best course of action would be to refer them to a clinician outside the internship program.

21. **D. Present the option to substitute teach to all of your graduate students and compensate them based on what you would have earned for teaching those classes**

    Because the APA Code Section 3.08 indicates that psychologists should not exploit persons over whom they have supervisory, evaluative, or other authority, the students would need to be compensated based on what the psychologist would have earned for the classes. So as to not demonstrate preference for certain graduate students, the option to substitute teach would need to be presented to all of them.

22. **B. Client**

    The client holds privilege unless he or she is a minor or has a legal guardian or conservator.

23. **D. The psychologist should update his lectures to include some more current literature**

    Section 7.01 of the APA Code states that in the design of education and training programs, psychologists take reasonable steps to ensure that programs are designed to provide the appropriate knowledge and proper experience, and to meet the requirements for licensure, certification, and other goals for which claims are made by the program. Classic or "timeless" readings could certainly be included in the lectures, but more current readings would also need to be included in order to ensure students are properly educated or trained.

24. **B. Unethical because of poor boundaries and being in a multiple relationship with significant potential for harm to the student**

    Although multiple relationships are not precluded, Section 3.05 of the APA Code states that a psychologist refrains from entering into multiple relationships if the multiple relationship could reasonably be expected to impair the psychologist's objectivity, competence, or effectiveness in performing his or her functions as a psychologist, or otherwise risk of exploitation or harm to the person with whom the professional relationship exists. Because the multiple relationship in this case is avoidable and there is significant risk for harm to the student, the psychologist's behavior is unethical.

25. **B. Inform your client that the other psychologist's behavior was unethical and discuss what action she may want to take**

The psychologist's behavior is clearly unethical as engaging in sexual intimacies with current therapy clients is prohibited by the APA Code 1.04. The psychologist and client should discuss how this has impacted the client, what requirements there may be in terms of mandatory reporting, as well as a consequence of actions that need to take place.

26. **B. The psychologist should discuss the benefits of maintaining confidentiality with group members**

Group participants do not have a clearly defined ethical or legal obligation to maintain confidentiality. The best course of action would be for the group to discuss the benefits of confidentiality to individual members and to the group as a whole.

27. **D. Both the student and the advisor**

Both the student and advisor are responsible as they both have an ethical obligation to protect research participants according to the APA Code 3.04. It states, "Psychologists take reasonable steps to avoid harming their clients, students, supervisees, research participants, organizational clients, and others with whom they work, and to minimize harm where it is foreseeable and unavoidable."

28. **D. Discuss the potential risks and benefits with your client**

There is no clear ethical probation against such behavior but there are risks, including possible breach of confidentiality and a blurring of boundaries.

29. **C. Are aspirational in nature**

In this section of the Code it states, "This section consists of General Principles. General Principles, as opposed to Ethical Standards, are aspirational in nature. Their intent is to guide and inspire psychologists toward the very highest ethical ideals of the profession. General Principles, in contrast to Ethical Standards, do not represent obligations and should not form the basis for imposing sanctions."

30. **C. The welfare of the client being seen by the trainee should get greater consideration than the welfare of the trainee**

The APA Code, Standard 7: Education and Training, focuses on psychologists' behavior to protect students' welfare. Nowhere in the APA Code is it mentioned that the clients' welfare is more important than that of students. Standard 3.04 of the code, Human Relations, Avoiding Harm states, "Psychologists take reasonable steps to avoid harming their clients, students, supervisees, research participants, organizational clients, and others with whom they work, and to minimize harm where it is foreseeable and unavoidable."

9

Preparation Strategies and Tips

Walter Penk and Dolores K. Little

Preparing for the Examination for Professional Practice in Psychology (EPPP) is among the most challenging rites of passage in one's career to become and to be a psychologist. Taking the EPPP is one of the last requirements to complete before being licensed or certified. It is the last hurdle to leap before crafting and creating one's career. Herein, we discuss techniques in test taking: Deliberate Practice Theory (or the 10,000-hour practice test), getting grit, learning the EPPP rules, domains of the EPPP, distributing your learning, exercising the body and mind, reading books and peer-reviewed journals in the Internet age, preparing through professional societies, learning with peers and professionals, and persevering until you pass.

Deliberate Practice Theory

It is not clear that deliberate practice theory, or the 10,000-hour practice rule (the amount of time it takes to become a world class expert), applies as much to psychologists as it does to expert musicians or other scientific thinkers (Ericsson, Krampe, & Tesch-Romer, 1993). What is clear is that the EPPP requires both natural endowment and hard work over many years in order to meet and to fulfill requisites to become a psychologist. As one prepares to take the EPPP, it is assuredly time to actualize as much of the 10,000-hour practice rule as one possibly can; however, research shows that approximately 400 hours is generally sufficient when preparing for an exam like the EPPP.

Getting Grit

It is also the time for grit, to access within one's self and to promote one's grit, defined as the personal characteristics of perseverance and passion for the long-term goal of becoming a psychologist (Duckworth, Kirby, Tsukayama, Berstein, & Ericsson, 2011). Psychology is both a profession and a science and it develops on case studies followed by randomized clinical trials, results from which must be learned and then applied.

Taking the EPPP is a time when one stands alone, outside the care and comfort of one's college, beyond facilities where one was trained to practice. The EPPP is the final place where one, alone, competes to demonstrate one has mastered qualifications to be called a psychologist. It is the last step, where one brings together, within one's self, focusing talent and experience, all the resources within one's mind and body, to demonstrate that one has, as an individual and as a person, the knowledge and the experience to practice as a psychologist. It is time to let go of your anxiety and worries and trust in your studies and abilities.

Understanding the EPPP and Test-Taking Strategies

Restrictions prevail about the extent to which any psychologist can write about and describe the test that comprises the EPPP. For, among the first steps taken when getting ready to take the EPPP, each candidate must promise, as part of ethical and legal duties, never to divulge the content of the exam. Hence, any descriptions provided beforehand must remain in keeping with guidance and primary source documents that the Association of State and Provincial Psychology Boards (ASPPB) provide to candidates. See www.asppb.net/InfoForCandidates

What may be written in advance is that the EPPP evaluates knowledge that the most recent practice analysis has determined as foundational to the component practice of psychology (www.asppb.net/PracticeAnalysis).

However, candidates may practice an equivalent of the current EPPP by taking, online, the PEPPPO Test, that is, the Preparatory Examination of the Professional Practice in Psychology Online Test. The PEPPPO is a 100-item facsimile test using items no longer included in the current version of the exam. Although it takes time to take the PEPPPO—and one has to pay a modest fee—nonetheless, such experiences are informative about the candidate's capacity. Further, it enhances one's experience in taking standardized tests under online conditions. In addition, such an experience yields important clues about the tasks and goals ahead. The PEPPPO provides experiences in taking multiple-choice tests. It tutors the candidate in how to plan ahead for the 4-hour time limit for finishing the 225-item EPPP. And it may inform the candidate about the time of day when it is best for each person to take the EPPP. Each candidate schedules in advance 4 hours for test-taking time, relative to the 8 a.m. to 8 p.m. span when a Prometric location is open for computer-assisted testing.

Finally, the candidate may readily integrate into the rules governing administration of the EPPP, and the test-taking strategies and skills the candidate learned about test taking long ago in middle or prep or high school. That is, the candidate can access "test-taking strategies videos" on Google or YouTube and relearn previous skills for answering multiple-choice items like, eliminating wrong answers, solving easy items first, coping with tricky words, coping with "all" or "none" answers, and setting a comfortable pace.

Learning Domains of the EPPP

Candidates must not only become acquainted with directions for taking the EPPP, but, further, one must study in advance about the various domains comprising the EPPP. Restated, the EPPP has 225 multiple-choice items. The candidate has up to 4 hours to answer from an online site provided by Prometrics, with an extra 15 minutes at the beginning for practice purposes. EPPP items are subcategorized into eight areas: (1) biological bases of behaviors; (2) cognitive–affective bases of behaviors; (3) social and cultural bases of behaviors; (4) growth and life span development; (5) assessment and diagnosis; (6) treatment, intervention, prevention, and supervision; (7) research methods and statistics; and (8) ethical, legal, and professional issues.

In preparing for the test, elements comprising each of these eight categories must be studied, learning the most recent developments that have been demonstrated as foundational to the science of psychology (see Appendix A in www .asppb.net for more details about each domain, which are invaluable when preparing to take the EPPP). These domains are central to the profession of psychology. Each constitutes both knowledge and skills that the student must demonstrate as having mastered in order to advance to levels of knowledge for becoming licensed or certified as a psychologist.

Likewise, in learning about the domains and their elements that are being assessed, the candidate needs to understand how the EPPP items were developed and validated.

Distribute Your Learning

Test-taking strategies for the EPPP require that you constantly improve your skills for learning. Cramming for the EPPP, indeed, will yield some positive results. However, what you learn fast, you forget quickly. Psychology is a marathon, not a walk around the block.

Research by such psychologists as Henry L. Roediger III has demonstrated that we remember more of what we learn when we distribute our learning over time and learn by frequently self-testing ourselves about the content that we are learning (e.g., Roediger & Butler, 2011; 2012 award address at www.psycho logicalscience.org/convention/videos). We must go beyond rereading, summarizing, outlining, and highlighting. Rather, we must also repeatedly test ourselves on the materials we are learning and the results and outcomes from what we practice. This principle, validated now by Roediger and others, is as old as psychology itself, for as William James taught us long ago, in *Principles of Psychology*, paraphrasing James: it is better to recollect from within than to look at a book again.

Updating observations by James from his time of books and journals to our time of the Internet and Apps, we improve our performance when we increase testing ourselves about the new materials we have just learned (Roediger, 2013). Our mastery of self-testing to improve working memory is just as important for each one of us to do as it is for us to facilitate performances of others whom we may be training by teaching them to test themselves. Learning is testing, as the EPPP reminds us (Simonton, 2008; Tsay & Nanaji, 2011). And the wisdom about learning required by preparing for the EPPP is confirmed by recent reviews about learning techniques that are effective (e.g., Dunlosky, Rawson, Marsh, Nathan, & Willingham, 2013). As noted by Roediger (2013), cognitive and educational psychology are demonstrating that learning to test ourselves has been empirically validated as effective for learning, along with other approaches; for example, distributed practice on tasks (not massed practice), the aforementioned retrieval practice (or testing), interweaved practice (i.e., interweaving topics while learning), elaborative interrogation (i.e., asking why information is true), and self-explanation (i.e., explaining information to one's self).

Exercise the Body and the Mind

Prior to taking the EPPP, one should exercise both body and mind. Taking the EPPP is likely to be improved when you yourself have mastered relaxation and meditation, when you yourself are exercising and practicing positive nutrition. Such mastery of mind and body is essential for the EPPP, and to practice psychology in general, because psychology is a field that confronts and copes with stress. Psychology is a discipline in which clinicians vicariously experience stress and trauma when providing services for clients who have been stressed and traumatized. Exercise and meditation not only facilitate organization in coping with personal feelings, emotions, and thoughts, but likewise improve relationships with others. As a consequence, when preparing for the EPPP, the candidate may improve performance by balancing reading and talking with exercising and meditation. Preparing for the EPPP is a matter of organizing one's life around the age-old principle of balancing time to create a sound body and sound mind. We all must learn how to balance rest and use the brain's default mode for our education (e.g., Immordino-Yang, Christodoulou, & Singh, 2012). One should confront the EPPP well rested and relaxed.

Reading Books and Peer-Reviewed Journals in the Internet Age

Successfully preparing for the EPPP means mastering the most recent knowledge about psychology as a profession. Planning beforehand for the EPPP, recalling the emphasis on "recent" knowledge foundational to psychology, suggests that such books as the *Annual Review of Psychology* are essential for reading and improving working memory and retention by constantly testing one's self about such content.

But, likewise, regularly reading journals in one's profession is essential for not just preparing for the EPPP, but for developing one's career as a psychologist. For the candidate seeking state licensure to practice as a clinical psychologist, journals from the American Psychological Association (APA) and the Association for Psychological Science (APS) are vital (e.g., *Journal of Abnormal Psychology, Journal of Consulting and Clinical Psychology, Professional Psychology, American Psychologist, APS's Observer, Psychological Review, Perspectives on Psychological Science,* and *Psychological Science*), as are journals in one's area of specialized focus (e.g., *Behavior Therapy*). And findings from such recent articles, like Dunlosky et al. (2013) and Roediger (2013) specify specific techniques (e.g., practice testing) that will improve learning needed for the EPPP.

Preparing Through Professional Societies

Becoming a psychologist also means that candidates for the EPPP prepare by learning from participating in professional societies. APA and APS are rich in providing resources to develop new psychologists. Likewise, state psychological associations, along with societies for specialized practice (e.g., International Society of Traumatic Stress Studies; Association of Behavior and Cognitive Therapies, etc.) are major contributors to the development of the discipline. Professional societies offer student rates for candidates, lowering dues, and providing support to prepare for licensing and certification. Newsletters from professional societies, divisions, state associations, and specialty societies are valuable resources when learning fundamentals for domains evaluated on the EPPP (e.g., APA's Practice Directorate).

Learning With Peers and Supervisors

It is important that you form social groups, not just of supervisors but also peers, from whom to learn, not just facts, but categories of principles to practice. Training is important from licensed supervisors but likewise there are peer interactions that take place, akin to training in business and industry (Salas, Tannenbaum, Kraiger, & Smith-Jentsch, 2012). Preparing for the EPPP, one is encouraged to form groups of doctoral candidates to study together; to develop tests to improve working memory; and to practice transferring principles of psychology from one kind of task to another, from one setting to another, and from one person to another. Peers are necessary to corroborate transfer of training, as well as feedback from supervisors and from clients whom the candidate is serving. Staff conferences in facilities training candidates are vital in transferring knowledge from texts to persons.

Persevere Until You Pass

A useful test-taking strategy, that you can accomplish at the outset, is agree to keep taking the EPPP until you pass. That means, from the beginning, that you plan for the worst possible outcome—not passing (although the statistics are definitely in your favor for passing the first time). You prepare by learning at the outset what you will do if you do not pass. From the beginning, you create your own personal support services from peers and supervisors. You obtain all the feedback you are able to amass. You constantly test with peers, supervisors, and clients the new skills you are learning. You learn Association of State and Provincial Psychology Board (ASPPB) rules about the EPPP before you pay your first dollar to participate. Your main EPPP test-taking strategy is that you will persevere until you pass.

References

Duckworth, A. L., Kirby, T. A., Tsukayama, E., Berstein, H., & Ericsson, K. A. (2011). Deliberate practice spells success: Why grittier competitors triumph at the National Spelling Bee. *Social Psychological and Personality Science, 2,* 174–181.

Dunlosky, J., Rawson, K. A., Marsh, E. J., Nathan, M. J., & Willingham, D. T. (2013). Improving students' learning with effective learning techniques: Directions from cognitive and educational psychology. *Psychological Science in the Public Interest, 14,* 4–58.

Ericsson, K. A., Krampe, R. T., & Tesch-Romer, C. (1993). The role of deliberate practice in the acquisition of expert performance. *Psychological Review, 100,* 363–406.

Immordino-Yang, M. H., Christodoulou, J. A., & Singh, V. (2012). Rest is not idleness: Implications of the brain's default mode for human development and education. *Perspectives on Psychological Science, 7*, 352–364.

Roediger, H. L. (2013). Applying cognitive psychology to education: Translational educational science. *Psychological Science in the Public Interest, 14*, 1–3.

Roediger, H. L., & Butler, A. C. (2011). The critical role of retrieval practice in long-term recall. *Trends in Cognitive Science, 15*, 20–27.

Salas, E., Tannenbaum, S., Kraiger, K., & Smith-Jentsch, K. (2012). The science of training and developments in organizations: What matters is practice. *Psychological Science in the Public Interest, 13*, 74–101.

Simonton, D. K. (2008). Scientific talent, training, and performance: Intellect, personality, and genetic endowment. *Review of General General Psychology, 12*, 28–46.

Tsay, C., & Nanaji, M. R. (2011). Naturals and strivers: Preferences and beliefs about sources of achievement. *Journal of Experimental and Social Psychology, 47*, 400–465.

1. The model that posits that any change in one context or domain of development can disrupt the entire system and prompt a reorganization that leads to more adaptive functioning is _____.

   A. The Selective Optimization with Compensation (SOC) model
   B. The dynamic systems theory
   C. The cognitive-developmental theory
   D. The theory of psychosocial development

2. What is pertinent in the effort to promote and enhance health?

   A. Encouraging healthy behavior and educating the public on problems in society
   B. Job satisfaction, building resilience, building self-esteem and social skills, addressing risk factors, and encouraging healthy behavior
   C. Implementing advocacy groups for health, only targeting problem groups, and encouraging healthy eating
   D. Advocating and educating the public on obesity

3. MRI is preferred over CT (computed tomography) in all of the following scenarios, EXCEPT:

   A. The detection of a small tumor
   B. The detection of a skull fracture
   C. The detection of acute cerebral infarct
   D. The detection of white matter abnormalities

4. Attentional load theory posits:

   A. The unity of our actions places limits on attentional resources
   B. The degree to which an ignored stimulus is processed depends on the extent of processing required by the attended stimulus
   C. Selective attention facilitates inhibition of return
   D. There is a general limit to the extent of attentional resources

5. An individual's genotype is _____.

   A. The 23 pairs of chromosomes one inherits from one's parents
   B. One's environmental context
   C. One's observable appearance and characteristics
   D. One's physical attributes

6. If a researcher conducted a study in which the criterion for statistical significance was set to 0.05 and statistical power was equal to 0.85:
   A. The probability of making a type I error is 0.15.
   B. The probability of making a type II error is higher than the probability of making a type I error.
   C. The probability of making a type II error is 0.85.
   D. The probability of type I and type II errors cannot be computed from the information given.

7. Social influence occurs when an individual's attitude, thoughts, feelings, or behaviors are affected by the persuasive effect of others. There are many responses. Which type of social influence represents the Milgram effect?
   A. Conformity
   B. Obedience
   C. Compliance
   D. Power

8. Psychologists call the pathway that connects the past with the present and the future a(n) _____.
   A. Organizational process
   B. Developmental trajectory
   C. Developmental approach
   D. Theoretical model

9. The presence of manic episodes is required for a diagnosis of:
   A. Depression
   B. Bipolar I
   C. Bipolar II
   D. Dysthymia

10. A patient wishes to use data from your recent neuropsychological evaluation in a civil hearing in which he is suing the supermarket where he slipped and fell. Which answer should be the first step in fulfilling this request after a release has been duly executed?
   A. Provide the data and test forms to the patient
   B. Provide the data and test forms to the patient's attorney
   C. Provide the data to an appropriately qualified psychologist as indicated on the release form
   D. Provide all data and test forms, if contacted directly by the attorney

11. An assessment that uses primarily observational methods to examine and understand the physical and psychological variables that impact behavior in a given environment or setting is a:
   A. Functional behavioral assessment
   B. Work sample
   C. Norm-referenced test
   D. Ecological assessment

12. Identify the only construct that is pertinent to developmental models on intelligence:

A. Investment theory
B. The positive manifold
C. G theory
D. Primary mental ability theory

13. Tonotopic processing of auditory stimuli occurs at which site:

A. Striate cortex
B. Heschel's convolutions
C. Calcarine sulcus
D. Pre-central gyrus

14. If you believe another psychologist has committed an ethical violation, you should first:

A. Report it to the APA Ethics Committee
B. Report it to his or her state professional standards board
C. Wait to see whether he or she commits a second violation
D. Discuss your concerns with him or her

15. Which is NOT a criticism of Piaget's theory of cognitive development?

A. Piaget may have underestimated young children's competence and overestimated adolescents' cognitive abilities
B. Piaget placed too much emphasis on the role of culture and social interactions in children's cognitive development
C. Cognitive development is more gradual and continuous rather than abrupt and stagelike as Piaget thought
D. Children actually have certain cognitive capabilities at particular ages that Piaget did not observe because he designed experiments that were too difficult

16. One of the key features for making a differential diagnosis between bulimia nervosa and anorexia nervosa is:

A. Purging
B. Maintaining a normal body weight
C. Bingeing
D. All of the above

17. Which of the following is true of strong organizational culture?

A. It can facilitate cultural and other types of change
B. It is correlated with low levels of job commitment
C. It is correlated with high levels of job performance
D. It is correlated with high levels of voluntary job turnover

18. In a study in which depressed individuals presenting for outpatient mental health treatment are randomly assigned to either cognitive behavioral or brief dynamic treatment and both groups are assessed at pretest and posttest:

A. A mixed model analysis of variance (ANOVA) could be used to analyze the data
B. The design includes one between-subjects factor and one within-subjects factor
C. Each factor comprises two levels
D. All of the above

19. A stroke that affects the posterior region of the corpus callosum, thus disconnecting the visual centers of the brain from the language centers of the brain, may result in this syndrome:

A. Agraphia without alexia
B. Alexia without agraphia
C. Aphasia
D. Apraxia

20. The idea that individuals may have different possible developmental trajectories, given the timing of an environmental experience or lack thereof, is the concept of _____.

A. Nature with nurture
B. Sensitive or critical periods
C. Discontinuity
D. Risk and resilience

21. The first standardized measure of assessment was:

A. Stanford Binet
B. Binet–Simon Scale
C. Wechsler Adult Intelligence Scale
D. Raven's Progressive Matrices

22. The assignment of a term paper with a known due date employs a _____ schedule of reinforcement.

A. VI
B. FI
C. FR
D. VR

23. Behavioral treatments for depression typically include:

A. Flooding
B. Increasing pleasurable activities
C. Social Skills training
D. Exposure and Response Prevention

24. When a psychologist doesn't feel he or she is competent to accept a case, the most justifiable option is to:

A. Try his or her best
B. Refer out
C. Read a chapter on the issue
D. Charge the client less

25. Attribution theories provide a framework for the important types of information used to assess behavior. One theory describes how people identify explanations of people's personal characteristics from behavioral evidence. This theory is _____.

A. Correspondent inference theory
B. Covariation model of attribution
C. Achievement attribution
D. Attribution of harm

26. A regression model predicting frequency of tantrums from (a) effectiveness of parental commands, (b) consistency of parental discipline, and (c) parental warmth, would result in a model with:

A. One *y*-intercept and one regression coefficient
B. Four regression coefficients
C. One regression coefficient and three *y*-intercepts
D. One *y*-intercept and three regression coefficients

27. The flaw in Anderson's ACT theory was that some considered it _____.

A. Only applicable to a motor system
B. Untestable and thus, of uncertain scientific value
C. Lacking in definition for its elements
D. Overly complex in explaining the operation of cognition

28. Which is NOT a contributor to individual differences in the development of vocal language skills?

A. Variation in the support for language acquisition in the social environment
B. Hearing loss
C. The quality of nonparental early care and education experiences
D. The particular native language in a child's environment

29. The following measure of general cognitive abilities would be most appropriate for use with a nonverbal adolescent:

A. Stanford-Binet Intelligence Scales–5
B. Leiter–R
C. Kaufman Assessment Battery for Children–II
D. Wechsler Intelligence Scale for Children–IV

30. An agonist is _____.

A. A drug that cannot produce 100% of the biological response
B. A drug that has no effect
C. Another name for antianxiety medication
D. A drug that binds to a receptor producing a change in activity

31. Which of the following is not represented in *DSM-5* diagnostic criteria for problem gambling?

A. Tolerance
B. Withdrawal
C. Legal problems
D. Lying

32. Any substance that can have a negative impact on fetal development is _____.

A. An Apgar
B. A teratogen
C. Only a problem in the first 6 weeks
D. A controlled substance

33. If a researcher implemented a brief motivational interviewing intervention to increase client motivation in the hopes that increased motivation would lead to lower levels of problem alcohol use, motivation would be a
_____.

A. Moderator
B. Mediator
C. Covariate
D. Construct validity threat

34. In cognitive dissonance theory, individuals will change their _____ to match their _____.

A. Behavior; belief
B. Cognition; emotion
C. Belief; motivation
D. Belief; behavior

35. You have been treating a teenage male you suspect may have some neurologic difficulties. You inform his parents about your concerns and suggest they send him to a neurologist for an evaluation. Sometime later, the neurologist contacts you and requests your progress notes. You should _____.

A. Tell the neurologist the parents need to request the records
B. Send the records as requested
C. Inform the neurologist that you would need a release of information signed by your client's parents
D. Ask your client whether he wishes to have the records released to the neurologist

36. The American health care system is primarily dominated by which network?

A. The public sector
B. The private sector
C. The VA system
D. None, all are equally important

37. A 5-year-old child is shown two identical rows of pennies each containing five pennies that line up. One row is lengthened and the child is asked whether one row has more objects than the other. The child answers that the longer row has more objects. According to Piaget, this child is in the
_____.

A. Sensorimotor stage
B. Preoperational stage
C. Concrete operational stage
D. Formal operational stage

38. Which of the following assessment measures is not used to assess symptom validity or malingering?

A. Test of Memory Malingering
B. The Differential Aptitude Test–5
C. Recognition Memory Test
D. Personality Assessment Inventory

39. What two theories provide the conceptual framework for the evolution of mating adaptations?

A. Long-term mating and short-term mating
B. Parental investment and ecological warming
C. Sexual selection and parental investment
D. Levels of analysis and sexual selection

40. A 20-month old clings nervously to her mother and does not want to explore a new play environment. She suddenly pushes her mother away and does not engage in any hugs her mother tries to give her. The infant's facial expression shows anxiety but she looks away from her mother. The mother turns away from the baby as well. This child most likely has which type of attachment to her mother?

A. Secure
B. Insecure avoidant
C. Insecure resistant
D. Insecure disorganized

41. Which of the following relies on internal resources to cope with a problem?

A. Problem-focused coping
B. Emotion-focused coping
C. Cognitive dissonance
D. Semantic differential

42. The seat of higher cortical functioning is typically associated with the _____.

A. Temporal lobe
B. Frontal lobe
C. Occipital lobe
D. Hippocampus

43. A child diagnosed with conduct disorder cannot receive an additional diagnosis of:

A. ADHD
B. Rett's disorder
C. Oppositional defiant disorder
D. Asperger syndrome

44. According to Vygotsky, a teacher's changing level of guidance based on the student's performance level is called _____.

A. Sociocultural development
B. Skill enhancement
C. Scaffolding
D. Synchronization

45. The belief that an unhealthy style of life stems from self-centered, competitive goals is most consistent with the theory of personality proposed by whom?

A. Freud
B. Jung
C. Rogers
D. Adler

46. The most automatic of the proposed memory systems is _____.

    A. Episodic memory

    B. Semantic memory

    C. Declarative memory

    D. Explicit memory

47. The primary value underlying the existence of ethical principles is:

    A. Confidentiality of therapist–client communication

    B. The continued prosperity of the field of psychology

    C. The advancement of the welfare of society as a whole

    D. The advancement and protection of the welfare of clients of psychologists

48. Standardized tests or measures that compare an examinee's performance to the performance of a specified group of participants are:

    A. Criterion-referenced testing

    B. Functional behavioral assessments

    C. Intellectual assessments

    D. Norm-referenced tests

49. A rattle that a 4-month-old is playing with is hidden underneath a blanket in front of the child. She looks at her mother. This child has not yet developed _____.

    A. Conservation

    B. Egocentrism

    C. Hand–eye coordination

    D. Object permanence

50. On average, men perform better than women on all the following tasks with the exception of:

    A. Simultaneous processing

    B. Mental rotation

    C. Target-directed motor skills

    D. Mathematical problem solving

51. What are the facets of primary prevention?

    A. Primary, secondary, and tertiary prevention

    B. Primary, universal, and indicative

    C. Universal, selective, and indicative

    D. None of the above

52. _____ has implications for internal validity and _____ has implications for external validity.

    A. Generalizability, causality

    B. Random assignment, random selection

    C. Random selection, random assignment

    D. Temporal precedence, nonspuriousness

53. A person who is actively rejecting the dominant culture and holds rigid, positive beliefs about the minority culture is most likely in what stage of racial/cultural identity development according to Atkinson, Morten, and Sue?

   A. Conformity
   B. Dissonance
   C. Resistance and immersion
   D. Introspection

54. Which of the following is not an available tool for assessing suicide risk?

   A. Beck Hopelessness Scale
   B. Beck Scale for Suicidal Ideation
   C. The Suicide Action Questionnaire
   D. Suicidal Ideation Questionnaire

55. According to Piaget, children are _____.

   A. "Blank slates"
   B. Less intelligent than adults
   C. "Little scientists"
   D. Shaped by culture

56. Benzodiazepines must be used cautiously as _____.

   A. They are expensive
   B. They can lead to dependence
   C. They can cause agranulocytosis
   D. There is never a use for them

57. What are the four tenets of analytical psychotherapy according to Jung?

   A. Self-regulating psyche, the unconscious, family, therapist–patient relationship
   B. Self-regulating psyche, the unconscious, therapist–patient relationship, stages of self-improvement
   C. Id, ego, superego, libido
   D. Archetypes, unconscious, self-esteem, social needs

58. A small bit of meat powder in the dog's mouth was Pavlov's _____.

   A. US
   B. CS
   C. UR
   D. CR

59. The following has been shown to be the most effective means of symptom reduction for obsessive-compulsive disorder:

   A. Dialectical behavior therapy
   B. Antidepressant medications
   C. Exposure and response prevention therapy
   D. Combination of exposure and response prevention therapy and antidepressant medications

60. Compared to individuals in their 20s, which of the following is an advantage to having children after the age of 30?

    A. Older parents typically have more income for additional expenses due to established careers

    B. Older mothers have fewer medical complications during pregnancy and birth

    C. Older parents have not had time to build up expectations about children's behavior

    D. Older parents have more physical energy and time to play with their young children

61. Which of the following best describes the best ethical position on bartering with clients?

    A. Bartering is ethical because both parties benefit

    B. Psychologists should never barter for services

    C. Bartering is ethical and acceptable if it is not clinically contraindicated and not exploitative

    D. Bartering is ethical only if the client is not otherwise able to pay for services

62. Research that demonstrates parents who play more roughly with male children and are more protective of female children is most consistent with which theory of gender-role identity development?

    A. Psychodynamic

    B. Social learning

    C. Cognitive development

    D. Gender schema

63. What factors increase the likelihood of burnout?

    A. External locus of control and insufficient praise

    B. Positive environment and micro-management

    C. Age and quality of life

    D. Lack of control and insufficient reward

64. The scoring criterion categories for the Exner Scoring System used to score the Rorschach Inkblot Test include all of the following except:

    A. Color

    B. Popular

    C. Content

    D. Location

65. The match between a child's temperament and the demands and responses of the environment in which she develops is known as _____.

    A. Attachment

    B. Goodness of fit

    C. Bidirectionality

    D. Developmental contextualism

66. Which of the following is NOT a component of Weiner's attributional style theory?

A. Globality/specificity
B. Internality/externality
C. Equity/inequity
D. Stability/instability

67. The classic triad of symptoms in Parkinson's disease is:

A. Tremor, executive dysfunction, and rigidity
B. Tremor, rigidity, and gait imbalance
C. Tremor, gait imbalance, and paresis
D. Tremor, rigidity, and bradykinesia

68. Which of the following is true?

A. Spirituality has been shown to act as a protective factor against disease, and it is imperative to put effort toward understanding and incorporating spirituality into clinical practice
B. Incorporating spirituality into evidence-based treatments has only been effective for religious individuals
C. Yoga, meditation, mindfulness, and acupuncture techniques are not very effective treatment for pain associated with a chronic illness
D. All choices are false

69. A female psychologist provides a 2-month course of brief behavior therapy for a driving phobia to a male client. Six months after termination they meet at an art opening reception and begin to date. Over the next few months, the relationship progresses and they become sexual. In this situation, the psychologist has acted:

A. Ethically because it had been 6 months since termination
B. Probably ethically since there was no coercion involved and the relationship was consensual
C. Unethically, because she engaged in a sexual relationship with a former client, which is prohibited under any circumstances
D. Ethically according to professional standards, but the psychologist exhibited poor professional judgment

70. Piaget's theory describes stages of cognitive development _____.

A. During infancy only
B. From birth to late childhood only
C. From birth through late adolescence only
D. Throughout the life span

71. The effects of crowding are influenced by a number of factors, including all of the following except _____.

A. Self-esteem
B. Age
C. Gender
D. Culture

72. Which of the following vocational interest inventories is not tied to Holland's theory of vocational interest?

A. Kuder Occupational Interest Survey
B. Strong Interest Inventory
C. The Campbell Interest and Skill Survey
D. Self-Directed Search

73. Which concept and stage are appropriately matched according to Piaget's theory of cognitive development?

A. Centration—concrete operational stage
B. Egocentrism—sensorimotor stage
C. Hypothetical-deductive reasoning—formal operational stage
D. Object permanence—preoperational stage

74. Cerebral spinal fluid is secreted by the _____.

A. Third ventricle
B. Basal ganglia
C. Choroid plexus
D. Pia mater

75. What treatment method has the best results with addressing anxiety symptoms?

A. Cognitive behavioral therapy
B. Social skills training
C. Behavioral activation treatment
D. Nondirective supportive treatment

76. The "needs" of both Murray and Maslow can be considered similar to _____ from operant conditioning theory.

A. "Oughts"
B. Latent conditioners
C. Reinforcers
D. Latent punishers

77. A researcher interested in examining the potential impact of parent alcoholism on child and family development recruits 12-year-olds ($n = 100$), 13-year-olds ($n = 100$), and 14-year-olds ($n = 100$)—half of whom have an alcoholic parent and half of whom do not—into a multiple-year longitudinal study assessing various outcomes. This study is best characterized as:

A. A true experiment
B. A cross-sequential cohort design
C. A natural experiment
D. A cross-sectional cohort design

78. Which is NOT an example of children actively shaping their own development?

A. Children selecting the contexts in which they participate
B. Children imposing their subjective appraisal on the context
C. Children affecting what takes place in the context
D. Children being conditioned to modify their behavior to the context

79. A psychologist places an ad in a local newspaper claiming a guaranteed cure for anxiety.

A. The ad is not ethical because psychologists are not allowed to advertise
B. The ad is ethical because the psychologist is an excellent psychologist
C. The ad is unethical because it makes misleading claims of effectiveness
D. The ad is ethical because even psychologists are protected by the First Amendment protecting one's freedom of speech

80. Life span developmental theories, such as Baltes's Selective Optimization with Compensation theory,

A. Focus mainly on the development of psychopathology over time
B. Describe development as a process of growth (gain) and decline (loss)
C. Do not account for environmental influences on development
D. All of the above

81. Which of the following is true of low-context communication?

A. It is grounded in the situation
B. It relies heavily on nonverbal cues
C. It is a less unifying form of communication
D. It is more typical of culturally diverse groups in the United States

82. Nonverbal and primarily nonculturally biased abilities are referred to as:

A. Fluid intelligence
B. Broad stratum abilities
C. Achievement or aptitude
D. Crystallized intelligence

83. A person who recognizes a need to change certain behavior but exhibits ambivalence would most likely be in which stage of change?

A. Precontemplation stage
B. Indicative stage
C. Contemplation stage
D. Maintenance stage

84. Which of the following is NOT true about the difference between traditional research and program evaluation?

A. Program evaluation questions are often identified through the needs of a program's staff and stakeholders, while traditional research questions are identified by researchers using previous, existing research.
B. Program evaluation uses unique quantitative and qualitative methodologies to collect data. These methods are different from those that are used in traditional research.
C. Traditional research and program evaluation have different aims. Traditional research aims to test existing theories and discover generalizable knowledge, while program evaluation aims to collect information important for timely decision-making.
D. Both traditional research and program evaluation may incorporate rigorous and systematic ways of collecting data in order to address their aims.

85. For Kohlberg, morality:

A. Develops independent of outside influence

B. Cannot be rationalized in every instance

C. Is independent from emotion

D. Shows a logical progression from egocentric thought to broad moral principles

86. The reticular formation and reticular activating system are associated with all of the following functions, EXCEPT:

A. Decussation of auditory stimuli

B. Alertness

C. Consciousness

D. Pain

87. Research into _____ has helped us understand paradoxical reward.

A. Frustration

B. Conditioning

C. Attachment

D. Homeostasis

88. Justice primarily involves _____.

A. Recognizing fairness for all persons

B. Promoting accuracy and truthfulness

C. Benefitting others and "do no harm"

D. Respecting cultural and individual differences

89. The following are methods of increasing reliability and validity in qualitative research designs, EXCEPT:

A. Triangulation

B. Audits

C. Inductive processes

D. Member checking

90. An aspect of development that is more plastic is an aspect that is _____.

A. More or less fixed and difficult to change

B. Not heavily influenced by the environment

C. Relatively malleable

D. Irrelevant to developmental processes

91. A person who has difficulty performing a purposeful skilled movement, such as opening a door with a key, despite having intact motor and sensory functioning, most likely has which of the following disorders:

A. Transcortical motor aphasia

B. Apraxia

C. Pure alexia

D. Agraphia

92. According to the *DSM-5*, patients who meet some but not all of the criteria for a particular diagnosis can still be assigned that diagnosis. This reflects the fact that:

A. The *DSM-5* relies on a dimensional rather than a categorical approach to diagnosis

B. The *DSM-5* relies on a categorical rather than a dimensional approach to diagnosis

C. The *DSM-5* integrates aspects of categorical and dimensional diagnosis

D. The *DSM-5*'s approach to diagnostic classification is not valid

93. A person in the pseudoindependent stage of White racial identity is currently _____.

A. Developing an awareness of the role of Whites in perpetrating racism

B. Unaware of race and racism

C. Exploring what it means to be White and confronting own biases

D. Attempting to resolve moral dilemmas associated with an awareness of race and racism

94. The body's stress response system:

A. Is vulnerable to influence during childhood, but not before birth

B. Cannot be affected by outside influences

C. Can mainly be regulated through prescribed selective serotonin reuptake inhibitors (SSRIs)

D. Can impact genetic predispositions to developmental disorders

95. Your client is on probation and your ongoing treatment is a condition of his probation. He informs you that he wishes to terminate treatment. You should _____.

A. Inform your client's probation officer

B. Insist that your client stay in therapy

C. Agree to termination because your client has free choice

D. Discuss the possible ramifications and legal consequences of terminating therapy without informing his probation officer

96. Selective serotonin reuptake inhibitors (SSRIs), monoamine oxidase inhibitors (MAOIs), tricyclics, norepinephrine–dopamine reuptake inhibitors (NDRIs), and serotonin-norepinephrine reuptake inhibitors (SNRIs) all describe _____.

A. Antipsychotics

B. Antidepressants

C. Anticonvulsants

D. Cognitive enhancing agents

97. All of the following brain regions are considered part of the limbic system except _____.

A. Mammillary bodies

B. Septal nuclei

C. Putamen

D. Hippocampus

98. It is a 3-year-old's first day of preschool. When she arrives at her classroom, she holds on tightly to her mother's hand and watches the other children play. After a few minutes and some coaxing from her teacher, she begins to help another child complete a puzzle. According to Thomas and Chess, what temperament style does this child have?

    A. Easy
    B. Difficult
    C. Slow to warm up
    D. Secure

99. What model of consultation can be used with couples?

    A. Supervisor-centered consultation
    B Treatment-centered consultation
    C. Problem-centered consultation
    D. Client-centered case consultation

100. A lateralized lesion in this lobe of the cerebrum will result in hemisensory loss:

    A. Frontal lobe
    B. The temporal lobe
    C. The parietal lobe
    D. The occipital lobe

Answers to Multiple-Choice Questions

1.   **B. The dynamic systems theory**

     (From Chapter 4): The dynamic systems theory of Esther Thelen posits that the child's mind, body, and physical and social worlds form an integrated system that guides mastery of new skills. Any change in one context or domain of development can disrupt the entire system, prompting a reorganization that leads to more adaptive functioning. In this model, dynamic *refers to the concept that a change in any part disrupts the current organism–environment relationship, which leads to active reorganization, so the system's components work together again, but this time in a more complex, effective way.*

2.   **B. Job satisfaction, building resilience, building self-esteem and social skills, addressing risk factors, and encouraging healthy behavior**

     (From Chapter 6): Doyle (2006) suggests that the promotion and enhancement of health should incorporate a variety of components, including job satisfaction, building self-esteem and social skills, addressing risk factors, and encouraging healthy behavior.

3.   **B. The detection of a skull fracture**

     (From Chapter 1): CT (computed tomography) is better at detecting acute intracranial hemorrhage and at visualizing bony structures (e.g., skull fracture). CT is also preferred for patients who have metallic implanted devices, such as a pacemaker. MRI is preferred in nonurgent situations in which a higher-resolution imaging method is required for better anatomical detail (e.g., white matter lesions, remote ischemic stroke, and tumor).

4.   **B. The degree to which an ignored stimulus is processed depends on the extent of processing required by the attended stimulus**

     (From Chapter 2): Attentional load theory posits the degree to which an ignored stimulus is processed depends on the extent of processing required by the attended stimulus. According to attentional load theory, reduction of interference caused by distractors is greatest when the processing demands to the attended stimulus are highest.

5.   **A. The 23 pairs of chromosomes one inherits from one's parents**

     (From Chapter 4): Genotype is the set of genes—the 23 pairs of chromosomes—an individual inherits from his or her parents.

6.   **B. The probability of making a type II error is higher than the probability of making a type I error.**

     (From Chapter 7): The criterion for statistical significance is a synonym for alpha and is the probability of a type I error (0.05 in this case). The probability of a type II error is β, which is equal to 1 – power (0.15 in this case).

7.   **B. Obedience**

     (From Chapter 3): Research shows that people tend to be obedient when there is a perceived legitimate authority figure regardless of the task they are being asked to perform.

8. B. Developmental trajectory

(From Chapter 4): The pathway that connects a person's past to his or her future is known as the developmental trajectory.

9. B. Bipolar I

(From Chapter 6): Only bipolar I disorder requires a history of manic episodes. In bipolar II disorder, hypomanic episodes occur.

10. C. Provide the data to an appropriately qualified psychologist as indicated on the release form

(From Chapter 8): Standard 9.04(a) allows for possible release of test data to the patient; however, psychologists are required to protect test forms. Therefore, the only answer that could be acceptable is the one identified.

11. D. Ecological assessment

(From Chapter 5): By definition, an ecological assessment uses primarily observational methods to examine and understand the physical and psychological variables that impact behavior in a given environment or setting.

12. A. Investment theory

(From Chapter 2): How does intelligence develop over time? Cattell (1987) proposed investment theory, in which a single relation-perceiving faculty (Gf) is applied to the development of other abilities, such as acquired knowledge (Gc).

13. B. Heschel's convolutions

(From Chapter 1): Heschel's convolutions are the site of primary auditory processing in which the processing is tonotopic.

14. D. Discuss your concerns with him or her

(From Chapter 8): Standard 1.04 suggests to first attempt an informal resolution by bringing the issue to his or her attention.

15. B. Piaget placed too much emphasis on the role of culture and social interactions in children's cognitive development

(From Chapter 4): Piaget may have underestimated children's competence and overestimated adolescents' cognitive abilities. Piaget placed an overreliance on the physical and motor skills of infants, and ignored learning through sensation, perception, and environmental input. Cognitive development is less abrupt and stagelike and more gradual and continuous than Piaget thought. Cognitive development is not necessarily a general process and new skills in one area may not translate to new skills in another area. Piaget required children to perform complex tasks and answer complex questions. When children are given real-world, less abstract tasks to complete, they are generally more successful at an earlier age than Piaget predicted. Piaget did not consider the influence of the environment, individual differences, cultural variations, and social trends on children's cognitive development.

16.   B. Maintaining a normal body weight

(From Chapter 6): Bingeing and purging behavior may be present in both disorders.

17.   C. It is correlated with high levels of job performance

(From Chapter 3): Strong organizational culture is associated with high levels of job performance, satisfaction, and organizational commitment.

18.   D. All of the above

(From Chapter 7): All statements are true—linking relevant ANOVA (analysis of variance) terminology to a design commonly used in clinical psychology.

19.   B. Alexia without agraphia

(From Chapter 1): Pure alexia refers to impairments with reading, whereas the ability to write is relatively preserved. The pathology is usually a stroke in the posterior region of the left hemisphere, affecting the posterior region of the corpus callosum, disconnecting the visual centers of the brain from the language centers of the brain.

20.   B. Sensitive or critical periods

(From Chapter 4): The concept of sensitive or critical periods encompasses the idea that individuals may have different possible developmental trajectories, given the timing of an environmental experience or lack thereof.

21.   B. Binet–Simon Scale

(From Chapter 5): The Binet–Simon scale was one of the first standardized assessment measures. It was developed in 1905 to assess intellectual functioning for children in the French school system.

22.   B. FI

(From Chapter 2): An FI schedule leads to intermittent behavior that, when graphed, looks scalloped because responses right after the reward are never rewarded, and as a result responses stop for a time. After a while, the responses start again slowly, reaching a very high rate just before the end of the interval with its reward. Responses are never rewarded at the beginning of an interval, but are always rewarded at the end, so responses stop at the beginning, and become rapid at the end. Then they stop again for a bit, and the cycle continues. Work on term papers nicely illustrates the schedule.

23.   B. Increasing pleasurable activities

(From Chapter 6): Scheduling and increasing pleasant events is a typical component of behavior therapy for depression.

24.   B. Refer out

(From Chapter 8): Standard 2.01(c) explains that psychologists are to practice within the boundaries of their competence and take relevant training, supervised experience, and so forth when learning a new skill. In an emergency, they may be able to work with a client so as to not deny services (consistent with 2.02), but this scenario is not identified in the question.

25. A. Correspondent inference theory

(From Chapter 3): Correspondent inference theory indicates that we infer that other people's behavior corresponds to their personality and character.

26. D. One *y*-intercept and three regression coefficients

(From Chapter 7): The y-intercept and the three regression coefficients would comprise the full set of regression constants from such a model.

27. B. Untestable and thus, of uncertain scientific value

(From Chapter 2): Although the theory was quite powerful, with a number of applications, to some it was untestable (Leahey & Harris 1993).

28. D. The particular native language in a child's environment

(From Chapter 4): Variation in the support for language acquisition in social environment is one of the key contributors to individual differences in language development, including both the home/parental and nonparental care environments; hearing loss may contribute in some cases.

29. B. Leiter–R

(From Chapter 5): The Leiter International Performance Scale–Revised is the only nonverbal measure of intelligence listed and thus would be the most appropriate choice for assessing this patient.

30. D. A drug that binds to a receptor producing a change in activity

(From Chapter 1): An agonist is a chemical that binds to a receptor of a cell and triggers a response by that cell.

31. C. Legal problems

(From Chapter 6): Negative legal consequences were removed from the DSM-5 as a symptom criteria.

32. B. A teratogen

(From Chapter 4): A teratogen is any substance that can have a negative impact on fetal development. An agent is teratogenic if it has the potential for producing congenital malformations or problems depending on the dosage and timing of exposure during pregnancy, including viruses, alcohol and nicotine, prescription drugs, controlled substances, and environmental toxins.

33. B. Mediator

(From Chapter 7): In this scenario, the distal predictor is the intervention, the mediator is motivation, and the outcome is problem alcohol use. In other words, the intervention is hypothesized to reduce problem alcohol use by increasing motivation (i.e., the intervention mediator).

34. D. Belief; behavior

(From Chapter 2): In cognitive dissonance theory, when individuals behave in a manner that is inconsistent with their values or beliefs, they will change their beliefs to manage the psychological tension created by the mismatch.

35. **C. Inform the neurologist that you would need a release of information signed by your client's parents**

(From Chapter 8): Because the client is a minor, the parents hold the privilege and would need to provide written consent to release records. Otherwise, the psychologist could not provide any information to the neurologist.

36. **B. The private sector**

(From Chapter 6): The private sector encompasses HMO (health maintenance organization) and PPO (preferred provider organization) networks that are implemented in places of employment. The private insurance model is financed based on premiums paid through private insurance companies, making it the dominant network in the American health care system.

37. **B. Preoperational stage**

(From Chapter 4): During the concrete operational stage (7–11 years), children are able to reason logically in specific or concrete examples. Conservation is the understanding that changing the appearance of an object or substance does not change its basic properties. A 5-year-old child is still in the preoperational stage and is not able to understand conservation. Instead, his thinking is controlled by centration and he is only able to focus on one aspect to the exclusion of all others.

38. **B. The Differential Aptitude Test–5**

(From Chapter 5): The Test of Memory Malingering and Recognition Memory Test are symptom validity tests. The Personality Assessment Inventory has validity indices that can be reviewed to determine invalid symptom reporting or response biases that may indicate malingering. The Differential Aptitude Test is an aptitude test that is used to assess aptitude or ability level in several areas and is unrelated to malingering.

39. **C. Sexual selection and parental investment**

(From Chapter 3): Mating is at the heart of the evolutionary process that has created many of the adaptations. Darwin's sexual selection theory provided the early framework that was followed years later by Trivers's parental investment theory.

40. **C. Insecure resistant**

(From Chapter 4): Attachment is an emotional bond between a child and his primary caregivers that endures over the lifetime. Child characteristics of an insecure resistant attachment include the inability to use the caregiver as a secure base from which to explore; distress on separation with ambivalence, anger, reluctance to be comforted by the caregiver, and resume play upon return; preoccupation with the caregiver's availability and seeking contact but resisting angrily when it is offered; and anxiety due to inconsistency in the caregiver's availability. The caregiver is inconsistent between appropriate and neglectful response and generally will only respond after the child displays increased attachment behavior.

41. **B. Emotion-focused coping**

    (From Chapter 2): The coping mechanisms of secondary appraisal may be identified as "emotion-focused" (use of internal resources to cope with situation) or "problem-focused" (intervene in the environment to solve a problem externally).

42. **B. Frontal lobe**

    (From Chapter 1): Although multiple regions of the brain are involved in higher cortical functioning, the frontal lobes are typically associated with higher cortical functioning, such as reasoning, judgment, and problem solving.

43. **C. Oppositional defiant disorder**

    (From Chapter 6): A child with conduct disorder will likely also meet criteria for a diagnosis of ODD (oppositional defiant disorder). However, conduct disorder is considered to be a more severe form of pathology and therefore, the child will only receive the Conduct Disorder diagnosis.

44. **C. Scaffolding**

    (From Chapter 4): Scaffolding *refers to the changing level of support an instructor provides as she adjusts to a child's current performance level based on his increasing skill level. Thus, in the beginning of a lesson, a teacher may use a great amount of direct instruction and offer less guidance as the student's competence increases.*

45. **D. Adler**

    (From Chapter 3): Adler suggested that "style of life" unified the various aspects of personality. A healthy style of life reflects optimism, confidence, and contributing to the welfare of others. An unhealthy style of life results when a person's goals reflect self-centeredness, competitiveness, and striving for personal power.

46. **A. Episodic memory**

    (From Chapter 2): Episodic memory was proposed by Tulving (1972) and is autobiographic memory. Everyday experiences are recorded here and are connected to other events of the day. These memories are essentially stored automatically.

47. **D. The advancement and protection of the welfare of clients of psychologists**

    (From Chapter 8): Although this is not stated explicitly in the APA Code, much of the Code is focused on protecting the welfare of clients as opposed to just confidentiality, the field of psychology, and society in general.

48. **D. Norm-referenced tests**

    (From Chapter 5): Although intellectual assessments may fit this definition, norm-referenced tests are the better response because this term encompasses a broad range of assessment measures that fit this definition. Norm-referenced tests are standardized tests or measures that compare an examinee's performance to the performance of a reference population.

49.   D. Object permanence

(From Chapter 4): During the coordination of secondary circular reactions substage of the sensorimotor stage of Piaget's theory of cognitive development, an infant becomes more capable of recognizing object permanence, the understanding that objects continue to exist even if they cannot be seen, heard, or touched. Object permanence develops around 8 to 12 months of age.

50.   A. Simultaneous processing

(From Chapter 2): Men tend to have a slight advantage over women on task performances of mental rotation, target-directed motor skills, and mathematical problem solving. Women have a slight advantage in vocabulary and arithmetic task performance, among others.

51.   C. Universal, selective, and indicative

(From Chapter 6): These are the three components within primary prevention. All three include primary preventative measures but differ in their target groups. Universal prevention strategies are designed to reach the entire population, selective prevention strategies target groups at risk, and indicative prevention strategies target individuals showing early signs of an illness.

52.   B. Random assignment, random selection

(From Chapter 7): Random assignment and random selection are often confused. Random assignment is relevant to internal validity because it probabilistically equates treatment groups on measured and unmeasured covariates. Random selection is relevant to external validity because it strengthens generalizability.

53.   C. Resistance and immersion

(From Chapter 3): Atkinson, Morton, and Sue identified five stages of racial/ cultural identity. The third stage is resistance and immersion, which is characterized by active rejection of the dominant society and appreciating attitudes toward self and members of own (minority) group.

54.   C. The Suicide Action Questionnaire

(From Chapter 5): Well-supported assessment tools that are available to help assess suicide risk include the Beck Depression Inventory–Second Edition, Beck Hopelessness Scale, Beck Scale for Suicidal Ideation, Suicidal Ideation Questionnaire, and the Suicidal Behavior History Form.

55.   C. "Little scientists"

(From Chapter 4): According to Piaget, cognitive development is not governed by internal maturation or external teachings alone; instead, children are "little scientists" who actively construct their cognitive worlds through exploration, manipulation, and trying to make sense of their environment.

56.   B. They can lead to dependence

(From Chapter 1): Benzodiazepines must be used with care as they are addictive.

57. B. Self-regulating psyche, the unconscious, therapist–patient relationship, stages of self-improvement

(From Chapter 6): According to Jung, analytical psychotherapy specifically entailed the self-regulating psyche, unconscious, therapist–patient relationship, and stages of self-improvement. These four tenets were central to successful outcome in analytical psychotherapy according to Jung.

58. A. US

(From Chapter 2): Pavlov would present the metronome (CS), and follow it with meat powder (US) in the dog's mouth. The dog would salivate (UR) in the course of eating the tiny amount of food. After a few trials, the dog salivated (CR) to the sound.

59. C. Exposure and response prevention therapy

(From Chapter 6): Exposure and response prevention therapy is the most effective way to reduce symptoms associated with obsessive-compulsive disorder. The addition of pharmacological treatments has not been shown to result in better outcomes.

60. A. Older parents typically have more income for additional expenses due to established careers

(From Chapter 4): Advantages of having children in the 20s include more physical energy, fewer medical problems during pregnancy and childbirth, and decreased likelihood of building up expectations for children. Advantages of childbearing in the 30s include parents who have more time to consider career and family goals, maturity, the benefit of their experiences to engage in more competent parenting, and more established careers and higher income for childrearing expenses.

61. C. Bartering is ethical and acceptable if it is not clinically contraindicated and not exploitative

(From Chapter 8): The APA Code Section 6.05 states that psychologists may barter only if it is not clinically contraindicated and the resulting arrangement is not exploitative.

62. B. Social learning

(From Chapter 3): Social learning theory suggests that gender-role development is the result of observational learning and differential reinforcement.

63. D. Lack of control and insufficient reward

(From Chapter 6): Along with lack of control and insufficient reward, work overload, breakdown of community, and conflicting values contribute to the likelihood of burnout.

64. A. Color

(From Chapter 5): Exner's Scoring System scores patient's responses to the Rorschach Inkblot Test based on a set of four criteria. These criteria are Location, Determinants, Content, and Popular.

65. **B. Goodness of fit**

*(From Chapter 4): Goodness of fit is the match between a child's tempera-
ment and environmental demands. Awareness of goodness of fit has implications for parenting, including ensuring parents are sensitive and flexible
to an infant's signals and needs, and structuring a child's environment so
that children who are classified as difficult or slow to warm up have additional time to adjust to a crowded or noisy environment.*

66. **C. Equity/inequity**

*(From Chapter 2): Weiner developed the concept of attributional style with
the following components: globality/specificity, stability/instability, and
internality/externality.*

67. **D. Tremor, rigidity, and bradykinesia**

*(From Chapter 1): The classic triad of PD includes tremor, rigidity, and
bradykinesia (i.e., slowness of movement). Postural instability is also usually present. PD is caused by degeneration in the basal ganglia, which are
involved in the regulation of voluntary movements.*

68. **A. Spirituality has been shown to act as a protective factor against
disease, and it is imperative to put effort toward understanding and
incorporating spirituality into clinical practice**

*(From Chapter 6): Spirituality has been empirically supported to be effica-
cious for nonreligious mental health consumers (Post & Wade, 2009) and
furthermore, Brawer et al. (2002) have suggested it as a protective factor against disease. Its clinical utility is promising toward mental health
treatment.*

69. **C. Unethically, because she engaged in a sexual relationship with a
former client, which is prohibited under any circumstances**

*(From Chapter 8): Sexual intimacy with former clients is prohibited accord-
ing to the APA Code 10.08(a) and (b).*

70. **C. From birth through late adolescence only**

*(From Chapter 4): Piaget developed a stage theory of cognitive development
from birth through adolescence.*

71. **B. Age**

*(From Chapter 3): Crowding is influenced by a variety of factors, including
self-esteem, gender, culture, and perception of control.*

72. **A. Kuder Occupational Interest Survey**

*(From Chapter 5): Responses B, C, and D all have some tie to John Holland's
work in terms of the theoretical underpinning of the scale or subscales. The
Kuder Occupational Interest Survey is a self-report measure of vocational
interest that was developed by measuring the similarity between an individual's responses and the average interests of people employed in a given
occupation.*

73.   C. Hypothetical-deductive reasoning—formal operational stage

(From Chapter 4): Individuals are capable of hypothetical-deductive reasoning, the ability to develop hypotheses and determine systematically the best way to solve a problem and arrive at a conclusion, during the formal operational stage (appears between 11 and 15 years of age and continues through adulthood). Centration and egocentrism are characteristics of the preoperational stage. Understanding of object permanence develops during the sensorimotor stage.

74.   C. Choroid plexus

(From Chapter 1): The choroid plexus, the linings of the lateral ventricles, secretes cerebral spinal fluid.

75.   A. Cognitive behavioral therapy

(From Chapter 6): Cognitive behavioral therapy or CBT is generally supported as effective treatment for a variety of disorders. However, Hunot, Churchill, Teiceira, and De Lima (2010) found that with anxiety specifically, CBT had better results in their review comparing psychodynamic, supportive, and CBT approaches.

76.   C. Reinforcers

(From Chapter 2): Prior to Maslow, Murray had developed a list of human motivations under the heading of needs (Murray, 1938). They can similarly be seen as a list of reinforcing activities.

77.   B. A cross-sequential cohort design

(From Chapter 7): The design is a cohort design because groups are formed as a function of exposure to some factor (parental alcoholism). Multiple cohorts are included, which are the cross-sequential elements.

78.   D. Children being conditioned to modify their behavior to the context

(From Chapter 4): Children are not passive recipients of environmental influence. Rather, they actively shape their own development by evoking responses and actively selecting the contexts in which they participate. Children also actively construct and organize their ways of thinking, feeling, and more to assist them in making sense of the world. They actively shape their own development: by selecting the contexts in which they participate, by imposing their subjective appraisal on the context, and most of all by affecting what takes place in the context.

79.   C. The ad is unethical because it makes misleading claims of effectiveness

(From Chapter 8): The APA Code 5.01 states that psychologists do not knowingly make public statements that are false, deceptive, or fraudulent concerning their research, practice, or other work activities or those of persons or organizations with which they are affiliated.

80. **B. Describe development as a process of growth (gain) and decline (loss)**

   (From Chapter 4): According to Selective Optimization with Compensation (SOC) theory, gains and losses are subject to considerable contextual influences, and can include: normative age-graded influences that occur during the same period of development in most individuals; non-normative life events, or occurrences such as illnesses that impact individuals' lives at different periods; and normative history-graded influences, which describe historical events that occur and affect entire cohorts or generations of individuals at once.

81. **C. It is a less unifying form of communication**

   (From Chapter 3): High-context communication helps to unify cultures and changes slowly. Conversely, low-context communication can change quickly and easily and is a less unifying form of communication.

82. **A. Fluid intelligence**

   (From Chapter 5): The Cattell–Horn Model (Horn & Cattell, 1967) postulates two types of intelligence: fluid and crystallized. Fluid intelligence refers to nonverbal and primarily nonculturally biased abilities, such as new learning and efficiency on novel tasks (Sattler, 2001). Crystallized intelligence refers to an individual's knowledge base or range of acquired skills, which are dependent on experience.

83. **C. Contemplation stage**

   (From Chapter 6): The precontemplative stage is incorrect because it involves individuals who do not recognize their behavior as problematic and therefore see no need to change. The maintenance stage is incorrect because it involves relapse prevention after an individual has sustained positive change for a significant amount of time. The indicative stage is incorrect because it is not included as a stage of change. The contemplative stage is the correct answer because at this stage the person has insight into the problematic behavior. However, the person in the contemplative stage is not ready to actively change his or her behavior.

84. **B. Program evaluation uses unique quantitative and qualitative methodologies to collect data. These methods are different from those that are used in traditional research.**

   (From Chapter 7): Many differences exist between program evaluation and traditional research, including the primary purpose of evaluation versus research. However, evaluators use many of the same qualitative and quantitative methodologies used by researchers in other fields.

85. **D. Shows a logical progression from egocentric thought to broad moral principles**

   (From Chapter 4): Kohlberg's stages of moral reasoning described moral thought processes that begin as largely egocentric "preconventional" cognitions, which become progressively more focused on societal expectations (i.e., "conventional" stage thinking), followed by abstract principles about right and wrong (e.g., protection of life, liberty, and justice typical of post-conventional moral reasoning).

86.   A. Decussation of auditory stimuli

(From Chapter 1): The reticular formation is associated with pain perception, consciousness, and alertness. Decussation of auditory stimuli occurs in another brainstem region (lateral lemniscus).

87.   A. Frustration

(From Chapter 2): Research in frustration helps to explain paradoxical reward effects, which occur when a reward seems to weaken a response rather than strengthen it.

88.   A. Recognizing fairness for all persons

(From Chapter 8): Recognizing fairness for all persons is part of the definition of justice in the General Principles.

89.   C. Inductive processes

(From Chapter 7): Inductive processes are the basis for qualitative research— they move from specific to broad generalizations.

90.   C. Relatively malleable

(From Chapter 4): Plasticity can be defined as sensitivity to the environment engendered by experience. This addresses the extent and under what conditions it is possible for the course of development to change as the result of intervention or accident. Certain aspects of development are more or less fixed and difficult to change, whereas other aspects of development are relatively malleable and easy to change. In the former, the environment may have less influence, or less influence over time, whereas in the latter, the environment can have great influence.

91.   B. Apraxia

(From Chapter 1): Apraxia is a cognitive motor disorder characterized by impairments in performing a purposeful skilled movement. This deficit cannot be attributed to a primary motor or sensory impairment. Transcortical motor aphasia is a disorder of speech, pure alexia refers to impaired reading with intact writing, and agraphia refers to a disturbance in writing.

92.   C. The *DSM-5* integrates aspects of categorical and dimensional diagnosis

(From Chapter 6): The DSM-5 integrates aspects of categorical and dimensional diagnosis. The DSM-5 uses an integration of both the categorical and dimensional approach. This approach allows clinicians to assess the severity of the disorder without the strict guidelines for "normal" and mental disorder.

93.   A. Developing an awareness of the role of Whites in perpetrating racism

(From Chapter 3): Helms's model of White racial identity development comprises six statuses. The pseudoindependent status occurs when an event causes a person to question his or her racist views and acknowledge the role that Whites have in perpetrating racism.

94.   **D. Can impact genetic predispositions to developmental disorders**

(From Chapter 4): Through the process of epigenesis, environmental influences such as a chaotic home environment that tend to result in hypo- or hyperactive stress responses can contribute to genetic predilection for a range of developmental disorders, including antisocial behavior disorder and oppositional defiant disorder.

95.   **D. Discuss the possible ramifications and legal consequences of terminating therapy without informing his probation officer**

(From Chapter 8): Your primary concern should be the client's welfare and you could not contact the probation officer without a release of information. The best course of action would be to discuss the ramifications and legal consequences to help him or her make a more informed decision.

96.   **B. Antidepressants**

(From Chapter 1): SSRIs, MAOIs, tricyclics, NDRIs, and SNRIs are all types of antidepressants.

97.   **C. Fornix**

(From Chapter 2): The limbic system is composed primarily of subcortical regions, including the following: amygdala, hippocampus, mammillary bodies, septal nuclei, parahippocampal gyrus, and cingulate gyrus. The fornix, meanwhile, carries signals from the hippocampus to the hypothalamus.

98.   **C. Slow to warm up**

(From Chapter 4): Thomas and Chess classified children into three temperament categories: easy, difficult, and slow to warm up. Easy children are generally in a positive mood, establish regular routines quickly, and adapt easily to new experiences. Difficult children often react negatively and cry frequently, have irregular routines, and are slow to accept change. Slow-to-warm-up children have low activity levels, are somewhat negative, and exhibit low mood intensity.

99.   **D. Client-centered case consultation**

(From Chapter 6): Client-centered case consultation will focus on conflict resolution. Couples may experience discord through conflicts in communication, and therefore the couple is seen as the client.

100.   **C. The parietal lobe**

(From Chapter 1): The frontal lobe is the largest of the four lobes, governs output, and is considered the seat of higher cortical and cognitive functioning. The temporal lobe is the site of primary auditory processing. The occipital lobe is devoted to primary visual processing. The parietal lobe processes visual information along dorsal and ventral pathways from the occipital lobes to help coordinate movements and behaviors with the environment. Lateralized lesions in the parietal lobe will result in hemisensory loss (loss of sensation on one side of the body).

Index

critically appraising research
  construct validity, 254
  description, 250–252
  evidence levels, 254–255
  external validity, 254
  threat to internal validity
    attrition, 253
    history, 252–253
    impact evaluation, 253–254
    instrumentation, 253
    maturation, 252
    selection, 253
    statistical regression, 253
    testing, 253
cross-cultural psychology, 92
crowding, 85
crystallized intelligence, 171
CT. *See* computerized tomography
CTT. *See* Classical Test Theory
culturally mediated communication
    patterns, 99
curriculum-based measurement, 175

DA. *See* dopamine
data interpretation factors, 187
decision making factors, 187
declarative memory, 51
defense mechanisms, 207
deliberate practice theory, 325
delirium, 22
dementia, 18–21
density intensity hypothesis, 85
depression, 211–212
descriptive statistics
  central tendency, 262
  definition, 261
  normal distribution, 263–264
  skewness, 264
  variability, 262–263
  z-scores, 263–264
developmental science
  description, 111–112
  research evidence, 113–114
Diagnostic and Statistical Manual of
    Mental Disorders (DSM), 185–187
diagnostic classification systems
  DSM, 185–187
  ICD, 184–185
Differential Aptitude Test–Fifth Edition, 176
differential diagnosis, 183
dimensional models of emotion, 55–56
disability models, 98
disconnection syndrome, 17
discontinuity, 115
discriminant validity, 257–258

discrimination, 94–95
dishabituation, 128
displacement, 207
dispositional attribution, 80
disruptive behavior disorder, 217
divorce, 140–141
domains of development
  cognitive development
    language and communication,
      129–130
    theory of mind, 130–131
  physical and motor development
    brain development, 125
    genetics, 125
    hypothalamic–pituitary–adrenal
      axis, 126
    malnutrition, 126
    motor development, 126–128
    sensory and perceptual development,
      128–129
  prenatal development
    birth complications, 124–125
    environmental impact, 123–124
    meiosis and mitosis, 123
    periods, 123
  social-emotional development
    aggression, 137
    attachment, 134–135
    emotional development, 131–134
    gender awareness, identity, and
      constancy, 131
    identity development, 138
    moral development, 135
    prosocial behavior, 137
    self-concept, 131
    self-regulation, stress, and
      environment, 134
    social competence and skills, 137–138
dopamine (DA), 7
double approach-avoidance conflict, 85
drive theory, 57–58
DSM. See Diagnostic and Statistical
    Manual of Mental Disorders
dynamic systems theory, 121–122

eating disorders, 213
ecological assessment, 161
EEG. *See* electroencephalography
EFA. *See* exploratory factor analysis
EFs. *See* executive functions
electroencephalography (EEG), 15–16
emotional regulation, 132
emotions
  brain systems, 56–57
  Cannon–Bard theory, 53–54

psychopharmacology, 7–8, 13–14
psychostimulants, 13
psychotic disorders, 215
PTSD. *See* posttraumatic stress disorder
pure alexia, 17

qualitative inquiry, 278
qualitative research
    description, 277–278
    qualitative inquiry, 278
    reliability/validity, 278
    thematic analysis, 278
quasi-experimental research studies,
    249–250

Racial/Cultural Identity Development
    Model, 94
rational emotive behavior therapy
    (REBT), 60
rationalization, 207
ratio scale, 261
reaction formation, 207
reality therapy, 90
REBT. *See* rational emotive behavior
    therapy
regression, 207
reinforcement schedule, 47–48
relatedness, 59
relational aggression, 137
reliability, 166
    alternate/parallel forms, 256
    internal consistency, 256
    inter-rater, 256
    test–retest, 256
reliability coefficient, 166
repression, 207
research dissemination, 282
research methodology
    Campbell's validity typology
        construct validity, 246
        external validity, 246
        internal validity, 246
        statistical conclusion validity, 246
    theory and hypotheses, 245–246
research process
    community partnerships, 281
    critical appraisal and application
        construct validity, 254
        description, 250–252
        evidence levels, 254–255
        external validity, 254
        threat to internal validity, 252–254
    ethics, 309–310
    presentation and dissemination, 282
    program evaluation, 279

sampling and recruitment strategies
    barriers to recruitment, 280
    outreach strategies, 281
    sample selection, 280
research study designs
    correlational studies
        case–control designs, 250
        cohort designs, 250
        uncontrolled case studies, 250
    group-based randomized experiments
        effectiveness trials, 247
        efficacy trials, 247
        intent-to-treat analyses, 247
    quasi-experimental studies, 249–250
    single-case experiments
        ABAB designs, 248
        multiple baseline designs, 248–249
        result evaluation, 249
resilience, 115–116, 227
response to intervention (RTI), 188
Rett's disorder, 216
risk, 115
    assessments, 181–182
    reduction, 227
Risperdal, 12
role schemas, 80
RTI. *See* response to intervention

Sameroff's Transactional Model, 137–138
SB-5. *See* Stanford-Binet Intelligence
    Scales–Fifth Edition
scaffolding, 119
schemas, 80
school psychologists, 160
school transitions, 142
SD. *See* standard deviation
SDT. *See* self-determination theory; signal
    detection theory
secondary emotions, 132
secondary prevention, 218
seizure disorders, 23–24
selective attention, 40
selective prevention, 218
selective serotonin reuptake inhibitors
    (SSRI), 10–11
self-concept, 131
self-determination theory (SDT), 59
self psychology theory, 89
self-report, 162
self-schemas, 80
self-serving bias, 81–82
semantic memory, 52
semistructured interview, 163
sensation, 37–38
sensitivity, 276–277